STRATEGIC

CO   CIAL
R   Y

Sara Miller McCune founded SAGE Publishing in 1965 to support the dissemination of usable knowledge and educate a global community. SAGE publishes more than 1000 journals and over 800 new books each year, spanning a wide range of subject areas. Our growing selection of library products includes archives, data, case studies and video. SAGE remains majority owned by our founder and after her lifetime will become owned by a charitable trust that secures the company's continued independence.

Los Angeles | London | New Delhi | Singapore | Washington DC | Melbourne

Debbie Haski-Leventhal

*Foreword by **David Cooperrider***

STRATEGIC CORPORATE SOCIAL RESPONSIBILITY

Tools & Theories for Responsible Management

Los Angeles | London | New Delhi
Singapore | Washington DC | Melbourne

Los Angeles | London | New Delhi
Singapore | Washington DC | Melbourne

SAGE Publications Ltd
1 Oliver's Yard
55 City Road
London EC1Y 1SP

SAGE Publications Inc.
2455 Teller Road
Thousand Oaks, California 91320

SAGE Publications India Pvt Ltd
B 1/I 1 Mohan Cooperative Industrial Area
Mathura Road
New Delhi 110 044

SAGE Publications Asia-Pacific Pte Ltd
3 Church Street
#10-04 Samsung Hub
Singapore 049483

© Debbie Haski-Leventhal 2018

First published 2018

Editor: Matthew Waters
Editorial assistant: Jasleen Kaur
Production editor: Sarah Cooke
Copyeditor: Solveig Gardner Servian
Proofreader: Sharon Cawood
Indexer: Silvia Benvenuto
Marketing manager: Alison Borg
Cover design: Francis Kenney
Typeset by: C&M Digitals (P) Ltd, Chennai, India
Printed in the UK

Library of Congress Control Number: 2017955499

British Library Cataloguing in Publication data

A catalogue record for this book is available from
the British Library

ISBN 978-1-47399-800-1
ISBN 978-1-47399-801-8 (pbk)

At SAGE we take sustainability seriously. Most of our products are printed in the UK using responsibly sourced papers
and boards. When we print overseas we ensure sustainable papers are used as measured by the PREPS grading
system. We undertake an annual audit to monitor our sustainability.

To my husband, Paul, who is the wind beneath my wings, and to our two daughters, Emily and Michaela, who inspire me in their compassion and sustainable mindset and who make the journey towards a world of CSR even more purposeful.

Contents

Expanded Contents

Visit **https://study.sagepub.com/businessandmanagement** for downloadable PowerPoint Slides prepared by the author to support your teaching.

Foreword

Strategic CSR is the Future of Management

This is a very special book. I say this to begin with because the book is written with such clarity and strategic relevance, in such an engaging yet intellectually advanced way, that you know you are holding in your hands one of those kinds of books, in management, that will become something of a timeless anchor point. Quite simply, Debbie Haski-Leventhal has written the best textbook on strategic CSR I've ever seen, one I've been waiting for *without quite knowing* it, for a long time. It's a book I'll now be using not just in my management courses on CSR and sustainable value creation, but in my courses *on business strategy* and *managing change*, and *the future of management*. For that's what this book is—it's about the future of management. Why this excitement?

Let me share three reasons: (1) This book is Drucker-like—it is transcendent; (2) It's about the biggest business opportunity of the 21st century—and this book captures it perfectly, not as a trend but as an unstoppable trajectory; and (3) it's a book written with such grace, such relevance, and so creative in terms of engaging questions that learners, and executive educators, will love it. Let me detail several of these achievements, by drawing on a couple of stories.

This book is Drucker like—it is transcendent. I had what I called my 'Peter Drucker Moment' in March of 2003 when I had my last conversation with the legendary father of management thought—he was 93 years old and it was shortly before his passing. Yet his mind was so cogent and active. That day I ventured into the corporate social responsibility question. And like today's ethical meltdown of Volkswagen (costing the company billions) there were, at that time, huge debates surrounding big corporations such as Enron.

More specifically I used the occasion to ask about the difference between two intellectual giants: Drucker himself, a huge advocate of high-purpose business, and the Nobel economist Milton Friedman. I knew that Drucker saw management as a noble profession—and that its birth was a pivotal event in history—where the transition to a pluralist and free society of organizations meant huge progress over totalitarianism. So, it seemed as though it would be easy enough; it would be a snap to pit Drucker's views against those of Friedman who, as we all know, drew the anti-social responsibility line in the sand, arguing that the only social responsibility of business is business profit. I waited anxiously for the response. I invited him to critique the black and white idea that 'the only social responsibility of business is business'. But Drucker did not bite. No matter how hard I pressed, I could not get him to say one word about Friedman, not even his name. Like an impressionist artist, Drucker painted a different picture. He spoke from a higher vantage point about management as a liberal art—as an art that draws from disciplines as diverse as history, human science and the humanities— and spoke about the corporation as an organ in a body (society), as an interdependent part of a whole, whereby if any part were sick every other part would no doubt be affected: 'you cannot have a healthy body with a cancerous organ, and oppositely it is a healthy body that provides the nutrients for the healthy organ', he said. He also shared a belief in the notion that great companies are among humankind's noblest inventions. And then the conversation surfaced a surprise insight. Again, nothing related to my question about Friedman but something more profound and game-changing. Drucker said: 'You know, I hinted at it many years ago:

> 'Every social and global issue of our day is a business opportunity, in disguise, just waiting for the entrepreneurship and innovation of business, the pragmatism, and the capabilities of good management.'

I called it my 'Drucker moment' because, in one sentence, Drucker transcended the old and tired debate over the profit or social responsibility pendulum swing. He completely re-framed the simplistic questions: 'Does social responsibility pay?' and 'Is corporate citizenship some kind of sideline to the real business of business?' Like Schumpeter's creative destruction or Clayton Christensen's disruptive innovation, Drucker's comment is paradigm shifting, and it makes the tired debates, frankly, irrelevant. Why? Because it's a statement that reunites: it reunites social responsibility and exciting business purpose; it reunites enterprise with an interconnected world where our social and global issues matter; and it reunites the strengths of markets—for example, the spirit of entrepreneurship and free and open mutual exchange of value—with a higher-altitude query: *how do good managers and industry-leading stars actually turn our most pressing social and global issues into business opportunities and game-changing innovation?*

Well, I say all of this because that's one of the great achievements of this book. In a world where we experience the overproduction of mountains of definitions and endless back and forth debates—often insignificant fragments magnified all out of proportion and one point of view trying to demolish the other—we have those rare and special synthetic minds, like Drucker's. How are they different? They are transcendent. It's as if they are not interested in primarily moving against and negating any point of view, especially if it might within it have some kernel of truth, but, instead of opposing and demolishing views, they include them in and elevate them to a larger theoretical structure. They are searching not for fragments but for those world-historical significant insights begging for attention.

And that's precisely what Debbie Haski-Leventhal's synthetic writing does. It's so refreshing. In an era of hyper-specialization, her work brings us into the history and exciting future of CSR, the useful debates, and ultimately, a higher-level synthesis, much like Drucker did in our conversation and throughout his prolific career. In this volume Debbie creatively spans fields and has relevance for every area of management practice—strategy, marketing, organization development, innovation, and the future of management—in ways where the insights seem like a gift. For example, her chapter on ethics. Instead of dragging us down, it radiates with energy and reality—and instead of an afterthought or feeling of obligatory 'have to' in management education, I found myself saying this is 'something else'.

This book helps us see what a special time we are living in. Could it be that there has never been a better time to be alive in the field of management? Could it be that we are on the eve of management's finest hour? Again, before I highlight it in this volume—how this book carefully and historically shows that strategic CSR, as it's grown, is perhaps the largest business opportunity of the 21st century and that it's not a simple trend but an unstoppable trajectory—let me share a story about the first time I experienced that potential.

Nearly two decades ago I was honored to be invited to bring the large group Appreciative Inquiry Summit method (see Chapter 12 in this book) to a UN World Summit with Nobel Laureate Kofi Annan, and hundreds of CEOs from corporations such as Green Mountain Coffee Roasters, Daiwa Asset Management Ltd, Siemens AG, Tata Industries, Novo Nordisk, China Mobile, Royal Dutch Shell, Dow, Coca-Cola, Starbucks, Novartis, IBM and others. Unexpectedly, at this business and society Summit in the General Assembly Hall of the UN, we learned that we all share a common conviction: *that business has the opportunity to 'stand up, step up, and scale up' and be one of the most positive forces on the planet—and that the epic transition to a world economy of 'full spectrum flourishing' is no longer a utopian urge or mini-trend, but an observable and astonishing trajectory.*

That day, in the 'discovery phase' of this summit in which we were collaboratively designing the growth strategy of the UN Global Compact, over 2,000 stories of business and society innovation poured in: there were win-win-win innovations in business as a force for eradicating extreme poverty; business as a net-positive force for eco-regeneration and human thriving; and business as a force for peace, reunion and healing in some of the most extreme conflict zones in the world. With stories of solutions, magnified strengths and system-wide breakthroughs in the room, there was a groundswell of what can only be described as the emotion of *urgent optimism.* And it inspired the plenary conversation. The 500 CEOs were then invited to paint a picture of the desired future economy—to think 30 years out: 'what's happening a generation from now in your most positive image of the future that *you* most want to help create?' Leveraging that same kind of AI process, we then repeated this exploration at three more Summits—at the 2006, 2009 and 2014 Global Forums for Business as an Agent of World Benefit. The thematic similarities were remarkable.

In a brief composite form, here is the guiding image of the future that resonated across each of these world summits:

> It's a bright green restorative economy that purifies the air we breathe; it has eliminated the very concept of waste and toxic byproduct; extreme poverty has been eradicated from the planet; the economy is powered by 100% renewable, abundant energy and is saving the decarbonized world trillions in lower costs; it is a world of freer and truer markets with signals that generate positive incentives aligned with the long-term greater good (thus, it has virtually eliminated 'perverse incentives'); the economy's industry-leading stars are celebrated as CSR leaders and creators of sustainable value where the word 'sustainability-as-less-bad' has been replaced with the 'sustainability-as-flourishing' net positive; what we see when we look around are resilient, bright green, and walkable cities, re-generative agricultural practices, and astonishing exponential technologies for advancing health and connections for supercooperation; and all of this is built on an economy of institutions that are widely trusted as *positive institutions*—workplaces that elevate, magnify, and refract our highest human strengths (wisdom, courage, humanity, compassion, inspiration, collaborative creativity, freedom, hope, joy, learning, integrity, love and meaning) into the world. Moreover, humankind has successfully built the bridge from an unsustainable industrial age to a future that embraces the idea of full-spectrum flourishing where business can excel, human beings can thrive and nature can flourish. We have re-designed the entire material basis of our civilization—*successfully*.

And all of this, as discussed in this book, was even before the Paris agreements and when Unilever's CEO Paul Polman addressed the General Assembly pointing to how the global goals represent $12 trillion dollars of business opportunity. He spoke about the business privilege of living at a time when we can be the first generation in history to eradicate extreme, grinding poverty, and can find ways to power up new innovation and ennoble our work as managers:

> There is no business case for enduring poverty. We have an opportunity to unlock trillions of dollars through new markets, investments and innovation. But to do so, we must challenge our current practices and address poverty, inequality and environmental challenges. Every business will benefit from operating in a more equitable, resilient world if we achieve the Sustainable Development Goals. (Unilever, 2016)[1]

As you might imagine—where you literally see the field of management changing in front of your eyes at summits such as these—each of these experiences leaves you with a profound sense of privilege. For me and the management students we've brought to these decisive moments, as part of their education, I heard over and over those special words every professor wants to hear: 'seeing this is life changing' or 'I today feel more hope about our world's future than I ever have' or 'I feel like we are on the eve of management's finest hour' or 'I'm so glad I entered this profession, this noble profession of management'. Each of these comments by our millennials, each taken alone or together, says it's an incredible time to be alive in this field.

I say all this because this book carries this same electric current. One of the book's great achievements—I think it's a big achievement—is the way the author traces the history of strategic CSR, makes sense of it from both a moral standpoint, global challenges, and good business framework, and leaves you with the feeling that somehow its growth totally makes sense and has perhaps followed a natural trajectory—somehow in the cards. No, it's not about putting a superficial sense of hope on a troubled time—loss of trust in business, volatile world currency markets, deep inequalities, predictions of climate catastrophe, unthinkable possibilities of nuclear nightmare, and more—because the book engages these in a clear-minded way. But it does provide hope. It acknowledges no company is perfect and then proactively lifts up the data, the stories, the business case, and the *model elements within the models* of hundreds of companies. I think this is one of the reasons students will respond and thrill to this book. Strategic CSR, as it is narrated and taught here, is filled with urgent optimism and epic meaning.

This book will make great teachers even greater. My last comment is a selfish one. This book will make me, and you too, into a better teacher. It unites the best in learning theory with the worldwide movement to educate globally responsible managers who possess the mindsets and mental models, the positive leadership qualities, and the intrinsic sense of purpose needed to unite success with significance. Just its format is a rich reservoir of resources for helping educators return to the deepest roots of the term education, that is *educare,* which in Latin means 'to lead forth' and 'to bring out from within'. So, beyond the volume's narrative richness in combination with just the right academic rigor—memorable models, rich citations, worksheets for doing strategic CSR—the parts I love most are the group discussion questions. Like the treasure hidden in broad daylight, remarkable questions are the heart and soul of education. Every one of Debbie Haski-Leventhal's leadership questions made me pause, instilled more love for the subject matter and made me want to learn more. Remember what the poet Rilke said about the power of questions: 'Be patient … try to love the questions themselves … live the questions now. Perhaps someday you will then gradually without noticing it, live along some distant day into the answers.'

As I said at the outset, this is an important book. It is an incredible time to be alive in this field.

It is essential that we enable managers and all our young people to see themselves as participants in one of the most creative episodes in management history.

I cannot wait to look back 30 years from now. We know our task. It's to create a future where business can excel, human beings can thrive and nature can flourish. What will that take? In hope theory, it requires two things: it requires willpower x waypower. One without the other will falter yet both together create a positive, self-reinforcing loop. That's what this book does—in the language of scenario planning terms, it makes the hopeful scenario the more probable scenario.

David L. Cooperrider
Fairmount Santrol Professor
of Appreciative Inquiry
Faculty Founder, Fowler Center for
Business as an Agent of World Benefit
Weatherhead School of Management
Case Western Reserve University

Note

1   Unilever (2016) Available at: www.unilever.com/news/news-and- features/?monthfrom=1& yearfrom=2001&monthto=12&yearto=2017&type=featuredArticle (Accessed: 19 May 2017)

Acknowledgements

This book would not have come into existence without the support, encouragement and work of so many people. First and foremost, I would like to thank my family and in particular my husband, Paul, who is the wind beneath my wings. He is a true partner in every sense of the word, providing unlimited support and encouragement. I would also like to thank my two daughters: Emily, who teaches me about compassion towards animals and about following passion, and Ella, who at the young age of 7 is concerned about sustainability and the environment. It is the world these girls will grow up into that drives my tireless work on CSR and sustainability. I would also like to thank my parents, Ziva and Nissim, for their support, and especially my sister, Meirav, who encouraged me to start this book and helped with the book proposal.

The book began with a meeting in Sydney with SAGE Editor Matthew Waters, who showed enthusiasm for the topic of the book from the minute we met. His support and guidance were an essential part of the creation of this book. I would also like to thank SAGE and the entire team for assisting in finalising this book and bringing it to print.

I am grateful to three women who contributed to this book. Firstly, Dr Irit Alony, who authored the case studies in Chapters 3 to 7 and 9 to 11. Irit has been a wonderful colleague, a friend and a teacher. Without her, the writing of this book would have been a lonesome task. I am grateful to have her in my life. Akriti Mehra has been my assistant for many years but with this book she was promoted to the position of my guardian angel. Akriti worked tirelessly to edit the chapters, work on the references, develop models and made me feel like I have a true partner in writing. Finally, Mehndi Premraj Shivdasani, one of my first students on the Masters of Social Entrepreneurship (of which I am the programme director), wrote cases 1, 8 and 12 and several small sections in the book. Her passion and work to make our world more sustainable are inspirational.

I would like to thank the MGSM CSR Partnership Network, a network of businesses, not-for-profits, governments and academia which I initiated in 2012 to create and share CSR knowledge and inspirational practices. With the generous support of Johnson & Johnson Family of Companies in Australia, the MGSM CSR Partnership Network conducted several empirical studies, held workshops and events. I have learned so much from these companies about CSR and some of the network member companies are featured in this book.

Last but not least, I would like to thank Macquarie University and the Macquarie Graduate School of Management (MGSM) for enabling me to work effortlessly on developing CSR knowledge, with industry, academics and students. Since I do not see my role as a lecturer standing before a class, instead as an enabler of shared learning, I have gained enormous knowledge from my students. Through their discussions and presentations, many of the ideas, concepts and cases presented in this book came to my knowledge. The passion of so many business students to ensure the sustainable development of our society makes me believe that a better world than the one I grew up in is possible and that the next generation of business leaders will understand, like no one before them, that the world that we want presents both an enormous responsibility and unprecedented opportunities.

Prologue: An Introduction to the Book

Businesses acting as businesses, not as charitable donors, are the most powerful force for addressing issues we face. (Porter and Kramer, 2011: 64)

On strategic corporate social responsibility (CSR)

Nearly half a century ago, an economics professor noted that the only social responsibility of a business is to maximise profit. This was Milton Friedman, a Nobel laureate who published an article with this title in the *New York Times* and many believed his statement to be true. Over these 45 years, we have seen the magnitude of corporate social *irresponsibility*. From companies such as Enron, which put profit maximisation above legal and ethical duties, to many other companies violating human rights, abusing young children through child labour and destroying our planet beyond recognition. These companies too thought the only responsibility they had was towards their shareholders.

But something else has happened in these 50 years: a counter movement with a few pioneers that have become an enormous force over time. At about the same time that Friedman's article was released, two young entrepreneurs, Ben Cohen and Jerry Greenfield, started a small ice cream company in Vermont. Instead of just focusing on making great flavours and yielding good profit, they saw the potential of business as a force for good. From the early days of Ben & Jerry's, the founders used their brand to also protest against what is wrong and promote what they felt was right. From anti-war protests to environmental sustainability, from fair trade to social inclusion, ice cream suddenly received a new and powerful flavour.

Anita Roddick did the same with Body Shop and other examples started to increasingly emerge. A growing number of businesses realised they can be a 'force for good' and an 'agent for world benefit'. Over time, these companies inspired other business entrepreneurs to follow by engaging their employees in a way unseen previously and creating emotional brand-loyalty among many consumers. Purpose and values became an important aspect of business and CSR was seen as an effective way to benefit both the business and its stakeholders, including society and the environment.

These pioneers and many others changed society and altered the market. The market signals are stronger than ever before, telling us that 'business as usual' is no longer an option. That growth at any cost, including to human lives and the environment, is no longer an option. That treating the planet as an open sewer is no longer an option. That having only one stakeholder group prioritised far and above everyone else, is no longer an option. Consumers, employees, community, interest groups and even shareholders are signalling clearly and loudly – we need change, we desire change, we must have change, because all this time, we are running out of time.

And the change is here. In the year 2000, the then United Nations (UN) Sectary-General Kofi Annan called for business to give a human face to a global market and become a 'force for good'. Together with 50 business leaders, the UN Global Compact was initiated – a compact between companies and the UN, aimed at increasing collaboration and responsibility by involving the business sector in achieving the Millennium Development Goals and subsequently the Sustainable Development Goals. The UN Global Compact has over 15,000 members and many are committed to being a force for good. Business leaders are expected to take part in achieving the 17 global Sustainable Development Goals.

Businesses have enormous power, resources, networks, knowledge and skills. If all of that was harnessed towards ending poverty, hunger and war, there is no limit to what could be achieved. With the changing expectations of consumers, employees and regulators, being best in the world is no longer enough. Businesses are now also expected to be best *for* the world: to be socially and environmentally responsible, sustainable and ethical. For financial, moral and other reasons, business leaders need to know how to be more strategic about their CSR, create shared value and work with their internal and external stakeholders.

Strategic CSR is not about doing less harm or giving some money to charity but it is focused on a holistic business approach that demonstrates responsibility in its strategy and core operations, while working from a multi-stakeholder perspective and with a long-term focus. It is not only a shift away from the narrow and short-term view of maximising profit, but it is also a transition from corporate philanthropy that is based on random acts of charity and CSR as a marketing strategy, which could lead to greenwashing. It is about tying the company's CSR to what it knows best and what it stands for. By achieving this alignment, the power of business can be effectively harnessed to benefit the world.

About this book

This book is based on the concept of strategic CSR as was developed by Werther and Chandler (2011). After close examination of many approaches to CSR, including creating shared value, conscious capitalism and others, it seems that strategic CSR offers the most holistic and comprehensive approach and that by working according to this approach, business could become much more powerful in addressing the most burning issues our global society faces today. Other approaches are also featured in this book to create a comprehensive CSR knowledge and practice.

The book came to be out of mere personal necessity. After years of teaching CSR to hundreds of CSR students, I could not find a CSR textbook that ties both theory and practice well enough together. Believing that students and practitioners need to know the concepts, theories and philosophical approaches to CSR but also acquire the practical tools that allow them to implement this knowledge is what motivated me to write this book. Since business schools have a growing duty to develop leaders who are responsible and ethical, a textbook providing theory and practical examples related to CSR was required.

Indeed, the book was developed based on the ideas and principles of responsible management education. After the business scandals and ethical meltdowns of the 2000s, a debate started about the role of business schools in ensuring their graduates are ethical and responsible. As the president of Texas A&M University, Robert Gates said in 2002: 'All of these liars and cheats and thieves are graduates of our universities'. The response was the formation of the Principle of Responsible Management Education, or PRME, at the UN Global Compact. Since its official launch in 2007 by the Former UN Secretary-General Ban Ki-moon, the initiative has grown to more than 650 leading academic institutions from over 85 countries. Signatories commit to six principles, which are organised around purpose, values, method, research, partnership and dialogue. As per the expectations of business schools to be part of the CSR movement, more teaching materials are required and this is one of the reasons to develop a CSR book which offers a strong connection between theory and practice as well as a holistic and positive approach. Together with PRME, I conducted a bi-annual international study on business students and their attitudes towards CSR and responsible management education. The results of these surveys demonstrated how eager many students are to learn more about CSR and sustainability, which motivated me further to write this book.

Inspired by positive psychology, positive management and positive frameworks such as Appreciative Inquiry, this book is aimed at showcasing what is good in business and what is possible with CSR. It does not imply ignorance of corporate irresponsibility nor does it imply naivety. It is based on the conviction that by showcasing mainly positive examples of CSR, more companies and business leaders will be inspired to become more ethical and responsible. The world does not yet have (and may never have) perfect companies, impeccable CEOs or flawless people.

However, by celebrating positive business aspects, we can show that CSR is possible and that it can have a positive impact on all stakeholders. While the book does also offer a critical approach and sporadically discusses cases of irresponsibility and the negative impact of business, the focus is primarily positive.

The book is both descriptive and normative. It is descriptive in the way it presents existing knowledge, models and concepts and in the way it describes the current and past events, behaviour and practices of corporations and organisations. However, it is also normative as it is based on certain values and worldview, according to which business has a remarkable opportunity to address the biggest issues that humanity faces, and it needs to take responsibility over its actions and impacts. Some CSR and business ethics books and articles take a more distant approach but there is a growing number of publications that offer a value-based thought. This book takes a stand on CSR and the role of business.

Finally, while the book is based on the term 'corporate social responsibility' (CSR), it is not focused only on corporations. As will be explained in Chapter 1, we use 'CSR' as it is the most commonly used term and the one used for strategic CSR. However, the models and tools in this book can serve small companies, social enterprises and various types of organisations.

The structure of the book

The book includes 12 chapters organised in three parts. The first part, CSR Thought, provides the theoretical background of CSR. Chapter 1 examines CSR thought, definitions, concepts and critical perspectives. Next, Chapter 2 focuses on CSR theories and models, including CSR stages, CSR congruence, creating shared value and strategic CSR. The following Chapter 3 is based on the stakeholder theory and examines various approaches to stakeholder management and integration.

The second part, CSR Approaches and Implementation, examines various CSR approaches and how they can be implemented to create and lead a responsible, ethical and sustainable organisation. It begins with Chapter 4 on business ethics, which examines the way that philosophy can assist us in making sound business decisions. Next, Chapter 5 focuses on environmental sustainability and the role of business in assuring the future of this planet. Chapter 6 thereafter focuses on responsible leadership and applies various leadership approaches and models to the context of CSR. Finally, Chapter 7 discusses the ways to practically involve stakeholders, particularly employees, consumers and investors, in the CSR efforts of the company.

The third and final part of this book is CSR Measurement and Communication. It begins with Chapter 8, which displays social impact and assessment methods, followed by Chapter 9 on benchmarking tools. Chapter 10 discusses CSR reporting and Chapter 11 focuses on CSR marketing, both of which can become powerful channels to involve more stakeholders in the CSR efforts of the company and inspire others to follow. Finally, Chapter 12 looks at making the shift towards CSR and the way forward. It also details the future of CSR and offers a conclusion to the book.

Each chapter begins with an opening case study: a positive example of what one company does in the topic discussed in that chapter. None of the companies presented here are perfect but they all do outstanding work in the area presented and this is what we focus on. Each case is followed by questions that can be discussed in class or in small groups. The chapter then begins with an introduction to the topic and why it is an important component of strategic CSR, followed by various aspects of these topics. All chapters also include mini case studies, questions for reflection and discussion, and exercises. Each chapter ends with a summary, key definitions, general questions, references and further reading and links, all of which can be used to enhance class discussion and learning.

References

Gates, R. (2002) Convocation address by Dr Robert M. Gates, President, Texas A & M University.

Porter, M. E. and Kramer, M. R. (2011) 'Creating shared value', *Harvard Business Review*, 89(1/2): 62–77.

Werther, W. B. and Chandler, D. (2011) *Strategic corporate social responsibility: Stakeholders in a global environment* (2nd edn). Thousand Oaks, CA: Sage.

Part I
CSR thought

Our Changing World and the Evolution of CSR 1

Learning outcomes

By the end of this chapter, students should be able to:

- articulate several definitions and names of CSR and understand the evolvement of the concept
- contextualise CSR thought in history
- explain what CSR is and what it is not, and why it is important to know the difference
- detail the importance of CSR in our changing world
- critically reflect on current approaches to CSR in theory and practice.

Case study   Ronald McDonald's House Charities – corporate philanthropy

In the early 1970s, the daughter of a Philadelphia Eagles' player, Fred Hill, was diagnosed with leukaemia. Fred found that in addition to facing every parent's worst nightmare, people whose children were severely ill had to spend nights on uncomfortable hospital benches and get food from vending machines. In addition to the medical care for such children, Fred realised there is a need for a place for their families to stay and get the physical, mental, emotional and even financial support they require. He approached Dr Audrey Evans from the Children's Hospital of Philadelphia and McDonald's – one of the biggest fast-food retailers in the world. Together they established the first Ronald McDonald House, a not-for-profit organisation, with the purpose of providing a 'home away from home' for families with seriously ill children at little or no cost.

Fast forward to 2016: there are currently 366 Ronald McDonald Houses in over 63 countries and regions operating in 90 per cent of the world's top children's hospitals. Additionally, there are 215 Ronald McDonald Family Rooms in 23 countries and regions offering families a peaceful place to regroup and regain the strength needed to support their children during their treatment. The charity also operates 50 Ronald McDonald Care Mobiles, which are state-of-the-art vehicles built to provide paediatric health care services to children in nine countries and regions including the US and countries such as Poland and Thailand. These mobiles have a reception, examination rooms, a laboratory and medical record areas, all designed to deliver preventative health care including immunisation and health education, diagnosis and treatment as well as referrals to patients. The charity also supports future generations by offering scholarships and grants for young and promising high school children in the US in need of financial assistance, enabling them to receive a college education. To date, they have awarded scholarships worth over US$60 million to an estimated 31,350 students, irrespective of race, colour, creed, religion, sexual orientation, gender, disability or national origin. They have served over 7.1 million children and their families, helping them save approximately US$700 million in lodging and meal services. The charity is operated by thousands of paid staff and engages 390,000 volunteers who assist with administrative and maintenance-related activities.

Ronald McDonald House Charities is operated by McDonald's, the largest fast-food restaurant chain in the world. With 36,899 restaurants worldwide serving almost 69 million people a day, the company had an annual revenue of US$24.6 billion in 2016. The Ronald McDonald's House Charities is an example of ongoing corporate philanthropy, focused on charitable giving that is aligned with the company's brand. Each year, McDonald's run the McHappy Day – an annual event in which a percentage of the day's Big Macs sales go to the charity. McDonald's contributes approximately US$1 million annually to the charity and its support extends from monetary contributions (philanthropy) and volunteerism to cause-related marketing promotions and the space to place donation boxes located in every restaurant. The organisation is also supported by various signature, official and friendly partners such as The Coca-Cola Company and Southwest Airlines that provide annual funding ranging from US$100,000 to $500,000. As part of its CSR, McDonald's has helped to positively impact millions of children and their families, enabling them to be an active part of their children's treatment and wellbeing. McDonald's has been a source of support that continues to provide valuable resources to help the organisation expand its core programmes and services.

Despite all the efforts being made by McDonald's to help families in need, its CSR is controversial. Since it is a fast food company, McDonald's has been criticised for its unhealthy food and beverage offerings (Howlett, 2016). The company markets its products to children from an early age so much so that most children in the US can recognise McDonald's even before they can speak (Robbins, 2011). It has been found that approximately every month, nine out of ten children in the US eat at a McDonald's restaurant (Howlett, 2016). The company generates over 460,500 tons of waste every year in the US alone (Ma, 2013), although according to its own website, McDonald's works on reducing waste and increasing in-store recycling.

The company is currently making efforts to offer its customers healthier food and drink options by opting to use cage-free eggs and Fairtrade ingredients, by reducing the preservatives in its core products, and to make environmentally conscious decisions regarding its supply chain, but there are still great opportunities for improvement. There is no taking away from the fact that the company's charity has had a positive impact on the lives of many; however, there also exists immense

(Continued)

scope for the company to operate more ethically and hold itself accountable for the impact its products have on its customers.

Questions

1. What do you find positive in the work that McDonald's is doing to help the community? Would you say that it makes the company more responsible?
2. Does Ronald McDonald House fit with your idea of what CSR should be?
3. What would you suggest the company does to become more responsible?
4. If stakeholders are defined as any individual, group or institution who is affected, positively or negatively, by the achievement of an organisation's purpose, who would you say the stakeholders of McDonald's are? Are they being affected more positively or negatively? What does it teach you about McDonald's CSR?

References

Howlett, A. (2016) Why are McDonald's foods and ingredients unhealthy for you? Available at: http://thenutritionalsource.com/what-food-ingredients-in-mcdonalds-hamburger-bad-unhealthy-for-you-and-why (Accessed: 7 May 2017)

Ma, C. (2013) McDonald's creates 1/2 million TONS of garbage each year in the U.S. alone. Available at: http://truthcdm.com/mcdonalds-creates-12-million-tons-of-garbage-each-year-in-the-u-s-alone (Accessed: 7 May 2017)

Robbins, J. (2011) How bad is McDonald's food? Available at: www.huffingtonpost.com/john-robbins/how-bad-is-mcdonalds-food_b_754814.html (Accessed: 7 May 2017)

Links

Dexter, S. C., Klein, K. A., Clark, D. A., Ross, S. L. and Veille, J. C. (2004) 'The Ronald McDonald House as an alternative to antepartum hospitalization', Journal of Perinatology, 24(10): 623–5.

Haski-Leventhal, D., Hustinx, L. and Handy, F. (2011) 'What money cannot buy: The distinctive and multidimensional impact of volunteers', Journal of Community Practice, 19(2): 138–58.

McDonald's (2015) Sustainability report. Available at: www.mcdonalds.co.jp/company/csr/pdf/MCD_CSR2015_English_0425.pdf (Accessed: 16 April 2017)

McDonald's (2017) McHappy day ad. Available at: www.youtube.com/watch?v=XGYMcjnuGcM (Accessed: 17 April 2017)

McDonald's (2017) Official corporate website. Available at: http://corporate.mcdonalds.com/mcd.html (Accessed: 16 April 2017)

McDonald's (2017) Ronald McDonald House Charities. Available at: www.youtube.com/watch?v=8wOCFS6SyzE (Accessed: 16 April 2017)

McDonald's (2017) Ronald McDonald House Charities. Available at: www.rmhc.org/ (Accessed: 3 April 2017)

McDonald's (2017) Ronald McDonald House Charities, Australia. Available at: www.rmhc.org.au (Accessed: 17 April 2017)

Introduction: The importance of corporate social responsibility (CSR)

CSR, once a do-good sideshow, is now seen as mainstream. But as yet, too few companies are doing it well. (*The Economist*, 2008)

CSR has been gaining attention, popularity and importance in the last few decades. It is perceived as important because it offers a remarkable opportunity to discuss the role of business in society after decades (if not centuries) during which business was not always acting in the best interest of our global society.

CSR illustrates a direction for business to take so it can help address the biggest challenges of our time. It is an important alternative to the extreme capitalism that possibly led markets to financial crises and ethical meltdowns in recent years. Social movements such as Occupy Wall Street and many others called for a reflection on the direction of capitalism and what alternatives should be considered. It is now acknowledged that responsible and ethical business is essential for the future of our world. In times of climate change, globalisation, frequent humanitarian crises and ongoing conflicts, business, with its resources, knowledge and power, can offer much more than doing less harm. There are growing signals from the market that companies are expected to be more responsible in their entire value chain, and CSR can be an effective pathway to meet these expectations.

In their book on strategic CSR, Werther and Chandler (2011: xxiii) wrote: 'Between the great good and the terrible harm businesses produce, lies concern about the proper role of corporations in society, especially in times of globalisation and technological innovation.' In 1999, Kofi Annan (the then UN Secretary-General) said that we need to give a human face to the global market (UN, 1999). As our world, economy and society rapidly change, CSR can offer a way for business to be responsible and ethical.

Furthermore, companies that genuinely contribute to the world, ensure responsibility and sustainability in everything that they do and in what they stand for, see many benefits for all stakeholders. As we will demonstrate in the following chapters, employees are more engaged when working in companies that have a strong purpose. Consumers often prefer to buy from companies that have a good reputation in the community and are willing to pay more for products that are sustainable. The community benefits from strong and ongoing partnerships with the corporations that operate within them. Governments and world organisations get a genuine partner to help them address society's biggest challenges, far beyond paying taxes. The environment is then looked after and our only planet is taken better care of. Consequently, shareholders benefit when all the other stakeholders are satisfied and should receive a better return on investment from a company that is sustainable and as such can yield profit (however, not necessarily maximise profit) for a longer term. CSR can contribute to positive outcomes for the company as well as to all its other stakeholders.

CSR is a growing trend in many big and small companies around the world, but the perceptions of what CSR is and related practices rapidly change. While some companies still continue with 'business as usual', many others understand that they need to step up and become part of the solution. Some companies still cause harm to humans, animals and the environment through their actions. Others are only using CSR for marketing and public relations purposes, while neglecting to fix harm caused by their core operations. Others yet see CSR only as philanthropy, focusing on the donations and volunteering of their employees. However, a growing number of companies are now adopting a holistic approach to their corporate responsibility, ensuring sustainability and responsibility in everything that they do and aligning their CSR to their business core mission and strategy. The latter is often referred to as 'strategic CSR', and it is this approach that this book is based upon.

In this chapter, CSR will be defined and debated, while shedding light on the aforementioned changes in CSR perceptions and practices and the drivers for this change. We will examine the shift from a narrow view to a broad view of business responsibility and observe the current motivations of business to engage in CSR.

Questions for reflection and discussion

1. What are other reasons besides the ones stated above that make CSR so important?
2. There are over 150 definitions of CSR. Why do you think so many different definitions of CSR exist?
3. What does having so many definitions tell us about CSR?

CSR defined and debated

Examining the evolvement of CSR definitions can assist us in gaining a better understanding of CSR approaches and trends and in capturing the underlying shifts in the role of business in society. While we cannot cover all the definitions of CSR in this chapter, we will examine four definitions of CSR and observe how they have evolved over time.

The first definition is from 1979 by Archie Carroll who claimed 'CSR encompasses the economic, legal, ethical and philanthropic expectations that society has of organisations at a given point in time' (Carroll, 1979: 500). The main point of this definition is that companies have responsibilities in addition to maximising profit: legal responsibility (to obey the law); ethical responsibility (to do the right thing); and philanthropic responsibility (to give money to charity). Listing these four responsibilities in this order could implicitly suggest that financial responsibility always comes first, even if it implies unethical behaviour. Another issue with this definition is that it puts organisations in a very passive position – CSR is about the expectations that society has of the organisation, not the responsibility that the organisation should have and act upon. Since what is acceptable today could become unacceptable very quickly, taking a passive position towards CSR instead of a proactive one could be risky.

A second definition of CSR was introduced by Edward Freeman in 1984. Freeman brought the term 'stakeholders' into this discourse and the approach according to which a corporate has a role in society and that it is larger than just pursuing profit. According to the stakeholder theory, CSR can be defined as 'a view of the corporation and its role in society that assumes a responsibility among firms to pursue goals in addition to profit maximisation and a responsibility of the stakeholders to hold the firm responsible for its actions' (Werther and Chandler, 2011: 5). In this definition we see that companies have a broad set of stakeholders they need to consider and whose expectations they need to meet. This would require a more holistic business management approach than just maximising profit. Since Freeman defined stakeholders as people who are affected by the company's achievement of its goals, it is not difficult to see that these stakeholders include other groups than just the shareholders/owners. However, even in this definition, the corporate is still in a passive position, and it is the role of the stakeholders to hold the firm responsible for its actions.

A more recent definition of CSR is found in an article by Aaronson (2003: 310), in which CSR is defined as 'business decision making linked to ethical values, compliance with legal requirements, and respect for people, communities, and the environment around the world'. Accordingly, CSR is about managerial practices such as decision making, but it is also aligned with ethical and legal responsibilities. While the first part is a reference to Carroll's definition, the second part about respect for people, communities and the environment could suggest a more holistic approach. This definition specifically includes the environment, which has become more relevant in recent years, while also referring to global responsibilities according to which companies are responsible for their employees and other stakeholders, regardless of their global location.

As the focus of this book is strategic CSR, it is important to know how it is defined. Werther and Chandler (2011: 40) defined strategic CSR as 'the incorporation of a holistic CSR perspective within a firm's strategic planning and core operations so that the firm is managed in the interest of a broad set of stakeholders to achieve maximum economic and social value over the medium to long term.' This definition offers a more holistic view of CSR while emphasising the importance of tying CSR to the company's strategic planning and core operations. This definition also includes a broad set of stakeholders, an extensive view of business responsibility and the importance of doing all of the above not only for short-term marketing benefits but also for long-term benefits for all.

These authors differentiated between strategic CSR and what can be seen as 'traditional CSR' or 'responsive CSR'. Responsive CSR occurs when the firm becomes involved in a generic social issue that is not related to operations or when it structures its value chain to avoid any negative social impacts. As such, responsive or traditional CSR can be seen as 'random acts of charity' that have nothing to do with what the company does and what it stands for.

Questions for reflection and discussion

Return to the case study of Ronald McDonald's House Charities and the mother company, McDonald's. Under which of the above definitions would this be a case of CSR? Would you say it is strategic or responsive CSR? Why?

CSR: What's in the name?

While this book is on CSR, and more specifically on strategic CSR, there are many other similar concepts that are often used interchangeably with CSR. These include (but are not limited to) corporate responsibility, corporate citizenship, sustainability, conscious business, social business and creating shared value or CSV. There are some shared meanings but also differences between these terms. Figure 1.1 details some of these alternative concepts and terms.

Many companies choose to use the concept of *corporate responsibility* (CR) instead of CSR. Their main rationale is that companies need to be fully responsible,

Figure 1.1   Alternative concepts and terms to CSR

not just socially, and therefore broaden their scope of responsibility by omitting the S. Some claim that CSR does not include environmental responsibility, while CR does, and they opt to use the latter instead. Similarly, some organisations started using social responsibility (SR) because it can be applied to any organisation, not just corporates.

Another common name is *corporate citizenship* (CC). CC has emerged as a prominent term in the management literature, particularly after the 2002 UN Global Corporate Citizenship summit in New York. It is based on the meaning of good citizenship behaviour (responsible, contributing to the community and obeying the law). Matten and Crane (2005) argued that CC is broader than CSR and includes more responsibilities. Maignan et al. (1999: 457) defined CC as 'the extent to which businesses meet the economic, legal, ethical and discretionary responsibilities imposed on them by their stakeholders.' While this is almost identical to Carroll's definition of CSR, it emphasises actively meeting responsibilities as opposed to detailing the responsibilities as a list.

Another relevant concept that has gained more support recently and will be referred to often in this book is conscious capitalism and *conscious business* (Mackey and Sisodia, 2014). This concept is based on a movement started by John Mackey, the founder and CEO of Whole Foods Market in the US, pushing for a values-based economy with social and environmental concerns at both global and local levels. Conscious business refers to business galvanised by higher purposes that serve and align the interests of all major stakeholders. This is one of the few concepts in the CSR literature that emphasises the importance of purpose and it will be vastly used in this book.

When searching for any company's description of its CSR, it is often found under a web page titled *sustainability*. While sustainability is often seen as related to the impact of a firm on the natural environment, it gained a more holistic perspective when it started to include the triple bottom line: financial, social and environmental sustainability (Elkington, 2004). As such, instead of speaking about responsible business, people sometimes speak about sustainable business, based on the idea that businesses that are more responsible would also be more sustainable in the long term.

Another way of describing a responsible business is through the terms *social business* and *social enterprise*. Social enterprises are about using business models and knowledge to achieve both financial sustainability and social purpose. Social enterprise seems to be somewhere in the middle between socially responsible business and a revenue-generating non-profit organisation (Dees, 1998). While a social business is more purpose driven than a business with CSR, it is sometimes difficult to tell the difference. There are socially responsible businesses that are now looking and behaving more like a social enterprise.

One more method of referring to responsible businesses is *creating shared value* (CSV), a concept developed by Michael Porter, a professor at Harvard University as well as a management thought leader, and Mark Kramer, founder and managing director of FSG, a consultancy agency in the US. The concept is covered extensively in Chapter 2 and focuses on identifying and expanding the link between economic and societal progress. It is based on the premise of making a positive change in society through creating innovative products and new markets (Porter and Kramer, 2011).

However, the term CSR was chosen for this book rather than its alternatives for several reasons. Firstly, it is the most commonly known and commonly used term by people who study and practise business responsibility. Using Google Scholar, CSR yields far more results than any other term mentioned above. In many business schools, CSR and business ethics are now taught as part of their commitment to responsible management education. More importantly, this book is mainly based on the concept of strategic CSR, and this is the concept used in this approach. However, it is important to know that scholars and practitioners use other terms and concepts, so that you can identify them and know the difference between them and CSR.

Brief history of CSR thought

Although the concept of corporate social responsibility and its acronym CSR have only been in use for several decades, the origins of CSR thought can be traced to early human thought, from religion and Greek philosophy, to scholars of the 17th and 18th centuries. To focus, we will start with Adam Smith (although we will get back to some older sources in Chapter 4 on business ethics) and only cover some highlights in the evolution of CSR thought. Figure 1.2 summarises some of the main events in this process.

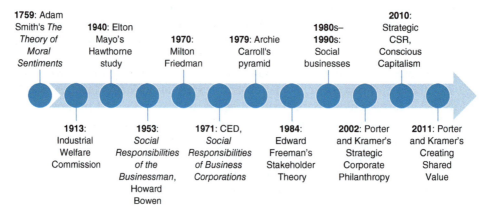

Figure 1.2   CSR thought timeline

Many business students and scholars know Adam Smith as the father of modern economy and capitalism. Born in 1723, his famous book *The Wealth of Nations* (Smith, 1776) is considered the first modern work of economics. It was the first book to introduce core concepts of economy, which are still used today, such as the division of labour, productivity and free markets. It is particularly the last concept (free markets and the invisible hand) that encouraged political and economic leaders in the last century to decrease regulation in the market (particularly in the US) and which we can carefully refer to as 'extreme capitalism' in which power and money are the most important goals. However, few people know Adam Smith's earlier work, which was the foundation of *The Wealth of Nations*. In *The Theory of Moral Sentiments* (1759), Smith talks about altruism and empathy, our need to care for others, and how, in addition to the famous 'invisible hand' of free markets, we also need a 'caring hand' for society. Smith outlined an ethical approach that is based on the human ability to empathise with others. When *The Wealth of Nations* is read with the moral foundations offered in *Moral Sentiments*, a more compassionate capitalism emerges. In the book *Conscious Capitalism* (Mackey and Sisodia, 2014), *Moral Sentiments* is used to argue that capitalism is not evil, and can be used in a way that contributes to all stakeholders.

Adam Smith wrote his book at the beginning of the industrial revolution and it is interesting to see how this revolution changed our society for better and for worse. While this revolution included the creation of machines and factories to produce items to make our life more convenient, it came at a cost. Moving from an agricultural society of farmers to the industrial society of employees, people somewhat became disposable machine parts. While the industrial revolution introduced and increased the standard of living, not everyone benefited from it. Women, children and other socially disadvantaged groups were particularly affected. At the beginning of the 20th century, concerns about the welfare of workers were more vocally raised. These issues were discussed by Karl Marx, particularly in his book *Capital* (1867) and captured in Charlie Chaplin's film *Modern Times* (1936). Consequently, in 1913 the Industrial Welfare Commission (IWC) was established in California to regulate working conditions for employees, including wages, hours and safety. This is an important step in the process in which CSR was directed towards employees (i.e. internal CSR).

This approach was strengthened by the Hawthorne study conducted by Professor Elton Mayo in the US (Mayo, 1945). In this study, which focused on the productivity of workers in an electric factory outside Chicago, the researchers studied the effect of light on the workers' performance (remember that the approach to employees at the time, led by scientific management, was as parts of a machine that need to perform better). What they eventually discovered was that it was not the physical conditions that impacted the results, but rather the attention given to the workers, treating them like human beings, asking them about their working conditions and how these can be improved. This and other studies laid the foundations for the development of organisational behaviour as a field of study and for the humanistic management approach.

In 1953, a book was published entitled *Social Responsibilities of the Businessman* by Howard Bowen. It was the first time that someone had written specifically about CSR and on social entrepreneurship, both of which only became popular years later. It is therefore often seen as the milestone of modern-era CSR. Bowen (1953) argued that the large corporations in the US are vital centres of power, which impact many lives every day. The key question that Bowen (1953) asked (and it is possible to say that it is still being asked today) was: what responsibilities to society are businessmen reasonably expected to assume?

Bowen's book started a debate on CSR, which was argued against most strongly in 1970 by the Nobel Laureate economist Professor Milton Friedman. In a well-known article in the *New York Times*, Friedman (1970) argued that the only social responsibility of a company is to make as much money for its stockholders as possible. CSR, unless used as a means to make more profit, is immoral. Friedman was a strong advocate of the 'narrow approach' to business responsibility (which will be further discussed next). His main argument was that shareholders invest money in the company, and the managers have no moral right to use this money in any other way than to maximise profits. Just as they cannot build a villa in Tuscany with this money, argued Friedman, they cannot use it to give to charities. They can use it for CSR only as a marketing strategy to maximise profit (Friedman, 1970).

A counter approach was that corporates have responsibilities beyond their financial duty to maximise shareholder value. In 1971 the Committee for Economic Development (CED) published the *Social Responsibilities of Business Corporations*. CED observed that business functions by public consent, and its basic purpose is to serve constructively the needs of society to the satisfaction of society. As such, the social contract between business and society was changing substantially and business was expected to assume broader responsibilities to society. Furthermore, the CED noted that business assumes a role in contributing to the quality of life and that this role is more than just providing goods and services.

Similarly, in 1979, Archie Carroll argued that in addition to financial responsibility, companies also have a legal responsibility (to obey the law and regulations), an ethical responsibility (to do what is right, fair and just) and a philanthropic or discretionary responsibility (to be a good corporate citizen, give back to the community). Later (Carroll, 1991, 1999) this was portrayed as a pyramid of responsibilities; as the first two responsibilities are required, the ethical responsibility is expected and the last one – the philanthropic responsibility – is only desired (by society, that is). Figure 1.3 captures the essence of this pyramid, which will be further discussed in Chapter 2.

In 1984 there was another leap forward in CSR thought, when Edward Freeman developed the stakeholder theory and argued that companies are not only accountable to their shareholders but to a broad set of stakeholders. Freeman defined stakeholders as any individual, group or institution who is affected, positively or

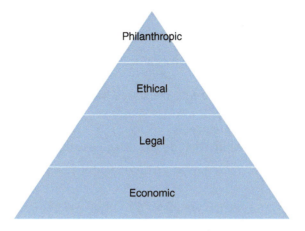

Figure 1.3   Carroll's pyramid of business responsibilities (based on Carroll, 1991)

negatively, by the achievement of an organisation's purpose. As such, stakeholders include employees, consumers, governments, the community in which the company operates and even the environment. This was another attempt to broaden the responsibility of business from financial alone, to social and environmental as well. Stakeholder theory will be further discussed in Chapter 3.

In the 1970s and 1980s there was an increase in the number of scholarly work on CSR, with theories, concepts and empirical studies starting to emerge. It slowly became an interest for companies, managers and other stakeholders. Some companies that were established at the time, such as Ben & Jerry's or The Body Shop, showed that having a social mission and working for a higher-level purpose instead of only maximising profit could be good business. The focus, however, was on corporate philanthropy and in 2002 Porter and Kramer published an article in *Harvard Business Review* (HBR) arguing that companies that are not good for society would not be able to maintain their competitive advantage in the future. However, to do so companies need to tie their giving (philanthropy) to their overall strategy and give to charities that are more aligned with their brand and what they stand for. In 2011 the two authors further developed their ideas and published another HBR article on 'creating shared value', which was about making financial value and social value at the same time (Porter and Kramer, 2011).

At the same time, another concept began to emerge, of 'strategic CSR' (Werther and Chandler, 2011). Similar to the previous HBR article by Porter and Kramer (2002), the writers on strategic CSR emphasised the importance of aligning the company's CSR (not just its philanthropic endeavours) to the company's strategy. However, over time this concept was further developed and it will be fully presented in the next chapter.

EXERCISE

Read Milton Friedman's *New York Times* article from 1970 on the Internet:

1. What are the main arguments he makes for the narrow view of business responsibility?
2. What are the counter arguments?
3. What do you agree with? What do you disagree with?

From a narrow view to a broad view of business responsibilities

As can be seen in the aforementioned evolution of CSR thought, there is a shift from a narrow view of business responsibility, being to only maximise profit, to a broader view that includes other responsibilities as well.

The narrow view

The narrow view, such as presented by Milton Friedman, argues that business exists to produce products and services, sell them and maximise profit. This is what they are legally bound to do. Shareholders invest money in the company so they can get a good return on investment, not to solve societal issues. As such, Friedman and others went as far as to call CSR immoral. Business responsibility is to provide people with jobs and salaries, allowing employees to live well and consume, and this is their contribution to society. As such, we do not need CSR.

Another argument for the narrow view is based on the concept of the invisible hand (Smith, 1776), according to which markets will ensure business responsibility, since if they behave illegally or immorally, the market will punish them. Others claim that societal issues are not business problems. Business pays taxes to the government and it is the government's role to address issues such as homelessness, food security and poverty. Not only is it not the responsibility of business, but business also lacks the knowledge, capacity and capability to deal with such issues. We are business people, they say, not social workers, and it is the government's responsibility to address societal and environmental issues, including the ones created by business.

Finally, an argument against CSR comes from another extreme perspective (one could say from a more left-wing one). Anti-capitalists argue that CSR is not good because it is mostly 'greenwashing', being used instrumentally to brainwash us, manipulate consumers to believe that the business is good for the world. It is often a lip service, allowing businesses to patch up their immoral behaviour and the harm they cause to people, animals and the ecosystem. Business needs to change more radically, they argue, rather than just give some money to charity. Moreover, CSR allows businesses to impose their capitalist values upon us, and they have enough power in the world already.

The broad view

On the other hand, there are many who argue, such as Carroll (Carroll and Shabana, 2010) and others, that businesses have additional responsibilities to making profit. Business operates within society and only thrives because of people who are employees, consumers and even shareholders. As such, business has an enormous responsibility to ensure the wellbeing of people and to avoid harm. A concept that has been used more frequently in the past two decades is business social licence to operate (Moffat and Zhang, 2014). In addition to the legal licences businesses need to operate, companies also need to be legitimate by societal standards, cause no harm and create positive impact on our society and the community in which they operate.

If we are going to use Adam Smith's idea of the invisible hand, we should also use his idea of the caring hand and promote a society that is built on morality, caring and empathy to drive our wealth and health. Furthermore, with information asymmetry (the inability of consumers, governments and others to know what truly occurs within a firm), companies can get away with immoral behaviour for years without being 'punished' by the market, if at all, and as such, the invisible hand is not always an effective regulator.

Even shareholders, who are often perceived as being profit-driven only, have started to shift towards a more holistic point of view of business responsibility. As we will see in Chapter 7, many investors are looking for sustainable businesses to invest in, not only because they are morally driven to do so, but also because they understand that sustainable companies have a better likelihood of survival in the future and in recent years also yielded better return on investment (at least in some parts of the world).

In addition, some companies have realised that they need a stronger purpose than just maximising profit. Many business leaders realise that being number one in the world and crashing all your competitors is no longer engaging. Instead of being best in the world, companies needed to be best *for* the world to really engage their stakeholders and create a trustworthy brand. While profit is extremely important for the survival of any business, it is only the result of a good business, not its purpose. We are not just profit-driven creatures, we are also purpose-driven ones, and companies that lack purpose will not be able to engage people for the long term. As Peter Drucker, the management guru, once said:

> Profit for a company is like oxygen for a person. If you don't have enough of it, you're out of the game. But if you think your life is about breathing, you're really missing something. (cited in Werther and Chandler, 2011: 15)

As for the claim that business lacks the capacity and capability to be socially responsible and address local, national and global needs, many argue otherwise. Porter and Kramer (2011) claimed that if a business acts as a business, not as a charitable donor to address societal challenges, there is no limit to what can be achieved. Business has remarkable resources, knowledge, talent, networks and power. If only some of these would be used to work with governments and non-profit organisations to address issues such as poverty, food insecurity and even conflict and war, these issues could be solved much faster. By using their existing value chains and resources, businesses could make a real contribution to a better humanity and society.

It is indeed true that often, perhaps too often, business sees CSR as an instrument to maximise profit. In a way, this practice is the remains of the narrow view. Companies use CSR to enhance their brand, create positive marketing campaigns and engage their employees through corporate volunteering. While there is nothing wrong in leveraging the benefits of CSR for the company, it is usually genuine and holistic CSR that gains these benefits, not an instrumental one. When a company known for unethical behaviour markets its CSR, not only will it not be trusted with its CSR, but also the overall cynicism towards CSR will grow. This is precisely why this book adopts the concept of strategic CSR, which is based on a holistic approach, tying CSR to the company's strategic planning and core operations.

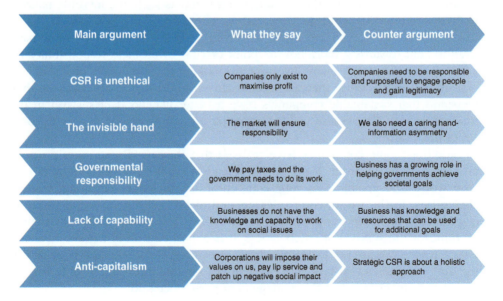

Figure 1.4   The main arguments for the narrow view and counter arguments (for a broad view)

Figure 1.4 shows the main arguments for the narrow view that were detailed above and the counter arguments, which are the basis for a broad view of business responsibilities.

Drivers for change

There have been many drivers for the shift towards the broader view of business responsibility, particularly in the last four decades. Some had a more direct effect while others had an indirect effect on the fast growth in CSR. To name a few, there were successful responsible companies; consumer growing awareness; globalisation and free flow of information; and financial crises and the results of unethical business (see Figure 1.5).

To begin with, the more positive drivers, *successful responsible companies,* inspired many others to become purpose-driven organisations and CSR leaders. In the 1970s, several companies emerged with a social purpose as their goal in addition to making profit. The Body Shop was founded by Anita Roddick in 1976, and became well known for its social activism, particularly after it aligned with Greenpeace in 1986 (Austin and Herman, 2008). While not without controversy, the company prides itself on products that are based on fair trade (with its slogan 'Trade, not aid'), are environmentally friendly and are not tested on animals. It is

Figure 1.5   Drivers for change

affiliated with several social causes, such as stopping human trafficking. In 2006 it was acquired by L'Oréal, and while many criticised the acquisition due to the mother company's animal testing and other practices, it was acknowledged that The Body Shop was a desirable brand due to its CSR. Similarly, Ben & Jerry's and Patagonia are 'social icons' with strong and popular brands (Austin and Herman, 2008). Other companies wanted to follow these practices and adopted a broad view of business responsibility and so these social icons became a driver for change.

In addition, the last few decades have witnessed a *rise in consumer awareness and activism*. In the 1980s, there was a report on the CBS channel in the US that showed the unethical practices and sweatshops used by Nike to make shoes and apparel. This was followed by a large consumer movement, calling on shoppers to boycott the company (with the slogan 'Boycott Nike, just do it!'). The company first denied these practices, but was still put under a lot a pressure. With the growing level of consumer awareness of social issues, labour and human rights and the environmental impact of business, many companies tried to take a proactive approach and to demonstrate CSR before they were scrutinised for their practices and boycotted like Nike (Zadek, 2004). Today, with social media this could happen a lot faster, and companies that only react to such criticism could lose face. This shift in consumer awareness and activism has led many companies to take a proactive approach and to change their practices towards CSR.

Globalisation is another strong driver for CSR. It is the increasingly global relationships of culture, people and economic activity. It is generally used to refer to economic globalisation: the global distribution of the production of goods and services, through a reduction of barriers to international trade such as tariffs, export fees and import quotas. In his book *The World is Flat*, Thomas Friedman (2005) argued that globalised trade, outsourcing, supply-chaining and political forces had permanently changed the world, for better and worse. He showed that there are three phases of globalisation (see Figure 1.6).

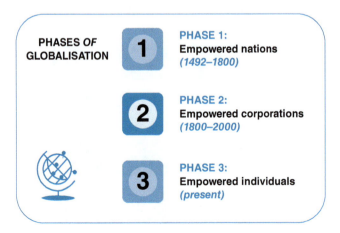

Figure 1.6   The three phases of globalisation (based on Friedman, 2005)

The second phase led many companies to work and have presence in various parts of the world, but also to outsource and offshore some of their manufacturing to the developing world, often without assuring the basic rights of employees in these places. In the third and current phase, the empowered individuals are well connected and can lead a global change to ensure CSR globally. In addition, globalisation was characterised by free flow of information, particularly after the fall of the Soviet Union and the rise of the Internet and social media, which also resulted in consumer awareness and activism.

Several *corporate ethical scandals and meltdowns* were prominent in the last two decades. The best-known example is Enron. In 2001, it was revealed that Enron's financial reports were based on institutionalised, systematic and creatively planned accounting fraud (known as the 'Enron scandal'). Enron has since become synonymous with corporate fraud and corruption, and the scandal brought to light the unethical accounting practices and activities of many corporations in the US. As the company collapsed, it took down with it the savings and retirement funds of many people, particularly in the US (McLean and Elkind, 2013). This led not only to new legislation and regulation, but also to a growing demand from the public that companies will not put their financial gain before their legal and ethical obligations. However, in 2008 the world witnessed new corporate scandals, particularly in financial institutions and home loan providers, which resulted in a global financial crisis. The discourse on capitalism and the responsibility of business was rapidly changing. The impact of irresponsible business and unethical behaviour was so evident that the public started demanding a much higher level of responsibility and ethics.

Business motivation for CSR

Based on their set of corporate values (see Chapter 4), companies develop various motivations to participate in CSR, which, according to Aguilera et al. (2007), can be divided into three groups: moral, relational and economical motivations (see Figure 1.7). The first set of motivations is seen as more altruistic, while the other two are seen as more egoistic.

The *moral motivation* can be found among companies with strong benevolence values, who often reflect on their role in society and are (or are becoming) socially and environmentally responsible because it is the right thing to do. Based on a strong sense of duty and gratitude, these companies know that society makes business possible and that it therefore has a reciprocal obligation to be responsible. Moreover, these companies and their leadership understand that in order to gain legitimacy and a 'social licence to operate' they need to behave morally and in accordance with the expectations of all stakeholders (McLean and Elkind, 2013).

Moral motivation	Relational motivation	Economic motivation
• It is the right thing to do • Society makes business possible and companies have a reciprocal obligation • Social license to operate	• Relationships with stakeholders • Minimise restrictions	• Brand and reputation • Employee engagement • Profits

Figure 1.7   Three CSR motivations (based on Aguilera et al., 2007)

Other motivations for CSR can be grouped under the *relational motivation*. Companies who are socially responsible because of relational motivation value the relationship they have with a broad set of stakeholders, and understand that to maintain this good relationship they need to respect people and the environment. Furthermore, by maintaining good relationships (with governments, consumers, employees and others) companies strive to minimise restrictions and regulations in the future, either directly on them or more in general on the business sector.

The last set of motivations is called *economic motivations* but can also be referred to as 'instrumental' and 'self-serving' CSR. There is a growing body of research showing the benefits of CSR: from financial performance and employee engagement to better brand and consumer loyalty. Some companies are therefore motivated to demonstrate higher levels of CSR to yield these benefits.

Some writers, such as Carroll (1999), call it the 'business case' for CSR. The business case refers to the underlying arguments and rationales that support the reasons for CSR. Its primary questions are: what do the business community and organisations get out of CSR? And how do they benefit tangibly from engaging in CSR policies, activities and practices? The business case often refers to the financial bottom-line and other reasons for businesses pursuing CSR strategies and policies. Scholars and practitioners who focus on the business case often strive to show a positive relationship between doing good (CSR) and doing well (in finance, reputation and performance).

Summary

CSR has become very prominent in the last few decades. It is important because it sets a direction for business to behave in the interest of our global society and all stakeholders; because it can address the growing criticism on extreme capitalism; and because it yields great benefits to everyone.

There are many definitions of CSR that demonstrate that business holds other responsibilities in addition to profit maximisation. However, the responsibilities, the focus of CSR and the position of the company as a passive or active player, vary between these definitions. The one adopted in this book is of strategic CSR.

There are also many other names and concepts that are used, such as corporate responsibility, social responsibility, corporate citizenship, social business and corporate business. However, CSR is best known and most commonly used and it is also the term used by strategic CSR and therefore used in this book as well.

The brief history of CSR thought demonstrates that while there was a growing interest in the role of business in society, its morality and consequences, some scholars thought that the only social responsibility of a business is to maximise profit. However, in recent years we see a shift away from this approach and CSR is becoming a more common discourse and practice. As such, there is a change from the narrow view of business responsibilities to a broad view. The main arguments for the narrow view are that CSR is unethical; there is an invisible hand; the government should do it; business lacks the capacity; and anti-capitalism. The broad view has counter arguments for each of the above.

There were several drivers for this change, including successful responsible companies; consumer growing awareness; globalisation and free flow of information; and financial crises and the results of unethical business. As such, the business motivation to be more socially responsible had grown. Such motivations can be divided into moral, relational and economic/instrumental.

General questions

1. Why is CSR a fast-growing phenomenon? What substantial underlying changes led to it being so?
2. What are the advantages and benefits of CSR? What are the dangers and risks?
3. Think of an example of a company that is, in your opinion, genuinely responsible. What makes it so? What can you learn from it?
4. In your opinion, why are there so many different definitions and terms for CSR? Why can't we agree on one term and one definition?
5. Reflect on one of the leaders of CSR thought, such as Carroll, Freeman or even Adam Smith. What would you like to ask them? Can you challenge their approach?
6. Reflect on the drivers for change from the narrow view to a broad view of business responsibility. What other drivers can you identify? What are the counter drivers?

Key definitions

- CSR encompasses the economic, legal, ethical and philanthropic expectations that society has of organisations at a given point in time (Carroll, 1979).
- CSR is a view of the corporation and its role in society that assumes a responsibility among firms to pursue goals in addition to profit maximisation and a responsibility of the stakeholders to hold the firm responsible for its actions (Werther and Chandler, 2011).
- CSR is business decision making linked to ethical values, compliance with legal requirements, and respect for people, communities and the environment around the world (Aaronson, 2003).
- Strategic CSR is the incorporation of a holistic CSR perspective within a firm's strategic planning and core operations so that the firm is managed in the interest of a broad set of stakeholders to achieve maximum economic and social value over the medium to long term (Werther and Chandler, 2011).
- Corporate citizenship is the extent to which businesses meet the economic, legal, ethical and discretionary responsibilities imposed on them by their stakeholders (Maignan et al., 1999)
- Conscious business refers to business galvanised by higher purposes that serve and align the interest of all major stakeholders (Mackey and Sisodia, 2014).

References

Aaronson, S. A. (2003) 'Corporate responsibility in the global village: The British role model and the American laggard', *Business and Society Review*, 108(3): 309–38.

Aguilera, R. V., Rupp, D. E., Williams, C. A. and Ganapathi, J. (2007) 'Putting the S back in corporate social responsibility: A multilevel theory of social change in organizations', *Academy of Management Review*, 32(3): 836–63.

Austin, J. E. and Herman, B. (2008) 'Can the virtuous mouse and the wealthy elephant live happily ever after?', *California Management Review*, 51(1): 77–102.

Bowen, H. R. (1953) *Social responsibilities of the businessman*. New York: Harper & Row.

Carroll, A. B. (1979) 'A three-dimensional conceptual model of corporate performance', *Academy of Management Review*, 4(4): 497–505.

Carroll, A. B. (1991) 'The pyramid of corporate social responsibility: Toward the moral management of organizational stakeholders', *Business Horizons*, 34(4): 39–48.

Carroll, A. B. (1999) 'Corporate social responsibility: Evolution of a definitional construct', *Business & Society*, 38(3): 268–95.

Carroll, A. B. and Shabana, K. M. (2010) 'The business case for corporate social responsibility: A review of concepts, research and practice', *International Journal of Management Reviews*, 12(1): 85–105.

Committee for Economic Development (CED) (1971) *Social responsibilities of business corporations*. Washington, DC: CED.

Dees, J. G. (1998) The meaning of social entrepreneurship. Available at: www.redalmarza.cl/ing/pdf/TheMeaningofsocialEntrepreneurship.pdf (Accessed: 7 May 2017)

Elkington, J. (2004) *Enter the triple bottom line. The triple bottom line: Does it all add up?* London: Earthscan.

Freeman, R. E. (1984) *Stakeholder management: Framework and philosophy*. Mansfield, MA: Pitman.

Friedman, M. (1970) *The social responsibility of business is to increase its profits*, *New York Times Magazine*, September 13.

Friedman, T. L. (2005) *The world is flat: A brief history of the twenty-first century*. London: Penguin.

Mackey, J. and Sisodia, R. (2014) *Conscious capitalism: Liberating the heroic spirit of business*. Boston, MA: Harvard Business Review Press.

Maignan, I., Ferrell, O. C. and Hult, G. T. M. (1999) 'Corporate citizenship: Cultural antecedents and business benefits', *Journal of the Academy of Marketing Science*, 27(4): 455–69.

Marx, K. (1867) *Capital*. London: Penguin.

Matten, D. and Crane, A. (2005) 'Corporate citizenship: Toward an extended theoretical conceptualization', *Academy of Management Review*, 30(1): 166–79.

Mayo, E. (1945) *The social problems of an industrial civilization*. Boston, MA: Harvard University.

McLean, B. and Elkind, P. (2013) *The smartest guys in the room: The amazing rise and the scandalous fall of Enron*. New York: Penguin.

Moffat, K. and Zhang, A. (2014) 'The paths to social licence to operate: An integrative model explaining community acceptance of mining', *Resources Policy*, 39: 61–70.

Porter, M. E. and Kramer, M. R. (2002) 'The competitive advantage of corporate philanthropy', *Harvard Business Review*, 80(12): 56–68.

Porter, M. E. and Kramer, M. R. (2011) 'Creating shared value', *Harvard Business Review*, 89(1/2): 62–77.

Smith, A. (1759) *The theory of moral sentiments*. Oxford: Clarendon Press.

Smith, A. (1776) *An inquiry into the nature and causes of the wealth of nations*. Oxford: Clarendon Press.

The Economist (2008) 'Just good business'. Available at: www.economist.com/node/10491077 (Accessed: 7 May 2017)

United Nations (1999) 'Secretary-general proposes global compact on human rights, labour, environment, in address to world economic forum in Davos'. Available at: www.un.org/press/en/1999/19990201.sgsm6881.html (Accessed: 7 May 2017)

Werther, W. B. and Chandler, D. (2011) *Strategic corporate social responsibility: Stakeholders in a global environment* (2nd edn). Thousand Oaks, CA: Sage.

Zadek, S. (2004) 'The path to corporate responsibility', *Harvard Business Review*, 82(12): 125–33.

Further reading and links

Aguinis, H. and Glavas, A. (2012) 'What we know and don't know about corporate social responsibility: A review and research agenda', *Journal of Management*, 38(4): 932–68.

Carroll, A. B. (2000) 'Ethical challenges for business in the new millennium: Corporate social responsibility and models of management morality', *Business Ethics Quarterly*, 10(01): 33–42.

Crane, A. and Matten, D. (2007) *Corporate social responsibility*, Vol. 2. London: Sage.

Crane, A., Palazzo, G., Spence, L. J. and Matten, D. (2014) 'Contesting the value of "creating shared value"', *California Management Review*, 56(2): 130–53.

Dahlsrud, A. (2008). 'How corporate social responsibility is defined: An analysis of 37 defini-tions', *Corporate Social Responsibility and Environmental Management*, 15(1): 1–13.

Falck, O. and Heblich, S. (2007) 'Corporate social responsibility: Doing well by doing good', *Business Horizons*, 50(3): 247–54.

Khan, M. T., Khan, N. A., Ahmed, S. and Ali, M. (2012) 'Corporate social responsibility (CSR): Definition, concepts and scope', *Universal Journal of Management and Social Sciences*, 2(7): 41–52.

Kotler, P. and Lee, N. (2008) *Corporate social responsibility: Doing the most good for your company and your cause*. Chichester: Wiley.

Porter, M. E. and Kramer, M. R. (2006) 'Strategy and society: The link between competitive advantage and corporate social responsibility', *Harvard Business Review*, pp. 5–16.

TEDGlobal (2013) The case for letting business solve social problems. Available at: www.ted.com/talks/michael_porter_why_business_can_be_good_at_solving_social_problems (Accessed: 7 May 2017)

TEDxCville (2013) R. Edward Freeman and stakeholder theory. Available at: www.youtube.com/watch?v=2VSBJY4kprs (Accessed: 12 April 2017)

TEDxCville (2014) Business is about purpose. Available at: www.youtube.com/watch?v=7dugfwJthBY (Accessed: 12 April 2017)

Werther, W. B. and Chandler, D. (2005) 'Strategic corporate social responsibility as global brand insurance', *Business Horizons*, 48(4): 317–24.

From CSR Pyramids to Shared Value and Beyond: CSR Models and Frameworks

2

Learning outcomes

By the end of this chapter, students should be able to:

- present several theories and frameworks of CSR
- articulate the main contributions and limitations of each model
- explain how CSR has changed based on the evolution of such models
- critically reflect on the current body of knowledge and on the way forward
- apply the theories and models to managerial practice.

Case study   Strategic CSR at Ben & Jerry's

Ben & Jerry's is an ice cream company that, since its humble beginnings in the 1970s in Vermont, US, has had a social goal as part of its core business. The co-founders, Ben Cohen and Jerry Greenfield, quickly realised the opportunity to embed values in the new business. The company aims to create linked prosperity for everyone who is connected to its business: suppliers, employees, farmers, franchisees, customers and neighbours. In the early days, the two founders were committed to a variety of social causes on both a local and large scale. People realised that this company was different, as it was not just there to maximise profit, but also to achieve social goals.

This notion was expressed years after the company was founded by one of the company's advisors: 'We are not just another ice cream company, but one that works hard to have our social mission expressed in all we do' (Austin and Herman, 2008: 84). The company received various awards for its social and environmental work and employees were highly involved in various social causes, including peace, equality and the environment. Due to it being a purpose-driven organisation, employees were highly engaged, as one of them said: 'I took quite a big pay cut to come to Ben & Jerry's, and I came because I had been working in corporate America for 17 years and I was sick of it. I wanted to see what was different and it was very, very, very different' (Austin and Quinn, 2005: 2).

Ben & Jerry's is founded on and dedicated to a sustainable corporate concept of linked prosperity (Ben & Jerry's, 2017). The company's goal is 'Making the best possible ice cream, in the nicest possible way'. The mission of the company consists of three interrelated parts: product, economic and social (see Figure 2.1).

In 2000, Unilever acquired Ben & Jerry's, and some argue that it was due to the company being a CSR icon (Austin and Herman, 2008). However, the acquisition led to a high level of criticism of the company: employees, customers, franchisees and social activists claimed that Ben & Jerry's was 'selling out'. At the time, a cultural gap existed between the parent company and its subsidiary in terms of their CSR levels and motivations. Four years after the acquisition, only 30 per cent of the employees felt that Ben & Jerry's had remained true to its roots and origins. According to Austin and Quinn (2005), Unilever imposed several restrictions on the company's CSR, and its code of ethics required that the company remained apolitical. Subsequently, employees were no longer allowed to use the brand name while participating in anti-war marches and similar activities.

In 2009, Paul Polman (see Chapter 6, Case Study) became the CEO of Unilever and emphasised the role of Unilever in creating environmental and social value. Polman launched a 'sustainable living plan' with the aim of doubling the size of the

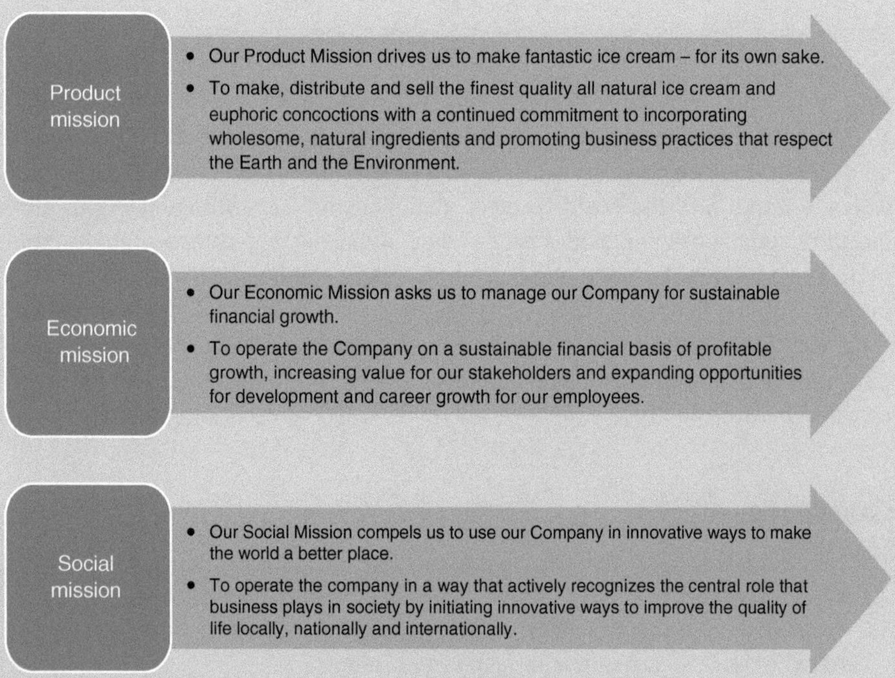

Product mission
- Our Product Mission drives us to make fantastic ice cream – for its own sake.
- To make, distribute and sell the finest quality all natural ice cream and euphoric concoctions with a continued commitment to incorporating wholesome, natural ingredients and promoting business practices that respect the Earth and the Environment.

Economic mission
- Our Economic Mission asks us to manage our Company for sustainable financial growth.
- To operate the Company on a sustainable financial basis of profitable growth, increasing value for our stakeholders and expanding opportunities for development and career growth for our employees.

Social mission
- Our Social Mission compels us to use our Company in innovative ways to make the world a better place.
- To operate the company in a way that actively recognizes the central role that business plays in society by initiating innovative ways to improve the quality of life locally, nationally and internationally.

Figure 2.1   Ben & Jerry's three-part mission (Ben & Jerry's, 2017)

business while reducing its environmental impact and footprint. Consequently, Ben & Jerry's was able to fully promote social and environmental causes, and employee engagement is now very high.

Today, the company's social mission is very strongly communicated on its website and in its reports and actions. The company is committed to peace: it celebrated the International Day of Peace and even launched a 'Peace, Love & Ice Cream' campaign. The brand is once again attached to a political stand, such as support for the Occupy Wall Street movement. It is also a strong advocate of environmental sustainability and uses its main products to communicate the urgency of addressing climate change with 'If it's melted, it's ruined'. It works to become more sustainable throughout its entire supply chain, including the introduction of carbon-neutral freezers. In 2010, the company committed to purchasing 100 per cent fair trade ingredients where possible, including vanilla, cocoa, sugar, fruits and nuts in its products, and also demonstrated consistent support for social enterprises. For example, the Ben & Jerry's brownies are produced by a social enterprise

(Continued)

that employs homeless people without consideration of any previous work history or time spent in prison. The bakery provides job skills, training and housing along with its unique open-door hiring practice.

Ben & Jerry's works with over 80 farms in Vermont to source 100 per cent of its dairy needs. The company has established a programme called Caring Dairy™ under which it works with the farms to meet guidelines for 13 sustainability indicators, including animal welfare, biodiversity, energy and water. The company guides farms in implementing sustainable practices that benefit the livestock, the land and the farmers. Farmers pledge not to treat their cows with hormones, learn how to conserve water, enrich the soil and run their farms more sustainably. Recently the company pledged to work with migrant workers in Vermont to implement a programme called Milk with Dignity to support a worker-led dairy sourcing programme.

Questions

1. How did Ben & Jerry's CSR change over the years and for what reasons?
2. Would you say that its CSR is holistic? What do you learn from its current mission?
3. What makes it a CSR icon? Why do you think being a social icon makes companies more desirable for acquisition by larger corporations?
4. What can the company still do to improve its CSR? Provide a list of three things it can do better.

Bibliography

Austin, J. E. and Herman, B. (2008) 'Can the virtuous mouse and the wealthy elephant live happily ever after?', *California Management Review*, 51(1): 77–102.

Austin, J. E. and Quinn, J. (2005) *Ben & Jerry's: Preserving mission & brand within Unilever*. Cambridge: Harvard Business School.

Ben & Jerry's (2017) Available at: www.benjerry.com (Accessed: 05 April 2017)

Carter, J. (2013) *Corporate social responsibility: Ben & Jerry's*. Munich: GRIN.

Kaye, L. (2012) Ben & Jerry's, now certified B Corp. Available at: www.triplepundit.com/2012/10/ben-jerrys-certified-corp (Accessed: 05 April 2017)

Page, A. and Katz, R. A. (2012) *The truth about Ben & Jerry's*. Indianapolis, IN: Indiana University Press.

Unilever (2017) Sustainable living. Available at: www.unilever.co.uk/sustainable-living (Accessed: 05 October 2017)

Links

SNHU (2017) Inside Ben & Jerry's social mission. Available at: www.youtube.com/watch?v=N_x3bOHBwRA (Accessed: 05 April 2017)

Ben & Jerry's YouTube Channel (2015) Our social mission: Ben & Jerry's. Available at: www.youtube. com/watch?v=Lu2VBQBpn7U (Accessed: 05 April 2017)

Ben & Jerry's YouTube Channel (2017) Join the climate movement! Ben & Jerry's. Available at: www. youtube.com/watch?v=80NLPNHpm0k (Accessed: 05 April 2017).

Introduction: There is nothing so practical as a good theory

In the first chapter of this book, we saw the shift from a narrow view of business responsibility to a broad one. The narrow view, mainly represented by Milton Friedman, claims that the only responsibility of a business is to maximise profit. However, this approach is not sustainable. If profit is the only motive, companies can do any harm to the environment and to the society just to make another dollar. If everyone behaves this way, the harm would be too great to overcome, in which situation we would not be able to run companies or make money at all. Since the 1970s, the realisation grew that businesses have other responsibilities and many firms, managers and scholars gradually adopted the broad view of business responsibility.

As CSR became more prominent in many large, medium and small enterprises, several frameworks started to emerge. These frameworks help us to better understand CSR and the various perspectives on the topic. More importantly, they can assist us in better implementation of CSR. As Kurt Lewin (1951), a well-known German scholar, said: 'there is nothing so practical as a good theory'.

In this chapter, we will examine several theories, models and frameworks of CSR, inspect the contribution and limitation of each one and develop a more comprehensive understanding of CSR. We will begin with Carroll's CSR pyramid; followed by Zadek's CSR learning stages; the CSR congruence model; and creating shared value. We will end this chapter by detailing strategic CSR, its meaning and components and explain why it is the basis of this book.

There are many others, of course, but the ones presented here will allow us to capture what CSR is, what is the meaning of CSR to business and other stakeholders, what the process of becoming more responsible is and what various aspects of the business need to change. These frameworks also enable us to measure CSR and understand how to improve it in any organisation.

The CSR pyramid

In 1979, Archie Carroll presented a four-part framework or definition of CSR, which he later used to create a graphic depiction of CSR in the form of a pyramid (Carroll, 1991). His definition of CSR is: 'CSR encompasses the economic, legal, ethical, and discretionary (philanthropic) expectations that society has of organisations at a given point in time.'

The pyramid is therefore based on *societal expectations*: economic, legal, ethical and discretionary (philanthropic). Furthermore, the order of responsibilities is based on a survey with over 200 executives and the way they ranked them. This set of four responsibilities creates a foundation that helps to characterise the nature of businesses' responsibilities to the society of which it is a part. The CSR pyramid is one of the best-known models of CSR and it is used broadly by CSR scholars, practitioners and educators.

Carroll later explained that the pyramid was selected as a geometric design because it is simple, intuitive and built to withstand the test of time (Carroll, 1999; Carroll and Shabana, 2010). The economic responsibility was placed as the base of the pyramid because it is a foundational requirement in business and the enabler of everything else. The main idea here is that the infrastructure of CSR is built upon the premise of an economically sound and sustainable business (see Figure 2.2).

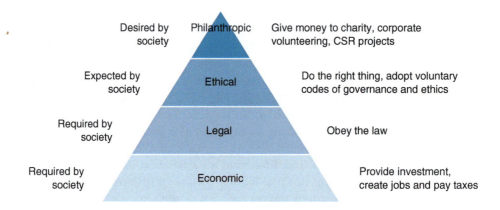

Figure 2.2   Carroll's pyramid of business responsibilities (based on Carroll, 1991)

The first set of responsibilities as portrayed in this pyramid is the *economic* responsibilities. Carroll argued that the strongest expectation that society has of a business is to be financially successful, produce goods that have value for society, provide investment, create jobs and pay taxes. It is argued that companies already contribute substantially to society by performing according to these expectations. Profit is, according to Carroll, the incentive and the reward for companies to do all of the above.

The second responsibility (or societal expectation) is *legal*. Since business did not always meet the expectations of society, governments regulate business through legislation and it is the duty of business to know and obey the law and the basic 'rules of the game'. The legal responsibilities include: performing in a manner consistent with the expectations of government and law; complying with various federal, state and local regulations; conducting business as law-abiding corporate citizens; fulfilling all legal obligations to societal stakeholders; and providing goods and services that at least meet minimal legal requirements.

The third responsibility in this pyramid is *ethical*. Being ethically responsible means performing in a manner consistent with the expectations of societal norms and ethical norms; recognising and respecting new or evolving ethical/moral norms adopted by society; preventing ethical norms from being compromised in order to achieve business goals; being good corporate citizens by doing what is expected morally or ethically; and recognising that business integrity and ethical behaviour go beyond mere compliance with laws and regulations.

The final responsibility is *discretionary*, which means it is voluntary and based on the goodwill of the company and its managers, mainly focused on philanthropy. It includes all forms of business giving (including money, in-kind and time) and voluntary activities. Carroll explains that philanthropy may not be a responsibility in a literal sense but it is normally expected by society of business and therefore is part of the pyramid. Business philanthropy is guided by the desire to participate in social activities that are not mandated, not required by law and not generally expected of business in an ethical sense. However, it should be noted that philanthropy could be driven by economic responsibility or ethical ones and for some countries, such as India, it is now indeed required by law. It is based on the unwritten social contract between business and society and part of the way business strives to achieve a social license to operate.

The pyramid is a useful model of CSR as it is easy to capture and remember. It made an important contribution to the shift from the narrow view of business responsibility to a broad one, while including crucial aspects such as ethical behaviour and philanthropy. However, there has been some criticism around it, part of which is due to a lack of understanding of Carroll's ideas, though part of the criticism still stands.

Question for reflection and discussion

What are the main issues that you see with Carroll's definition and model of CSR? Reflect before reading onwards.

Criticism of the CSR pyramid

Hierarchy

The foremost issue with the CSR pyramid is that it is, indeed, a pyramid. As such, it implies some level of hierarchy between the four responsibilities, with economic being the most important responsibility of all. Some people argue that it encourages companies to make profit, even if it means disobeying the law or being unethical. The fact that philanthropy is the last in order puts it as less important. One could even argue that working in accordance with this pyramid could result in corporate behaviour such as that portrayed by Enron and other unethical companies, as they functioned according to the order of responsibilities as defined in the pyramid.

However, Carroll later explained that the pyramid should be viewed from a stakeholder perspective wherein the focus is on the whole and not the different parts, arguing that CSR is about engaging in decisions, actions, policies and practices that *simultaneously fulfil all four component parts*. Carroll argued that the pyramid should not be interpreted to mean that business is expected to fulfil its social responsibilities in some sequential, hierarchical fashion, starting at the base. Rather, business is expected to fulfil all responsibilities simultaneously. Consequently, Carroll said that his definition of CSR should read as follows: Economic Responsibilities + Legal Responsibilities + Ethical Responsibilities + Philanthropic Responsibilities = Total Corporate Social Responsibility. Furthermore, although the ethical responsibility is depicted in the pyramid as a separate category of CSR, it should also be seen as a factor, which cuts through and saturates the entire pyramid. Ethical considerations are present in each of the other responsibility categories as well. This does solve the above criticism, but most people only know the graphic of the pyramid and implement it as such.

Philanthropy, not sustainability

Another point of criticism against the pyramid is the emphasis on corporate philanthropy. This, in a way, promotes traditional CSR in which the focus of responsibility is in giving money and time, just as we saw in the McDonald's case in Chapter 1. However, CSR can (and some would say should) be more holistic than this. Even the ethical responsibility does not cover all the various aspects of being a truly responsible business. Furthermore, there are some aspects missing from these four responsibilities. What about the responsibility towards the environment? Is it part of ethical behaviour or something greater/different? And if CSR is about social responsibility, where is that in the pyramid? Should the responsibility towards the community and society be included in the existing four parts, or should it be a separate one?

Overlap

Looking at the lists that appear in some of Carroll's articles on what falls under each of the four responsibilities, there is some overlap between them. For example, under legal responsibility there is also the obligation to make a sound profit for the shareholders and to create good products. Under ethical responsibility, there is also the moral obligation to obey the law. Carroll further suggested that philanthropy could be driven based on ethical responsibility. It could be rather confusing to follow which responsibility includes what kind of activities.

Tensions

Carroll argued that while his CSR model is portrayed as a pyramid, companies should simultaneously fulfil all four components. However, we know that reality does not always allow for this to happen and tensions between the four responsibilities could inevitably arise. What if doing the right thing decreases sales? What if we could use philanthropy to patch up our negative behaviour – is this ethical? Carroll explained that the way companies decide to balance their responsibilities defines their CSR orientation and reputation. As such, it can be seen again that if companies put their economic responsibility first, they may be perceived as having lower levels of CSR.

Culture and ethical relativism

The four-part construct of CSR and the pyramid are based on American-type capitalistic societies. However, several writers have proposed (e.g. Visser, 2006) that the pyramid needs to be reordered to meet the conditions of other countries or smaller businesses. It was shown that in some parts of Europe and in the developing world, different ways of portraying business responsibilities are present, consequently giving way to the development of a different pyramid. This was also true for different organisations from other sectors (governmental and civil society) and sizes. In addition, when we discuss the ethical responsibility of a company, we need to ask ourselves: according to whose morality and ethics? Ideas of what is right and wrong vary drastically not only between societies, but within societies as well. Ethical relativism is a broad field of study and debate, which should be taken into account when saying that society has ethical expectations of business (see Chapter 4).

Alternative pyramid

In a study conducted with the UN Principles for Responsible Management Education (or PRME) another pyramid emerged (Haski-Leventhal, 2014). The study targeted business students from all around the world in 2012, 2013 and 2015 and each time they were asked to rank business responsibilities in the order they perceive to be right. In addition to Carroll's four responsibilities, environmental responsibility and social responsibility were added to the list. The results of the three surveys are consistent and the same alternative pyramid emerged every time, portrayed in Figure 2.3. Business students around the world say that ethical responsibility should be at the base of the pyramid, followed by legal and economic. Students also placed social and environmental responsibilities ahead of philanthropy. This could be seen as an alternative pyramid, adopted by the business leaders of tomorrow.

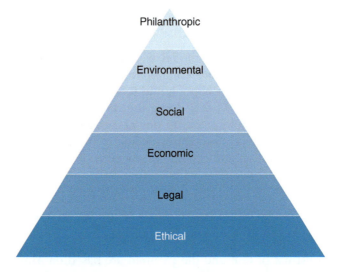

Figure 2.3   Alternative pyramid of business responsibility according to business students (Haski-Leventhal, 2014)

CSR stages: Pathways to being more responsible

In 2004, Simon Zadek offered a different CSR pyramid, with five levels or stages of CSR: defensive, compliance, managerial, strategic and civil. This model was primarily based on a case study of Nike, a world-famous shoe and apparel company that sponsors many athletics and sport teams. Nike was accused many times (particularly in the 1990s) of not providing its employees with basic conditions and liveable wages. Nike's factories were firstly based in South Korea, then in China until they were moved to Indonesia in the 1990s, where Nike could pay people who develop its products very low wages. However, the conditions in the factories or 'sweatshops' as they were referred to became public knowledge via news reports and investigations, resulting in many people boycotting the company and refusing to buy the company's products or even receive its sponsorship.

In 2004, after working with Nike for a few years, Zadek argued that Nike went through a learning curve with its CSR and moved away from the stage in which it was initially at – defensive to becoming fully responsible: 'Nike's metamorphosis from the poster child for irresponsibility to a leader in progressive practices reveals the five stages of organisational growth' (Zadek, 2004: 125). Figure 2.4 illustrates the five stages, which are explained below.

Based on this case and other business cases, Zadek developed a pyramid of five stages, each showing a higher level of CSR. The *defensive stage* usually takes place when a company is accused of behaving unethically, when consumers and/or employees are unhappy with the corporate conduct or after some actions had been taken, such as consumers and other stakeholders boycotting the company. Companies with the lowest levels of CSR will only deny practices ('we did not do it') or responsibility ('everyone is doing the same'). In this case, the company's view is short-term, during which it attempts to avoid additional harm to its reputation and performance. This was initially the reaction of Nike when people boycotted the company in the 1990s.

At the *compliance stage*, managers and leaders understand that denial will not result in rebuilding trust and fixing the reputational damage. As such, the company then agrees to comply with laws, regulations and policies (be it external or internal). The company usually feels forced into such actions, but it does understand that it must follow these actions to mitigate the erosion of economic value in the medium term because of ongoing reputation and litigation risks. In the 2015 scandal of Volkswagen, during which the automobile company was accused of cheating in pollution tests, the company moved into the compliance stage to mitigate damages. The CEO resigned and the company agreed to comply with the law and change its policies (BBC, 2015).

Stage	Focus	Purpose
Defensive		Risk mitigation, economic value and reputation
Compliance	The past	Risk mitigation, economic value and reputation
Managerial		Risk mitigation, economic value and reputation
Strategic	The future	Value creation and social impact
Civil	The future	Value creation and social impact

Figure 2.4   **CSR stages and learning process (based on Zadek, 2004)**

At the *managerial stage*, companies embed societal issues in their core management processes, develop CSR departments, give large amounts of money to philanthropy and communicate their efforts in corporate citizenship to their stakeholders. The goal at this stage is still to mitigate the erosion of economic value in the medium term and to achieve longer-term gains by integrating responsible business practices into their daily operations. Nike did the same and its current website communicates the company's responsibility, particularly around environmental sustainability and innovation. In 2005, Nike was the first company in its industry to demonstrate transparency, when it published a complete list of its contract factories. In the same year, it also published its first version of a CSR report, detailing pay scales and working conditions in its factories and admitting continued problems.

The first three stages are risk averse. Companies engage in such practices to reduce risk and engage in some level of damage control. However, the next two stages, strategic and civil, are aimed at value creation. At the *strategic stage* companies integrate the societal issue into their core business strategies. Similar to the practice of strategic CSR, companies align their responsibility, sustainability and philanthropy with what they do and what their mission is. At this stage, the companies examine their value chain and strive to be responsible throughout it.

Table 2.1   The content and motivation of each CSR stage (based on Zadek, 2004)

Stage	Defensive	Compliance	Managerial	Strategic	Civil
Organisation Actions	Deny any wrongdoing, taking no responsibility	Comply with CSR norms and legislation	CSR is embedded in management processes	Integrate CSR into business strategy and core operations	Lead and inspire industry participation and strategic CSR
Reasons for Actions	Short-term defense against attacks to reputation and brand due to negative impact	Mid-term defense against economic value decrease due to ongoing reputation and litigation risks	Mid-term defense against economic value decrease by integrating responsible business practices into core operations	Enhance long-term economic and social value by aligning strategy and process innovations with the societal issues	Enhance long-term economic value and social value

The final and highest stage of all five is *civil*. Companies at this stage are considered CSR leaders that inspire others to be more responsible and pave the way in becoming CSR icons. Zadek speaks about companies that have a meta-strategy and examine the future role of business in society and the stability and openness of global society itself. Nike continues to publish its commitments, standards and audit data as part of its CSR reports.

The contribution of Zadek's model is in the ability to see CSR as part of organisational learning and to understand that a company's level of ethics and responsibility could change (see Table 2.1). While Zadek does not fully provide the transitions in this model (what could cause companies to move from one stage to the next), we can see from the examples he provides that stakeholder pressure, change of leadership and change of societal norms are some of the drivers for companies to move up this CSR ladder. In addition, the model seems to be linear, and as such, companies always move upwards. However, there are examples of companies that started as civil from their early days and there are companies that moved backwards, towards a lower level of CSR (although they are the minority of cases).

EXERCISE

Go back to the Ben & Jerry's case at the beginning of the chapter. Where would you place the company on these stages prior to and post the acquisition? Why? Can you think of other companies to place in each stage?

CSR congruence model

While the first two models, by Carroll and Zadek, are vertical in nature, going from low to high on one dimension, the more recent CSR congruence model offers a bi-dimensional model to capture social responsibility (Haski-Leventhal et al., 2017). Based on the fast growing CSR literature, the model offers two dimensions on which companies and their CSR should be measured: CSR identity and CSR behaviour. Putting it simply, this model can assist us in assessing companies that 'talk the talk', 'walk the walk', 'walk the talk' or do neither. CSR is not just about what you say you do, but also what you actually do (according to what you say).

In the article presenting the model, *CSR behaviour* is defined as the ways in which a company actually behaves towards its various stakeholders, both external and internal. It involves a variety of CSR activities, such as corporate philanthropy, addressing social issues, ethical behaviour, sustainability and community involvement. *CSR identity* refers to the company's strategy, culture and values that are aligned with responsibility and sustainability. Companies with ethical corporate identities are regarded as ethical according to their social connectedness, openness, critical reflexivity and responsiveness. Companies with socially responsible organisational identities are perceived as helpful, caring and benevolent.

Companies can be high or low on CSR identity and high or low on CSR behaviour. As such, the CSR matrix offers four patterns of CSR: low social responsibility, identity-based social responsibility, behaviour-based social responsibility and entwined social responsibility (see Figure 2.5). Companies with a *low social responsibility* pattern are low on both CSR identity and behaviour – they do not present themselves as socially responsible nor do they engage in any giving, volunteering, ethical behaviour, and so on. These companies simply avoid CSR all together. Companies with *identity-based social responsibility* have a great set of espoused values on their websites, telling the world how responsible they are, but do not have the behaviour to match. In other words, they just 'talk the talk'. *Behaviour-based social responsibility* means that companies are engaged in phi-lanthropy or other types of CSR behaviour, but they do not really believe in it or do not have the set of values and ethos to match. People sometimes refer to such actions as 'greenwashing' or instrumental CSR. Finally, *entwined social responsibility* is what you find in companies that are high on both CSR behaviour and CSR iden-tity. These would be the companies that 'walk the talk', the ones that are perceived as CSR leaders and icons.

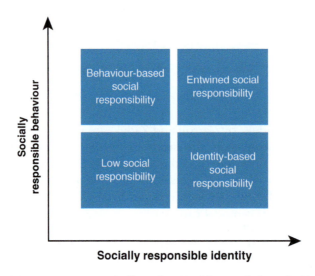

Figure 2.5   The CSR engagement matrix (based on Haski-Leventhal et al., 2017)

The CSR congruence model does not only typologise companies, it also offers the same typology for employees. Just like companies, employees (and people in gen-eral) have socially responsible identity and behaviour and can be placed on any of the four patterns. The proximity between the employees' social responsibility (ESR) pattern and that of their employer can result in congruence or lack thereof and consequently in desired and undesired workplace outcomes, which will be further discussed in Chapter 7.

Obviously, companies and employees can change their pattern by increasing or decreasing their CSR identity levels, their CSR behaviour levels, or both. There are three groups of determinants of CSR patterns: internal factors (such as background variables, motivation and leadership style), relational factors (mutual effects of companies and employees and processes such as socialisation) and external factors (such as stakeholder pressure or changes in the market). For example, a change of CEO can completely change the CSR identity and behaviour of a company.

The contribution of this model is twofold. Firstly, it offers a multidimensional model of CSR, tying identity and behaviour, both of which are very important to CSR and the perception of a company as socially responsible. Secondly, it is the first one to offer one model, which applies to both employees and employers, allowing us to compare the two and examine the impact of a match between them on the employees and the employers.

EXERCISE

Read the Ben & Jerry's case above and the Nestlé mini case below. On which pattern would you place each of these companies? Can you think of other examples for each of these patterns?

Creating shared value

Michael Porter and Mark Kramer have published several articles on CSR and strategic philanthropy, however their best-known work is the *Harvard Business Review* article from 2011 on creating shared value or CSV (Porter and Kramer, 2011). In a nutshell, the idea behind CSV is a shift away from CSR that is focused on philanthropy and is a sideshow to CSV that creates financial and social value at the same time. It is not about making money and then giving money to charity, but rather about making a positive change in society through creating innovative products and new markets.

CSV involves creating economic value in a way that also creates value for society by addressing its needs and challenges. CSV recognises that societal needs, not just conventional economic needs, define markets. A global society in which so many cannot afford basic goods is not only a societal issue, but also implies that many companies are missing out on potential markets.

CSV unleashes the power of business to do good for the world. Porter and Kramer write: 'Businesses acting as businesses, not as charitable donors, are the most powerful force for addressing issues we face' (2011: 64). Indeed, if businesses use their power, resources, knowledge and skills to address the most burning global issues we face, then there is no limit to what can be achieved. Porter and Kramer believed it such a powerful idea that the cover of the *Harvard Business Review* issue promised to 'fix capitalism'.

To do so, Porter and Kramer suggested three key ways for creating shared value (Figure 2.6). The first one is to *redefine productivity in the value chain*. According to Porter (1985), a value chain is a set of activities that a firm operating in a specific industry performs in order to deliver a valuable product or service for the market. Productivity in the value chain is determined by the activities that are carried out. CSV is about reconceiving productivity by improving resource efficiency and reducing cost of operation and its impact. This can be achieved by being more sustainable and less wasteful. For example, Unilever found innovative ways to create laundry detergents that use smaller quantities per wash, are more effective in a cold wash and are sold in smaller packages. This means the company reduces costs and waste throughout the entire value chain, including the end use by the consumer. It promotes the brand and increases its competitive advantage, and as such creates financial value and social value at the same time.

CREATING SHARED VALUE	
Reconceiving products and markets	Increase revenue with new/improved products and services to address social and environmental issues *Example: Unilever body care products in rural India*
Redefining productivity in the value chain	Improve resource efficiency in the supply chain (more for less) and reduce operation costs and negative impacts *Example: Unilever laundry detergents*
Enabling local cluster development	Activate supply chain to enable growth and productivity, work with various stakeholders to create impact *Example: Unilever Lipton Tea*

Figure 2.6   **Three levels of CSV (based on Porter and Kramer, 2011)**

The second pathway is to *recreate products and markets*. Companies can grow revenue through new or improved products and services to address social issues. To illustrate this, many people in rural India could not afford bodycare products because of relative high costs together with low income. For example, a bottle of shampoo costs a two-week salary and so only a few can afford to wash their hair, resulting in poor hygiene and health. Unilever then reconceived the product and instead of selling shampoo in big plastic bottles, which had been the standard form of packaging, it offered small, disposable sachets of body wash and shampoo, which were affordable. As such, the company addressed a social issue while creating a new market and financial growth.

The third and final pathway is to *enable local cluster development*, which means activating the company's supply chain to enable growth and productivity. This implies working with suppliers and stakeholders, creating successful collaborations from which everyone gains. Another example from Unilever is the work the company has done in enabling local clusters around its Lipton Tea brand. Unilever worked closely with farmers and suppliers of tea leaves to develop and build local communities. This work went beyond just paying the farmers a fair trade price, to even building schools for their children and creating local groups of farmers. The result is a more sustainable supply chain, improved wellbeing of farmers and communities, and a better product and brand. The company thus creates financial value and social value at the same time.

Questions for reflection and discussion

1. Find examples from other companies of achieving the three pathways.
2. Are the three pathways enough to create genuinely responsible companies?
3. What is missing in the model?
4. Can companies address all three and still demonstrate low levels of CSR?

Importance and limitations

The idea of creating shared value became very popular after the publication of Porter and Kramer's article in 2011. Some companies, such as Nestlé (see mini case study below), completely moved away from CSR, replacing it with CSV. There are CSV networks, conferences, workshops and tools to help companies and managers to adopt the idea of CSV. The concept gained strong academic acceptance and in its first five years the article was cited nearly 5,000 times by other academics. It became one of the most popular *Harvard Business Review* (HBR) articles and the video in which Porter speaks about CSV became the most watched video at Harvard Business School. When Porter speaks about social issues, the world listens, and as such the article had a huge impact on companies' policies and practice around responsibility and creating social value. CSV offers a different perspective on corporate responsibility, while proposing practical tools and examples to move forward with this. When an HBR article states that the capitalist system is under siege and needs to be fixed, the impact is immense, even if the solution is not perfect.

Indeed, while CSV attracted support and followers, there was some strong criticism of it. Firstly, critics said that it does not fix capitalism as was promised on the cover. Rather, it sits comfortably within the capitalist system. The subtitle of the HBR issue in which Porter and Kramer's article was published (2011) was 'How to fix capitalism' followed by 'And unleash a new wave of growth'. A careful reading shows that the language and discourse of CSV is profit-focused and that it continues the discourse of greed while simply offering another way to make strong corporations even stronger.

The second line of criticism was that the idea is not original. Reading theories and models of social entrepreneurship and strategic CSR, there are many similarities to the idea of CSV. Social enterprises have been creating financial value and social value at the same time for decades. Strategic CSR is also about being innovative and responsible throughout the entire value chain 'to achieve maximum economic and social value'. Furthermore, when Porter and Kramer compare CSV to CSR, they use a traditional view of CSR, mainly focusing on philanthropy, instead of comparing it to strategic CSR, which could have been more appropriate. Furthermore, companies can (and some of them do) implement all three key ways to creating shared value while still demonstrating unethical behaviour. *The Economist* also highly criticised CSV, calling the idea 'undercooked', while *Management Next* went as far as calling Porter a 'pirate' for stealing other people's ideas with no acknowledgement (as cited in Crane et al., 2014).

In 2014, Crane et al. published an article in the *California Management Review* entitled 'Contesting the value of creating shared value' and it accused Porter and Kramer of being unoriginal, for not holding up to their promise to fix capitalism and for making unfounded assumptions. Porter and Kramer responded at the end of that article and an interesting debate unfolds there. Crane et al. explained that Porter and Kramer ignore the tensions between social and economic goals – as if these goals could always be aligned and achieved at the same time. The authors further argued that the HBR article is naive about business compliance, as Porter and Kramer (2011: 75) say that 'creating shared value presumes compliance with the law and ethical standards, as well as mitigating any harm caused by the business, but goes far beyond that'. That is a lot to presume of business, given the unethical scandals we have witnessed in the last two decades.

The alternative view is that we need to fundamentally examine the rules of the capitalist game. As Porter and Kramer themselves say, the capitalist system is under siege. People do not trust the big corporations, and extreme capitalism has resulted in too many scandals and too much corruption, violation of human and animal rights, environmental damage and other harm. It seems right to conclude that the system is broken and that the business approach needs to change. Concepts such as conscious capitalism and strategic CSR offer a more holistic option.

Mini case study   Nestlé

Nestlé is a food and beverage company headquartered in Switzerland. It is the largest food company in the world measured by revenues. With a market capitalisation of US$239.6 billion, Nestlé was ranked as the 11th largest company in the world in 2014 by the *Financial Times* (Global 500).

Nestlé was one of the first companies that claimed to create shared value and served as a case study, which later helped Porter and Kramer develop the CSV concept. It has a CSV Council (of which Michael Porter is a member) and tries to implement the three key ways of CSV. Today it no longer has a CSR report, but a CSV report. The company states that:

> Being a global leader brings not only a duty to operate responsibly, but also an opportunity to create long-term positive value for society. We call this Creating Shared Value, and we embed it firmly across all parts of our business. (Nestlé, 2017)

To create shared value, Nestlé made 39 commitments that go beyond compliance and work according to their value. According to Nestlé, some of its key achievements in 2015 included: adopting the UN Guiding Principles reporting framework for human rights issues; activating 81 Healthy Kids programmes around the world to promote healthy diets and lifestyles; finalising Nestlé Guidelines for Respecting the Human Rights to Water and Sanitation; working to eliminate child labour; and strengthening its commitment to reduce food loss and waste.

However, Nestlé has been criticised over the years for alleged unethical or irresponsible behaviour by many people and organisations. From the baby formula controversy in the 1980s (in which the company was accused of aggressively promoting baby formula to the poor, resulting in a long boycott, which is ongoing for some groups); through smear campaigns against Nestlé's usage of palm oil from forests which harms the orangutans' habitat; to strong recent criticism of Nestlé's irresponsible use of water, particularly in some parts of the US (*Guardian*, 2013; Coombs and Holladay, 2015; Samson, 2016). It is interesting to see a company that commits to creating shared value and all three key ways to achieve it, being strongly criticised for unethical behaviour.

References

Coombs, W. T. and Holladay, S. J. (2015) *Corporate social responsibility in the digital age*. Bingley: Emerald Group.

Nestle (2017) CSV. Available at: www.nestlé.com/csv (Accessed: 27 February 2017)

Points for discussion

1. What are the positive and negative aspects of Nestlé's CSR?
2. Do you think it creates shared value?
3. What can Nestlé do differently?
4. What does this case teach us about CSV?

Strategic CSR

While strategic CSR is not a theory or a model, it is important to elaborate on this concept and approach as it is the basis of this book. You may recall that strategic CSR is defined as 'the incorporation of a holistic CSR perspective within a firm's strategic planning and core operations so that the firm is managed in the interest of a broad set of stakeholders to achieve maximum economic and social value over the medium to long term'. If you read the definition carefully, you will find that it has six important components that are summarised in Figure 2.7.

Figure 2.7   The six components of strategic CSR (based on Werther and Chandler, 2011)

Holistic perspective: As CSR recently became more popular, some companies realised they needed to appoint a CSR officer or open a CSR department. They started publishing CSR reports in addition to their general reports and engage in some form of philanthropy. However, a holistic CSR perspective is much broader than this. It is about having social responsibility embedded in every aspect of the company. Every decision made is based on responsible and ethical thinking. Every employee, from entry level to the CEO, lives the values of social responsibility and ethics and acts upon them.

Strategic planning: Every company in the world has a mission or a goal. Some define it in terms of the products and services that they sell and some do so in broader terms of stating their purpose. For example, Ben & Jerry's mission statement is 'Making the best possible ice cream, in the nicest possible way'. Nestlé declares that its mission of 'Good Food, Good Life' is to 'provide consumers with the best tasting, most nutritious choices in a wide range of food and beverage categories and eating occasions, from morning to night'. Companies then develop a full strategy on how to achieve this mission, with tactics as the means to the end goal. This helps the company to clarify to all stakeholders what it is, what it stands for, what it does and for what reason. As such, strategic CSR is about tying the company's social responsibility to its mission and strategy. Instead of concentrating on 'random acts of charity', the company uses its competitive advantage and strategy to define its involvement in society and the community. If the company is a food and beverage company, it makes sense that its CSR and giving would focus, for example, on food security.

Core operations: Core operations are what the company does every day in order to achieve its mission and act upon its strategy. It is the part of a company's business that is central to its overall strategy and typically generates the bulk of its revenues. This could be, for example, manufacturing products or delivering services. Strategic CSR means that companies behave responsibly, sustainably and ethically in all of their core operations. A company will not be trusted upon its CSR activities if it mistreats employees in offshoring factories or if it trashes the planet through its manufacturing. For companies to be more strategic about their CSR, the entire supply chain needs to be examined and fixed so it is conducted in the most responsible and sustainable way possible.

Broad set of stakeholders: As was explained in Chapter 1, moving from the narrow view of business responsibility to a broad view meant accepting the idea that companies should care about stakeholders other than just shareholders. Stakeholders are people (or groups or organisations) that are affected by the company achieving its mission. If we look at Nestlé's mission to provide consumers with food and beverage from morning to night, you can see how many people and organisations could be affected by it (both positively and negatively): consumers, employees, governments, various non-profit organisations, health organisations, competitors, the community and the environment. For the company to have strategic CSR, it needs to keep in mind all these stakeholder groups and to work with them to ensure that they all benefit from the company's actions with the least harm possible (see Chapter 3).

Maximum economic and social value: similar to what was said above, moving away from the narrow view of business responsibility meant that companies do not only maximise economic value. Firstly, we need to accept that maximising financial value at any cost may no longer be an option and that making enough money to ensure the company's financial sustainability could also be a possibility. Many companies and social enterprises are now shifting away from 'profit maximisation' to 'profit making', which requires a shift in mindset. Secondly, strategic CSR is about maximising social value as well. While making products and delivering services to make profits, companies can also deliver social value at the same time. Finding innovative ways to benefit all stakeholders while doing so is at the core of strategic CSR. This is the same idea that later appeared in the creating shared value concept – to create financial value and social value at the same time.

Medium to long term: When Paul Polman joined Unilever as its new CEO in 2009, one of the first things that he did was to get rid of the quarterly reports that seem to determine everything in so many companies (see Chapter 6). Polman later said to the *Washington Post*:

The issues we are trying to attack with our business model and that need to be solved in the world today—food security, sanitation, employment, climate change—cannot be solved just by quarterly reporting. They require longer-term solutions and not 90-day pressures. (Cunningham, 2015)

Strategic CSR is about shifting away from the very short-term thinking of quarterly performance to long-term outcomes and impact. If companies really embrace responsibility for global issues, a long-term approach is needed.

Questions for reflection and discussion

1. Looking at the case studies you have seen so far, which companies have strategic CSR?
2. Examine Ben & Jerry's – would you say that it is an example of strategic CSR? Why or why not?
3. Which of the six components of strategic CSR does Ben & Jerry's demonstrate and which ones need to be improved?

Summary

Since the 1970s, several CSR theories, models and frameworks have emerged to assist in capturing and measuring CSR. Carroll's CSR pyramid (Carroll, 1991) shifted away from a narrow view of business responsibility to an approach that business has no fewer than four responsibilities: economic, legal, ethical and discretionary (philanthropy). It is one of the best-known models of CSR, but there is also a vast amount of criticism around it.

Another CSR pyramid was presented by Zadek (2004), but his pyramid was around CSR levels and stages as part of the learning journey companies undergo. Using the case study of Nike and other examples, Zadek offered a model with five levels from low CSR to high: defensive, compliance, managerial, strategic and civil. The first three levels are all about mitigating damage and averting risk while the last two create value for the company and society.

The CSR congruence model (Haski-Leventhal et al., 2017) included a CSR matrix built on CSR identity (strategy, values and culture) and CSR behaviour (action, philanthropy and ethical behaviour). The result is four patterns of CSR: low social responsibility, identity-based social responsibility, behaviour-based social responsibility and entwined social responsibility. The model can be applied to both employers and employees and used to examine the congruence between them and the impact of such congruence or the lack thereof.

In 2011, Porter and Kramer published an HBR article on creating shared value (CSV), which had a vast impact on CSR scholars and practitioners. CSV is a transformation from corporate philanthropy to creating financial value and social value at the same time. This can be achieved via three key ways: redefining productivity in the value chain; recreating products and markets; and enabling local cluster development. Although this idea became very popular (and perhaps because of it), there is also strong criticism of it.

Strategic CSR is the approach selected for this book because it is more holistic in nature than others. It includes six key components: incorporating a *holistic* CSR perspective within a firm's *strategic planning* and *core operations* so that the firm is managed in the interest of a *broad set of stakeholders* to achieve *maximum economic and social value* over the *medium to long term*.

General questions

1. Why do we need different models and theories of CSR?
2. Examining the models and concepts that were detailed in this chapter, how are they all helping to develop CSR as a field of study and practice?
3. In your opinion, which one is the most applicable to business? Why?
4. What are we still missing in the existing models and concepts? What do you think the next theory will be?
5. Do you agree that 'there is nothing so practical as a good theory'? How can these models and theories assist companies in implementing CSR? Choose one model to demonstrate its applicability.

Key definitions

- CSR encompasses the economic, legal, ethical and philanthropic expectations that society has of organisations at a given point in time (Carroll, 1979).
- Zadek's CSR pyramid includes five levels or learning stages of CSR: defensive, compliance, managerial, strategic and civil (Zadek, 2004).
- The CSR congruence model and its CSR matrix is based on CSR identity and CSR behaviour, resulting in four patterns that can be applied to employers and employees: low social responsibility, identity-based social responsibility, behaviour-based social responsibility and entwined social responsibility (Haski-Leventhal et al., 2017).
- Creating shared value (CSV) involves creating economic value in a way that also creates value for society by addressing its need and challenges. This can

be done through three key ways: redefining productivity in the value chain; recreating products and markets; and enabling local cluster development (Porter and Kramer, 2011).

- Strategic CSR is defined as the incorporation of a holistic CSR perspective within a firm's strategic planning and core operations so that the firm is managed in the interest of a broad set of stakeholders to achieve maximum economic and social value over the medium to long term (Werther and Chandler, 2011).

References

BBC (2015) Volkswagen: The scandal explained. Available at: www.bbc.com/news/business-34324772 (Accessed: 24 February 2017)

Carroll, A. B. (1979) 'A three-dimensional conceptual model of corporate performance', *Academy of Management Review*, 4(4): 497–505.

Carroll, A. B. (1991) 'The pyramid of corporate social responsibility: Toward the moral management of organizational stakeholders', *Business Horizons*, 34(4): 39–48.

Carroll, A. B. (1999) 'Corporate social responsibility: Evolution of a definitional construct', *Business & Society*, 38(3): 268–95.

Carroll, A. B. and Shabana, K. M. (2010) 'The business case for corporate social responsibility: A review of concepts, research and practice', *International Journal of Management Reviews*, 12(1): 85–105.

Coombs, W. T. and Holladay, S. J. (2015) *Corporate social responsibility in the digital age*. Bingley: Emerald Group.

Crane, A., Palazzo, G., Spence, L. J. and Matten, D. (2014) 'Contesting the value of "creating shared value"', *California Management Review*, 56(2): 130–53.

Cunningham, L. (2015) 'The tao of Paul Polman', *Washington Post*, 21 May. Available at: www.washingtonpost.com/news/on-leadership/wp/2015/05/21/the-tao-of-paul-polman/?utm_term=.2262c07941f8 (Accessed: 16 May 2017)

Guardian (2013) Nestlé baby milk scandal has grown up but not gone away. Available at: www.theguardian.com/sustainable-business/nestle-babymilk-scandal-food-industry-standards (Accessed: 27 February 2017)

Haski-Leventhal, D. (2014) 'MBA student values, attitudes and behaviors: A cross-cultural comparison of PRME signatory schools', *SAM Advanced Management Journal*, 79(4): 29–41.

Haski-Leventhal, D., Roza, L. and Meijs, L. C. (2017) 'Congruence in corporate social responsibility: Connecting the identity and behaviour of employers and employees', *Journal of Business Ethics*, 143(1): 35–51.

Lewin, K. (1951) *Field theory in social science*. New York: Harper & Row.

Nestlé (2017) CSV. Available at: www.nestle.com/csv (Accessed: 27 February 2017)

Porter, M. E. (1985) *Competitive advantage: Creating and sustaining superior performance*. New York: Free Press.

Porter, M. E. and Kramer, M. R. (2011) 'Creating shared value', *Harvard Business Review*, 89(1/2): 62–77.

Samson, K. (2016) The privatization of water: Nestlé denies that water is a fundamental human right. Available at: www.globalresearch.ca/the-privatisation-of-water-nestle-denies-that-water-is-a-fundamental-human-right/5332238 (Accessed: 27 February 2017)

Visser, W. (2006) 'Revisiting Carroll's CSR pyramid', in E. R. Pederson and M. Huniche (eds), *Corporate citizenship in developing countries*, Copenhagen: Copenhagen Business school press, 29–56.

Werther, W. B. and Chandler, D. (2011) *Strategic corporate social responsibility: Stakeholders in a global environment* (2nd edn). Thousand Oaks, CA: Sage.

Zadek, S. (2004) 'The path to corporate responsibility', *Harvard Business Review*, 82(12): 125–33.

Further reading

Beschorner, T. (2014) 'Creating shared value: The one-trick pony approach', *Business Ethics Journal Review*, 1(17): 106–12.

Brammer, S., Jackson, G. and Matten, D. (2012) 'Corporate social responsibility and institutional theory: New perspectives on private governance', *Socio-Economic Review*, 10(1): 3–28.

Burke, L. and Logsdon, J. M. (1996) 'How corporate social responsibility pays off', *Long Range Planning*, 29(4): 495–502.

Falck, O. and Heblich, S. (2007) 'Corporate social responsibility: Doing well by doing good', *Business Horizons*, 50(3): 247–54.

McWilliams, A., Siegel, D. S. and Wright, P. M. (2006) 'Corporate social responsibility: Strategic implications', *Journal of Management Studies*, 43(1): 1–18.

Michelini, L. and Fiorentino, D. (2012) 'New business models for creating shared value', *Social Responsibility Journal*, 8(4): 561–77.

Pfitzer, M., Bockstette, V. and Stamp, M. (2013) 'Innovating for shared value', *Harvard Business Review*, 91(9): 100–7.

Polonsky, M. and Jevons, C. (2009) 'Global branding and strategic CSR: An overview of three types of complexity', *International Marketing Review*, 26(3): 327–47.

Sekhar Bhattacharyya, S., Sahay, A., Pratap Arora, A. and Chaturvedi, A. (2008) 'A toolkit for designing firm level strategic corporate social responsibility (CSR) initiatives', *Social Responsibility Journal*, 4(3): 265–82.

Siano, A., Vollero, A., Conte, F. and Amabile, S. (2017) '"More than words": Expanding the taxonomy of greenwashing after the Volkswagen scandal', *Journal of Business Research*, 71: 27–37.

Moving Beyond Shareholders: Internal and External Stakeholders

3

Learning outcomes

By the end of this chapter, students should be able to:

- define and list the stakeholders of any organisation
- articulate the importance of responsible stakeholder management as part of strategic CSR

- explain stakeholder theory and corporate stakeholder responsibility
- develop the stakeholder management capacity and stakeholder integration of an organisation
- detail CSR issues, which are specifically related to certain stakeholder groups.

Case study   Johnson & Johnson's stakeholder approach

Johnson & Johnson is an international healthcare company, which was founded in 1886 by three brothers. For over 130 years, the company has been pioneering healthcare innovation in fields ranging from dental care to cutting-edge cancer treatments. The company is organised into three business segments: consumer, pharmaceutical and medical devices.

One of the most unique aspects of Johnson & Johnson's is its credo, a statement of beliefs and aims regarding the company's responsibility towards its various stakeholders, which guides its actions. Johnson & Johnson's credo declares the company's responsibility towards four stakeholders groups: 1. customers and suppliers; 2. employees; 3. the community in which the company works as well as the world community; and 4. the shareholders of the company. According to the company's website:

> Robert Wood Johnson, former chairman from 1932 to 1963 and a member of the Company's founding family, crafted 'Our Credo' himself in 1943, just before Johnson & Johnson became a publicly traded company. This was long before anyone ever heard the term 'corporate social responsibility'. 'Our Credo' is more than just a moral compass. We believe it's a recipe for business success. The fact that Johnson & Johnson is one of only a handful of companies that have flourished through more than a century of change is proof of that.

The first responsibility stated in the credo is towards the company's *customers*: 'We believe our first responsibility is to the doctors, nurses and patients, to mothers and fathers and all others who use our products and services.' Addressing this responsibility, Johnson & Johnson develops safe and healthy products, maintains affordable prices and controls distribution of its products in order to allow fair access.

(Continued)

The second responsibility is towards the *employees*: 'We are responsible to our employees, the men and women who work with us throughout the world. Everyone must be considered as an individual. We must respect their dignity and recognize their merit.' Johnson & Johnson employs over 127,000 employees worldwide and exhibits internal CSR practices towards them. The company's 2016 annual report states: 'All of our compelling strategies and strong results would not be possible without our talented, diverse and dedicated employees. Their commitment and passion has helped Johnson & Johnson to be named by top industry.' The company's citizenship report details high levels of workplace health and safety, how the company improves employees' health and wellbeing and how it recruits for diversity.

In addition, Johnson & Johnson offers its employees corporate volunteering opportunities, paid leave to volunteer and skill-based volunteering. The employees can also participate in a payroll giving programme (in which the employees donate directly from their monthly salary and the company matches their donations) and in disaster relief, as many did after hurricane Sandy in New York in 2012, for example. These efforts can be seen as beneficial to both the employees and the community.

The third responsibility is towards the *community* and the environment: 'We are responsible to the communities in which we live and work and to the world community as well. (...) protecting the environment and natural resources.' In line with this responsibility, Johnson & Johnson champions various local, national and global initiatives to advance health and sustainability along three main dimensions: people, places and practices. In the *people* dimension, Johnson & Johnson created research partnerships and licensing agreements to provide treatment of neglected diseases in the developing world and made HIV medicines more accessible to people in more than 100 developing countries. The company also donated 200 million doses of its treatment for intestinal worms to children in more than 30 countries in the course of one year. In terms of environmental sustainability, Johnson & Johnson declares that, as a company, it recognises the need to identify, prevent and plan for environmental challenges, including constraints on natural resources, climate change and water scarcity and their impacts on human health. The company states that to create healthier societies, we must have an unwavering commitment to protecting the natural resources upon which we all rely, today and in the future.

The fourth responsibility is towards its *shareholders*: 'Business must make a sound profit. (...) When we operate according to these principles, the stockholders should realize a fair return.' As part of its responsibility towards the shareholders, in 2016 Johnson & Johnson invested approximately US$5 billion in acquisitions and major licensing deals and US$9.1 billion in research and development; paid US$8.6 billion in dividends; and completed two-thirds of its US$10 billion share repurchase programme.

The credo represents the underlying approach that guides the company and its operations in looking after all its stakeholders – the customers, suppliers, employees and the environment – which in turn will result in shareholder profit. Although written in 1943, it captures a stakeholder integration approach that few companies can demonstrate even today.

Our credo

We believe our first responsibility is to the doctors, nurses and patients, to mothers and fathers and all others who use our products and services. In meeting their needs everything we do must be of high quality. We must constantly strive to reduce our costs in order to maintain reasonable prices. Customers' orders must be serviced promptly and accurately. Our suppliers and distributors must have an opportunity to make a fair profit.

We are responsible to our employees, the men and women who work with us throughout the world. Everyone must be considered as an individual. We must respect their dignity and recognize their merit. They must have a sense of security in their jobs. Compensation must be fair and adequate, and working conditions clean, orderly and safe. We must be mindful of ways to help our employees fulfill their family responsibilities. Employees must feel free to make suggestions and complaints. There must be equal opportunity for employment, development and advancement for those qualified. We must provide competent management, and their actions must be just and ethical.

We are responsible to the communities in which we live and work and to the world community as well. We must be good citizens – support good works and charities and bear our fair share of taxes. We must encourage civic improvements and better health and education. We must maintain in good order the property we are privileged to use, protecting the environment and natural resources.

Our final responsibility is to our stockholders. Business must make a sound profit. We must experiment with new ideas. Research must be carried on, innovative programs developed and mistakes paid for. New equipment must be purchased, new facilities provided and new products launched. Reserves must be created to provide for adverse times. When we operate according to these principles, the stockholders should realize a fair return.

(Johnson & Johnson, 2017)

(Continued)

Questions

1. Read Johnson & Johnson's credo and identify all the company's listed stakeholders. Which stakeholders are missing?
2. Try to prioritise them. Whom do you think is more important and why?
3. The credo was written in 1943 and has hardly changed since. Why is this revolutionary in terms of stakeholder management?
4. How would you, as a senior manager in Johnson & Johnson, explain the importance of the credo to a newly recruited manager in your team?

Bibliography

Akerstrom, A. (2009) Corporate governance and social responsibility. Available at: www.grin.com/en/e-book/137651/corporate-governance-and-social-responsibility (Accessed: 07 May 2017)

Berry, D. (2007) 'CSR should be part of the way a company works and thinks' (reprinted with permission from The Chartered Secretary Malaysia, Nov.–Dec. 2006), *Keeping Good Companies*, 59(7): 416.

Johnson & Johnson (2017) Johnson & Johnson credo. Available at: www.jnj.com/about-jnj/jnj-credo (Accessed: 05 May 2017)

Katsoulakos, P., Koutsodimou, M., Matraga, A. and Williams, L. (2004) 'A historic perspective of the CSR movement', CSRQuest Sustainability Framework. Athens: Athens University of Economics and Business.

Links

CNBC (2017) Johnson & Johnson talc-powder trial. Available at: www.cnbc.com/2017/05/05/johnson-johnson-ordered-to-pay-110-million-in-us-talc-powder-trial.html (Accessed: 08 May 2017)

Johnson & Johnson (2017) CSR. Available at: www.jnj.com/caring/citizenship-sustainability (Accessed: 08 May 2017)

Johnson & Johnson (2017) CSR report. Available at: www.jnj.com/_document?id=00000159–6a1e-dba3-afdb-7aff1b270000 (Accessed: 08 May 2017)

Introduction: Every business has stakeholders

The definition of strategic CSR states that the firms must be managed in the interest of a broad set of stakeholders and therefore understanding who the stakeholders are, where their interests lie and how to manage the company to address these interests (which can sometimes be contradictory) is an essential part of responsible management.

Not every business has *shareholders*, however they all have *stakeholders*. While we all take this for granted nowadays, it was only in the 1980s that this concept became popular and made such a huge impact, not only on CSR scholars and practitioners, but also on business management all over the world. The idea resonated with people because it made sense and touched on our basic notion of family, tribe and community. Whilst the term had been used in business literature since the 1930s to discuss the different duties companies hold towards shareholders, customers, consumers and employees, it was only after stakeholder theory was presented in the 1980s that it became a popular business term.

The stakeholder theory's main contribution, as it emerged in the 1980s, was the novel idea that a company is responsible towards more stakeholders than just its shareholders. And if it is so, we can no longer say that its sole responsibility is to maximise profit. But the concept was not accepted immediately. For example, in 1996, Albert J. Dunlap, the CEO of Scott Paper who was later accused of serious unethical behaviour, wrote:

> The most ridiculous word you hear in boardrooms these days is 'stakeholders'. A stakeholder is anyone with a stake in a company's well-being. That includes its employees, suppliers, the communities in which it operates, and so on. The current theory is that a CEO has to take all these people into account when making decisions. Stakeholders! Whenever I hear that word, I ask 'How much did they pay for their stake?' Stakeholders don't pay a penny for their stake. Shareholders do. (Dunlap, 1996: 12)

Well, Mr Dunlap, all stakeholders pay for their stake. Employees 'pay' to be stakeholders with their time, efforts and sometimes with their best years and their lives. Their families pay the price of not seeing them often enough or of dealing with the impact of stress and health and safety issues. Consumers pay, not only with money for the products they buy, but also with the impact these products have on their wellbeing. The environment pays a heavy price of detrition due to unsustainable business practices and governments pay billions to fix business's 'externalities'. They all pay, but most also get 'dividends' from their stake – with access to jobs, better quality of life, products that serve them and tax money. As such, all major stakeholder groups deserve a 'seat at the table', to have their voices heard and to have companies who take them into consideration as the minimum benefit of a company's CSR.

Stakeholders defined

Due to the hold that stakeholders have over the company or the way they are affected by it, the stakeholder theory suggested that they (the stakeholders) have a 'stake' in the company. This is quite different to the 'shareholder theory of the firm', which dominated business and the debate over its purpose, particularly in the 1960s, according to which the main responsibility of a company is to increase shareholder value. In contrast, stakeholder theory offers an alternative approach, asserting that the firm has material and moral reasons to consider its relationship with stakeholders other than the investors. It does not mean in any way that CSR suggests companies do not have a responsibility to their shareholders, but rather it broadens their responsibility.

Stakeholders are individuals, groups or organisations (or even countries) that are affecting a company or being affected by a company achieving its goals. This can be a positive effect: employees get a job and liveable wage; consumers buy products that they need or that can improve their lives; and communities receive funds from the firm's philanthropic activities. However, the effect can also be negative: employees get treated badly and work for slavery-level pay; consumers buy products that are unhealthy or unsafe; and the community and the environment are negatively impacted by the firm's manufacturing or waste management. All of these stakeholders and many others could be affected by the company achieving its goal to sell as many products as it can while making maximum profit.

However, stakeholders can also affect the company: consumers can choose to buy a product as soon as it hits the shelf or boycott it; employees can decide to work as hard as they can for a company or go on strike; and the government can decide to regulate the company or turn a blind eye to unethical behaviour.

As such, Freeman's (1984: 46) definition of stakeholders is easy to remember: 'any group or individual who can affect or is affected (positively or negatively) by the achievement of the organisation's objectives.'

Another definition of stakeholders has some additional aspects: 'the stakeholders in a firm are individuals and groups that contribute, either voluntarily or involuntarily, to its wealth-creating capacity and activities, and who are therefore its potential beneficiaries and/or risk bearers' (Post et al., 2002: 8).

This definition emphasises the contribution of stakeholders to a company's wealth-creating capacity or its goal to maximise profits. Shareholders, consumers, employees, suppliers, governments and others can all contribute, directly and indirectly, to the company's wealth-creating capacity. To illustrate, consumers can contribute to a company's wealth by buying its product and recommending it through word of mouth: telling their friends about the product and sharing positive reviews of it on social media.

This definition also adds the aspect of 'voluntarily or involuntarily' and it is indeed important to remember that some stakeholders do not voluntarily contribute to the wealth creation of a company. Many employees in developing countries (what is often referred to as 'offshoring') do not choose to work for a certain company, but do so due to lack of choice. They definitely do not choose to do so with very low pay and in inhumane and unsafe conditions. Some farmers do not choose to sell their produce to corporates at the price offered to them, however they have very low 'supplier power' and as such involuntarily help the company to create more wealth. Instead of defining stakeholders as being affected negatively or positively, this definition divides them into 'beneficiaries' (those who enjoy the fruits of the company) and 'risk bearers' (those who are negatively affected or bear the risk of being negatively affected).

These two definitions refer to stakeholders as people (individuals and groups), but we should bear in mind that companies also affect the environment, animals and bio-diversity with their actions. For example, there is a growing awareness around the animal cruelty which goes hand in hand with many companies' operations: from endangering natural habitats and using animal testing to selling them as produce. Billions of animals suffer every year and many organisations and consumers are trying to be the voice of these voiceless stakeholders. The environment was also identified as an important stakeholder and will be further discussed in Chapter 5.

It is important to note that stakeholder theory is *descriptive*, in the sense that it describes what is (i.e. that every corporation has stakeholders). It describes the corporation as a constellation of cooperative and competitive interests possessing intrinsic value. It is also *normative*, as it suggests what companies should do (they should strive to meet the expectations of a broad set of stakeholders or work with them to come up with the best possible solution for all). Stakeholder theory is *instrumental*, as it establishes a framework for examining the connections that may exist between the practice of stakeholder management and the achievement of various corporate performance goals. It is *managerial* because it recommends attitudes, structures and practices that, taken together, constitute stakeholder management (Donaldson and Preston, 1995).

Questions for reflection and discussion

1. In your opinion, why do the definitions of stakeholders include negative aspects?
2. Do you think stakeholders affect a company or are more affected by it?

Who the stakeholders are: Lists and typologies

When examining the definitions above, lists of individuals and groups that may be affected by the company achieving its goals start to emerge. They include (in no particular order): employees, consumers, suppliers, owners and shareholders, governments, the community in which they operate as well as the environment and animals. There were a few attempts to classify stakeholders and offer several stakeholder typologies, some of which will be detailed next.

Three groups of stakeholders

In their book on strategic CSR, Werther and Chandler (2011) divided stakeholders of any company into three groups: organisational (internal to the firm), economic and societal (both external to the firm). The *organisational stakeholders* are within the organisation and as such the organisation works inwards when addressing its needs. As can be seen in Figure 3.1, organisational stakeholders include employees, owners and managers as well as employee unions, which are sometimes listed as employees and sometimes as additional stakeholders. Trade unions have different levels of power to individual employees due to their 'coalition' power base (power in the numbers) and as such can serve the individual employees better (although there are cases of corruption and political behaviour, which lead to poor service). In this group we can also include employees' families as being affected by the company's actions (e.g. if single mums in developing countries are forced to work 15–20 hours a day, their children will be affected by these actions as well).

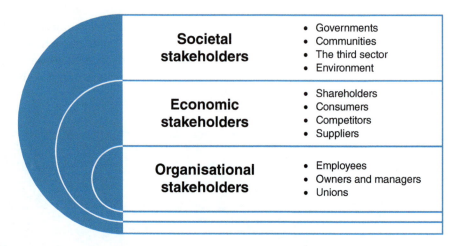

Figure 3.1   Three types of stakeholders (based on Werther and Chandler, 2011)

The *economic stakeholders* include the *shareholders*, who legally own a share of stock in a public or private corporation. Shareholders may be referred to as members of a corporation, in which case they could be placed in the first group of organisational stakeholders. The shareholders provide the company with financial resources, which allow it to operate, and in many countries, corporations are legally bound to maximise shareholder value. It is no wonder that for so many companies the shareholders become the primary priority, although one could argue that without (satisfied) employees and consumers, companies cannot operate either.

In this group, we also find *consumers*, who use the economic services or commodities offered by the firm. Consumers pay money to consume goods and services and are therefore essential stakeholders. When developing a company, a product or service, it is usually with the consumer in mind, trying to address an unmet consumer demand. When companies use marketing strategies, they try to show consumers that they will get a better value proposition by buying from them instead of buying from their competitors. This does not necessarily imply that the companies always work with the consumer's best interest in mind. However, strategic CSR indicates that consumer expectations are to be met in a way that creates positive value for them and other stakeholders.

Other economic stakeholders are the *competitors* that are affected by the company achieving its goals. If we look at business as a 'zero sum game', then the success of one company results in its competitors (the ones that strive to sell similar goods in similar markets) being negatively affected. If the company's goal is to maximise profit, then it might follow that all is fair in war and business competition. Companies such as Walmart were often criticised in the past for 'crashing' their competitors, including small local businesses, sometimes resulting in the local 'main street' being economically destroyed. The conscious business movement presents another approach to competitors, and it will be discussed next.

The last economic stakeholders listed are the *suppliers*. Suppliers could be vendors who sell companies' goods (which are then sold to the end consumer at a profit) or local farmers who grow produce that are then being used or sold by the company. The way that a company works with and treats its suppliers could be a strong indicator of its CSR. When Ben & Jerry's started its ice cream company, it was always important for it to buy milk from local dairy farmers for a fair price and the company later moved to 100 per cent fair trade in most of the ingredients it used. To date, the company works closely with the dairy farmers to ensure sustainability and help them thrive. Some companies try to bring down the suppliers' 'seller power' in order to reduce the price of the supplied goods and thus make more profit, however this is a short-term strategy.

The third group in this figure are *societal stakeholders*. These could be seen as less direct stakeholders, but they are still very important for the company's success and responsibility. *Governments* affect business and are being affected by business. Corporations pay taxes that are used by governments to deliver public goods, such as education, health and infrastructure. There is a growing expectation that business will help local government achieve its goals through CSR and philanthropy. However, governments also have the duty to regulate business and enforce the law. Big corporations and business people pressure governments through lobbying and financial support, which make this relationship more complicated.

The *local communities* in which businesses operate can also be negatively or positively affected by the company, through employment and financial support on the one hand and strong competition, impact on the environment and community wellbeing on the other. Think of a big factory opening up in a small rural area and the positive and negative impacts that this could have on the local community. Figure 3.1 lists the *third sector,* which are the not-for-profit organisations and non-government organisations (NGOs) that could be the beneficiaries of corporate philanthropy or those that need to fix/address problems created by the company.

Internal and external stakeholders

Similar to the above typology, stakeholders can be divided into internal and external ones (de Chernatony and Harris, 2000). *Internal stakeholders* include individuals and groups within the organisation that affect or are affected by the organisation's actions and goals. Internal stakeholders comprise employees (including offshore and outsourced employees), leadership and management, owners and corporate members, and trade unions. Being internal stakeholders implies that they are often perceived as particularly important for the organisation to achieve its goals, but also as extremely powerful stakeholders whose expectations need to be addressed. Of course, not in every company do employees have the power to act or associate (in some cases they cannot join or create unions, voice their concerns or go on strike) and the freedom and power of employees are considered a major issue of CSR.

External stakeholders include individuals and groups that have no direct affiliation to the organisation. Consumers, suppliers, governments, competitors, communities and the third sector are external to the organisation and fall under this category.

Based on this categorisation, another dual definition of CSR emerges: internal and external CSR. *Internal CSR* is a company's ethical behaviour towards its internal stakeholders, mainly employees. *External CSR*, on the other hand, encompasses ethical behaviour towards external stakeholders, and includes philanthropy and community contributions. It also reflects the way in which the firm interacts with the physical environment and its ethical stance towards consumers and other external stakeholders.

When companies are only engaged with external stakeholders, with an emphasis on philanthropy, and ignore the rights of their employees, their CSR may be perceived as hypocritical. As was said in 2011 by the then Australian Foreign Minister, Kevin Rudd:

> If companies do not act fairly with their own employees, consistent with industrial laws, they will not be believed more broadly on any matter of corporate social responsibility.

Questions for reflection and discussion

1. Why do you think it is important to differentiate between internal and external stakeholders and CSR?
2. Why will companies not be believed on their external CSR if their internal CSR is lacking?
3. What are the implications for managerial practices?

Primary and secondary stakeholders of a conscious business

In their book *Conscious Capitalism*, Mackey and Sisodia (2014) divide stakeholders into two groups: primary and secondary stakeholders, or inner-circle and outer-circle stakeholders. The primary stakeholders in the inner circle include six stakeholders which the authors describe as: 1. loyal, trusting customers; 2. passionate, inspired team members; 3. patient, purposeful investors; 4. collaborative, innovative suppliers; 5. flourishing, welcoming communities; and 6. a healthy, vibrant environment. All of these were covered above, but it is interesting to see how the authors refer to these six stakeholders in a positive way and how employees are perceived as 'team members'.

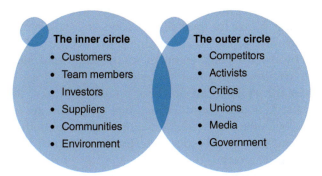

Figure 3.2 **Primary and secondary stakeholder typology (based on Mackey and Sisodia, 2014)**

The outer circle includes stakeholders that are not so commonly used in stakeholder mapping: competitors, activists, critics, unions, media and government (see Figure 3.2). They are seen as stakeholders due to their impact on the organisation and their influence on the inner-circle stakeholders. However, they do not routinely engage in voluntary exchange with the organisation for mutual benefit and are therefore categorised as outer-circle stakeholders. We need to add *academia/universities* to this list, particularly business schools that train many of the company's future and current employees and managers.

When it comes to competitors, conscious business treats them as allies rather than the 'enemy', striving for mutual excellence and learning:

> A far better attitude to have toward competitors is to zero in on what they're doing right, what they do better than us. It takes high emotional intelligence, self-awareness, and humility to recognize when a competitor is actually superior and can teach us and help our organisation to become better. (Mackey and Sisodia, 2014: 154)

The authors further suggest aligning with activists and critics. While these stakeholders could make the business uncomfortable and defensive, they could also be a remarkable source of knowledge on how to improve decisions and actions, resulting in a better and more ethical business.

The importance of stakeholder management in strategic CSR

Understanding that every company has many groups of stakeholders to consider and that it is important to manage their expectations and ensure their wellbeing is at the core of strategic CSR. When Edward Freeman published the stakeholder theory in 1984, it was more than a mere addition to the CSR body of knowledge. It contributed to the shift of mindset which was previously limited to defining the corporates' need only to care for their shareholders and have only one responsibility, which is to maximise profit. By discussing other people and groups that need to be considered by any company, Freeman contributed to the shift from a narrow view of corporate responsibility to a broad view.

The stakeholder theory is based on three related premises: that organisations have a number of stakeholder constituencies that affect and are affected by them; that processes and outcomes of these interactions impact on both stakeholders and the organisation; and that stakeholder perceptions influence the viability of the organisation's strategy (Freeman, 1984, 1994).

It is therefore apparent why stakeholder management is an essential part of CSR. Since the 1980s, there is a growing understanding that a company cannot be considered socially responsible if it only focuses on its shareholders. Some companies, such as Johnson & Johnson (see case study), have spoken for decades about other stakeholders, but others only came to acknowledge their stakeholders and the need to work with them in more recent years. CSR defines society in its widest sense and therefore responsible companies need to include all stakeholders and constituent groups that maintain an ongoing interest in the organisation's operations.

Some have argued (e.g. Jensen, 2001) that holistic stakeholder management requires a shift away from the profit maximisation doctrine. A focus on only one dimension, profit, will make it impossible to work with all stakeholders effectively. Firms need to make profit, but not maximise profit at any cost, as the latter approach will make it impossible to create (social) value for all stakeholders. Many companies now understand that they need to be purpose-driven, not only profit-driven, in order to engage all their stakeholders.

According to the conscious capitalism movement, a conscious business treats the needs of all its major stakeholders as ends in themselves, while a traditional business treats stakeholders only as a mean to maximise profit. Stakeholder integration is an essential component of a conscious business, together with purpose, leadership and culture. Stakeholders make up a company and must be honoured as people first. This will be elaborated upon in the following sections of this chapter.

It is important to understand that stakeholders are not only passive in their relationship with the company. Stakeholders constantly observe the company and its actions, evaluate its responsibility towards them and other stakeholders, and when they are not pleased with what they see they can be active (as long as they have basic freedoms to do so). Furthermore, stakeholders' evaluation of the firm depends not only on *what* the firm does but also on *how* it does it, including its general activities, its CSR and its stakeholder management. Vision statements must therefore appeal to multiple stakeholders.

Firms are not compelled (legally or otherwise) to comply with every stakeholder demand. However, affected parties who are ignored long enough may take action against the firm. It is also not socially responsible to ignore an important group of stakeholders. As such, companies need to learn how to improve their stakeholder management capacity, as discussed next.

Stakeholder management capacity

How well an organisation manages and works with all its stakeholders is a strong indicator of its CSR level. But what does it mean to manage the organisation's stakeholders and what does it mean to do it well?

'Stakeholder management' is the term given to the system by which organisations pursue their objectives whilst considering the interests of their stakeholders. For a company to develop strategies to manage its stakeholder relationships, it first needs to determine who its stakeholders are and what the nature of the relationship is between this company and its stakeholders.

Stakeholders can have contradicting expectations and it is challenging to work with all of them to find a solution with which everyone is happy. For example, consumers, suppliers and shareholders might have contradicting expectations regarding the pricing of a product.

EXERCISE

Stakeholder prioritisation in Delight coffee

A food and beverage company, which we will call *Delight*, sells coffee to consumers at $5 per jar and pays suppliers $1 per kilo of coffee beans. Suppliers demand fair trade pay for their coffee, which will be $2 per kilo. The firm agrees, bringing the price of a jar to $6. Consumers then become angry about the rising cost, and *Delight* decides to keep the price of the jar as it was and cut down its profits. The profits are decreased and the shareholders then become unhappy with the firm. How do you solve this triangle in the best way possible?

Stakeholder prioritisation

One solution is to prioritise stakeholders according to their importance and meet the expectations of the most important stakeholder group first. For a very long time, this seemed to be a good stakeholder management approach. Stakeholder prioritisation is particularly important when there is conflict in the interests of different stakeholders. It was found that businesses are most likely to succeed in the global environment if they learn how to balance the conflicting interests of multiple stakeholders.

Stakeholder prioritisation includes three steps. Firstly, the firm needs to list all its major stakeholders. Secondly, it needs to decide how important they are for which aspect of its strategy and CSR. Thirdly, it needs to use this prioritisation to decide which stakeholders to work with and whose expectations to meet first.

Table 3.1 can be used to prioritise stakeholders according to Carroll's (1979) four responsibilities, where in each row all stakeholders are ranked from 1 to 4 (1 being first in importance and 4 being last). In the above example, Delight listed four groups of major stakeholders: shareholders, consumers, suppliers and the community. It then prioritised each stakeholder group according to the four responsibilities. Firstly, it asked 'to whom do we hold our greatest economic responsibility?' Delight then prioritised the shareholders first (1), followed by suppliers, consumers and only then the greater community. Similar prioritisation is then done for legal, ethical and discretionary responsibilities. Stakeholder prioritisation of Delight is clear when examining the total points given to each stakeholder group, with the lowest number indicating the highest priority. As such, Delight prioritised its stakeholders in this order: suppliers, shareholders, consumers and the community. Of course, other firms will have different lists of stakeholders and responsibilities, resulting in different priorities.

Table 3.1   Stakeholder prioritisation (based on Carroll, 1979)

CSR component	Shareholders	Consumers	Suppliers	Community
Economic	1	3	2	4
Legal	1	3	3	4
Ethical	3	2	1	4
Philanthropic	4	3	2	1
Total	9	10	8	13
Priority	2	3	1	4

The third step is for the firm to act according to the prioritisation results. Delight may have assumed that shareholders are its most important stakeholders, and they are in some aspects, but when examining all four aspects of its responsibility, Delight discovered that its suppliers are the most important stakeholders. As such, Delight will need to make business decisions that are aligned with this result, working closely with the suppliers and paying fairly for the coffee.

It should be noted that the table could be used more broadly by adding as many stakeholders as needed. Rather than using Carroll's four responsibilities, companies may use any other aspects of the business that are important for them, such as financial performance, brand loyalty, employee engagement and corporate reputation, to name just a few.

Similarly, Mitchell et al. (1997) argued that stakeholder salience is based on attributes of power, legitimacy and urgency. Stakeholders vary in their perceived power to influence the organisation, the extent to which their claims are regarded as legitimate and the time frame available to respond to their demands. As such, organisations tend to prioritise stakeholders that have more power, legitimacy and urgency over stakeholders who lack these attributes or have them to a lesser degree. However, it is arguable whether prioritising powerful stakeholders over others is always the right and ethical thing to do. If companies want to be more responsible and ethical in their stakeholder management capacity, they may examine who their most powerful stakeholders are, but decide to prioritise others for the purpose of justice.

Three levels of stakeholder management

Freeman (1994) offered a different way of managing the company's stakeholders, which includes three levels of stakeholder management capacity: the rational level, the process level and the transaction level (see Figure 3.3). Freeman suggested shifting away from the instrumental process-driven approach to one that

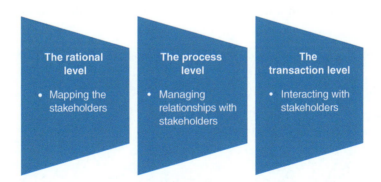

Figure 3.3 Three levels of stakeholder management (based on Freeman, 1994)

adopts a strategic view of understanding the resources and capabilities needed to effectively deal with conflict and dissent between an organisation and its stakeholder groups.

At the *rational level*, managers map their stakeholder groups and accurately define the interests each has in its operations. Whilst this may appear a simple task at first glance, effective stakeholder management capability requires extensive market research to understand the nature and the source of each stakeholder's interest.

At the *process level*, stakeholders are included in the firm's strategic decision-making process with a view to using their multiple perspectives as a resource for the organisation. This can be done by inviting consumers and community representatives to take part in executive meetings and boardroom discussions and to have their voice heard on business decisions which could affect them.

At the *transaction level* of analysis, companies with good stakeholder management capability establish and execute 'win-win' transactional exchanges with their stakeholders. This would require a more innovative and holistic approach compared to simply prioritising the stakeholders and preferring one group's expectations to others. It is important to note that the three levels must be consistent. A philosophical view and approach, such as strategic CSR, can act as the underlying glue to connect all three levels and to establish a relationship with the stakeholders.

According to Freeman (1994), some organisations are better than others in the way they manage their stakeholders. Based on some extensive research, Freeman concluded that organisations with high stakeholder management capability:

- design and implement communication processes with multiple stakeholders
- negotiate with stakeholders on critical issues and seek voluntary agreement
- integrate boundary spanners into the strategic formulation processes in the organisations
- are proactive – they anticipate stakeholder concerns and try to influence the stakeholder environment
- allocate resources in a manner consistent with stakeholder concerns.

Questions for reflection and discussion

1. Based on Johnson & Johnson's case study at the beginning of the chapter, which level of stakeholder management capacity does the company demonstrate – rational, process or transaction?
2. Which criteria of effective stakeholder management capacity does Johnson & Johnson's meet?

Stakeholder integration and the Win[6] approach

Whole Foods Market is one of North America's fastest growing supermarket chains but is not a typical supermarket. In 1980, John Mackey opened a health food store, *SaferWay*, in Austin, Texas, which later grew into Whole Foods Market. In 2015, the company had 91,000 employees and 431 stores in the US, Canada and the UK. The company is well known for selling healthier food (including organic food) and for its CSR activities, including the Whole Kids Foundation, Whole Planet Foundation and the Whole Cities Foundation. Whole Foods Market also works to minimise the harm to animals, through its Global Animal Partnership. In 2007, the company launched the Whole Trade Guarantee, a purchasing initiative emphasising ethics and social responsibility for products imported from the developing world. Whole Foods Market is committed to environmental sustainability and in 2008 it was the first supermarket in the US to ban plastic bags (Mackey and Sisodia, 2014).

It was in the early days of the company that Mackey realised the importance of stakeholders. In his book *Conscious Capitalism* (Mackey and Sisodia, 2014), he tells the story of how the store was affected by a natural disaster, resulting in near destruction, with no insurance. Mackey was devastated; he thought his business was finished. But the next day, his employees, consumers, neighbours and people from the local community showed up, helped to clean and rebuild the store, saving it and allowing it to thrive again (and for Whole Foods Market to emerge). They did this because they cared about the store and because it affected them. Mackey realised the profound importance of stakeholders to any business. It was this early experience together with his business approach that later led to the development of the conscious capitalism movement, of which stakeholder integration is such a prominent part.

Stakeholder integration is one of the three tenets of conscious capitalism at the centre of which is a higher purpose and core values (see Figure 3.4). It is quite different from stakeholder prioritisation. It is based on the assumption

Figure 3.4 **Stakeholder integration is one of the three tenets of conscious capitalism (based on Mackey and Sisodia, 2014)**

that business does not have to be a zero-sum game with winners and losers, but rather an opportunity for everyone to thrive and win (similar to Freeman's transaction level above). If business is managed effectively, there are opportunities to create value for each and every stakeholder of the organisation and the result is greater than the sum of individual value.

Stakeholder integration is based on the philosophical and practical approach that conscious businesses should treat satisfying the needs of all their major stakeholders as ends in themselves, not as the means to achieve an ultimate goal of profit maximisation. When we examine different approaches to ethics in Chapter 4, we will see that this resonates with the deontological approach, according to which we should not use another human being as a means to an end, but only as the end in itself. According to the integrated stakeholder approach, stakeholders make up a company and therefore must be honoured as people first, before being treated according to the role they happen to be playing.

The second important assumption at the basis of stakeholder integration is that we need to move away from zero-sum thinking and trade-offs to finding synergies in a positive-sum game instead. 'Conscious businesses understand that if we look for trade-offs, we always will find them. If we look for synergies across stakeholders, we can usually find those too' (Mackey and Sisodia, 2014: 70). When synergies are created, all stakeholders can win and no one has to lose, not even competitors.

The role of public relations in stakeholder integration is in cultivating and stewarding relationships with key publics, not in isolation but with mindfulness about the effects on the broader system. Recognising the interdependent nature of life and the human foundations of business, a business needs to create value with and for all its various stakeholders.

Figure 3.5 shows how Whole Foods Market created a situation in which all stakeholders could benefit from the company at the same time. Based on finding synergies between them, the company showed that when *employees* are happy and motivated (because they work in a company that is known for its good practices and are proud to have such an employer), and when the company creates partnerships with vendors and *suppliers* in which they are happy, *customers* are satisfied and delighted. *Investors* then receive a better return on their investment, and the *community* and the *environment* benefit as well. This is referred to as Win[6] (short for a win-win-win-win-win-win situation).

EXERCISE

Using the Delight coffee example, what can the company do to achieve stakeholder integration and Win[6]?

Figure 3.5   Stakeholder integration and Win⁶ (based on Mackey and Sisodia, 2014)

Multi-stakeholder initiatives

Multi-stakeholder initiatives (MSIs) have recently become a popular concept and CSR tool in helping businesses and governments address complex societal and environmental challenges (Mena and Palazzo, 2012). MSIs were devised to address the governance gap that exists due to the failure of existing systems and structures to solve global business and social issues. They bring together various stakeholder groups such as governments, businesses, civil society organisations, local communities and individuals to promote responsible, inclusive and sustainable governance as well as business operations (Mena and Palazzo, 2012).

Governments provide experience, influence and often local knowledge to MSIs. They can also help endorse, convene, facilitate or even finance an MSI. Governments have the power to make policy or regulatory changes to help facilitate the smooth functioning of an MSI and can contribute to increasing the demand for MSI-certified products or services through endorsements.

Companies are often motivated to participate in an MSI when they or their consumers recognise that components of their supply chain or operations adversely affect the environment and people. They play a crucial role in MSIs due to their ability to fund the process of piloting a proposed solution to an identified problem. The private sector can also reach out to a wider range of people and help increase the scale and positive impact of a proposed solution.

Not-for-profit organisations and other stakeholders represent the interests of local communities, individuals, vulnerable and marginalised groups, women and indigenous people. They help balance the needs of these different groups, the government and the private sector. They hold all the other stakeholders accountable for their actions and ensure that the solutions implemented by an MSI have minimal unfavourable impacts.

According to CSR Asia (2015), MSIs have specific characteristics and benefits:

- They bring together different stakeholders to collaborate and combine their varied skills, resources and expertise to address issues of importance and relevance to all.
- The different opinions and proposed solutions to problems are discussed without one particular stakeholder group overpowering the discussion or exerting their influence.
- The concerns and participation of women and vulnerable groups are of vital importance to an MSI platform or structure.
- Most MSIs are designed with a common purpose and are characterised by codes of conduct, certification systems, common standards and funding for research.
- They are established to make business value chains comprising of the production, consumption and distribution of goods and services ethical and sustainable.
- MSIs inform policy making and governance by enabling governments to interact with the different stakeholder groups and acquire an understanding of their problems, needs and wants.

MSIs assist in organising forums and in facilitating dialogue on social and environmental issues to communicate challenges and collectively devise possible solutions to overcome those challenges. These initiatives can help stakeholders to engage in institution building by developing mutual understanding, trust and respect amongst different stakeholder groups. They can also result in organising opportunities for learning, teaching, training and capacity building across different sectors and stakeholders to encourage knowledge sharing and open communication channels. MSIs can be very useful for bringing different groups with diverse perspectives together to develop solutions applicable for all. It is important to develop a culture of transparency and accountability within the system so that all the participating stakeholders can accrue the benefits of the MSI.

Some examples of MSIs are The Forest Stewardship Council, The Marine Stewardship Council, and the Ethical Trading Initiative. The Marine Stewardship Council works with its partners to develop fishing practices and establish standards for fishing and tracing seafood in an effort to increase the supply of seafood for current and future generations. It uses a blue eco-label to certify that the seafood has been handled in an ethical manner. It was created by Unilever as a single stakeholder initiative but now involves collaboration amongst multiple organisations. This initiative involves collaboration with fishermen, producers, retailers and consumers in an effort to influence the way resources are utilised and consumed.

Stakeholder-related CSR issues

When examining the stakeholders mentioned in this chapter, each one bears different challenges and implications for strategic CSR. In this chapter we will examine CSR issues related to three groups of stakeholders: employees, suppliers and consumers.

We should keep in mind that there are two important aspects to the connection between stakeholders and strategic CSR. Firstly, responsible companies behave responsibly towards all stakeholders, throughout the entire value chain. This can be referred to as 'corporate stakeholder responsibility'. The S in CSR might imply responsibility towards society in general ('social'), but corporate stakeholder responsibility is focused on all stakeholders.

Secondly, many stakeholders, from employees to suppliers and consumers, have their own high or low levels of social responsibility. As strategic CSR is about adopting a holistic approach to CSR, embedded in all of the company's core operations and activities, it is important to work with responsible stakeholders. This would include the attraction and selection of employees with high social responsibility and aligned values as well as working with responsible suppliers that treat employees fairly. It also means educating all stakeholders about the company's CSR and involving them in it as much as possible. This aspect will be covered in Chapter 7.

Employees: Fair employment

When companies direct their responsibility towards their employees, including offshored employees, we refer to it as 'internal CSR'. In this context, ethical management and fair employment are the most important CSR issues. Many CSR scholars and practitioners argue that before companies engage in external philanthropy, they should ensure high levels of internal CSR by treating their employees well. There are a vast number of industrial laws, regulations, standards and guidelines on fair employment, which also vary from place to place, and we cannot cover them all. However, employees need to be treated fairly and ethically, assuring their physical and psychological wellbeing and allowing them to thrive in the workplace. The second paragraph of Johnson & Johnson's credo summarises these responsibilities well:

> We are responsible to our employees, the men and women who work with us throughout the world. Everyone must be considered as an individual. We must respect their dignity and recognize their merit. They must have a sense of security in their jobs. Compensation must be fair and adequate, and working conditions clean, orderly and safe. We must be mindful of ways to help our employees fulfill their family responsibilities. Employees must feel free to make suggestions and complaints. There must be equal opportunity for employment, development and advancement for those qualified. We must provide competent management, and their actions must be just and ethical.

Employees (or 'our people' or 'team members') should be paid at least a liveable wage, which is the minimum income necessary for a worker to meet their basic needs. Often, companies pay the minimum required to employees according to their national law, but it is not always enough to meet the basic needs of housing, food, education and transportation. For example, in Cambodia, garment workers earned US$140 per month in 2015, but this was not enough to meet their most basic needs. Local labour unions pushed for a mild increase to US$160, which would be closer to a liveable wage, but were unsuccessful (Bloomberg, 2014).

In addition, as will be demonstrated in Chapter 7, a great opportunity exists to involve employees in the company's CSR while educating and engaging them. There is currently a growing demand of employees to be involved in their employer's CSR. Employees in many organisations come to expect that their employers would not only offer them good working conditions, dignity and job satisfaction, but also allow them to act on their values at work and create meaningfulness in their jobs. Many employers nowadays offer employees opportunities to volunteer, donate money, fight for social and environmental causes, and even initiate employee-led CSR. It is important to educate employees about the company's CSR, allowing them to know what the company does and in particular what their social impact is. Often, CSR reports are directed outwards, to investors and consumers, and not even shared with employees. Having internal CSR reports that let the employees know what their employer is doing, why and what it achieves can be an effective way to not only engage employees in CSR, but also to create employee engagement, enthusiasm, trust and pride.

It is important to educate employees about social responsibility and sustainability issues so that they can be intrinsically motivated to be involved in everything the company does. In outstanding socially responsible companies, newcomers are social-ised to take part in the company's CSR from the time they join the organisation and to learn and adopt the CSR ethos, values and culture. Employees can be educated about social and environmental issues and how the company is striving to address them. Only by creating a real partnership with the company's people and team members can it embed CSR throughout every part and aspect of the organisation.

Suppliers: Fair trade

Companies should continually look for creative ways to craft mutually beneficial relationship with suppliers. (Mackey and Sisodia, 2014: 117)

Suppliers are major stakeholders to any company that needs the goods they grow, create, manufacture and/or sell, and as such suppliers have a major effect on the company. In a way, they can be seen as very close to the employees whose labour allows the company to thrive. Sometimes, the suppliers work closely with the firm, on a personal basis, but often the suppliers deliver the goods through a third party or a supply chain and there is no direct relationship. It is usually in the latter case that companies sometimes ignore the rights and the needs of suppliers, despite their importance to the company. Suppliers sometimes work in the same country as the company, but often their goods are imported, usually from the developing world. This is case with a lion's share of tea, coffee, chocolate, vanilla, cotton and many other produce used by numerous companies and consumers.

In Porter's (1985) five forces model, 'supplier power' refers to the pressure suppliers can exert on businesses by raising prices, lowering quality or reducing availability of their products. When working with poor suppliers from the developing world, or even with local suppliers, big corporations usually have the upper hand with much more power than the suppliers. This does not mean that they necessarily need to 'squeeze' and exploit suppliers. Not only is it not a socially responsible business practice, it is usually not a financially sound practice either, at least not in the long run.

Being socially responsible towards suppliers implies, above all, paying them fairly for their goods, treating them with respect and helping them to grow and thrive. Paying suppliers fairly requires an understanding of the market in which they operate so that the payment is fair and just in the context of their needs, costs and competition. It also requires paying suppliers on time, as so many companies make a profit by delaying payment, sometimes resulting in the financial collapse of the supplier. Some refer to this as 'fair trade'.

According to the fair trade movement, fair trade is about stable prices, decent working conditions and the empowerment of farmers and workers around the world. Fair trade advocates for better working conditions and improved terms of trade for farmers and workers in developing countries. It is about supporting the development of thriving farming and worker communities to have more control over their futures, and protecting the environment in which they live and work.

As we will see in Chapter 9, there is a growing number of certifying and accrediting bodies which allow companies to use their labels on products so consumers know that what they are buying is from a company that supports farmers and workers, works to improve their livelihoods and provides support to their communities. For example, the fair trade standards include protection of workers' rights and the protection of children, the preservation of the environment, payment of the Fairtrade Minimum Price and an additional Fairtrade Premium to invest in initiatives to support local communities or business development. Companies that have genuine fair trade work closely with all the suppliers and their suppliers as well to audit the way they treat their employees and the environment.

Some companies such as Whole Foods Market, Ben & Jerry's and The Body Shop work closely with their suppliers to ensure their rights, freedoms and prosperity. They develop local clusters of suppliers, paying them fairly and on time. They also help to build local communities and schools. In the case of vanilla (the substance obtained from vanilla pods), when many companies moved to fair trade practices, the farmers thrived. This allowed the farmers to invest more in growing high-quality vanilla, and the companies and consumers using this produce benefit as well.

According to Mackey and Sisodia (2014), as conscious businesses change the parameters of their relationship with suppliers, these changes can have a ripple effect throughout the supply chain. When companies with strategic CSR work with their stakeholders, partnering with them and educating them on sustainable practice, one of the impacts is that these suppliers can now treat their own employees and their own suppliers better. If practices such as child labour are abolished, children can go to school, gain education and the next generation can come out of poverty. However, this would only work if it is realised that 'profit maximisation at any cost' is not a sustainable way of doing business.

Since this is not always the case (at least not yet and not everywhere), third parties often intervene to make sure companies treat their suppliers fairly. Such third parties include *certification and auditing bodies* and *consumer and competition 'watchdog' organisations*. The *media* is also engaged in giving a voice to powerless suppliers. It was a CBS report about Nike's treatment of its suppliers in Indonesia that started a big public debate on offshoring and responsibility towards suppliers. Last (but definitely not least) are the *consumers*, many of whom care to buy products that are based on fair trade practices and are willing to pay higher prices for such products.

It is important to note that these four groups (and others) work together to achieve corporate stakeholder responsibility, but that they also hold each other accountable for the same purpose. For example, the *Financial Times* (media) audited Fairtrade certified companies and their suppliers to check if these practices were being followed in the developing world. The results of this report in 2006 were so poor (ten out of the ten mills they visited had sold uncertified coffee to co-operatives as certified), it led to a wide discourse on the topic and a change in auditing practices.

Consumers: Ethical trade and ethical marketing

Consumers are a major stakeholder group, including for companies that only focus on maximising profit. Without consumers, there are no sales and no revenue. However, this could be the Achilles' heel of socially responsible companies, as the pressure to sell is sometimes greater than the ethical obligation to ensure the wellbeing of consumers.

Being responsible towards consumers implies first and foremost that the firm needs to ensure their wellbeing, safety and health, and practise ethical behaviour in marketing and sales. Ethical marketing will be discussed more broadly in Chapter 11, but the basic component of it is to always communicate to consumers with honesty and integrity (avoiding deceptive marketing is always a good practice), not to market to vulnerable groups in an unethical way (e.g. targeting children to buy unhealthy food) and to use marketing methods that are not offensive.

In addition to responsible and ethical marketing, there is the product itself that must not harm consumers. This may sound easy, but almost all food and beverage companies nowadays sell products that are seen by some groups (large or small) as unhealthy and unsafe. For example, while it has been acknowledged for decades now that cigarettes pose a big health risk, the growing criticism around sugary food and drinks has only begun. In the developed world, 80 per cent of products sold in supermarkets have added sugar in them, some at levels condemned by the World Health Organisation as unhealthy and dangerous. These products are sold directly to kids, and could be related to obesity, diabetes, severe dental decay and other health issues. Interestingly, some claim that the defensive approach of the sugar industry today is very similar to what the tobacco industry did 50 years ago: a denial of practices and their health impact, funding and fighting research to serve its agenda, and blaming consumers for irresponsible consumption, while knowing full well that they manufacture demand of, what could be, addictive products.

In addition, CSR and stakeholder integration mean working with consumers, informing them and involving them in what seems to be a growing interest for these stakeholders. Recent surveys demonstrate a strong consumer demand for CSR. According to Forbes (2014), 88 per cent of consumers think that companies should try to achieve their business goals while improving society and the environment. Furthermore, 83 per cent of consumers think that companies should support charities and non-profit organisations with financial donations.

An international study conducted in 2015 with over 10,000 citizens showed that 81 per cent of consumers would make personal sacrifices to address social and environmental issues (Cone Communications, 2015). Nine in ten consumers expect companies to do more than make a profit and to operate responsibly to address such issues.

This data shows that consumers in many parts of the world expect companies to have high levels of CSR, but also understand that they have a role to play. Consumer awareness of CSR-related issues is higher than ever before, and for many people the price and quality of products are not the only determinants of their decision to buy. In addition to these two important aspects, consumers also look for the 'goodness' of the product: how good it is for them (e.g. organic, healthy), how good it is for society and how good it is for the environment (see Figure 3.6). Some consumers prefer to buy products that sit in the middle of all three aspects, and are willing to pay a higher price for products of high quality and goodness.

Figure 3.6   Three aspects of a product now determine the consumer decision to buy

Many consumers refer to certifications and labels on products when they decide what to buy, such as Fairtrade, but also look at the company's website and reports. Nearly 80 per cent of consumers tell family and friends about the CSR of a company they buy from, such as ethical fashion (Cone Communications, 2015). Companies need to realise that in order to tap into the fast-growing market of socially aware consumers, they need to change their behaviour and communicate about it clearly with consumers:

> Companies are still relying on traditional forms of consumer engagement primarily tied to the product shelf, yet consumers are looking for more diverse ways to get involved with CSR efforts. Companies can serve as a catalyst for sparking donations, volunteerism and advocacy by giving consumers a spectrum of ways to get involved. (Alison DaSilva, Cone EVP)

Summary

Every business in the world, large or small, has stakeholders, which are individuals, groups and organisations that affect the company or are being affected by the company achieving its goals. This can be positively or negatively, voluntarily or involuntarily.

Stakeholders can be divided into organisational stakeholders (e.g. employees and managers), economic stakeholders (e.g. customers and suppliers) and societal stakeholders (e.g. governments and communities). Similarly, stakeholders can be divided into internal and external groups or into major and secondary stakeholders. These divisions allow us to list the stakeholders and later prioritise them.

Stakeholder management is a key component of strategic CSR. It is part of the shift towards a broad view of business responsibility and a more holistic approach to business management. It also makes good business sense to manage all the stakeholders of a company and to strive to satisfy the needs of every stakeholder group, although this could be challenging.

Just as we saw various CSR levels of different companies in the previous chapter, we can also find various corporate stakeholder responsibility levels in different companies. Freeman detailed three levels of stakeholder management capacity: the rational level, the process level and the transaction level. Companies with strong stakeholder management capacity work closely with their stakeholders, partner with them, educate them and create opportunities for them to be involved in the company's CSR. While a common solution to contradicting stakeholder expectations is to prioritise them and meet the strong stakeholders' expectations, it is not always the best, most ethical or most responsible option. Adopting an approach according to which responsible companies can benefit all their stakeholders and finding innovative ways of doing so could create better results.

There are CSR issues that relate directly to each stakeholder group. Employee-related issues include internal CSR and fair employment, ethical management and obeying industrial law. They also include employee engagement in CSR, through channels such as corporate volunteering and payroll giving. Supplier-related issues include fair trade practices, such as paying suppliers fairly and on time, while also helping them to develop their communities and thrive. In the case of suppliers, it is important to work closely with suppliers to ensure that their social responsibility is high, and to ensure that all of the suppliers treat employees and the environment in a way that is aligned with the main company's CSR. Consumer-related issues are firstly about selling products that are safe and healthy. In addition, there is a growing consumer demand to buy products that are socially and environmentally responsible, and companies are expected to rise to this opportunity.

In summary, corporate stakeholder responsibility requires courage, innovation and integrity. Strategic CSR is a holistic approach and cannot be adopted without a real partnership with all stakeholders. Stakeholders do not only pose some CSR challenges, they mainly offer some great CSR opportunities.

General questions

1. Why is stakeholder theory so important? How did it change the discourse and practice of business management?
2. Strategic CSR is managing an organisation in the interests of a broad set of stakeholders. Do you agree that these two are inherently connected?
3. Is it useful to divide stakeholders into subgroups (such as internal/external or primary/secondary)? What are the advantages and disadvantages of doing so?
4. While the term 'stakeholder management' is commonly used, so are stakeholder involvement, engagement and integration. Why does the verb matter? Which one do you think is more aligned with strategic CSR and why?
5. If you were a newly recruited manager in an organisation that does not work with stakeholders, how would you convince the senior team to adopt different managerial practices?

Key definitions

- A stakeholder is any individual, group or institution who is affected, positively or negatively, by the achievement of an organisation's purpose (Freeman, 1984).
- The stakeholders in a firm are individuals and groups that contribute, either voluntarily or involuntarily, to its wealth-creating capacity and activities, and who are therefore its potential beneficiaries and/or risk bearers (Post et al., 2002).

- Internal CSR is about the company's ethical behaviour towards its internal stakeholders, mainly employees. External CSR, on the other hand, encompasses ethical behaviour towards external stakeholders and includes philanthropy and community contributions. It also reflects the way in which the firm interacts with the physical environment and its ethical stance towards consumers and other external stakeholders (de Chernatony and Harris, 2000).
- 'Stakeholder management' is the term given to the system by which organisations pursue their objectives whilst considering the interests of their stakeholders (Freeman, 1994).
- Stakeholder integration is based on the philosophical (and practical) approach that conscious businesses treat satisfying the needs of all their major stakeholders as ends in themselves, not as the means to achieve an ultimate goal of profit maximisation (Mackey and Sisodia, 2014).
- Win[6] refers to the goal of the enterprise to achieve winning conditions for all six categories of stakeholders (Mackey and Sisodia, 2014).

References

Bloomberg (2014) Cambodians risk their lives for $160 a month. Available at: www.bloomberg.com/news/articles/2014–01–09/cambodians-risk-their-lives-for-160-a-month (Accessed: 22 March 2017)

Carroll, A. B. (1979) 'A three-dimensional conceptual model of corporate performance', *Academy of Management Review*, 4(4): 497–505.

Cone Communications (2015) Cone Communications/Ebiquity Global CSR study. Available at: www.conecomm.com/research-blog/2015-cone-communications-ebiquity-global-csr-study (Accessed: 22 March 2017)

CSR Asia (2015) *Multi-stakeholder initiatives cooperating to achieve responsible and inclusive business*. Hong Kong: CSR Asia.

de Chernatony, L. and Harris, F. (2000) 'Developing corporate brands through considering internal and external stakeholders', *Corporate Reputation Review*, 3(3): 268–74.

Donaldson, T. and Preston, L. E. (1995) 'The stakeholder theory of the corporation: Concepts, evidence, and implications', *Academy of Management Review*, 20(1): 65–91.

Dunlap, A. J. (1996) *Mean business: How I save bad companies and make good companies great*. New York: Times Business Books.

Forbes (2014) Consumers overwhelmingly want CSR. Available at: www.forbes.com/sites/csr/2010/12/15/new-study-consumers-demand-companies-implement-csr-programs/#454d8f8465c7 (Accessed: 7 May 2017)

Freeman, R. E. (1984) *Stakeholder management: Framework and philosophy*. Mansfield, MA: Pitman.

Freeman, R. E. (1994) 'The politics of stakeholder theory: Some future directions', *Business Ethics Quarterly*, 4(4): 409–21.

Jensen, M. C. (2001) 'Value maximization, stakeholder theory, and the corporate objective function', *Journal of Applied Corporate Finance*, 14(3): 8–21.

Mackey, J. and Sisodia, R. (2014) *Conscious capitalism: Liberating the heroic spirit of business*. Boston, MA: Harvard Business Review Press.

Mena, S. and Palazzo, G. (2012) 'Input and output legitimacy of multi-stakeholder initiatives', *Business Ethics Quarterly*, 22(3): 527–56.

Mitchell, R. K., Agle, B. R. and Wood, D. J. (1997) 'Toward a theory of stakeholder identification and salience: Defining the principle of who and what really counts', *Academy of Management Review*, 22(4): 853–86.

Porter, M. E. (1985) *Competitive advantage: Creating and sustaining superior performance*. New York: Free Press.

Post, J. E., Preston, L. E. and Sachs, S. (2002) 'Managing the extended enterprise: The new stakeholder view', *California Management Review*, 45(1): 6–28.

Rudd, K. (2011) 'Bringing accountability to responsibility: The new challenge for corporate social responsibility', Qantas Social Impact Lecture, 6 October. Available at: https://foreignminister.gov.au/speeches/Pages/2011/kr_sp_111006a.aspx?w=GYLX0mNSz4nLQK YuPOSgLQ%3D%3D (Accessed: 19 October 2017).

Werther, W. B. and Chandler, D. (2011) *Strategic corporate social responsibility: Stakeholders in a global environment* (2nd edn). Thousand Oaks, CA: Sage.

Further reading and links

Berman, S. L., Wicks, A. C., Kotha, S. and Jones, T. M. (1999) 'Does stakeholder orientation matter? The relationship between stakeholder management models and firm financial performance', *Academy of Management Journal*, 42(5): 488–506.

Carroll, A. B. (1991) 'The pyramid of corporate social responsibility: Toward the moral management of organizational stakeholders', *Business Horizons*, 34(4): 39–48.

Clarkson, M. B. (1991) 'Defining, evaluating, and managing corporate social performance: The stakeholder management model', *Research in Corporate Social Performance and Policy*, 12(1): 331–58.

Clarkson, M. E. (1995) 'A stakeholder framework for analyzing and evaluating corporate social performance', *Academy of Management Review*, 20(1): 92–117.

Deutsche Post (2014) Delivering tomorrow – exchange, engage, excel: Creating value through stakeholder engagement. Available at: https://delivering-tomorrow.de/wp-content/uploads/2015/08/delivering-tomorrow_stakeholder-engagement_en.pdf (Accessed: 23 March 2017)

Dohnalová, Z. and Zimola, B. (2014) 'Corporate stakeholder management', *Procedia-Social and Behavioral Sciences*, 110: 879–86.

Ethical Trading Initiative (2017) Available at: www.ethicaltrade.org (Accessed: 23 March 2017)

Freeman, R. E. (1984) *Stakeholder management: Framework and philosophy*. Mansfield, MA: Pitman.

Freeman, R. E., Wicks, A. C. and Parmar, B. (2004) 'Stakeholder theory and "the corporate objective revisited"', *Organization Science*, 15(3): 364–9.

Hillman, A. J. and Keim, G. D. (2001) 'Shareholder value, stakeholder management, and social issues: What's the bottom line?', *Strategic Management Journal*, 125–39.

Michael Porter YouTube Channel (2010) Creating shared value. Available at: www.youtube.com/watch?v=z2oS3zk8VA4 (Accessed: 23 March 2017)

Post, J. E., Preston, L. E. and Sauter-Sachs, S. (2002) *Redefining the corporation: Stakeholder management and organizational wealth*. Stanford, CA: Stanford University Press.

Preston, L. E. and Sapienza, H. J. (1991) 'Stakeholder management and corporate performance', *Journal of Behavioral Economics*, 19(4): 361–75.

Simmons, J. and Lovegrove, I. (2005) 'Bridging the conceptual divide: Lessons from stakeholder analysis', *Journal of Organizational Change Management*, 18(5): 495–513.

The Arthur W. Page Center (2016) Finding the impact CSR and CSV have on stakeholder trust. Available at: http://comm.psu.edu/page-center/article/impact-csr-csv-stakeholder-trust (Accessed: 23 March 2017)

The Forest Stewardship Council (2017) Available at: http://fsc.org (Accessed: 23 March 2017)

The Marine Stewardship Council (2017) Available at: www.msc.org (Accessed: 23 March 2017)

Part II

CSR approaches and implementation

Business Ethics: How Philosophy Can Help Us Make Ethical Decisions in Today's Business

4

Learning outcomes

By the end of this chapter, students should be able to:

- explain what ethics and business ethics are and describe their prominence in business conduct
- describe the significance of personal and corporate values to business ethics and ethical decision making
- detail the three philosophical approaches to ethics and how they direct business decision making today
- discuss business ethics in practice and ethical and unethical behaviour in the workplace
- identify ethical dilemmas and use frameworks to address such dilemmas
- apply knowledge to create and lead ethical organisations.

Case study   Business ethics at the Commonwealth Bank Australia

The Commonwealth Bank of Australia (CBA) was established in the early 1900s as a government bank but privatised in the 1990s. The bank currently employs over 52,000 people and has more than 800,000 shareholders. It is one of the largest listed companies on the Australian Securities Exchange. The bank is a leading provider of integrated financial services, including retail, premium, business and institutional banking, funds management, superannuation, insurance, investment and share-broking products and services.

Similarly to other large organisations, the CBA publically presents its vision and strategy, which guides its business tactics and daily operations. The bank's vision is to 'excel at securing and enhancing the financial wellbeing of people, businesses and communities', indicating its various responsibilities. The bank's values, as stated on its website, are summarised in Figure 4.1. They highlight integrity, accountability and service to customers and the community. These values are essential to the organisation and CBA recently introduced value-based awards to employees.

CSR takes many forms at CBA, as the bank looks for ways to use its capabilities and resources to make a positive contribution beyond its core business. This is done through society, the environment, communities, customers and employees. The CBA funds and runs various education programmes aimed at improving financial literacy among young Australians and providing financial consultation pro bono for indigenous businesses. Environmentally, CBA tracks its greenhouse gas emissions in all national locations, in order to reduce them. The Bank facilitates employee volunteering in its communities, supports them with targeted activities and forms partnerships with community initiatives such as clown doctors. As for internal CSR, CBA aims to increase its diversity and inclusion, and therefore monitors the percentage of women overall and in key roles, age diversity and ethnic diversity.

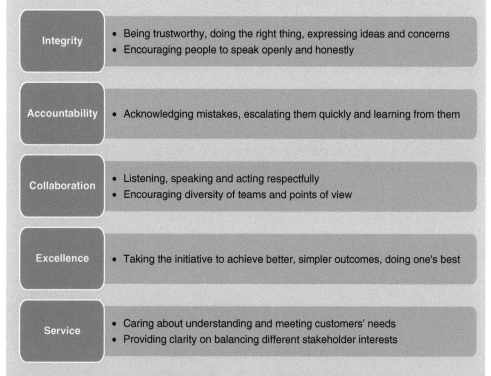

| Integrity | • Being trustworthy, doing the right thing, expressing ideas and concerns
• Encouraging people to speak openly and honestly |

| Accountability | • Acknowledging mistakes, escalating them quickly and learning from them |

| Collaboration | • Listening, speaking and acting respectfully
• Encouraging diversity of teams and points of view |

| Excellence | • Taking the initiative to achieve better, simpler outcomes, doing one's best |

| Service | • Caring about understanding and meeting customers' needs
• Providing clarity on balancing different stakeholder interests |

Figure 4.1   Commonwealth Bank of Australia's values (based on CBA, 2017)

Ethics is continuously becoming a major pillar of the Bank. The Bank's chairman, David Turner, in his address at the 2016 Annual General Meeting, referred to the growing importance of ethics to CBA and to the recent aim to lift ethical standards and behaviour. Continuing from 2014, when the bank introduced a Vision and Values programme, it is now making sure every employee is trained, either face-to-face, in groups, or, in remote cases, online, in business ethics and socialised into the values and ethos of the organisation. The bank has also established a new customer

(Continued)

advocate function, to ensure a more customer-centric focus across the organisation. This includes advocating for better customer outcomes, taking action where there is potential for concerns to arise and where things have gone wrong. In addition, the bank has an independently managed whistleblower policy, and whistleblower protection is central to how this function operates.

In 2017, the Bank's chairman, David Turner, told shareholders that ethics is a source of the bank's 'competitive advantage':

> We see it down the road as being an ultimate competitive advantage. We think we will be the ethical bank, the bank others look up to for honesty, transparency, decency, good management, openness. That is exactly where we are trying to go. (*Sydney Morning Herald*, 2015)

In a publicly available document, 'Our Commitments', CBA provides a practical tool and guidelines to assist employees in making the right decision (see Figure 4.2). In this document CBA explains that 'making the right decisions individually and collectively is essential to secure the trust of our stakeholders, and to enable us to realise our vision.' To help employees demonstrate all aspects of the organisational vision and values, they are asked to go through this process and ask themselves two imperative questions: Can we do this? Should we do this?

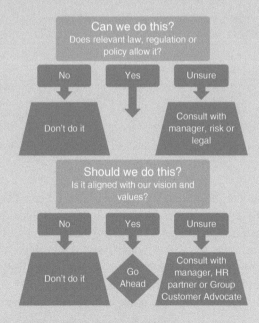

Figure 4.2   The CBA tool for ethical decision making

The CBA also recently joined forces with the St James Ethics Centre and several other major financial services (wealth management) players to develop the Ethical Professional programme. A key part of this programme is helping financial planners/advisers to understand their own personal ethical 'style' and to read and understand the ethical styles of other people. Accordingly, the programme builds ethical capacity, rather than concentrating on issues of rules/compliance. The programme is developed industry-wide, as opposed to by a single competitor, perhaps indicating a shift in the view of ethics.

Questions

1. CBA strives to be the most ethical bank in Australia. How does it do it? Do you agree that this is the best pathway to achieve this high-level goal?
2. What can CBA do better to improve its ethical standing?
3. Do you see a contradiction between being a bank and being ethical? Why? If you do, what needs to systematically change?
4. How does the CBA support ethical decision making?
5. If you were the CEO of the Bank, what would you do to improve the ethical approach to CBA?

Bibliography

Commonwealth Bank of Australia (CBA) (2014) Shareholder review. Available at: www.commbank.com.au/content/dam/commbank/about-us/shareholders/pdfs/shareholder-information/CBA-shareholder-review-2014-single-page-view.pdf (Accessed: 18 March 2017)

Sydney Morning Herald (2015) CBA wants to be 'the ethical bank'. Available at: www.smh.com.au/business/banking-and-finance/cba-wants-to-be-the-ethical-bank-20151117-gl11rc.html (Accessed: 7 May 2017)

Links

ABC News (2015) CBA denying compensation to victims of financial planning. Available at: www.abc.net.au/news/2015-10-28/cba-denying-compensation-to-victims-of-financial-planning/6892624 (Accessed: 7 May 2017)

Commonwealth Bank (2014) Our values. Available at: www.commbank.com.au/content/dam/commbank/microsite/2014shareholderreview/pdf/our-values.pdf (Accessed: 7 May 2017)

Commonwealth Bank (2016) Corporate Responsibility Report 2016. Available at: www.commbank.com.au/cr-report2016/cs-build-capability.html (Accessed: 7 May 2017)

Commonwealth Bank (2016) Corporate Responsibility Report 2016 – Fairness. Available at: www.commbank.com.au/cr-report2016/cs-fair.html (Accessed: 7 May 2017)

Commonwealth Bank (2017) About us. Available at: www.commbank.com.au/about-us/our-company/strategy.html (Accessed: 7 May 2017)

Sydney Morning Herald (2015) Committee hears of Commonwealth Bank's $82 billion fraud. Available at: www.smh.com.au/business/banking-and-finance/committee-hears-of-commonwealth-banks-82-billion-fraud-20151113-gky7df.html (Accessed: 7 May 2017)

Introduction: The importance of business ethics to CSR

Business ethics is about 'doing the right thing' in business, according to duty and norms, and it is therefore an essential part of CSR. However, what does it mean to be ethical? Who defines right and wrong? And what do we do when we need to choose between two rights or two wrongs, and whichever way we go could be undermining our ethos?

When we think about business ethics, often what comes to mind is *unethical behaviour*. Unethical corporate behaviour, such as by Enron and Volkswagen, or the business conduct that led to the mortgage crisis in the US, is what we usually think about. Looking through dozens of cases on business ethics for this book, we could not find one example of an ethical corporation. All the written case studies that we found were focused on *unethical* behaviour. Searching for 'business ethics' on YouTube results in videos that show unethical behaviour. However, as the goal of this book is to focus on positive examples of CSR instead of corporate social irresponsibility, it was essential to look for a company that while not perfect, offers an example of positive business ethics.

The impact of unethical behaviour in the workplace can be extremely negative, harmful and long lasting for individual employees, consumers, shareholders and the firm and its reputation. When behaving unethically towards an employee, for example, with unfair treatment or bullying, the effect on the employee's physical and psychological wellbeing could last for years, even after leaving the organisation. The impact of unethical behaviour by the leadership of a company could haunt the company and sabotage its reputation years after that leadership has changed.

Companies that emphasise their values and ethos to newcomers and existing employees develop a strong compass that provides a clear direction and guides behaviour. Clarifying what is ethical or not in a company will not only help avoid unethical behaviour, scandals and legal action against the company, but it will also assist in developing a strong organisational culture, employee engagement and wellbeing.

It is therefore the goal of this chapter to discuss business ethics; explain the philosophical approaches to ethics and define how they affect our behaviour; and discuss implications for managerial practices and offer some pathways for ethical behaviour and decision making.

EXERCISE

The Institute for Business, Technology and Ethics (IBTE) in Washington state listed 'Nine Good Reasons' for business to learn about business ethics and run the company in the most ethical way possible. These reasons can also be seen as a multi-stakeholder perspective on ethics.

- Litigation/indictment avoidance
- Regulatory freedom
- Public acceptance
- Investor confidence
- Supplier/partner trust

- Customer loyalty
- Employee performance
- Personal pride
- It is the right thing to do

In your opinion, which are the three most important reasons? Why? What other reasons can you think of?

Ethics and business ethics defined

Ethics is the study of right and wrong, duty and obligation, moral norms, individual character and responsibility. As such, it is highly relevant to CSR and for being ethical and responsible. To be professionally ethical means to act in accordance with the accepted principles of right and wrong that govern the conduct of a professional, while being unethical is defined as not conforming to approved standards of social or professional behaviour (Hartman et al., 2014).

Ethics was discussed mainly in philosophy and religion for thousands of years, and it is only in the last century that the topic was brought into the discipline of business management. As such, it is a form of applied ethics, similar to applied ethics in other disciplines, such as psychology or medicine. Business ethics is a form of applied ethics that examines ethical principles and moral or ethical problems that arise in a business environment. It applies to all aspects of business conduct and is relevant to the conduct of individual employees, managers and leaders as well as to entire organisations. In addition, business ethics examines business decision making and the solving of ethical dilemmas, which we will elaborate on further in this chapter.

Business ethics has both normative and descriptive dimensions. *Normative ethics* tells us what is right or wrong and instructs us what to do in general and in specific situations in particular. For example, normative ethics guides against fraud or insider information to gain profit. *Descriptive ethics*, on the other hand, describes what is considered ethical or unethical in certain contexts, why people behave ethically or not, without commanding certain behaviours (Hartman et al., 2014).

What guides our behaviour in the workplace?

When we consider how to behave in our profession, role and/or workplace, there are a few sources that guide us: etiquette, moral principles, values, ethics, professional codes and the law.

Rules of *etiquette* are guidelines for socially acceptable behaviour. Etiquette tells us what good manners in a workplace are – for example, how to greet people, how to behave in a meeting, whether it is acceptable to smoke, eat or tell jokes in certain situations. Of course, what is considered good manners will vary not only from culture to culture, and from one organisation to another, but also between situations, with people from various job levels, and so on. In most workplaces, people demonstrate a different etiquette in the presence of the CEO and with their peers. It should be noted that some types of behaviour, which would be considered bad manners in the past, like sexual harassment or smoking in the workplace, are now illegal in many countries.

The other source of guidance is the moral principles of a given culture or workplace. Accepting *moral principles* is not just a matter of intellectual recognition, but of profound individual commitment to a set of *values*. There are some universally accepted moral principles, such as not to do to others what you do not want to be done to you.

In addition, *ethics*, as was mentioned above, guides us on what the accepted principles of right and wrong are. Ethics are relativist, as will be discussed below, and what is wrong in one society could be seen as morally acceptable in another, and vice versa.

In certain professions, the *professional codes* are the rules that govern the conduct of their members. This could be a professional code of ethics that tells people what they can and cannot do. Such professional members include lawyers, psychologists, doctors and many others, but also some business roles, such as accountants, people in finance and managers.

Moving to the next level of behaviour guidance is the *law*: a system of rules and guidelines which are enforced through social institutions to govern behaviour. The laws of a given country tell us what is right or wrong in the eyes of that particular country's legislators, and the government and other institutions have the power to enforce these rules by taking away people's liberties and other rights when not obeyed. Over the years, as governments legislated many more laws, certain behaviour has shifted from being unethical to now being illegal.

However, it should be noted that 'legal' and 'ethical' are not the same. There may be instances in which something is legal but could be considered unethical (e.g. it is legal to test products on animals while causing them harm in many countries) and vice versa: there are examples of acts that would be illegal but considered moral by many (e.g. helping people escape countries that limit their freedoms and rights). In 2015, many multinational corporations, such as Google and Apple, were accused of avoiding taxes. While it was legal, many said it was immoral.

Morality and personal values

Morality in the narrow sense is the moral principles or rules that do, or should, govern the conduct of individuals in their relation to others. In a broader sense, morality is the values, ideals and aspirations that influence the decisions and lifestyles of individuals and entire societies. It originated from the Latin word *moralis*, meaning manners, character and proper behaviour. Morality, be it our individual moral standards or those of the society in which we live, helps us distinguish moral and proper actions, intentions and decisions from those that are immoral and improper. As such, morality can affect our behaviour and ethical choices in life as well as in business and in the workplace. Morality can be based on our culture, history, religion, worldview, philosophy, ideals, aspirations and values.

Values

Values are stable, evaluative beliefs that guide our preferences and behaviour (Schwartz, 1992). They can be described as desirable, trans-situational goals that vary in importance as guiding principles in people's lives. Values are based on our self-concept, or the way we would like to see ourselves and for others to see us. They are trans-situational in the sense that people usually do not change their values in different situations and in that the same values would be important in a personal or professional situation. Even when people feel they need to act against their values in the workplace, the same values still hold.

Values define what is right and wrong, what is good or bad, and therefore are the basis of our moral approach and behaviour. People hold a set of values in which there is a hierarchy, and some values are more important than others. We do not often think about our values or list them, but when facing, for example, a dilemma between honesty and friendship, we might need to choose and the choice implies our value system.

Shalom Schwartz (1992) developed the theory of basic human values, according to which ten values are the most dominant universally. This basic values inventory is widely used to test people's values and to compare nations, people with various backgrounds, variables (e.g. gender, age, ethnicity) and organisations. The ten values are organised in a circle on two different dimensions (see Figure 4.3) or four higher-order groups. The first axis is between openness to change and conservation, examining the tendency to cling to the past (including security, tradition and religion) or to open up to a different future. People who are strong on openness to change have high levels of self-direction (independent thought and action) and stimulation (the desire for excitement and challenge in life) values.

The second axis is between self-enhancement, which is the more egoistic side of the circle (values are hedonism, achievement and power), and self-transcendent values, which are about overcoming our selfishness and being occupied with the welfare of others. Self-transcended values include benevolence (preserving and enhancing the welfare of those with whom one is in frequent personal contact) and universalism (understanding, appreciation, tolerance and protection of the welfare of all people and of nature). It is clear why self-transcended values are attributed to companies and individuals with high levels of social responsibility. In a way, the values on the opposing sides of the scale should contest each other, and as such, for example, people, nations or companies that are very high on achievement should be low on universalism. However, people often have high scores on opposing values. For example, one can be high on achievement and benevolence and become a professor or director of CSR.

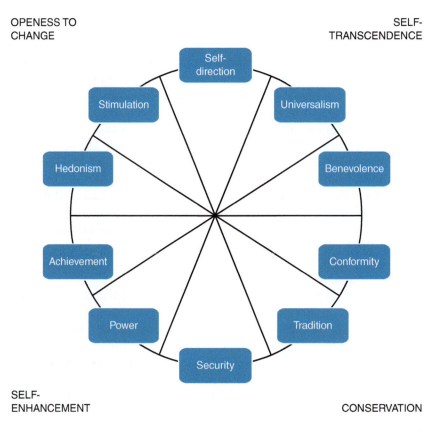

Figure 4.3   The basic human values model (based on Schwartz, 1992)

EXERCISE

1.   Write down your five 'commandments' or the five values that guide you the most in life.
2.   Reflect: How hard was it to write them down?

3. Delete one.
4. Then another one.
5. And another one.
6. Why did you delete these values and not others? What did it teach you about your value system?
7. Reflect: How difficult was it to delete those values? What did you learn from it?
8. Try listing the most important values of your current/past workplace. Do you think there is congruence (alignment) between your values and the values of the organisation you work(ed) for? How does it make you feel?

Corporate values

Since the 1990s there has been a growing business trend to set the core values of the company (Lencioni, 2002) and today we cannot imagine a large company without a set of values, stated on its website, sometimes printed on wall plaques. Every new employee needs to memorise these values. But that does not necessarily make them meaningful, as explained by Lencioni in a *Harvard Business Review* article from 2002:

> Take a look at this list of corporate values: Communication. Respect. Integrity. Excellence. They sound pretty good, don't they? Strong, concise, meaningful. Maybe they even resemble your own company's values, the ones you spent so much time writing, debating, and revising. If so, you should be nervous. These are the corporate values of Enron, as stated in the company's 2000 annual report. And as events have shown, they're not meaningful; they're meaningless.

Corporate values can set a company apart from the competition by clarifying its identity and serving as a reference point for employees. However, for values to be meaningful they need firstly to mean something. Using big words such as *integrity* and *leadership* does not necessarily lead to employees and other stakeholders knowing what the firm stands for. Most companies' values include integrity, teamwork, ethics, quality, customer satisfaction, and innovation (Lencioni, 2002). Consequently, this does not make them different from their competitors, and such values become meaningless.

Furthermore, corporate values need to have a meaning that is relevant and understood by all the stakeholders. It is therefore important to differentiate between *espoused values*, which are desirable by the company, employees and society at large, and *enacted values*, which most staff truly rely on to guide decisions and behaviours (Simons, 2002). Companies with espoused values that are not enacted could lose employee and public trust and be perceived as insincere. If a company puts 'integrity' in its set of values but encourages salespeople to be dishonest with buyers, then these are empty values. Empty values fail to meet people's need to work with a company that stands for something, but could also lead to cynicism and lack of trust and commitment over time. As such, corporate values need to be well known, meaningful, specific, authentic and acted upon. Similarly, there is a difference between core values and aspirational values. Core values are the deeply ingrained principles that guide all of a company's actions; they serve as its cultural cornerstones. Aspirational values need to be carefully managed to ensure that they do not dilute the core values (Joyner and Payne, 2002).

It is important that employees are rewarded for acting upon the company's values while leadership sets an example. This should create a strong organisational culture in which the values are lived by. For companies that are about to set or change their values, a good reflection process is useful to understand what they stand for and what their real values are. It is important to involve employees and other stakeholders in this process.

Furthermore, as both employers and employees have a set of values, the proximity between the individual values of the employee and those of the employer create *value congruence* or the lack thereof (Valentine et al., 2002; Edwards and Cable, 2009). Value congruence is the extent to which individuals can behave at work in ways consistent with their own personal values and self-image. When value congruence exists, employees find it easier to identify with their employers and develop stronger emotional commitment and affiliation. In contrast, it is very difficult for employees to experience meaningfulness and satisfaction at work if they are expected to behave in ways inconsistent with their highest values.

Questions for reflection and discussion

1. Go back to the case study and examine the values of Commonwealth Bank Australia.
2. Are these the values of a company you would like to work for?
3. Do you think they are espoused or enacted values?

Three philosophical approaches: Implications for management

Ethics has been a major stream in philosophy for thousands of years. For centuries, philosophers, including the early Greeks, have been trying to answer questions such as: What is good? What is right? What makes a person virtuous and ethical?

With so many different answers and approaches to these questions, scholars tend to group them into three: deontological ethics (non-consequentialist and action-based theories), utilitarian ethics (consequentialist and action-based theories) and virtue ethics (agent-based theories) (Christensen et al., 2007; Hartman et al., 2014). These three philosophical approaches are summarised in Figure 4.4.

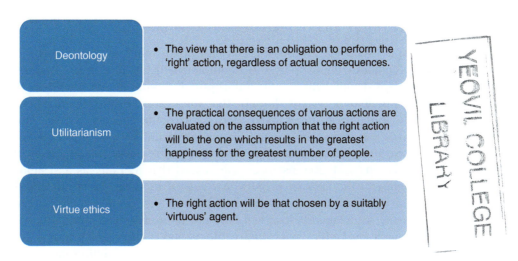

Deontology
- The view that there is an obligation to perform the 'right' action, regardless of actual consequences.

Utilitarianism
- The practical consequences of various actions are evaluated on the assumption that the right action will be the one which results in the greatest happiness for the greatest number of people.

Virtue ethics
- The right action will be that chosen by a suitably 'virtuous' agent.

Figure 4.4   Three philosophical approaches that impact business ethics

Consequentialist theories determine the moral rightness or wrongness of an action based on the action's consequences or results, while non-consequentialist (or deontological) theories determine the moral rightness or wrongness of an action based on the action's intrinsic features or character. Consequentialism holds that the action's results are the basis for moral judgement, promoting the rationale that 'the ends justify the means'. Extreme consequentialists may believe any method used to achieve a moral goal is acceptable. Deontology, or non-consequentialism, holds the view that the basis for moral judgement is the intent and motivation of one's actions, not the results.

In other words, the non-consequentialist approach would look at an action and determine whether it is right or wrong due to the action itself and the motivation behind it. As such, stealing is wrong no matter what, even if it is stealing from the rich to give to the poor, as was done by Robin Hood (although this somewhat oversimplifies deontology). On the other hand, the consequentialist approach will determine whether the stealing was right or wrong based on how many people were better off due to stealing, and as such will deem Robin Hood's action as moral.

Deontology

Deontological ethics or deontology is based on the Greek concept of *deon* (obligation, duty). It is the normative ethical position that judges the morality of an action based on the action's motivation and intent based on some rules. As such, it is often described as duty- or obligation- or rule-based ethics. According to deontological ethics, to act morally means to act according to our duty, morality and values. It is not the consequences of actions that make a person right or wrong but the motives of the person who carries out the action.

Immanuel Kant (1724–1804), a German philosopher, is considered the central figure of modern philosophy and deontology. In his 1797 book *Metaphysics of Morals*, Kant detailed his moral philosophy and what is considered as the foundation of deontology. Kant thought that there are moral obligations, which he called the 'categorical imperatives', derived from the concept of duty. Categorical imperatives are principles that are intrinsically valid and are good in themselves. To observe a moral law means that these imperatives must be obeyed by everyone in all situations and circumstances. He argued that morality as a system of laws is analogous to the laws of physics in terms of their universal applicability. Just as gravity will work everywhere and every time, the moral principles (categorical imperatives), as detailed below, will hold always and in every situation.

In deontological ethics, *maxims* are understood as subjective principles of action. A maxim is part of a person's thought process for every action taken, indicating in its standard form: (1) the action, or type of action; (2) the conditions under which it is to be done; and (3) the end or purpose to be achieved by the action, or the motive. The maxim of an action is often referred to as the agent's intention. In Kantian ethics, the categorical imperative provides a litmus test on maxims for determining whether the actions they refer to are right, wrong or permissible.

Kant's most well-known moral principle is the universal law: 'Act only according to that maxim whereby you can at the same time will that it should become a universal law' (Kant and Ellington, 1994: 30). In other words, act only in a way in which you are happy for everyone to act. This is similar to the basic golden rule of 'do unto others as you would have them do unto you'. It is basic moral rule and, according to Kant, if people's actions and motives are always aligned with it, then they should always be moral.

Another important principle is the second imperative, known as the formula for humanity: 'Act in such a way that you treat humanity, whether in your own person or in the person of any other, never merely as a means to an end, but always at the same time as an end' (Kant and Ellington, 1994: 36). Putting it simply, this means to never use another human being as just a means to an end but also as an end in itself. Considering some of the unethical treatment of human beings, particularly in the developing world by some large corporations that are mentioned in this book, this could be a very good business ethical principle to act upon.

Questions for reflection and discussion

1. What do you see as the main advantages of deontology?
2. What are the main issues that arise with it?
3. Think from a managerial point of view: What does it mean to act according to the deontological approach?

Criticism

A common criticism against deontological ethics is that it does not provide a clear pathway to resolve conflicts between moral duties. For example, both lying and harming people are against the deontological principles, but what should we do when we must choose between the two? Sometimes you must lie to avoid harming people. One solution is to choose the option that, according to you, will give the least worst results, but in this case we are shifting to a consequentialist approach.

A second criticism is that deontology does not allow for grey areas where the morality of an action is questionable. It is a system that is based upon absolute principles and absolute conclusions, however in real life ethical decision making usually involves some grey areas instead of black-and-white choices. Conflicting duties, obligations, interests and issues could lead to challenging decisions.

Implications for practice

So what does deontology mean for business management today and for CSR? Firstly, it means to act from a moral point of view. Not seeing CSR as a public relations activity or marketing instrument, but as the right thing to do. There are increasing numbers of companies that fully understand and adopt this approach to their social responsibility, shifting away from instrumental CSR. Another implication for business is that business decision makers need to ask themselves: Are we willing for all the companies in the world to behave this way? Are we willing that whatever we are doing to others will be done to us and to our families? Are we willing that our children will be used for cheap labour the way that we are using children to maximise profit?

Not to use another human being solely as a means to an end involves a complete transformation of mindset and business approach for many companies. It means treating people as human beings that deserve dignity, freedom and access to their basic needs and rights, and not as money-making machines, which is how many corporations currently see employees, consumers and other stakeholders. Having good corporate stakeholder management, as was discussed in Chapter 3, is about adopting the formula for humanity in every business decision and action. Obviously, it is challenging and not always possible; however, having this as a corporate aspirational value could lead to more ethical behaviour.

Utilitarianism

Utilitarian ethics is the moral theory according to which we should act in ways that produce the most pleasure or happiness for the greatest number of people affected by our actions. Its main representatives are the British philosophers Jeremy Bentham (1748–1832) and John Stuart Mill (1806–1873). It is based on the idea (strongly promoted by Bentham) that the only motivation for human behaviour is one's pleasure. In other words, hedonism is the only drive and value that makes people act. As such, if we are to ask people to behave morally, we need to appeal to their sense of pleasure. According to this line of thought, even when people serve others and volunteer, they do it to derive the pleasure of feeling good about themselves.

The morality of an action is determined by the utility of the result. The principle of utility asserts that actions are morally praiseworthy if they promote the greatest human welfare, and blameworthy if they do not. However, 'utility' is defined in many ways: it can be perceived as greater happiness, pleasure or wellbeing or as the number of people that are better off as a result of the action. In his 1789 book *An Introduction to the Principles of Morals and Legislation*, Bentham described utility as the sum of the pleasure that results from a certain action minus the suffering of anyone involved in it. This is known as the *hedonic calculus* (hedonistic calculation). In addition, Mill argued that 'some kinds of pleasure are more desirable and more valuable than others' (Mill, 1863: 11), and as such we need to discuss the quality and the quantity of the utility caused by the action to determine its morality. However, as observed by Henry Sidgwick (1907), this is impossible to do.

Some scholars divide utilitarianism into a number of variant forms, including act and rule utilitarianism. *Act utilitarianism* is straightforward, advising us to judge each individual action based on its outcome/results alone and choose the one which yields the most happiness for the most people. Notably, this kind of approach could lead to extreme unethical behaviour by individuals, corporates and societies. It could be argued that even Hitler thought he was serving humanity by abolishing Jews and other peoples. Many companies believe it is moral to use child and forced labour or to pay people very little, as long as they maximise profit to a large number of shareholders and keep many consumers happy with low prices.

Rule utilitarianism attempts to resolve the moral issues that arise in act utilitarianism. Rule utilitarianism assesses the utility of a rule for action as follows: if everyone were to obey this rule, would the general happiness be maximised? As such, it can be seen as a combination of the deontological universal law and utilitarianism. Applying it to the same example above, one could argue that using child labour is immoral even by the standards of utilitarian ethics, as the general good would decrease if every company in the world were to employ children. We could even argue that if every company were to give money to charity and large tax exemptions, general society would not be better off, and therefore this could be seen as an immoral act.

Questions for reflection and discussion

1. What do you see as the main advantages of utilitarianism?
2. What are the main issues that arise?
3. Think from a managerial point of view: What does it mean to act according to the utilitarian approach?

Criticism

There is quite a lot of criticism against utilitarian ethics, although when examining business practice today, it is not difficult to conclude that a lion's share of it is based on utilitarianism.

Firstly, happiness and pleasure cannot always be qualified and compared. It is a subjective term and it is impossible to decide if a long-term contentment is lesser or greater than short-term ecstasy. Secondly, pleasure is neutral and all people are equal, and as such pleasing many immoral people would be considered moral. Thirdly, this approach puts minorities and excluded groups at a distinct disadvantage, as it is only the majority's happiness that counts. As long as a majority of people are happy and safe, slavery and torture, which many people would see as immoral, could be justified. In fact, it could be argued that utilitarianism often requires action that is contrary to our moral 'common sense'. Fourthly, the utilitarian focus on consequences and results ignores motives and intention. It dismisses their significance for determining the rightness/wrongness of an action and motivation can be very important for ethics. Fifthly, happiness is not the only goal for humans and many would agree to sacrifice personal happiness to do what they see as right. In addition, people are not necessarily egoists and hedonism is not the only motivation for many of us. In an article on altruism I argued that:

> If we were all egoistic, working for our own interests and satisfaction, then we no longer need to speak about egoism. We rather need to ask why some people derive selfish satisfaction by helping and giving, while others derive it from self-centred behavior. That is, the egocentric approach contradicts itself: if everyone is egoistic, then

we only have to differ between those who enhance their own good by helping others (which should be called altruistic) and those who do that by self-centred behavior (egoistic). (Haski-Leventhal, 2009: 289)

Implications for managerial practice

As the basis of this book is strategic CSR and not instrumental CSR, utilitarian ethics is not going to be our guidance for managerial practice. However, there are some positive aspects that we can extract from it when implementing CSR. Firstly, it is important to strive to minimise pain for all beings – humans and animals – everywhere. The concept of pain reduction is a good beacon for doing business. It is important for each company to reflect on the pain caused by its actions, directly and indirectly, and to find measures to reduce this pain. Secondly, it is important for corporates to use rule utilitarianism and ask: Would we be happy for every company in the world to do what we are doing and for our actions to become the norm? Thirdly, it is useful to acknowledge that our nature can be very selfish, and to be aware of actions taken for selfish motivation alone. However, while we are capable of serving our hedonism and our selfishness, we are also capable of adopting self-transcendent values and of serving others, and feeling good about it does not make us selfish. Fourthly, the utilitarian behaviour of people, societies and corporations in the past occasionally led to catastrophic results and this too is an important lesson for business.

Mini case study   Ford Pinto

The case of Ford Pinto is often used to teach business ethics (although, as was explained in the introduction, it is about unethical behaviour). In the 1970s, Ford Motor Company developed a small car to compete with Volkswagen and other companies, which was marketed as a 'carefree car'. While conducting some crash tests, Ford learned that the Pinto introduced a severe hazard – in a case of rear collision, even at low speed, the car would burst into flames. Ford officials faced a moral decision: should they go ahead with the existing design, thereby meeting the production schedule but possibly jeopardising consumer safety, or should they delay production of the Pinto and redesign the car to make it safer? They knew that if they chose the latter, the cost would be about US$11 per car (Ladenson, 1995).

According to a memo, which was later leaked, Ford did an informed calculation to decide which action to take. In this calculation, the company estimated that 180 people would die each year and that the cost per death would be about US$200,000 (remember, this is the 1970s). Their calculations in the leaked memo were as follows (all sums are in US$):

Benefits

Savings:	180 burn deaths, 180 serious burn injuries, 2,100 burned vehicles
Unit cost:	$200,000 per death, $67,000 per injury, $700 per vehicle
Total benefit:	(180 × $200,000) + (180 × $67,000) + (2,100 × $700) = $49.5 million

Costs

Sales:	11 million cars, 1.5 million light trucks
Unit cost:	$11 per car, $11 per truck
Total cost:	12.5 million × $11 = $137.5 million

Given these numbers, Ford decided to move ahead and sell the dangerous car, knowing very well that it would cause deaths. The Ford Pinto ended up killing many more people than estimated (over 1,000) and the damages caused to customers and the company far exceeded the calculation.

Reference

Ladenson, R. (1995) *Ford Pinto case*. Chicago, IL: Center for the Study of Ethics in the Professions, Illinois Institute of Technology.

Points for discussion

1. What would you do if you were working in the Ford team at the time?
2. Analyse how ethical Ford was in its actions around the Ford Pinto from a deontological point of view. Is there an ethical justification to what they did using this approach?
3. Now apply the utilitarian approach to answer the same question.
4. What did you learn from this case about business ethics?
5. What did you learn from your responses about each of the moral approaches discussed in this chapter?

Virtue ethics

Virtue ethics refers to normative ethical theories, which emphasise virtues of mind and character and examine what a moral person is. Virtue ethics originated mainly with the ancient Greek philosophers, particularly Aristotle. Instead of asking what defines a moral action, as was later done by deontology and utilitarianism, virtue ethics focuses on the virtues (or traits) of the moral person. As such, deontology and utilitarianism can be seen as 'action-based' approaches, whereas virtue ethics is described as an 'agent-based' approach. Unlike the previous two approaches, virtue ethics is not a list of constraints on behaviour (Whetstone, 2001).

The basic approach to morality is that virtue is not just the tendency to be honest or noble, it is also a character trait. One of these important traits is the moral (and practical) wisdom that guides a person in any given situation to do the 'right thing'. Virtue ethics is concerned with pursuing morally inclusive excellence. A little similar to utilitarianism, virtue ethics is based on the idea that happiness, wellbeing and flourishing (*eudaimonia*) is the ultimate human goal, which characterises a well-lived life.

According to Aristotle, 'virtue' is defined as some desirable character trait, for example courage, which lies between two extremes, such as rashness and cowardice. To be a 'virtuous' agent entails a constant quest to achieve a balance between the two extremes. Virtue ethics is not about applying specific 'rules', but rather attempting to make decisions that are consistent with the pursuit of virtues, such as courage, wisdom, temperance, fairness, integrity and consistency (Goodpaster, 1994). Figure 4.5 shows virtues that are relevant to business management as a balance between two extremes. For example, businesses and managers need to find a good balance between having sole loyalty to shareholders and a social responsibility for public good; between focusing too much on the next quarterly results and too much on long-term results while ignoring the present; and between being too materialistic driven (profit oriented) and too purpose-driven.

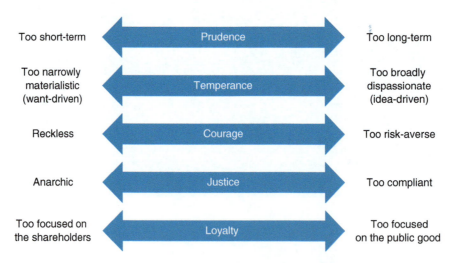

Figure 4.5   Virtues as a balance between two extremes (based on Goodpaster, 1994)

Various lists of virtues exist and we will not detail them all here. Socrates thought that the only virtue required is knowledge, while Aristotle identified nearly 20 virtues that enable a person to live a moral and well-lived life. Among these are moral virtues (including courage, temperance, ambition and honour, patience and truthfulness) and intellectual virtues (intelligence, reasoning and wisdom). When responsible and sustainable leadership is discussed in Chapter 6, some of these traits will become relevant.

The main criticism against virtue ethics is that it focuses too much on who a person is rather than on what a person does (or should do) and ignores the consequences of these actions. The discussion around morality and ethics needs to also include actual moral behaviour and not just traits. Others criticise the approach for not being culturally sensitive (these virtues are not universal as assumed) and for being too narrow and anachronistic. The virtue lists do not necessarily predict moral behaviour, as was shown by both history and research. There is also a risk in idolising a person for her or his virtues, instead of focusing on the work that needs to be done.

Ethical relativism

As was already raised in the criticism of the three aforementioned ethical approaches, what is perceived as good, right, moral and ethical in one place, organisation or culture, may not be so in a different context. As such, we need to understand that ethics is culturally based and may therefore be relativist. The notion of ethical (or moral) relativism attempts to be more culturally sensitive when discussing what the right business decision is, for example (Shaw and Barry, 2015).

Ethical relativism is the view according to which moral norms derive their ultimate justification from the customs of the society in which they occur (Pearson, 1989). Morality is relative to the norms of one's culture, and whether an action is right or wrong depends on the moral norms of the society in which the action is taken. The same action may be morally right in one society but be morally wrong in another. According to this approach, there are no universal moral standards that can be applied to all people at all times and the only moral standards against which a society's practices can be judged are its own. Our moral values and behaviours are deeply rooted in our upbringing and in the culture in which we grow up. This is referred to as 'descriptive cultural relativism' (Hartman et al., 2014; Shaw and Barry, 2015).

For example, you may think that taking another person's life is always morally wrong. Yet in some societies it is considered moral to take a human life with a death penalty, for various reasons (e.g. from murdering others to infidelity). In some cultures, it is considered merciful and moral to help a suffering human being to end his or her life (euthanasia), but in others it is illegal and considered immoral.

In some societies, young girls are killed to protect the 'honour' of the family. While in the society that you live this may be considered wrong, in other societies it is the norm.

Similarly, in business conduct, some actions can be seen as morally right or wrong depending on the social norms. As will be detailed below, in many cultures taking or giving a bribe to promote business would be associated with corruption and immoral behaviour. However, in other societies if you are offered a 'gift' to affect your behaviour or decision (which many would see as a bribe), the right thing to do is to accept this 'gift'. Rejecting it could be seen as bad manners or unethical. As such, conducting business internationally while behaving in accordance with our moral values could be more challenging than it may appear.

Ethical relativism is based on both ethics and anthropology, combining the knowledge of different societies with ethical approaches. It raises some important questions about universal moral values and whether there are any universal moral principles, or rather that morality is a matter of 'cultural taste'.

In addition, ethical relativism could be applied not just to place and culture but also to time. It is interesting to see how business conduct, such as using slaves from Africa in the plantations in the US, considered moral over 200 years ago is now immoral in today's society. Businesses that still use forms of modern slavery, child labour and abused and underpaid offshore workers need to remember that what is morally acceptable today may become unacceptable very quickly.

While ethical relativism has merit as it aims to be more culturally sensitive and to debate what is important for all of us as humanity, there is also some strong criticism against it. Some people argue that universal moral standards can exist even if some moral practices and beliefs vary among cultures. Others claim that while the moral practices of societies may differ, the fundamental moral principles underlying these practices do not (e.g. the underlying principle in the death penalty and euthanasia could still be seen as respect for life) (see Shaw and Barry, 2015).

In addition, ethical relativism is criticised due to its implications for individual moral beliefs: if the rightness or wrongness of an action depends solely on specific social norms, then it could be immoral to act against such norms, even when they are wrong. To take an extreme example, it could have been seen as immoral at the time for Germans not to support Nazism, and yet most people would agree today that supporting Nazism was immoral.

Quick question

Do you agree that ethical relativism contradicts personal responsibility? Explain.

Business ethics in practice: Ethical and unethical conduct

So far, we have looked at what ethics and business ethics are, why it is important to understand ethics and develop an ethical business, and the three philosophical approaches that could guide us in doing so. It is important to also understand what ethical behaviour actually means for business in the current global market and how to ensure that everyone in the company behaves ethically. In order to do so, this section will cover several common ethical challenges that managers often face and offer pathways to addressing them. This section can be perceived as a practical guide to ethical behaviour, offering some tools that can be implemented in every business, big or small.

Ethical people management

Since ethics are the moral principles or rules that govern the conduct of individuals in their relation to others, people management can be seen as an ethical issue and may present some ethical challenges. Understanding how to manage your staff ethically will not only result in lower risk, but will also ensure employee wellbeing, happiness, commitment and retention.

As was explained above, there are several sources of ethical behaviour in the workplace, from good etiquette to ethics and the law. All of these could be applied to managing people in the workplace. Although what is considered good manners, ethical and legal will vary from one place to another, there are some common rules that always apply. *Treating people with respect* can never be wrong. If you start there, you will avoid bullying employees, using them as disposable goods, harassing them and taking away their legal rights. For this reason, many companies have stopped using the term 'human resources' and 'human resource management' and have started referring to their employees as 'our people' or 'team members'. By genuinely treating people as human beings with dignity and rights, most of the issues that are detailed below can be avoided.

In addition, it is vital that managers and employees know the local and international laws, regulations and human rights principles and act in accordance with them. There are many industrial laws that guide managers in what is legal and permitted and what is not – from paying wages (what the minimum pay is, how often you need to pay it, what other benefits employees must receive) to workplace bullying and sexual harassment. If you disobey these laws, you might find yourself in a labour court or in the media, but more importantly, you could also destroy a good organisational atmosphere that leads to higher performance.

Employees have rights, not just duties and obligations. In 1995, the Heads of State and Government attended the World Summit for Social Development in

Copenhagen and adopted specific commitments to 'basic workers' rights' which included the following: the prohibition of forced labour and child labour; freedom of association; the right to organise and bargain collectively; equal remuneration for work of equal value; and the elimination of discrimination in employment (Kellerson, 1998). These are the basic rights accepted internationally and adopted by the UN and the UN Global Compact. There are many other rights that need to be observed but these are the basic ones that should never be ignored, regardless of where the employees are based in the world.

Another important aspect of ethical management is fair management. Fair management requires the assurance that all employees receive an equal opportunity, regardless of gender, ethnicity, age, disability and other background. *Equality* is about everyone receiving the same, while *equity* means that people receive what they need to get the same opportunity to succeed. For example, if a person with a disability and a person without a disability receive the same terms and opportunities, that would be equality, but it could still put the person with a disability at a disadvantage. Equity, on the other hand, indicates that the person with a disability receives the extra assistance needed so they can be at the same starting point as everyone else. Equity and diversity in the workplace are gaining momentum in many parts of the world, not only because it is the right thing to do but because it has been shown that they lead to many benefits, such as diverse thinking, innovation, open-minded employees and a great reputation.

Another important aspect of fair management is avoiding biases in the workplace, discrimination or favouritism. Employees need to be treated according to their performance, not in terms of how much the boss personally likes them (or not). Due to categorical thinking which makes us judge people too quickly, we are all likely to think stereotypically (assigning similar traits to everyone in a social group) and have biases such as the like-me effect (liking people who remind us of ourselves) or the halo effect (allowing one trait or action to determine our overall assessment of someone). Such biases often lead managers to create an 'in-group' and 'out-group' of employees, where only the former are close to the manager and receive certain privileges. While it is natural for humans, including managers, to like some people and not others and to have biases and judge too quickly, ethical people management implies that an active effort must be made to avoid acting upon these in the workplace (Banaji et al., 2003).

This does not mean that all employees should be treated the same, and reward by performance is still an ethical practice as long as it is fair and transparent. According to the equity theory of Adams, employees compare their own input (e.g. job level, responsibilities, time given, effort; achievements, experience, education etc.) with that of their peers and then compare their own output (salary, bonuses, treatment, recognition, promotion, etc.) with that of their peers as well (Adams, 1963). When employees feel that they put in the same input as their peers but that their peers receive better output, they feel underpaid and angry. Such employees might then try to decrease their input (absenteeism, poor performance), increase their own output (ask for a raise or take office supplies) or quit the situation (look for another job). You might think that the people who receive better output to their peers might feel obliged to work hard, but according to this theory and related research, such employees feel guilt at first but over time develop a sense of entitlement and take the extra output for granted. As such, it is better to provide all employees with a fair and transparent system in which everyone knows what input leads to what output.

There are many other aspects of ethical people management that cannot be discussed here, but managers should be aware of them and act accordingly. While we cannot detail all of them in this book, it is important to also refer to ethical people management in the context of *offshoring*. Offshoring is the removal of jobs from one country to another to 'exploit' lower-paid workers. In the last 50 years, many corporations have realised that they can shift work from developed countries, where the minimum wage could be as much as US$20 per hour and US$200 per day, to poor and developing countries, where they can pay employees less than US$1 per day, and even less to children. These employees can be forced to work extra hours without pay and be treated as disposable goods, since their rights in these countries are not monitored and enforced like they are in developed countries. To be ethical, companies should treat employees with respect and dignity and ensure that they receive liveable wages, and even when they are 'out of sight' they need not be 'out of mind'. As Dunning (2003: 12) said: 'Globalisation is a morally neutral concept. In itself it is neither good nor bad, but it may be motivated for good or bad reasons and used to bring about more or less good or bad results.'

Fraud

A common unethical behaviour in the workplace is fraud, which can be committed by managers or employees at all job levels. In criminal law, a fraud is an intentional deception made for personal (including the company) gain or to damage another individual (Albrecht et al., 1995). It should be noted that fraud is not only a crime, but also a civil law violation, and as such, people who commit fraud may be prosecuted by both the state and those citizens who were affected by the fraud. Defrauding people or entities of money or valuables is a common purpose of fraud, but there have also been fraudulent 'discoveries' (e.g. in science) to gain prestige rather than immediate monetary gain.

Common financial frauds in business include (Albrecht et al., 1995):

- *Embezzlement*: the illegal use of funds by a person who controls those funds, such as using company money for personal needs. This could be direct stealing by a bookkeeper, for example, or a more sophisticated fraud such as abusing reimbursement systems by human resource managers.

- *Internal theft*: the stealing of company assets by employees, including money, office supplies or products the company sells without paying for them (note that this is sometimes done when people feel underpaid by the company, according to the equity theory above, but it is still classified as fraud).
- *Payoffs and kickbacks*: employees accepting cash and/or other benefits in exchange for access to the company's business (e.g. helping another company sell its products to the company in which the employee works). A 'payoff' is paid before the sale is made and a 'kickback' is paid after the sale is made. This is a form of bribery that will be further discussed below.
- *Skimming*: skimming occurs when employees take money from receipts and do not record the revenue in the books.

There are many other business frauds such as payroll fraud, taxation fraud, over ordering, and so on. It is not the goal of this section to detail all of them but rather to exemplify that when profit becomes the means, the end and everything in between, unethical behaviour may emerge.

The Fraud Triangle, illustrated in Figure 4.6, demonstrates that for someone to commit fraud, three main conditions usually occur together (Albrecht et al., 1995). Firstly, there is *rationalisation*. People who commit fraud usually convince themselves that 'adjusting the books' is good for the company and that it is for the greater good, to give one example. It will make the company look more profitable and will benefit the shareholders. Another rationalisation is that 'everyone does it' and as such they need to do the same (use the company's resources for their own benefit) to not lag behind. People might also tell themselves that there is no 'visible harm' in doing so and what people do not know will not harm them.

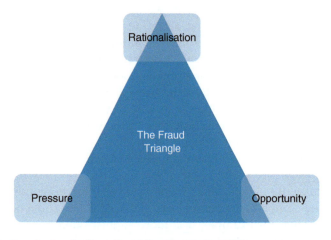

Figure 4.6   The fraud triangle (based on Albrecht et al., 1995)

This might have been the case with the 2015 fraud committed by Volkswagen, in which the company intentionally programmed diesel engines to activate certain emissions controls only during laboratory emissions testing (Gates et al., 2017). This was perceived as an intentional deception made for corporate gain. When Volkswagen managers and employees decided to do this, they might have rationalised that this was best for the company, that other automobile companies do it and that there is no 'visible harm' in doing so. As is often the case with a large-scale fraud, it turned into a scandal (known as the 'Volkswagen Emissions Scandal'), resulting in several managers stepping down and enormous damage to the company's reputation, after which all attempted rationalisations seemed poor.

It should be noted that rationalisation is based on people's values and belief systems, which is the reason why some people rationalise fraud as morally justified while others do not. A good boundary system, be it internal (a strong conscience) or external (a monitoring system in the company), may also stop rationalisation for fraud and the action that follows.

The other corner of the fraud triangle is the *pressure*, be it real or perceived. This could be market pressure, with fierce competition from other companies; company pressure that pushes employees to achieve certain quotas/profits at any cost; or a personal pressure to succeed, achieve and be rewarded. There could also be a direct pressure to commit fraud or lose one's job, or just general pressure that leads some employees to find ways to achieve difficult goals. In order to break this part of the triangle, companies need to reduce pressure on employees and avoid setting impossible goals. Diagnostic and interactive control systems could also assist in overcoming this pressure.

For someone to commit fraud, an *opportunity* usually needs to present itself. When employees discover weak internal control over the financial or safety systems in the company, the temptation to take advantage of this weakness could be great, particularly if both a rationalisation and pressure exist. If there is no auditing, or the auditing can be easily manipulated, employees might be tempted to deceive the system. In the Volkswagen case, it is possible to imagine that when it was discovered how relatively easy it was to deceive the emissions test and that by doing so the company could save millions of euros, the opportunity, together with the rationalisation and the pressure to outperform other companies, led to fraud.

Corruption

Corruption is a major ethical issue for many businesses, and it includes several types of bribery and corrupt behaviour. Corruption usually takes the form of dishonest or unethical conduct by a person entrusted with a position of authority, often to acquire personal benefits. It may include activities such as bribery and embezzlement and although some kinds of corruption are legal in some countries, it still stops people from doing what they are entrusted and paid to do. For example, the corruption and bribery of law enforcement people (e.g. police) stops them from doing what they are supposed to do: enforce the law on everyone and keep peace.

Corruption is strongly negatively associated with the share of private investment and therefore lowers the rate of economic growth. It may get to a point where the return on corruption exceeds the return on production, resulting in lower stock of producible input like human capital in corrupt countries. In addition, corruption increases inequality and, in turn, makes corruption activities more attractive. It is no wonder that the UN Global Compact included 'anti-corruption' as its tenth principal, particularly as corruption issues need to be addressed collectively and globally by business (see Chapter 9).

Corruption might serve individuals (unless they get caught, of course) but will always harm the collective. Going back to the Kantian categorical imperatives of the universal law, a driver might want to bribe a policeman to avoid a speeding fine, but would still not want to live in a society in which it is so easy to bribe police officers to a point where no one keeps order anymore. Similarly, where political corruption occurs and governments and politicians are corrupt, the state will not be governed in the best interests of its citizens.

The same issue applies in business corruption, in which business people receive or give benefits in order to influence behaviour and decisions. This could undermine fair competition, ethical business conduct or the overall governance of business and state. When a large corporation bribes a government representative, they only do so trusting that not everyone is doing the same. Otherwise, the bribe would have no effect and everyone would be living in chaos. Bribery is unethical in any case, but it will also be ineffective if everyone did the same. Adopting the Kantian maxim means that companies would not bribe as they do not accept it as a universal law.

In 2006, German prosecutors conducted a large-scale investigation of the German company Siemens to determine if its employees paid bribes in exchange for business. The investigation found questionable payments of roughly €1.3 billion from 2002 to 2006, and in May 2007 a German court convicted two former executives of paying about €6 million in bribes from 1999 to 2002 to help Siemens win natural gas turbine supply contracts with Enel, an Italian energy company. The contracts were valued at about €450 million. Siemens was fined €38 million and its reputation was harmed. The company would not have bothered to bribe had it known that all its competitors were using the same bribe as it would have had no impact on the result (Verschoor, 2007).

A bribe is a payment in some form for an act that runs counter to the work contract or the nature of the work that is to be performed. This payment can take the form of monetary rewards, getting business done, goods and gifts, services (including sexual services), and so on. A bribe could also take the form of prevention of negative actions, such as not revealing information that the person or the company does not want revealed.

Working in global markets and conducting international business could be challenging, as what is considered corruption and bribery in one culture is seen as 'simply doing business' in another. Furthermore, not accepting the gift would be considered offensive and unethical. Companies that send employees overseas to do business where it is likely they would be offered various kinds of bribe need to prepare them on how to act in a way that would be both ethical and aligned with the company values but also culturally sensitive. Having a clear company policy on what to do with gifts given in the course of doing business is essential to address these challenges.

Some factors are related to the moral acceptability of gifts: the value of the gift; its purpose (is the purpose to thank the person for services provided or to direct decisions and behaviour?); the circumstances under which it is given; the likelihood of influencing the person receiving the gift; the accepted business practice; and company policy and legal obligations.

Conflict of interest

Conflict of interest occurs when employees have a personal interest in a transaction substantial enough that it might reasonably be expected to affect their judgement or lead them to act against the interests of the organisation.

The employment contract creates various obligations to one's employer. In addition, employees often feel loyal to the organisation in which they work. On the other hand, an opportunity may occur for an employee to gain personal benefits or to benefit a third party they are close to, such as family and friends. When employees have financial investments in suppliers, customers or distributors with whom the organisation does business, conflict of interest can arise (Velasquez and Velazquez, 2002).

Company policy needs to determine the permissible limits of such financial interests and the disclosure policy for conflicts of interest. It is important to always ask employees to declare any conflict of interest and then make a decision as to whether or not this employee can be involved in certain decisions or activities based on the likelihood, strength and possible results of such conflicts. Doing so can help avoid ethical dilemmas, corruption and possible negative results for the employee and the company.

Insider trading

Another example of unethical (and illegal in many countries) business conduct is insider trading, which is buying or selling shares based on non-public information likely to affect share prices (Velasquez and Velazquez, 2002). It is seen as unethical because it is unfair to other investors who do not share the same access to information. It can injure other investors and undermine public confidence in the stock market and some research shows that overall it can harm economic growth. In practice, determining what counts as insider trading is not always easy but it typically involves misappropriating sensitive information.

The rules which govern insider trading are complex and vary from country to country, as does the extent of enforcement. The definition of who is an 'insider' in one jurisdiction can be broad and may cover not only insiders themselves but also any persons related to them, such as brokers, associates and even family members. For example, the European Union adopted legislation that sanctions insider trading and all member states agreed to introduce maximum prison sentences of at least four years for serious cases of market manipulation and insider dealing. In India, insider trading is an offence defined as when someone with access to non-public, price-sensitive information about the securities of a company subscribes, buys, sells or deals, or agrees to do so or counsels another to do so as principal or agent (Wherry and Schor, 2015). The penalty for insider trading is imprisonment, which may extend to five years. In the US insider trading is illegal and there are many famous cases in which people were convicted, sentenced and imprisoned.

Whistleblowing

Unlike some of the unethical behaviours listed here, whistleblowing is often seen as both ethical and unethical, and it is often used as an example of an ethical dilemma. It happens when an employee informs the public about the illegal or immoral behaviour of an employer or organisation (Miceli et al., 2013).

Whistleblowers may inform on unethical or illegal behaviour internally or externally. Internally, the accusations are brought to the attention of other people within the accused organisation, such as the CEO or other people with the power to act. Externally, allegations are brought to light by contacting a third party outside of an accused organisation, such as the government, police or the media.

Whistleblowers frequently act out of a sense of professional responsibility and an act of whistleblowing can be presumed to be morally justified if the whistleblower:

- has a moral motive
- has executed internal channels first (if possible)
- has compelling evidence
- has carefully analysed the dangers
- has some chance of success.

Some people see whistleblowers as selfless martyrs, scarificing themselves for public interest and organisational accountability. However, others view them as 'traitors' or 'defectors'. Some even accuse them of solely pursuing personal glory and fame, or view their behaviour as motivated by greed.

While in many countries there is legal protection and support organisations for whistleblowers, research shows that over time most of them suffer a hit to their career and often to their personal life as well (Miceli et al., 2013). While whistleblowers may win a civil case in court, they often find it very difficult to ever find another job. This demonstrates that many companies see whistleblowers as disloyal employees instead of as people who strengthen the ethical behaviour and boundaries of the organisation.

It is therefore difficult to start blowing the whistle when you find that the company you work for is involved in unethical or illegal conduct. On the one hand, your values and moral compass tell you that you have the responsibility to do something, particularly when such unethical behaviour could cause harm to many people. On the other hand, you want to be loyal to your employer. You know that you are damned if you do and damned if you don't, and it is usually a choice between two evils, leading to an ethical dilemma, as will be discussed below.

One famous case of whistleblowing in business is the story of Sherron Watkins, the former Vice President of Enron Corporation. Watkins knew about the accounting irregularities within Enron but decided to only blow the whistle internally, alerting the then-CEO, Kenneth Lay, via an email that Enron 'might implode in a wave of accounting scandals'. Watkins has been criticised for not reporting the fraud to government authorities and for not speaking up publicly sooner about her concerns. In 2002 *Forbes Magazine* wrote: 'Sherron Watkins had whistle, but blew it', blaming her for knowing only too well what was going on at Enron but not doing anything substantial to stop it, and in fact warning the CEO so the CEO would not get caught (Ackman, 2002).

Ethical dilemmas and decision making

Reading through this chapter, it is clear that doing the right thing is not always easy and a serious challenge occurs when a person needs to decide between two important values, knowing that whichever path is chosen, some negative consequences may occur. Choosing between right and wrong is not so difficult; choosing between two rights or two equally undesirable alternatives is what defines a dilemma. Dilemma means a 'double proposition' in Greek, being a problem with two possible solutions, neither of which is unambiguously acceptable or preferable (Ford and Richardson, 1994).

An ethical dilemma is a complex situation that often involves an apparent mental conflict between two or more moral imperatives, in which to obey one would result in defying the other (Velasquez and Velazquez, 2002). As such, ethical dilemmas can be broadly defined as situations in which two or more values are in conflict. As was explained above, we have a set of values that could be colliding in certain situations. Choosing action according to one value and not another could also indicate and define our value hierarchy, and yet sometimes making such a choice seems impossible.

To illustrate, euthanasia is the source of many ethical debates as there is a need to choose between two undesirable choices: letting someone suffer greatly with no hope of recovery and taking their life, both of which collide with many people's personal, cultural and religious values. While some countries have made an ethical decision to allow it, signalling that the quality of life is more important than the length of life and that people have the right to die in certain circumstances, these decisions are not easily made and usually lead to wide public debate. This is also the reason some countries decided against legalising euthanasia or did not decide on it (and not deciding on an ethical dilemma is also a decision).

Ethical dilemmas can occur in every aspect of business conduct, although there are several business areas in which such dilemmas are more common: finance and accounting, human resources, customer confidence, conflicts of interest, and the use of corporate resources. For example, when downsizing, who should be made redundant may present an ethical dilemma. Imagine you are in a position to decide between an older person who wouldn't be able to get another job, a pregnant woman (assuming it is legal in your country to dismiss a pregnant woman) and a young person who holds great promise for the company but was the last one to join. Who would you dismiss and why? What is the dilemma here?

In order to resolve the dilemma, it is important to gather as much information as possible, reflect on personal and organisational values, consult with as many people as possible and evaluate the possible solutions (including the costs, benefits and impacts of each) before and after the decision is made. Using everything presented in this chapter – sources of moral behaviour, values, philosophical approaches and business ethics in practice – could help you address such an ethical dilemma.

The four paradigms approach

Kidder (1995) offered a four paradigm approach that demonstrates how most ethical dilemmas are usually a battle between four sets of alternatives, as detailed in Figure 4.7.

The first set of colliding values is truth and loyalty. On the one hand, it is important to speak the truth: it builds self-respect and professionalism. On the other hand, people feel loyal to the company and its employees. This can be exemplified by a dilemma around whether or not to speak the truth about the company when you know there will be negative consequences for doing so for both the employees and the company.

Figure 4.7   The four paradigms approach (based on Kidder, 1995)

The next set of colliding values is between the individual and the community. On one hand, people are worried about their own careers, success and ambition. On the other hand, there is a responsibility towards the general community and society, which also refers to our sense of social justice. This was probably the dilemma the designers of Ford Pinto faced: between saving people's lives and advancing their own careers and success.

Thirdly, there is short term versus long term. Often, people feel that benefiting short-term results and profits could harm the long-term reputation and success of the company, or even the long-term results for society and the planet. This is why so many companies are still not environmentally sustainable, as they cannot find a solution to address both long-term and short-term issues.

Fourthly, ethical dilemmas can occur between justice and mercy. You know that one of your colleagues is doing wrong but if you disclose the colleague's behaviour to your manager your colleague may lose their job. In addition, your colleague is an older person that battles with cancer. Do you opt for justice or mercy?

Ethical decision-making frameworks

In addition to all the tools detailed here, there are some suitable frameworks that can be used to make ethical decisions and for solving dilemmas. As can be seen in Figure 4.8, Hartman et al. (2014) offered a decision-making model for business ethics, which includes six important stages.

Figure 4.8   The ethical decision-making model (based on Hartman et al., 2014)

In addition, Hartman and her colleagues suggest using business ethics concepts and theories and considering the following aspects (in brackets is a suggestion of related topics discussed in this chapter):

1. The consequences of the decision (consequentialist theories)
2. Duties, rights and principles (deontology)
3. The legal system (legal responsibility; see Carroll, 1991)
4. Professional duties and codes of conduct
5. Which principles are most obligatory? (hierarchy of values)
6. Treating people fairly, with respect for autonomy and equality (Kant)
7. Implications for personal integrity and character (virtue ethics)
8. Personal values, principles and purpose (Schwartz)

This is a good summary that demonstrates the importance and applicability of everything that you have learned in this chapter.

In addition, some companies develop their own frameworks to help people evaluate their decision making and how ethical it is. In the opening case study of this chapter, you saw that the Commonwealth Bank provides all employees with such a framework. When the bank employees make any decision or take any action that could be ethically difficult, they are required to assess it according to its consistency with the company's policies (Policies); its acceptability by relevant laws and regulation (Legal); its conformity with the company's values (Universal); and its satisfaction of own values and ethics (Self). Other ethical frameworks include additional questions such as: 'Would I be comfortable if the decision were published in the newspaper?' That is a good way to think about and weigh up solutions to an ethical dilemma.

Creating and leading an ethical organisation: Managerial tools

As ethical conduct and decision making are an essential part of strategic CSR, it is important to embed ethical behaviour in the organisational culture among all employees and to apply it to and implement it in the ongoing activities of the company. Doing so requires time and effort, but the benefits of ethical management, as were detailed throughout this chapter, are worthwhile. Furthermore, it is the right thing to do. By now, you should be able to see how this captures the two philosophical approaches to business ethics.

Practical guide to enhancing workplace ethics

There are many actions that companies, managers and all employees can take to build an organisational culture of ethics. Some were detailed in this chapter and some were not, but we will summarise them all in Table 4.1.

Table 4.1 **Actions for building a culture of ethics**

Action	Description
Values	<ul><li>Set a clear mission statement of the organisation that is purpose driven.</li><li>Involve your employees in developing a strong and relevant set of values.</li><li>Ensure corporate values are well known (by all employees and preferably by other stakeholders), meaningful, specific, authentic and acted upon.</li></ul>
Policies	<ul><li>Develop clear policies and procedures for ethical behaviour and decision making.</li><li>Introduce a professional or organisational code of conduct that is specific and practical.</li><li>Present guidelines to solving ethical dilemmas, which can be general (such as the PLUS tool) or specific to common dilemmas your employees face.</li></ul>
Human resource management	<ul><li>Recruit and select employees that are aligned with the company's values and ethos. Ask potential employees about their values and congruence with the company values.</li></ul>

(Continued)

Table 4.1   (Continued)

Action	Description
	• Train all employees in ethical behaviour and decision making. Use the knowledge from this chapter and share it with your employees. Present all employees with common ethical dilemmas and practise solving them before they actually occur.
	• Reward and recognise employees that demonstrate ethical behaviour, work in alignment with the company's values and ethos and exhibit ethical conduct (see the case study on how CBA rewards according to its values).
Ethical leadership	• Lead by example. It is essential that the leadership of the organisation walk the talk and exhibit ethical values and behaviour while acting upon the company's values.
	• Discuss the company's values and ethics at every opportunity (see the opening case study).
Support systems	• Appoint ethics officers and ethical committees to which people can turn to consult on ethical dilemmas or report on unethical behaviour.
	• Create open channels of communication in which people are supported when ethical issues arise.
Organisational culture	• Celebrate the company's values and ethos and communicate them to internal and external stakeholders.
	• Go beyond legal and risk averse: avoid immoral behaviour even if there is a legal loophole that allows you to do it.
	• Discuss your approach to ethics: is it utilitarian or duty-based?

Summary

Ethical behaviour is an essential part of strategic CSR and yet companies, managers and even CSR scholars often overlook it. It is essential for business students and managers to learn what business ethics is, what the ethical approaches are and how to implement ethics in the workplace so they can lead ethical organisations.

Ethics is the study of right and wrong, duty and obligation, moral norms, individual character and responsibility. Being professionally ethical requires acting in accordance with the accepted principles that govern the conduct of a profession. Specifically, business ethics is one form of applied ethics that examines ethical principles and moral or ethical problems that arise in a business environment. It includes ethical behaviour in the workplace as well as ethical decision making.

Being ethical in business requires an understanding of what morality personally means and what the sources of moral behaviour in the workplace are (such as etiquette, values, codes of conduct, ethics and law). Strong and acted-upon corporate values inspire employees to act ethically. It is also important to recruit employees that exhibit value congruence with the company.

In this chapter, three main ethical approaches were presented. Firstly, deontology is the normative ethical position that judges the morality of an action based on the action's motivation and intent based on some rules (non-consequentialist theory). Secondly, utilitarianism is the moral theory according to which we should act in ways that produce the most pleasure or happiness for the greatest number of people affected by our actions (consequentialist theory). Thirdly, virtue ethics emphasises virtues of mind and character and examines what a moral person is.

In addition, it is important to remember that what is considered moral and ethical in one culture and society may not be so in other cultures. Ethical relativism is the view according to which moral norms derive their ultimate justification from the customs of the society in which they occur. It combines knowledge of ethics with anthropology and assists us in being more culturally sensitive.

While these philosophical approaches create the foundations for business ethics, managers and employees need to know what it actually means to be ethical in the workplace. For this reason, the chapter detailed ethical and unethical behaviour and explained how to implement the former and avoid the latter, such as fraud, conflict of interest and whistleblowing.

In addition, an important part of business ethics is ethical decision making and solving ethical dilemmas. Ethical dilemmas are complex situations that involve a mental conflict between two or more moral imperatives, in which to obey one would be to defy the other. There are often colliding values and the choice is between two evils. Frameworks for understanding and solving ethical dilemmas can assist managers and employees who face them. Such frameworks and other practical tools detailed here could help in leading an ethical organisation, particularly for those who desire to do so because it is the right thing to do.

General questions

1. Business ethics is an essential part of strategic CSR and yet it does not receive adequate positive attention. Why do you think this is so?
2. Why is business ethics so important? Answer this from the deontological and utilitarian points of view.
3. What is the difference between ethical and legal? Can you think of an illegal action that is moral and an immoral action that is legal? What does it mean for business conduct that legal and ethical are not synonyms?
4. What makes great corporate values? Search for a company with a set of values that you find inspirational. What makes it so? What does it teach you about corporate values?
5. Is it possible for an organisation to be ethical or unethical or is it only the people who work in it and manage it that can be described as such?
6. Do you think humans have a natural tendency to be ethical or unethical? Based on your answer, what can companies do to ensure ethical behaviour?
7. Have you ever been confronted with an ethical dilemma, in or outside the workplace? Why was it a dilemma? Which values collided? How did you solve it? What did you learn from it?

Key definitions

- Ethics is the study of right and wrong, duty and obligation, moral norms, individual character and responsibility.
- Business ethics is a form of applied ethics that examines ethical principles and problems that arise in a business environment.
- Morality in the narrow sense is the moral principles or rules that govern the conduct of individuals in their relation to others. In a broader sense, morality is the values, ideals and aspirations that influence the decisions and lifestyles of individuals and entire societies.
- Values are stable, evaluative beliefs that guide our preferences and behaviour. They are desirable, trans-situational goals that vary in importance as guiding principles in people's lives (Schwartz, 1992).
- Value congruence is the extent to which individuals can behave at work in ways consistent with their own personal values and self-image (Edwards and Cable, 2009).
- Deontological ethics or deontology is the normative ethical position that judges the morality of an action based on the action's motivation and intent based on some rules.
- Utilitarian ethics or utilitarianism is the moral theory according to which we should act in ways that produce the most pleasure or happiness for the greatest number of people affected by our actions.
- Virtue ethics refers to normative ethical theories, which emphasise virtues of mind and character and examine what a moral person is.
- Ethical relativism is the view according to which moral norms derive their ultimate justification from the customs of the society in which they occur.
- An ethical dilemma is a complex situation that often involves an apparent mental conflict between two or more moral imperatives, in which to obey one would result in defying the other (Kidder, 1995).

References

Ackman, D. (2002) Sherron Watkins had whistle, but blew it. Available at: www.forbes.com/2002/02/14/0214watkins.html (Accessed: 5 May 2017)

Adams, J. S. (1963) 'Towards an understanding of inequity', *The Journal of Abnormal and Social Psychology*, 67(5): 422.

Albrecht, W. S., Wernz, G. W. and Williams, T. L. (1995) *Fraud: Bringing light to the dark side of business*. Burr Ridge, IL: Irwin Professional.

Banaji, M. R., Bazerman, M. H. and Chugh, D. (2003) 'How (un)ethical are you?' *Harvard Business Review*, 56.

Bentham, J. (1789) *An introduction to the principles of morals and legislation*. London: T. Payne & Son.

Carroll, A. B. (1991) 'The pyramid of corporate social responsibility: Toward the moral management of organizational stakeholders', *Business Horizons*, 34(4): 39–48.

Christensen, L. J., Peirce, E., Hartman, L. P., Hoffman, W. M. and Carrier, J. (2007) 'Ethics, CSR, and sustainability education in the *Financial Times* top 50 global business schools: Baseline data and future research directions', *Journal of Business Ethics*, 73(4): 347–68.

Dunning, J. H. (2003) *Making globalisation good: The moral challenges of global capitalism*. Oxford: Oxford University Press.

Edwards, J. R. and Cable, D. M. (2009) 'The value of value congruence', *Journal of Applied Psychology*, 94(3): 654–77.

Ford, R. C. and Richardson, W. D. (1994) 'Ethical decision making: A review of the empirical literature', *Journal of Business Ethics*, 13(3): 205–21.

Gates, G., Ewing, J., Russell, K. and Watkins, D. (2017) 'How Volkswagen's "defeat devices" worked', *New York Times*, 16 March. Available at: www.bbc.com/news/business-34519184 (Accessed: 19 October 2017)

Goodpaster, K. E. (1994) 'Work, spirituality, and the moral point of view', *International Journal of Value-Based Management*, 7(1): 49–62.

Hartman, L. P., DesJardins, J. R. and MacDonald, C. (2014) *Business ethics: Decision making for personal integrity and social responsibility*. New York: McGraw-Hill.

Haski-Leventhal, D. (2009) 'Altruism and volunteerism: The perceptions of altruism in four disciplines and their impact on the study of volunteerism', *Journal for the Theory of Social Behaviour*, 39(3): 271–99.

Joyner, B. E. and Payne, D. (2002) 'Evolution and implementation: A study of values, business ethics and corporate social responsibility', *Journal of Business Ethics*, 41(4): 297–311.

Kant, I. (1797) *The metaphysics of morals*. Cambridge: Cambridge University Press.

Kant, I. and Ellington, J. W. (1994) *Ethical philosophy: The complete texts of grounding for the metaphysics of morals, and metaphysical principles of virtue, part II of The metaphysics of morals, with On a supposed right to lie because of philanthropic concerns*. Indianapolis, IN: Hackett.

Kellerson, H. (1998) 'The ILO Declaration of 1998 on fundamental principles and rights: A challenge for the future', *International Labour Review*, 137(2): 223.

Kidder, R. M. (1995) *How good people make tough choices*. New York: Morrow.

Ladenson, R. (1995) *Ford Pinto case*. Chicago, IL: Center for the Study of Ethics in the Professions, Illinois Institute of Technology.

Lencioni, P. M. (2002) 'Make your values mean something', *Harvard Business Review*, 80(7): 113–17.

Miceli, M. P., Near, J. P. and Dworkin, T. M. (2013) *Whistle-blowing in organizations*. Hove: Psychology Press.

Mill, J. S. (1863) *Utilitarianism*. London: Parker, Son & Bourn.

Pearson, R. (1989) 'Beyond ethical relativism in public relations: Co-orientation, rules, and the idea of communication symmetry', *Journal of Public Relations Research*, 1(1–4): 67–86.

Schwartz, S. H. (1992) 'Universals in the content and structure of values: Theoretical advances and empirical tests in 20 countries', *Advances in Experimental Social Psychology*, 25: 1–65.

Shaw, W. H. and Barry, V. (2015) *Moral issues in business*. Boston, MA: Cengage Learning.

Sidgwick, H. (1907) *The methods of ethics*. Indianapolis, IN: Hackett.

Simons, T. (2002) 'Behavioral integrity: The perceived alignment between managers' words and deeds as a research focus', *Organization Science*, 13(1): 18–35.

Valentine, S., Godkin, L. and Lucero, M. (2002) 'Ethical context, organizational commitment, and person–organization fit', *Journal of Business Ethics*, 41(4): 349–60.

Velasquez, M. G. and Velazquez, M. (2002) *Business ethics: Concepts and cases* (Vol. 111). Upper Saddle River, NJ: Prentice Hall.

Verschoor, C. C. (2007) 'Siemens AG is the latest fallen ethics idol', *Strategic Finance*, 11–14.

Wherry, F. F. and Schor, J. B. (2015) *The SAGE Encyclopedia of Economics and Society*. London: Sage.

Whetstone, J. T. (2001) 'How virtue fits within business ethics', *Journal of Business Ethics*, 33(2): 101–14.

Further reading and links

College Binary YouTube Channel (2009) Three-minute philosophy – Immanuel Kant. Available at: www.youtube.com/watch?v=xwOCmJevigw (Accessed: 9 May 2017)

Kretchmer, H. (2015) 'The man who discovered the Volkswagen emissions scandal', *BBC News*, 13 October. Available at: www.bbc.com/news/business-34519184 (Accessed: 19 October 2017)

Schiermeier, Q. (2015) 'The science behind the Volkswagen emissions scandal', *Nature News*, 24 September.

Stead, W. E., Worrell, D. L. and Stead, J. G. (1990) 'An integrative model for understanding and managing ethical behavior in business organizations', *Journal of Business Ethics*, 9(3): 233–42.

TEDxLondonBusinessSchool (2015) The social responsibility of business. Available at: www.youtube.com/watch?v=Z5KZhm19EO0 (Accessed: 9 May 2017)

TEDxPresidio (2012) Creating ethical culture in business. Available at: www.youtube.com/watch?v=wzicXbnmllc (Accessed: 9 May 2017)

TEDxSMU (2015) Legal vs. ethical ability: A crisis of leadership and culture. Available at: www.youtube.com/watch?v=veXPk4Zeqtk (Accessed: 9 May 2017)

Trevino, L. K., Hartman, L. P. and Brown, M. (2000) 'Moral person and moral manager: How executives develop a reputation for ethical leadership', *California Management Review*, 42(4): 128–42.

Valentine, S., Godkin, L. and Lucero, M. (2002) 'Ethical context, organizational commitment, and person–organization fit', *Journal of Business Ethics*, 41(4): 349–60.

Watkins, S. (2003) 'Former Enron vice president Sherron Watkins on the Enron collapse', *The Academy of Management Executive*, 17(4): 119–25.

Watkins, S. (2003) 'Ethical conflicts at Enron: Moral responsibility in corporate capitalism', *California Management Review*, 45(4): 6–19.

Environmental Sustainability: The Role of Business in Sustainable Development

5

Main topics

Case study

Learning outcomes

By the end of this chapter, students should be able to:

- explain the urgency of environmental sustainability for business and society
- define sustainability, sustainable development and the sustainable development goals

(Continued)

- detail why the natural environment is a major stakeholder of business and the business case for sustainability
- describe the green and blue economy as innovative solutions towards sustainability
- detail how business can address environmental issues through the supply chain
- apply sustainability theories and models to managerial practice.

Case study   Patagonia – sustainability as a main stakeholder

Founded by Yvon Chouinard in 1973, Patagonia is an American outdoor apparel company based in California. From the outset, the company was an instrument of social responsibility and sustainability. In Chouinard's view, business was to blame for many of the world's social, economic and environmental problems. At the same time, Chouinard believed that if done right, business has the potential to address these problems and inspire positive change. For Chouinard, Patagonia as a business was an opportunity to challenge the conventional way of doing business and showcase responsible business making (Chouinard and Stanley, 2013).

'For some companies, such as Patagonia, the environment or planet is the ultimate stakeholder' (Mackey and Sisodia, 2014: 139). Patagonia's sustainability efforts are recognised globally. In 2008, Patagonia won the 'Eco Brand of the Year' and the best award at the Volvo Ecodesign Forum. It is a member of several environmental movements and is a certified B Corp, which means it is a for-profit company certified by the non-profit B Lab and meets rigorous standards of social and environmental performance, accountability and transparency.

How does Patagonia conduct responsible business? Firstly, it focuses on sustainability alongside its profit motives, and views profit as a means to continue providing value to its customers and to advance its social and environmental causes. The company takes the life cycle of its products very seriously, from conception to ultimate disposal. Its current CEO, Casey Sheahen, said: 'we take complete responsibility for every product we make. We repair our products, recycle them, help people sell them when they no longer need them. We are trying to protect all of embodied energy in the product and not have it end up in a landfill' (Mackey and Sisodia, 2014: 139). Patagonia commits 1 per cent of its total sales or 10 per cent of its profit, whichever is higher, to environmental causes.

Patagonia often features environmental issues in its catalogues and marketing campaigns. In addition to large global initiatives, Patagonia also supports several smaller initiatives such as the Conservation Alliance, the World Trout Initiative and the Organic Exchange, to name a few. Recently, the company launched a worldwide recycling initiative, titled 'The Common Threads Recycling Program', and has a site devoted to the explanation of its recycling process name 'The Footprint Chronicles'. Another initiative, 'Worn Wear', was launched as a six-week repair tour involving more than 10,000 participants, aiming to prolong the useful life of its clothing and change people's relationships with their stuff.

The way Patagonia does its business is consistent with its philosophy of sustainability and responsibility. Patagonia strives to be sustainable throughout its supply chain. The company prioritises ethical and business standards equally. It only works with factories that follow certain social and environmental practices as well as maintaining quality standards, financial stability and fair pricing. To achieve this, Patagonia audits all its factories and subcontractors and its social/environmental responsibility team can veto a decision to work with a new factory based on the factory not complying with Patagonia's sustainability standards. The company also demonstrates its environmental consciousness in the design and construction of its own facilities. Patagonia uses sustainable and recycled materials and the products it sells are designed to be high-quality and endurable.

Patagonia's true care for the environment was well illustrated in the 2014 Climate March, during which 400,000 people took to the streets of New York City to march for climate change action. Inspired by a request from employees in its New York City stores to join the march, Patagonia supported the march and even kept its retail doors in the city shut till 3 pm to ensure that its employees could participate in the march. Patagonia also invited customers to its Upper West Side store for a pre-march community gathering with representatives from several environmental activist organisations (Protect Our Winters, Catskill Mountainkeeper, New Yorkers Against Fracking and HeadCount) and supported the gathering with giveaways, coffee and bagels before taking to the streets.

The company funds extensive employee volunteering. As part of an environmental internship programme, employees are allowed up to two months away from their regular roles to work for environmental groups of their choice, while their pay and other benefits continue. In 2015, 34 employees, 12 stores, one work group and one department took advantage of the programme and put in almost 10,000 volunteer hours for 43 organisations, including The Renewable Resources Foundation and Pocono Environmental Education Center. The company also provides environmental grants to

(Continued)

groups working worldwide to restore forests and rivers, mitigate the effects of climate change and educate the public in 18 countries.

Questions for reflection

1. How does Patagonia's business philosophy drive the company's strategy?
2. Examining the supply chain of Patagonia, from resource extraction to the disposal of products by end users, what does Patagonia do at each step of the chain to ensure sustainability?
3. Watch this video titled 'Why Patagonia tells customers its coats are toxic': www. youtube.com/watch?v=0bk7SwcpdSc
4. Is it smart business to disclose negative impacts? Why?
5. Examine Patagonia's CSR and the aforementioned elements of strategic CSR. Is this an example of strategic CSR? How so?
6. Examine Patagonia's Environmental and Social Initiatives Report (2015). Which stakeholders has the company been engaging?
7. If you were a senior manager at Patagonia, what initiative(s) would you suggest for the next financial year?

Bibliography

Chouinard, Y. and Stanley, V. (2013) *The responsible company: What we've learned from Patagonia's first 40 years*. Ventura, CA: Patagonia.

Fowler, S. J. and Hope, C. (2007) 'Incorporating sustainable business practices into company strategy', *Business Strategy and the Environment*, 16(1): 26–38.

Mackey, J. and Sisodia, R. (2014) *Conscious capitalism: Liberating the heroic spirit of business*. Cambridge, MA: Harvard Business Review Press.

Reinhardt, F. L, Casadesus-Masanell, R. and Kim, H. (2010) Patagonia. Available at: https://ssrn.com/abstract=2025181 (Accessed: 4 March 2017)

Links

Patagonia (2015) Environmental and Social Initiatives Report. Available at: www.patagonia.com/on/demandware.static/Sites-patagonia-us-Site/Library-Sites-PatagoniaShared/en_US/PDF-US/patagonia-enviro-initiatives-2015.pdf (Accessed: 19 October 2017)

Patagonia (2017) Corporate responsibility. Available at: www.patagonia.com/corporate-responsibility.html (Accessed: 4 March 2017)

Patagonia YouTube Channel (2009) What's done in our name? Social responsibility and Patagonia supply chain. Available at: www.youtube.com/watch?v=S6sEWDRhhxs (Accessed: 4 March 2017)

Patagonia YouTube Channel (2011) Patagonia corporate responsibility. Available at: www.youtube.com/watch?v=WexueycQgmY (Accessed: 4 March 2017)

Introduction: Environmental sustainability – an urgent matter

> When the last tree is cut, when the last river has been poisoned, when the last fish has been caught, then we will find out that we can't eat any money. (Native American saying)

Three decades ago, most business organisations did not hear of sustainability issues or climate change, let alone conceive these as a business matter. However, as the discourse about urgent matters regarding our planet started to become more vocal and as tools and solutions were offered so that business can become more sustainable, this approach has changed (at least to some extent) for most business organisations. Many firms started examining their contribution to the damage done and how they can avoid further harm. Some companies have moved beyond the do-less-harm approach to making genuine contributions to environmental sustainability.

While not all companies and business leaders are yet on board, it is clear to many others that this is an urgent matter. According to the Living Planet Report (WWF, 2004), we are currently using 150 per cent of the capacity of the Earth to meet our global needs and it is estimated to grow to 200 per cent in a few decades. It is clear that this cannot be sustained over the long term and that if we continue to do so, we jeopardise our planet and there is no Planet B. If businesses keep manufacturing regardless of air and water pollution, climate change will continue to affect us and the Earth's temperature will rise to extremely dangerous levels. Many environmental experts warn that this is our very last chance to do something on the burning matter of environmental sustainability. It doesn't take much to understand that without a planet, we have no business, money and shareholder value.

It should be noted that when speaking about sustainability in the context of CSR, some refer to the triple bottom line, or the three aspects of sustainability: financial, social and environmental (Colbert and Kurucz, 2007). However, in this chapter we refer to the sustainability of our natural environment, as this is what the term is most commonly used for.

Sustainability defined

There are many definitions of sustainability. From the point of view of CSR, corporate sustainability can be seen as business operations that can be continued over the long term without degrading the ecological environment (Werther and Chandler, 2011). This is the definition adopted in strategic CSR literature and it is not difficult to see how this definition of sustainability relates to some key aspects of it: sustainability needs to be part of every business decision and operation, embedded in the entire value chain with a long-term perspective in mind.

Indeed, for too long two business approaches undermined environmental sustainability. The first one was *short-term* thinking: making profit in the next quarter without thinking what it means for the next year, let alone future generations. The other one was the issue of *externalities*: when a company pollutes the local river, it is someone else's business to clean it up (usually the government) or to suffer from it (usually the local community). The definition above shows that in order to really be sustainable, both these approaches need to thoroughly change. If they do, the natural environment then becomes a key issue and stakeholder for businesses, and no business decision is made without a consideration of the environmental impact.

A commonly used and cited definition of sustainability or sustainable development was offered in 1987 in the Brundtland Commission report (also known as 'Our Common Future') and by the World Commission on Economic Development (WCED). This definition of sustainability, which was later adopted by the World Business Council for Sustainable Development, is: 'meeting the needs of the present without compromising the ability of future generations to meet their own needs' (Brundtland, 1987: 16).

This is not just a theoretical and practical definition but also a call for a change of mindset. We started this chapter with a Native American quote about eating money, and there is another one that says 'We do not inherit the Earth from our ancestors but borrow it from our children'. When perceiving our planet not as something that we own and use but rather as what we must pass on to the next generations in a way that will meet *their* needs, it changes the way that we think, feel and behave towards the environment, including the way we conduct our business. It is a shift from a sense of entitlement to a sense of duty and responsibility.

It should be noted that the first part of this definition is about meeting the needs of the present. This is not only about the consumption needs of current generations and not just the needs of the developed world. To meet the needs of the present, we need to ensure equity to people of all backgrounds and from all countries, including basic needs (safe water, healthy food, clean air, shelter and safety, etc.) as well as growth needs, such as self-fulfilment.

The second part of this definition is about the ability of future generations to meet their own needs. If we continue using 1.5 Earths every year, it will not be long before the natural and other resources of the Earth will terminate and future generations everywhere will not have their basic needs met. The notion that our planet has a finite capacity to absorb or to process the results of human and industrial activities is at the core of the definition of sustainable development, as was noted by the WCED (1987: 8):

> Humanity has the ability to make development sustainable to ensure that it meets the needs of the present without compromising the ability of future generations to meet their own needs. The concept of sustainable development does imply limits – not

absolute limits but limitations imposed by the present state of technology and social organization on environmental resources and by the ability of the biosphere to absorb the effects of human activities.

The Brundtland report (1987) included several additional terms that should be explained, such as eco-justice, eco-efficiency and eco-effectiveness. *Eco-justice* refers to the fairness applied to the distribution of benefits that accrue from the development of the world's resources (unlike what was done in the long history of colonialism and by many companies to date).

Eco-efficiency seeks to reduce the intake of raw materials and energy, reduce the emission of all types into the air, water and soil, and result in a smaller amount of waste. This concept may appeal to many businesses that want to reduce costs and be more efficient in this value chain since it makes both business and environmental sense. It is about 'getting more for less', creating products using fewer resources as well as renewable and more efficient energy, and so on. As we have already demonstrated in previous chapters, many companies have risen to this challenge in the last few decades and are now finding innovative ways to create products and packages, sell them and have consumers use them in a more sustainable and efficient way.

Eco-effectiveness, on the other hand, focuses on reducing consumption, and may therefore seem less attractive to today's business, at least initially. While eco-efficiency puts most of the responsibility on the firm to reduce waste and pollution while manufacturing goods, this concept passes a lot of the responsibility to the consumer – if we consume fewer goods, stop replacing usable goods with new ones, we will inch closer to achieving our sustainability goals. However, eco-effectiveness also has an impact on business, as companies will need to stop driving consumers to buy as much as possible and may therefore see a decline in income.

The most common way to push consumers to buy more, which undermines eco-effectiveness, is through *planned and perceived obsolescence* (Bulow, 1986). Planned obsolescence, the strategy of designing products with low durability to induce repeat purchases from consumers, became very popular in the 1970s and 1980s as a way to sell more and increase profit. It is essentially the production of goods with uneconomically short useful lives. If in previous generations people bought furniture and appliances to last for a lifetime or decades, companies now make goods that will only last a few years. Television sets, for example, are often designed to start having technical problems after several years so that consumers will have to buy a new television and contribute to the profit maximisation of the firm. Another way of creating planned obsolescence is to offer new technology that will make the old appliance obsolescent, even if it is still working. Furthermore, through sophisticated marketing, companies create perceived obsolescence, which is about the desire to upgrade perfectly working products. Even if our old TV works just fine and matches all the new technology, we still desire (or are manipulated to desire) a new set every few years because our old one is no longer the most fashionable, the biggest or the best on the market. The whole concept of 'fashion' is based on 'perceived obsolescence' and, consequently, the average American throws away about 30 kg (65 pounds) of clothing per year, and along with other textiles that get tossed, like sheets and bedding, the total comes out to 14.3 million tons of textile waste per year. Despite this, planned and perceived obsolescence are still taught in business schools as good business practices and only recently have people started raising the ethical and environmental issues with such practices.

Questions for discussion

1. Using the case of Patagonia and the definitions above, would you say that the company is sustainable? In what way? How can it improve?
2. Can you find an example of a company that calls for eco-effectiveness and fights the ideas of planned and perceived obsolescence? Why is it so hard to find one?

Sustainable development and global goals

Since the Brundtland Commission Report (1987), much attention has been given to sustainability and sustainable development, particularly from governments and the UN. The Commission called for three pillars of action: economic growth, environmental protection and social equality. Most countries and businesses focus on the first pillar. As a result, the protection of the environment and social equality have suffered. There is a need to shift the focus of society and to achieve this a whole system approach is required. To facilitate this, the Brundtland Commission called for an international meeting to take place where more concrete initiatives and goals could be mapped out. The UN took a leadership role in facilitating the way forward.

In 1992, 189 states joined forces to address climate change in an international summit in Rio de Janeiro, known as the Earth Summit, organised by the UN. As part of this summit, the heads of states committed to the UN Framework Convention on Climate Change (UNFCCC), aimed at addressing climate change by limiting average global temperature increases and to cope with the 'inevitable impacts' of climate change. Over 190 states reconfirmed this commitment along with that of the sustainable development goals 20 years later in the Rio+20 Summit at the same place.

By 1995, many countries had collaborated to strengthen the global response to climate change, and, two years later, adopted the Kyoto Protocol. The Kyoto Protocol legally binds developed countries to emission reduction targets. The Protocol's first commitment period started in 2008 and ended in 2012. The second commitment period began on 1 January 2013 and will end in 2020. There are currently 197 Parties to the Convention and 192 Parties to the Kyoto Protocol. Notably, the US would not sign the Kyoto Protocol, fearing it would harm its economic development, and several states followed (Australia, Japan, China, South Korea and India), although some have changed course since.

In 2015, the Paris Agreement was adopted, marking the latest step in the evolution of the UN climate change regime and building on the work undertaken under the Convention. The Paris Agreement charts a new course in the global effort to combat climate change, as it seeks to accelerate and intensify the actions and investment needed for a sustainable and low-carbon future. Its central aim is to strengthen the global response to the threat of climate change by keeping the global temperature rise this century well below 2 degrees Celsius above pre-industrial levels, and to pursue efforts to limit the temperature increase even further to 1.5 degrees Celsius. The Agreement also aims to strengthen the ability of countries, including developing ones, to deal with the impacts of climate change. The US initially committed to the Paris Agreement, however the Trump administration withdrew this commitment in 2017.

In September 2015, the UN General Assembly formally adopted the 'universal, integrated and transformative' 2030 Agenda for Sustainable Development (UN, 2015a), a set of 17 sustainable development goals (SDGs). The SDGs replace the millennium development goals (UN, 2015b) and are to be implemented and achieved in every country from the year 2016 to 2030. The 17 SDGs (and their 169 related targets) offer a massive leap forward, including 'no poverty' and 'zero hunger' by 2030 (see Figure 5.1). If the MDGs were perceived as mainly a governmental task, the key to the SDGs was that in order to achieve them we must have the collaboration of government, the business sector, civil society and individuals. All these players are encouraged to focus simultaneously on the three dimensions of sustainable development: economic prosperity, social inclusion and environmental sustainability (Griggs et al., 2013). The particular role of business was clearly communicated by the UN:

> We call on all businesses to apply their creativity and innovation to solving sustainable development challenges. We will foster a dynamic and well-functioning business sector, while protecting labour rights and environmental and health standards. (UN, 2015a)

The first role of business is to avoid creating further problems and harm for governments to fix (externalities), such as pollution, contribution to poverty, human rights violation and even support for war and conflict. Strategic CSR means that each company chooses the SDGs that are most aligned with its core operations, capabilities and what it stands for and strives to help achieve these goals in collaboration with other entities.

Figure 5.1   The 17 sustainable development goals (UN, 2015b)

The SDGs not only present business with duties, but also with great opportunities (Haski-Leventhal, 2016). Strong markets and thriving societies go hand in hand. If the SDGs are achieved and with them the end of poverty, hunger and war, the prospects for doing business and building markets will likewise be stronger. Some SDGs are more relevant to doing business than others. For example, Goal 8 (SDG-8, Decent work and economic growth) is particularly relevant to the business sector: 'to promote sustained, inclusive and sustainable economic growth, full and productive employment and decent work for all.' Similarly, SDG-9 (Sustainable industrialisation) is about significantly raising 'industry's share of employment and gross domestic product, and double its share in least developed countries.' In addition, some SDGs are important to specific industries: SDG-3 (Health) is more relevant to pharmaceutical and healthcare companies, while SDG-6 (Water and sanitation) is more relevant to the food and beverage industry and to companies addressing sanitation through bodycare products. It is important for companies in the world to know the 17 goals and to decide which ones to focus on as part of their own strategic CSR.

There are some outstanding examples of business commitment to the SDGs. Unilever took an active part in forming the SDGs and in creating commitment to achieve them, organising an extensive business consultation process and ensuring the voice of business was included when the SDGs were designed. According to Unilever, the SDGs set out a positive vision for the future of our world, but require collective action to achieve this future (Unilever, 2017). Unilever states that it is in the interests of business, government and civil society alike to accelerate progress towards this vision. Based on Unilever's bodycare brands (such as Dove), the company collaborated with a range of organisations to campaign for the sixth goal (SDG-6, Clean water and sanitation), including measurement of hand-washing with soap facilities. CEO Paul Polman said:

> There is no business case for enduring poverty. We have an opportunity to unlock trillions of dollars through new markets, investments and innovation. But to do so, we must challenge our current practices and address poverty, inequality and environmental challenges. Every business will benefit from operating in a more equitable, resilient world if we achieve the sustainable development goals. (Unilever, 2016)

Nestlé committed to several SDGs, which are aligned with its core business, namely Nutrition (SDG-2), Water (SDG-6) and Climate (SDG-13) (Nestlé, 2016). On its website, Nestlé details how it is going to achieve each of these goals. For example, regarding water, Nestlé promised to achieve water efficiency and sustainability across its operations; advocate for effective water policies and stewardship; treat the water it discharges effectively; engage with suppliers; and raise awareness on water conservation as well as improve access to water and sanitation. Nestlé is also contributing to SDG-2 (Zero hunger), achieving food security, improving nutrition and promoting more sustainable agriculture. The company pledged to introduce micronutrient-fortified foods, to roll out its Rural Development Framework to understand farmers' needs, and to implement sustainable sourcing and preserve natural capital.

EXERCISE

Find another company that is committed to the SDGs:

1. Which goals did they choose and how are they going to achieve them?
2. Is this choice logical from a strategic CSR point of view?
3. Which other goals should they focus on and how can they be achieved using the company's current resources?
4. Are there any other global goals that business needs to consider?

The environment as a major stakeholder

If strategic CSR is about working with a broad set of stakeholders, then understanding that the environment is a major stakeholder is essential for the sustainability levels of a responsible corporation. Since stakeholders are defined as those who affect and are being affected by the company, it becomes clear how the natural environment is a major stakeholder. Without a thriving environment, most companies would not have the required resources to manufacture and create the goods they sell or use. With a rapid increase in natural disasters and extreme weather conditions, the environment affects business operations in every corner of world. Munich Re, a German insurance company, estimated that the effects of climate change could cost companies US$300 billion each year due to weather damage, pollution, industrial and agricultural losses (Werther and Chandler, 2011). On the other hand, it is also easy to see how current business operations and individual consumption affect the planet, and many scientists argue that industry contributes to climate change.

Climate change has now become an accepted fact. It is defined as 'a change in global or regional climate patterns, in particular a change apparent from the mid to late 20th century onwards and attributed largely to the increased levels of atmospheric carbon dioxide produced by the use of fossil fuels' (OECD, 2017). It should be clarified that the science on climate change is not disputed. Climate change scepticism and the claim that there is not enough evidence to connect it to human activities were addressed by the Fourth Assessment Report by the IPCC in 2007 (Parry et al., 2007), although some people still insist on disputing the science and facts on climate change, mainly around the consequences of climate change, the role of humans in this change and their ability to reverse the trend. However, it is undeniable that humans pollute water, air and land; deforest large parts of the Earth (thus contributing to desertification); bring many fauna and flora to levels of extinction and endangerment – and the list goes on and on. Not all of these actions are to serve the profit goals of business, but much of it is. For example, research shows that raising animals for food consumes more than half of all the water used in the US (PETA, 2017). It takes up to 20,000 litres of water to produce one kilogram of meat (Butler, 2013). This is before we begin talking about all the other negative impacts of the 'meat industry', such as the destruction of soil, pollution, animal welfare and human health.

In their book *Conscious Capitalism*, Mackey and Sisodia (2014) argue that business must take full responsibility for its environmental impact and start devising innovative ways to alleviate that impact. Business needs not accept trade-offs for the environment, but rather minimise its environmental impact as sustainability can improve the business relationship with consumers, create employee engagement and lower costs. To do so, the firm needs to study the full impact it has on the environment, take responsibility for its actions and fix related issues. Once the negative impact is clear, it is impossible to ignore it and the natural environment becomes a major stakeholder.

Whole Foods Market does sell meat but acknowledges the negative impact of such products. Since it perceives both the environment and its consumers to be major stakeholders, the company tries to address the needs of both and balance consumer demand for meat with its environmental responsibility. To do so, the company educates its customers and team members about the health advantages of plant-based diets; it strives to sell meat that is not sourced from factory farms and to improve animal welfare. Its Global Animal Partnership certifies each product by the level of animal welfare from 1 (no crates/cages) to 6 (animal welfare is the primary concern), keeping consumers informed (for more information, see www. globalanimalpartnership.org). When the environment becomes a major stakeholder of a company, it usually follows that the supply chain and the entire business operation needs to change. It requires a shift from a trade-off approach to a holistic approach in which the environment is part of the Win[6] scheme of the company (see Chapter 3).

In 2007, Marks & Spencer (M&S), the British multinational retailer, replaced its corporate responsibility with 'Plan A', 'because there is no Plan B' for this planet. The plan covered 100 commitments over five years to address the key social and environmental challenges facing the company and the world: climate change, waste, sustainable raw materials, fair partnership and health. The ambitious goal was for M&S to become carbon-neutral; send no waste to landfills; extend sustainable sourcing; help improve the lives of people in their supply chain; and help customers and employees live a healthier lifestyle. In 2012, M&S was awarded the European Business Award for the Environment by the European Union for Plan A. Recently, the company introduced Plan A 2020, which consists of 100 new, revised and existing commitments, with the ultimate goal of becoming 'the world's most sustainable major retailer' (Wills, 2011). In launching Plan A, M&S signalled how the environment is a major stakeholder and showed that a holistic approach throughout the entire supply chain is possible if the company works with all its stakeholders to achieve this: 'We work with our partners, employees and customers around the world to achieve our goals.' As M&S says on its website: 'By sourcing responsibly, reducing waste and helping communities, we believe we can do our bit to help protect the planet.'

The green, blue and circular economy

Circular economy

The circular economy is defined as 'a regenerative system in which resource input and waste, emission, and energy leakage are minimised by slowing, closing and narrowing material and energy loops. This can be achieved through long-lasting design, maintenance, repair, reuse, remanufacturing, refurbishing, and recycling' (Geissdoerfer et al., 2017: 764).

According to Stahel (2016), the circular economy system is designed to create environmental, economic and social value by eliminating waste from the life cycle of a product. It aims to shift away from the linear take-make-dispose economy, which generates high levels of energy, labour and material waste. Instead, circular economy promotes maintaining the highest utility and value of materials through restorative and regenerative design. This a closed-loop approach to the economy, which focuses on the optimal use of resources, enhancing the use and preservation of natural capital and limiting risks by effectively managing finite resource stocks and renewable energy (Webster, 2015). The circular economy differentiates between technical and biological cycles: it urges the production of goods such that the technical and biological components can be separated and recirculated in the supply chain and consequently the manufacturing process (Webster, 2015).

Lacy and Rutqvist (2015) explained that in the circular economy, customers are considered as users who should return products to companies when they are done using them. Instead of owning, users return, lease, rent or share their products and return them back into the supply chain. The circular economy harnesses all the potential it can from materials through predetermined processes. Through natural or controlled processes, biological materials are broken down to extract energy and nutrients from them. This business model is designed to rid the world of one-time-use products.

The circular economy is based on three principles for action (Ellen Macarthur Foundation, 2012):

1. *Natural capital should be preserved* and enhanced by exerting control on limited stocks of natural resources and utilising resources that are renewable in nature. The circular system selects materials and resources that are likely to perform better and have multiple uses to allow for regeneration of those resources.
2. *Using resources optimally* so that products and their components can be of high utility both in the technical and the biological stages of a product's life cycle. It is a zero-waste economy, which ensures that biological materials such as paper or fabric are composted and technical materials such as alloys, polymers and other man-made materials are of high-quality design so that they can be retained and reused.
3. *Fostering system effectiveness* by encouraging industries to design products in a way that they can be remanufactured, refurbished and recycled for use in a new supply chain and circulated continuously in the economy. This places great importance on access to food, shelter, education, mobility and human utility. The preservation of land, air and water along with efforts to reduce pollution and manage climate change are important components of this economy.

The green economy

The term *green economy* was first coined in a pioneering 1989 report for the British government by a group of leading environmental economists, entitled *Blueprint for a Green Economy* (Pearce et al., 1989). According to the UN Environment

Programme (UNEP), the green economy is defined as 'one that results in improved human well-being and social equity, while significantly reducing environmental risks and ecological scarcities' (Allen and Clouth, 2012: 9). In its simplest expression, a green economy can be thought of as one which 'is low carbon, resource efficient and socially inclusive' (Allen and Clouth, 2012: 9). Its aim is reducing environmental risks and ecological scarcities as well as sustainable development without degrading the environment. In addition to an emphasis on the natural environment, the green economy also emphasises the importance of justice, fairness and equity, and it is therefore often referred to as an 'inclusive green economy'.

In 2010, the UN General Assembly agreed that green economy in the context of sustainable development and poverty eradication would form one of the two specific themes for Rio+20 (resolution 64/236; see UN, 2015a). This led to vast international attention on green economy and related concepts and the publication of numerous reports and other literature aiming to further define and demystify the concept.

From a practical point of view, in a green economy the growth in income and employment is driven by public and private investments that reduce carbon emissions and pollution, enhance energy and resource efficiency and prevent the loss of biodiversity and ecosystem services. These investments need to be catalysed and supported by targeted public expenditure, policy reforms and regulation changes. This development path should maintain, enhance and, where necessary, rebuild natural capital as a critical economic asset and source of public benefits, especially for poor people whose livelihoods and security depend strongly on nature.

The green economy is based on six main sectors (Miller et al., 2010):

1. Renewable energy
2. Green buildings
3. Sustainable transport
4. Water management
5. Waste management
6. Land management

As can be seen in Figure 5.2, green companies and institutions fall into two broad categories:

1. The *core green economy* contains companies and institutions that provide products and services that conserve resources, offer clean alternatives, reduce pollution and repurpose waste. Companies that sell and install solar panel systems and automobile companies that offer hybrid cars allow other companies to be more sustainable.
2. The *adaptive green economy* encompasses companies and institutions that undertake serious efforts to 'green' their products, processes and supply chains

(making them more environmentally sustainable). These companies adopt a philosophy that green operations are good for business and good for the future. Adaptive green companies and institutions drive demand in the core green economy.

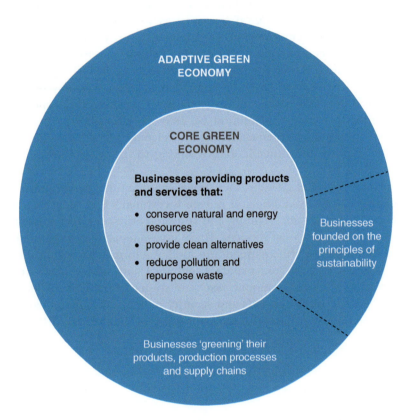

Figure 5.2   **The green economy (based on Collaborative Economics, 2010)**

The blue economy

In 2010, Gunter Pauli published a book that offered a leap forward from the green economy: *The Blue Economy: 10 years, 100 innovations, 100 million jobs*. The idea of the blue economy (based on the notion that the sky, oceans and Earth from space all look blue) is that we can shift from scarcity to abundance with what is locally available. The main argument is that some of the sustainable issues and solutions mentioned in this chapter have trade-offs. Renewable energy is not yet affordable to all and there are some issues with current technology that might affect people's health and the environment. Instead, the blue economy offers circular solutions with no negative trade-offs.

Pauli (2010) argues that there are potential benefits in connecting and combining seemingly disparate environmental problems with open-source scientific solutions based upon physical processes common in the natural world to create solutions that hold environmental and financial benefits. He claims that we can change the way in which we run industrial processes and tackle environmental issues, by using simpler and cleaner technologies. Instead of only focusing on cutting costs and reducing harm, the blue economy focuses on value creation and economic benefits via job creation and reduced energy use while benefiting the communities involved.

There are 200 cases on The Blue Economy website to inspire business people and entrepreneurs to work according to their principles. One such case is the innovative use of coffee waste to grow mushrooms. This reduces waste, creates food and offers sustainability and financial gain at the same time.

EXERCISE

Read one of the cases at www.theblueeconomy.org:

1. How does this example demonstrate the principles of the blue economy?
2. Does it offer a holistic and circular solution to an environmental issue?
3. What benefits and limitations of the blue economy concept do you perceive after reading the case?

The business case for sustainability

Often, when executive management discusses sustainability in the firm boardroom, people only talk about how costly it is to become more sustainable. In a world in which profit maximisation is often still the main motive, it is essential to develop a business case for sustainability, demonstrating that sustainability is also good for the financial bottom line, in order to gain broader consent for action.

There is an emerging body of research showing a relationship between CSR and sustainability with improved financial performance. It should be noted that not all studies find a positive correlation between the two and that some that do find such correlation cannot prove the causality (or direction) of such correlation. It is possible that companies that are socially and environmentally responsible perform better financially, but it is also possible that companies that do well financially tend to contribute more to society and adopt sustainable practices. However, there is now accumulating evidence that such a relationship does exist. One longitudinal study, for example, showed that companies with high levels of sustainability performed

4.8 per cent higher on the stock market compared to companies with low sustainability (Eccles et al., 2012).

One of the explanations for the connection between sustainability and financial performance is reduced costs. Eco-efficiency could lead, in the medium and long term, to major reductions in costs. When companies shift to renewable energy, green buildings and reduced waste, costs decline. When companies strive to use the resources needed for manufacturing (such as timber or water) in the most efficient way possible, they also increase their profitability. When companies such as IKEA innovate on flat packaging, the result is not only reduced costs of transportation (both to the company as well as to consumers) but also lower carbon emissions. Some of these solutions require upfront spending, but they usually provide an excellent return on investment within a few years or less.

Even when companies seem to be taking additional responsibilities to ensure their sustainability, they may gain from it financially. For example, Puma and H&M allow customers to return old shoes and apparel to their shops, so that some of the products can be recycled while others can be donated. In doing so, these companies take responsibility at the far end of the supply chain. It does increase costs to offer such services to their customers (and the environment), but in doing so companies also incentivise people to come back to the shops and consumers might use this opportunity to buy new products.

According to the financial literature, markets respond to signals, which are interpreted from information about the activity of a company (Blowfield and Murray, 2014). Companies strive to signal to the market that they are stable, trustworthy and profitable and that their products are of high quality and good value for money. On the other end, the markets signal to companies what the market demands are, what kind of products they would like to consume and from which kind of companies. There is an emerging view that the signals from the markets have changed and that consumers are increasingly demanding that companies be more sustainable. In addition to products that are good value for money, many consumers also want to choose to buy products that are good for the environment and for society. As such, some (like Porter and Kramer, 2006) argue that unless companies are environmentally sustainable (as well as socially responsible), they will lose their competitive advantage in the future. Data show that the next generation of consumers (particularly people who were born in the 1990s onwards) will not tolerate unsustainable corporate behaviour as much as previous generations (Agenti, 2016).

Sustainability as the key driver of innovation

Most environmental challenges cannot be solved unless business fully commits to addressing them through entrepreneurial innovations. (Mackey and Sisodia, 2014: 146)

According to a *Harvard Business Review* article, 'Why sustainability is now the key driver of innovation' (Nidumolu et al., 2009), sustainability does not pose the burden on bottom lines that many executives believe it does. Studying 30 companies for several years, the authors conclude that 'sustainability is a mother lode of organisational and technological innovations' and that becoming environmentally friendly may result in innovative ways to lower costs and increase revenues.

1
- Viewing compliance (e.g. legislation and regulation) as an opportunity to grow and innovate

2
- Creating sustainable supply chains

3
- Sustainable design thinking for products and services

4
- New and sustainable business models

5
- Leading innovative (next-practice) platforms

Figure 5.3   **The five-stage process of becoming sustainable (based on Nidumolu et al., 2009)**

Sustainability should be a touchstone for all innovation because in the future, only companies that make sustainability a goal will achieve competitive advantage. Sustainability can lead to innovative business models as well as products, technologies and processes. Becoming sustainable is a five-stage process (see Figure 5.3) and each stage has its own challenges, required competencies and innovation opportunities. For example, Stage 4 is 'Developing new business models'. The central challenge for business is to find novel ways of delivering and capturing value, which will change the basis of competition. To do this, business needs the capacity to understand and address the new consumer demand. The related innovation opportunities are new delivery technologies that change value-chain relationships in significant ways; monetisation models that relate to services rather than products; and business models that combine digital and physical infrastructures.

Sustainability business tools: Sustainable managerial practices

In order to meet the needs of the present generation without compromising the ability of future generations to meet their own needs, companies need to adopt sustainable managerial practices throughout the entire value chain. It starts with a shift in mindset, with a change of leadership approach and in company culture and values. However, it is ultimately about what the company actually does. Based on the CSR congruence model we saw in Chapter 2 (Haski-Leventhal et al., 2017), it is about sustainable identity and behaviour combined.

The journey to sustainability

How does a company become more sustainable? An article in the *MIT Sloan Management Review*, 'How to become a sustainable company' (Eccles et al., 2012), shows that only a few companies are born with a broad-based commitment to sustainability (although this has been changing in recent years) while the rest need to work hard to get there. Developing a sustainable company requires leadership commitment, an ability to engage with multiple stakeholders along the value chain, widespread employee engagement and disciplined mechanisms for execution. The authors' research shows that sustainable organisations are effective at engaging with external stakeholders and employees, have cultures that are based on innovation and trust and have a track record of implementing large-scale change.

Based on over 200 interviews in 60 companies, the study identified two interconnected stages in becoming more sustainable (see Figure 5.4). Stage One, 'Reframing identity', is composed of two elements: leadership commitment (which will be discussed further in Chapter 6) and external engagement of stakeholders, such as non-profit organisations. This stage is necessary but not sufficient to implement a long-lasting change towards sustainability. Stage Two, 'Codifying new identity', is therefore required and includes building internal support for the new identity through employee engagement (to be discussed in Chapter 7) and mechanisms for execution. The two stages should, over time, result in a strong culture and identity as well as in sustainable behaviour and positive outcomes for the company, employees and the environment.

Sustainable supply chain management

A supply chain is a system of organisations, people, activities, information and resources involved in moving a product or services from supplier to customer (Seuring and Müller, 2008). It encompasses all activities associated with the flow and transformation of goods from the raw materials stage (extraction) through to the end user, as well as the associated information flows. In short, supply chain

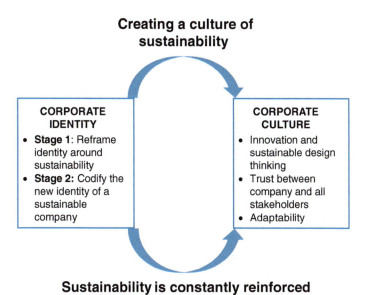

Creating a culture of sustainability

CORPORATE IDENTITY
- **Stage 1**: Reframe identity around sustainability
- **Stage 2**: Codify the new identity of a sustainable company

CORPORATE CULTURE
- Innovation and sustainable design thinking
- Trust between company and all stakeholders
- Adaptability

Sustainability is constantly reinforced

Figure 5.4   How to become a sustainable company (based on Eccles et al., 2012)

activities involve the transformation of natural resources into a finished product that is delivered to the end customer. It usually contains 5 to 6 main components and each of these can be high or low on sustainability levels: raw materials and resources are extracted from earth (usually through suppliers); manufacturing (with employees and suppliers); distribution (to direct customer, often retail companies); customer (selling the products); and use by end consumer (like individual households) and waste.

Seuring and Müller (2008) define sustainable supply chain management as the management of material, information and capital flows as well as cooperation among companies along the supply chain, while taking goals from all three dimensions of sustainable development (i.e. economic, environmental and social) into account. Supply chain sustainability examines an organisation's supply chain or logistics network in terms of environmental, risk and waste costs. Sustainable supply chain management has to take into account a wider range of issues and therefore look at a longer part of the supply chain while considering all stakeholders.

There is a growing need and demand, by both business and its stakeholders, for integrating environmentally-sound mechanisms into each stage of the supply chain. To be more sustainable, companies need to examine the entire supply chain and take responsibility for what occurs at each stage and the impact of that on the environment and society. For example, when examining raw materials, companies can assess the direct and indirect damage of current resource-extraction practices; find alternative resources with a lesser environmental impact; replace resources with new ones; use fast, renewable resources; and work with internal and external stakeholders to achieve a positive impact on everyone involved.

To illustrate, we will use the case of palm oil. Originally from Western Africa, palm oil trees now grow in other parts of the world, and 85 per cent of all palm oil globally produced and exported comes from Indonesia and Malaysia. It is a very popular resource for the food industry, but for many decades it was not extracted sustainably, resulting in enormous damage to bio-diversity. The vast usage of palm tree oil by industry is related to deforestation, habitat degradation, climate change, animal cruelty and indigenous rights abuses in the countries where it is produced. According to the World Wildlife Fund (WWF), an area equal to 300 football fields of rainforest is cleared each *hour* to produce palm oil (Kim, 2015). This large-scale deforestation is endangering many species, including orangutans and Sumatran tigers, and if nothing changes they could become extinct in the wild in the next decade. The palm oil industry has been linked to major human rights violations, including child labour in remote areas of Indonesia and Malaysia. Strong pressure by advocate groups, consumers and even some business leaders, led to the development of sustainable palm oil. To develop a sustainable supply chain, corporations need to understand the impact of each resource they use, such as palm oil, and find alternatives, such as using other oil types or certified sustainable palm oil. Sustainable palm oil is an approach to oil palm agriculture that aims to produce palm oil without causing deforestation or harming people. There is certified sustainable palm oil (CSPO) available to those companies and consumers that want to be more sustainable.

Palm oil is just one example of one resource in one stage of the supply chain that can become more sustainable. The same process needs to be applied to all resources used and all other stages as well. Examining the environmental and societal impact of manufacturing is another important issue for sustainability. How much does a company pollute the air, water and soil while manufacturing? Are toxic chemicals being used in the process, which could harm the environment and people's health during that stage and in all the following stages? Is manufacturing done while maintaining people's rights, safety and wellbeing, even when the factories are in a developing country? Is the factory using clean energy? There are sustainable and responsible ways to address these issues and to create sustainable and safe products in a sustainable way.

Similarly, a sustainable supply chain strives to make the distribution of goods more environmentally friendly. The longer the distance between raw materials, manufacturing and the customer, the less sustainable the supply chain is. This is why some restaurants and hotels, aiming to be more sustainable, have shifted to buying mainly local produce. Working with local farmers means fewer carbon emissions due to transportation and also a thriving local community. Investment in alternative modes of transportation, such as the use of canals and airships, can play an important role in helping companies reduce the cost and environmental impact of their deliveries. Another innovative solution is to create products that can be distributed more efficiently. The aforementioned flat packaging used by IKEA helps make its supply chain more sustainable. Alternatively, some companies avoid distribution all together: Amazon's Kindle, e-books and audio books lead to a reduction in the manufacturing and distribution of paper books, which mainly use trees to print.

Some companies see their responsibility over supply chain sustainability as terminating with the customer and end user, but others find innovative ways to reduce the negative environmental impact even at these end stages. In sophisticated supply chain systems, used products may re-enter the supply chain at any point where residual value is recyclable. Allowing customers to return old products so they can be recycled or donated, creating sustainable packaging to decrease environmental harm for the end user and developing products which require less energy are some examples which are already being implemented by some companies to ensure sustainability throughout the entire supply chain.

Recycle, downcycle and upcycle

When thinking about what happens to products after they leave the factory and the warehouse, after they are sold to the retail company and end up in people's houses, and particularly after they are no longer needed, the concept of recycling comes to mind. Some companies offer recycling options to consumers while others might only encourage buyers to dispose responsibly. It should be noted that putting a package or a product in the recycling bin does not always mean that it gets recycled. *Recycling* is the process of converting waste materials into reusable materials and objects. Taking an empty plastic bottle, for example, recycling means that the plastic is being used to create new bottles. However, in most cases the plastic bottles we recycle end up in someone else's backyard (usually somewhere in the developing world) or are *downcycled* and used in lower-quality products. There are innovative solutions nowadays that actually *upcycle* the empty bottles to build houses or create irrigation systems.

A key requirement of successful sustainable supply chains is collaboration with all stakeholders, including competitors. One great example is sharing distribution with other companies to reduce waste by avoiding half-empty vehicles being sent out and deliveries going to the same address in several trucks. Such practices of collaboration are not widespread, due to a fear of loss of commercial control by working with others, but in many places such collaboration platforms are emerging.

In 2008, The Future Laboratory Ltd produced a ranking system for the different levels of sustainability being achieved by organisations. This was called the 'Three tiers of sustainability' (The Green Market Oracle, 2011):

Tier 1: Getting the basics right. This is the base level and is the stage at which the majority of organisations are. Companies employ simple measures such as switching lights and PCs off when left idle, recycling paper and using greener forms of travel, with the purpose of reducing their day-to-day carbon footprint.

Tier 2: Learning to think sustainably. At this level, companies start to embed sustainability throughout the supply chain operations. Companies tend to achieve this level when they assess their impact across a local range of operations. In terms of the supply chain, this could involve supplier management, product design, manufacturing rationalisation and distribution optimisation.

Tier 3: The science of sustainability. Here, companies use auditing and benchmarks to provide a framework for governing sustainable supply chain operations. The framework gives clarity around the environmental impact and allows supply chain agility, flexibility and cost in the supply chain network. At this level, companies collaborate with others, including competitors and the government, to achieve higher levels of sustainability for all.

Working with all stakeholders to increase sustainability

The various stakeholder groups that were discussed in Chapter 3 could all be related to higher levels of sustainability and sustainable supply chain management. Often, companies start their sustainability journey due to stakeholder pressure, such as from not-for-profit organisations and consumers. For example, apparel distributors such as Nike, Disney, Levi-Strauss, Benetton, Adidas and C&A have been blamed in recent years for problems occurring during the production of their clothing, including contamination of the environment and inhumane working conditions. Sometimes scrutinised companies change their practices to become more sustainable, while others take another step forward and work closely with their stakeholders to achieve higher levels of sustainability. Such companies listen to stakeholders' concerns, learn from them and educate them in order to sustain their practices.

Moving beyond reacting to stakeholder pressure, sustainable companies work with their stakeholders, effectively communicating what they are doing in the area of sustainability, and educate stakeholders to achieve great results for sustainability. Whole Foods Market educates its customers about the sustainable supply chain, a healthy plant-based diet (which is also more environmentally friendly) and animal rights. Since consumers choose this brand because of its sustainability, it is important to constantly communicate sustainability practices.

In addition to consumers, many companies work with and educate their employees, without whom the shift towards sustainability would be limited. Employees have a remarkable role to play in helping the company become more sustainable through their actions both in the workplace, outside the workplace and in between. The way employees get to and from work, what they eat and drink while they are there and the energy they consume or save all have a huge impact on their employer's sustainability levels. That is why some companies, such as the Australian bank Westpac, work with their employees to educate them about issues and offer solutions, including sustainable transport (i.e. enabling car sharing and encouraging public transport usage) and a sustainable lifestyle at home.

Businesses have the resources, knowledge, skills and networks to support a more sustainable world. If these were harnessed to work with governments, not-for-profit organisations, competitors, consumers and employees, we could see a substantial change in business conduct, a reduction in global carbon emissions and a better future for the next generations.

Summary

The sustainability of our natural environment has become an important and urgent matter not only to governments and the UN but to many companies as well. As sustainability is about meeting the needs of the present without compromising the ability of future generations to meet their own needs, a long-term and holistic approach is required for business to become more sustainable. It involves the creation of a fair and just world in which humans, animals and the natural environment are all treated with respect and not as a means to a profitable end.

There is a growing expectation of business to take part in sustainable development and to help governments and the UN achieve the global SDGs, including ending poverty and hunger and addressing climate change. From a strategic CSR point of view, companies need to know the SDGs and identify those that they are most capable of addressing. To do so, there is a need for a shift in the mindset of business. The natural environment should not be perceived as something to be extracted and used as much as possible in order to maximise profit. Instead, it should be viewed as a major stakeholder. Without our planet there is no business and there is no Planet B or Plan B.

As part of the movement towards sustainability, the concept of circular economy has emerged. It is a regenerative system in which resource input and waste, emission and energy leakage are minimised by slowing, closing and narrowing material and energy loops. At the same time, the green economy has also become a popular concept to describe companies that help to increase sustainability by offering sustainable solutions to the whole industry. However, there is some criticism about the trade-offs of such solutions, which is why the concept of the blue economy was developed, to offer a holistic solution without negative side-effects for the environment.

When examining the business case for sustainability, sustainable companies are not just doing good, they are also doing well. They usually have better financial and organisational performance, due to reduced costs (at least in the long run), higher motivation of employees and brand loyalty of those consumers who care about our planet enough to make informed choices. Sustainability can also enhance the company's innovation and collaboration and lead to remarkable products and services.

To achieve all of the above benefits, business needs to change actions and practices. Companies can become more sustainable as they change their culture and work with internal and external stakeholders. Sustaining the entire supply chain is not an easy task, but only such a long-term and holistic approach can result in genuine sustainability. Working with, communicating with and educating consumers, employees and other stakeholders is the key to achieving these important goals.

General questions

1. Are profit maximisation and sustainability contradictory terms? If so, what can be done to change this?
2. The definition of sustainability incorporates an intergenerational connection. How does it impact sustainability perceptions and actions? What else does this definition imply for business management?
3. Whose role is it to ensure sustainability in general and the impact of business on sustainability in particular?
4. In addition to the role of governments and business, what can individuals do to increase business sustainability?
5. Do you think multinational corporations understand the importance and urgency of sustainability? If so, how do you see the change? If not, why not and what can be done about it?
6. If you were striving to make the company you work for more sustainable, how would you present the case for sustainability to the executive management?

Key definitions

- Sustainability is business operations that can be continued over the long term without degrading the ecological environment (Werther and Chandler, 2011).
- Sustainability is meeting the needs of the present without compromising the ability of future generations to meet their own needs (World Business Council for Sustainable Development, based on Brundtland, 1987).
- Eco-efficiency seeks to reduce the intake of raw materials and energy, reduce the emission of all types into the air, water and soil, and results in a smaller amount of waste. Eco-effectiveness, on the other hand, focuses on reducing consumption (Brundtland, 1987).
- Planned obsolescence is the strategy of designing products with low durability to induce repeat purchases from consumers (Bulow, 1986).

- Sustainable development is the process of meeting human development goals while sustaining the ability of natural systems to continue to provide the natural resources and ecosystem services upon which the economy and society depend. It is the organising principle for sustaining finite resources necessary to provide for the needs of future generations of life on the planet (Brundtland, 1987).
- Climate change is a change in global or regional climate patterns, in particular a change apparent from the mid- to late 20th century onwards and attributed largely to the increased levels of atmospheric carbon dioxide produced by the use of fossil fuels (OECD, 2017).
- A circular economy is a regenerative system in which resource input and waste, emission and energy leakage are minimised by slowing, closing and narrowing material and energy loops. This can be achieved through long-lasting design, maintenance, repair, reuse, remanufacturing, refurbishing and recycling (Geissdoerfer et al., 2017).
- The green economy is defined as one that results in improved human wellbeing and social equity while significantly reducing environmental risks and ecological scarcities (Allen and Clouth, 2012).
- The blue economy is the shift from scarcity to abundance with what is locally available (Pauli, 2010).
- A supply chain is a system of organisations, people, activities, information and resources involved in moving a product or service from supplier to customer. It encompasses all activities associated with the flow and transformation of goods from the raw materials stage (extraction) through to the end user, as well as the associated information flows (Seuring and Müller, 2008).
- Sustainable supply chain management is the management of material, information and capital flows as well as cooperation among companies along the supply chain, while taking goals from all three dimensions of sustainable development (i.e. economic, environmental and social) into account which are derived from customer and stakeholder requirements (Seuring and Müller, 2008).
- Recycling is the process of converting waste materials into reusable materials and objects. Downcycling is the recycling of waste in cases where the recycled material is of lower quality and functionality than the original material. Upcycling, also known as creative reuse, is the process of transforming by-products, waste materials, useless or unwanted products into new materials or products of better quality or for better environmental value.

References

Agenti, P. A. (2016) *Corporate responsibility.* Singapore: Sage.

Allen, C. and Clouth, S. (2012) *A guidebook to the green economy.* New York: UN Division for Sustainable Development.

Blowfield, M. and Murray, A. (2014) *Corporate responsibility.* Oxford: Oxford University Press.

Brundtland, G. H. (1987) *Report of the World Commission on Environment and Development: 'Our common future'*. New York: United Nations.

Bulow, J. (1986) 'An economic theory of planned obsolescence', *The Quarterly Journal of Economics*, 101: 729–50.

Butler, S. (2013) 'Plan A integral to the rebirth of Marks & Spencer, says CEO', *The Guardian*, 7 July. Available at: www.theguardian.com/business/2013/jul/07/plan-a-integral-rebirth-marks-spencer (Accessed: 19 May 2017)

Colbert, B. A. and Kurucz, E. C. (2007) 'Three conceptions of triple bottom line business sustainability and the role for HRM', *People and Strategy*, 30(1): 21–9.

Collaborative Economics (2010) The St. Louis region green economy profile. Available at: www.globalurban.org/StLouisGreenEconomy.pdf (Accessed: 19 May 2017)

Eccles, R. G., Perkins, K. M. and Serafeim, G. (2012) 'How to become a sustainable company', *MIT Sloan Management Review*, 53(4): 42–50.

Ellen Macarthur Foundation (2012) *Towards the circular economy*. Cowes: Ellen Macarthur Foundation Publishing.

Geissdoerfer, M., Savaget, P., Bocken, N. M. P. and Hultink, E. J. (2017) 'The circular economy – A new sustainability paradigm?', *Journal of Cleaner Production*, 143: 757–68.

Griggs, D., Stafford-Smith, M., Gaffney, O., Rockström, J., Öhman, M. C., Shyamsundar, P., Steffen, W., Glaser, G., Kanie, N. and Noble, I. (2013) 'Policy: Sustainable development goals for people and planet', *Nature*, 495(7441): 305–7.

Haski-Leventhal, D. (2016) 'Sustainable development goals: The roles and opportunities for business', *European Financial Review*, Oct.–Nov.: 48–50.

Haski-Leventhal, D., Roza, L. and Meijs, L. C. (2017) 'Congruence in corporate social responsibility: Connecting the identity and behaviour of employers and employees', *Journal of Business Ethics*, 143(1): 35–51.

Kim, G. J. (2015) Palm oil: Issues of climate change and human rights violation. Available at: www.huffingtonpost.com/grace-jisun-kim/palm-oil-issues-of-climat_b_7007354.html (Accessed: 19 May 2017)

Lacy, P. and Rutqvist, J. (2015) *Waste to wealth: The circular economy advantage*. New York: Palgrave Macmillan.

Mackey, J. and Sisodia, R. (2014) *Conscious capitalism: Liberating the heroic spirit of business*. Boston, MA: Harvard Business Review Press.

Miller, P. F., Vandome, A. F. and McBrewster, J. (2010) *Green economy*. Saarbrücken: VDM.

Nestlé (2016) Nestlé in society: Creating shared value and meeting our commitments 2016. Available at: www.nestle.com/asset-library/documents/library/documents/corporate_social_responsibility/nestle-in-society-summary-report-2016-en.pdf (Accessed: 19 May 2017)

Nidumolu, R., Prahalad, C. K. and Rangaswami, M. R. (2009) 'Why sustainability is now the key driver of innovation', *Harvard Business Review*, 87(9): 56–64.

OECD (2017) Glossary of statistical terms. Available at: https://stats.oecd.org/glossary/detail.asp?ID=360 (Accessed: 17 May 2017)

Parry, M., Canziani, O., Palutikof, J., van der Linden, P. and Hanson, C. (2007) *Climate change 2007: Impacts, adaption and vulnerability*. Cambridge: Cambridge University Press.

Pauli, G. A. (2010) *The blue economy: 10 years, 100 innovations, 100 million jobs*. Brookline, MA: Paradigm.

Pearce, D. W., Markandya, A. and Barbier, E. (1989) *Blueprint for a green economy* (Vol. 1). London: Earthscan.

PETA (2017) How does eating meat harm the environment? Available at: www.peta.org/about-peta/faq/how-does-eating-meat-harm-the-environment (Accessed: 14 May 2017)

Porter, M. and Kramer, M. (2006) 'Strategy and society', *Harvard Business Review*, 84(12): 42–56.

Seuring, S. and Müller, M. (2008) 'From a literature review to a conceptual framework for sustainable supply chain management', *Journal of Cleaner Production*, 16(15): 1699–1710.

Stahel, W. R. (2016) 'The circular economy', *Nature*, 531(7595): 435–8.

The Green Market Oracle (2011) Available at: www.thegreenmarketoracle.com/2011/10/three-tiers-of-sustainability-and.html (Accessed: 19 May 2017)

Unilever (2016) Available at: www.unilever.com/news/news-and- features/?monthfrom=1&yearfrom=2001&monthto=12&yearto=2017&type=featuredArticle (Accessed: 19 May 2017)

Unilever (2017) UN global goals for sustainable development. Available at: www.unilever.com/sustainable-living/our-approach-to-reporting/un-global-goals-for-sustainable-development (Accessed: 19 May 2017)

United Nations (UN) (2015a) *Transforming our world: The 2030 Agenda for Sustainable Development*. Resolution A/RES/70/1. New York: United Nations.

United Nations (UN) (2015b) The millennium development goals report 2015. Available at: www.un.org/millenniumgoals/2015_MDG_Report/pdf/MDG%202015%20rev%20(July%201).pdf (Accessed: 28 September 2017)

Webster, K. (2015) *The circular economy: A wealth of flows* (2nd edn). Cowes: Ellen Macarthur Foundation Publishing.

Werther, W. B. and Chandler, D. (2011) *Strategic corporate social responsibility: Stakeholders in a global environment* (2nd edn). Thousand Oaks, CA: Sage.

Wills, J. (2011) 'M&S – wholly embracing staff in plan to become the world's most sustainable retailer', *The Guardian*, 26 May. Available at: www.theguardian.com/sustainable-business/staff-plan-worlds-sustainable-retailer (Accessed: 19 May 2017)

World Commission on Environment and Development (WCED) (1987) *Our Common Future*. New York: Oxford University Press.

WWF (2004) Living Planet Report 2004: The alarming state of the world. Available at: http://wwf.panda.org/about_our_earth/all_publications/living_planet_report_timeline/lpr_2004 (Accessed: 19 October 2017)

Further reading and links

Butler, S. (2013) 'Plan A integral to the rebirth of Marks & Spencer, says CEO', *The Guardian*, 7 July. Available at: www.theguardian.com/business/2013/jul/07/plan-a-integral-rebirth-marks-spencer (Accessed: 19 May 2017)

Carter, C. R. and Rogers, D. S. (2008) 'A framework of sustainable supply chain management: Moving toward new theory', *International Journal of Physical Distribution & Logistics Management*, 38(5): 360–87.

Epstein, M. J. and Roy, M. J. (2001) 'Sustainability in action: Identifying and measuring the key performance drivers', *Long Range Planning*, 34(5): 585–604.

Fitzherbert, E. B., Struebig, M. J., Morel, A., Danielsen, F., Brühl, C. A., Donald, P. F. and Phalan, B. (2008) 'How will oil palm expansion affect biodiversity?', *Trends in Ecology & Evolution*, 23(10): 538–45.

IKEA (2016) IKEA Group sustainability report. Available at: www.ikea.com/ms/en_US/img/ad_content/IKEA_Group_Sustainability_Report_FY16.pdf (Accessed: 19 May 2017)

Koh, L. P. and Wilcove, D. S. (2008) 'Is oil palm agriculture really destroying tropical biodiversity?', *Conservation Letters*, 1(2): 60–4.

Marks & Spencer (2011) Marks & Spencer – Plan A. Available at: www.youtube.com/watch?v=w2EGIkIO7Sw (Accessed: 19 May 2017)

Marks & Spencer (2017) Welcome to Plan A. Available at: https://corporate.marksandspencer.com/plan-a (Accessed: 19 May 2017)

Morana, J. (2013) *Sustainable supply chain management*. Hoboken, NJ: Wiley.

Nestlé (2016) Nestlé in society: Creating shared value and meeting our commitments 2016. Available at: www.nestle.com/asset-library/documents/library/documents/corporate_social_responsibility/nestle-in-society-summary-report-2016-en.pdf (Accessed: 19 May 2017)

Pauli, G. (2010) The blue economy. Available at: www.youtube.com/watch?v=1af08PSlaIs (Accessed: 19 May 2017)

TED (2005) The route to a sustainable future. Available at: www.ted.com/talks/alex_steffen_sees_a_sustainable_future (Accessed: 19 May 2017)

TED (2009) The business logic of sustainability. Available at: www.ted.com/talks/ray_anderson_on_the_business_logic_of_sustainability (Accessed: 19 May 2017)

TED-ed (2017) Re-thinking progress: The circular economy. Available at: http://ed.ted.com/featured/2Yy019iv (Accessed: 19 May 2017)

Veleva, V. and Ellenbecker, M. (2000) 'A proposal for measuring business sustainability', *Greener Management International*, 31(3): 101–20.

Wills, J. (2011) 'M&S – wholly embracing staff in plan to become the world's most sustainable retailer', *The Guardian*, 26 May. Available at: www.theguardian.com/sustainable-business/staff-plan-worlds-sustainable-retailer (Accessed: 19 May 2017)

Responsible Leadership: Inspiring CSR

6

Learning outcomes

By the end of this chapter, students should be able to:

- explain the importance of leadership for strategic CSR
- describe the various leadership styles that are most applicable to strategic CSR

(Continued)

- define each leadership style and list its components, principles and aspects
- discover which leadership styles appeal to them the most
- use a holistic CSR leadership approach to achieve strategic CSR.

Case study   Paul Polman, Unilever – Genuinely responsible leadership

'The world we want is an enormous responsibility.' (Paul Polman)

Unilever is a multinational consumer goods company co-headquartered in Rotterdam and London. With 400 brands sold in 190 countries, 2.5 billion people around the world use a Unilever product on any given day, including brands such as Dove, Omo and Lipton. Over the years, Unilever has made numerous corporate acquisitions, including Ben & Jerry's (2000), Alberto Culver (2011), and more recently Dollar Shave Club (2016), Seventh Generation (2016) and Quala (2017), amongst others.

Unilever's CEO Paul Polman, who stepped into this role in 2009, is an outstanding global example of genuine CSR leadership. Polman has, over the years, won many awards for his contribution to sustainability. He is Chairman of the World Business Council for Sustainable Development and sits on the Board of the UN Global Compact and the Consumer Goods Forum, where he co-chairs the Sustainability Committee.

He was asked by the former UN Secretary-General Ban Ki-moon to be part of the panel for developing the sustainable development goals (SDGs) adopted in 2015, aiming to irreversibly eradicate poverty in a sustainable and equitable way. He helped to launch the SDGs in the UN General Assembly in 2015 with an inspirational speech, an excerpt of which is here:

Every day that we continue to abide poverty, thousands of children under the age of five die and with them, their dreams and our dignity. Every day that we continue to treat the atmosphere as an open sewer, we are irretrievably pushing our planet beyond its limits. And every day that business as usual continues, we delay the opportunities that we know await us in the New Climate Economy. It's not about doing less harm. It's about moving to positive contributions. [...] We are doing what we can, but not what we must and all this time, we are running out of time. (UN Global Compact, 2015)

In 2016, Paul was asked by the UN Secretary-General to be a member of the SDG Advocacy Group, tasked with promoting action on the 2030 Agenda.

Polman often emphasises the need to balance sustainability and profitability: 'We cannot choose between [economic] growth and sustainability – they are mutually dependent.' Polman consistently delivers the message that businesses cannot ignore their contribution to climate change because the impact of climate change will affect their business, whatever it is. To achieve both responsibilities, Polman focuses on long-term goals and did away with the practice of quarterly profit reporting with the intention of encouraging long-term investors:

> The issues we are trying to attack with our business model and that need to be solved in the world today – food security, sanitation, unemployment, climate change – cannot be solved just by quarterly reporting. They require longer-term solutions and not 90-day pressures. (Cunningham, 2015)

As the CEO of Unilever, Polman led the Unilever Sustainable Living Plan (USLP), setting an ambitious goal to halve Unilever's overall environmental footprint by 2020, while growing its business at the same time. Polman sees business opportunities in creating a sustainable global society because it is the only way society can exist in the long run. This includes issues like food security, sanitation, poverty, employment and climate change. For example, food companies that address food security issues can survive in the long run, but those who do not will not be able to exist in a global economy. Unilever's USLP specifically aims to lift a million small farmers out of poverty and to help a billion people improve their health and wellbeing ('It is unacceptable that more than 1 billion people are hungry every day while another billion are obese'), halve its environmental impact and enhance the livelihoods of millions of people in its supply chain.

Polman creates a clear vision to guide Unilever's actions. This vision of using Unilever's business to improve humanity globally while expanding the company's growth has resulted in clear global recognition. When Polman became CEO, Oxfam's report expressed concern and criticisms of Unilever's labour practices in Vietnam. But since then, when its Behind the Brands ranking report was released, looking at the top ten food companies' impact on small farmers, women's rights, the use of land and water and greenhouse emissions, Unilever was ranked the first in the world to tackle these issues, ahead of Nestlé, Coca-Cola, Kellogg's and Mars.

Unlike many CEOs worldwide, whose pay packages make headlines for their increases (sometimes at the same time as their companies experience massive layoffs),

(Continued)

Polman has chosen not to take a pay increase since he joined Unilever. Perhaps his personal background is a major contributor to this decision. Polman is one of seven children born to a hard-working father who worked two jobs his whole life and insisted all of his children attend university. Polman admits this taught him 'not to be lazy'. He grew up in a city in the eastern Netherlands, where the culture is for people to remain modest and this undoubtedly contributed to his servant leadership.

Servant leadership inherently respects all employees, which is something Polman constantly demonstrates through his personal behaviour and Unilever's organisational structure. There are only five job levels in this giant multinational corporation, making the entry-level employees relatively close to the executive managers. Polman conducts random employees selection interviews for any of these job levels, in which he asks potential employees about their values and ethos. Unilever regularly holds focus groups and dinners with people from all job levels, giving substance to Polman's statement that 'not one job is more or less important'. His attention to employees and other stakeholders provides a consistent message of caring, serving and respecting all individuals. He said:

> The moment you discover in life that it's not about yourself, that it is about investing in others, I think you're on the way to becoming a great leader.

Bibliography

Cunningham, L. (2015) 'The tao of Paul Polman'. Available at: www.washingtonpost.com/news/on-leadership/wp/2015/05/21/the-tao-of-paul-polman/?utm_term=.2262c07941f8 (Accessed: 16 May 2017)

Mirvis, P. H. (2008) 'Commentary: Can you buy CSR?' *California Management Review*, 51(1): 109–16.

Mirvis, P. (2011) 'Unilever's drive for sustainability and CSR – changing the game', in S. A. Mohrman and A. B. Shani (eds), *Organizing for sustainability* (Vol. 1, pp. 41–72). Bingley: Emerald.

UN Global Compact (2015) Address by Paul Polman, CEO of Unilever. Available at: www.unglobalcompact.kr/wp/?pageid=1&page_id=8223&lang=en&uid=1271&mod=document&ckattempt=1 (Accessed: 19 October 2017)

Unilever (2017) Sustainable living. Available at: www.unilever.co.uk/sustainable-living (Accessed: 5 October 2017)

Financial Times (2016) Unilever CEO Paul Polman the optimistic pessimist. Available at: www.ft.com/content/e6696b4a-8505-11e6-8897-2359a58ac7a5%20https:/www.theguardian.com/business/2016/jan/25/unilever-ceo-paul-polman-the-optimistic-pessimist (Accessed: 15 May 2017)

Forbes (2015) Unilever's Paul Polman: CEOs can't be 'slaves' to shareholders. Available at: www.forbes.com/sites/andyboynton/2015/07/20/unilevers-paul-polman-ceos-cant-be-slaves-to-shareholders/#20b8bc89561e (Accessed: 14 May 2017)

McKinsey & Company (2014) Committing to sustainability with Unilever CEO Paul Polman. Available at: www.youtube.com/watch?v=nShlnBJko5s (Accessed: 15 May 2017)

TED (2014) Harish Manwani: Profit's not always the point. Available at: www.youtube.com/watch?v=ihoR9B7p-1Q (Accessed: 15 May 2017)

Unilever (2017) Sustainable living strategy. Available at: www.unilever.com/sustainable-living/the-sustainable-living-plan/our-strategy (Accessed: 19 May 2017)

Unilever (2017) Reports and publications. Available at: www.unilever.com/sustainable-living/our-approach-to-reporting/reports-and-publications-archive (Accessed: 19 May 2017)

Murray Edwards College, University of Cambridge (2015) Paul Polman – We can end poverty. Available at: www.youtube.com/watch?v=GQEOExqXLqU (Accessed: 15 May 2017)

Unilever (2015) USLP report. Available at: www.unilever.com/Images/uslp-mobilising-collective-action-summary-of-progress-2015_tcm244–424809_en.pdf (Accessed: 19 May 2017)

Questions for reflection

1. Which actions indicate Polman's commitment to CSR? How have these actions affected Unilever's operation and performance?
2. How does Polman create and communicate his vision for Unilever and the world?
3. Polman interviews and communicates with people at all job levels. What does this practice signal to the company's employees? How do you think this affects the company success, and how do these elements affect Unilever's CSR?
4. How would you expect Polman's leadership at Unilever to affect the way other businesses operate? Describe possible mechanisms affecting individuals and organisations outside of Unilever.

Introduction: The role of responsible leadership in CSR

Leadership is one of the most researched, and possibly the most complex, topics in management. Great leaders, whether political, social or business leaders, inspire people and bring out the best in others and in the organisations/societies/countries they lead. If you think about leaders you admire, you will see that they usually have the ability to make a difference in people's lives. However, there is a limited discussion on leadership in the context of CSR.

One well-accepted definition of business leadership sees it as 'influencing, motivating and enabling others to contribute to the effectiveness and success of the organisations of which they are members' (House et al., 2004: 56). Great leaders apply various forms of influence to motivate people and achieve a great vision that brings everyone to higher levels of success. Peter Drucker once said that the task of leadership is to create an alignment of strengths so strong that it makes the system's weaknesses irrelevant (Cooperrider and Fry, 2009).

Waldman et al. (2006b) argued that empirical studies of CSR have largely ignored the place of the corporate leaders in CSR. Examining existing CSR textbooks, none had a chapter on leadership. We do not have enough knowledge on leadership styles, values and ethics that create socially responsible companies. And yet, the best examples of socially responsible companies (some of which are featured in our case studies) are usually based on strong leadership that genuinely believes in the responsibility of a business to do good for the world.

Being a responsible leader in today's business world can be very challenging. On the one hand, there is pressure to perform well financially and to show loyalty to the shareholders. On the other hand, business leaders are held accountable for (un)ethical behaviour more so than ever before. They are expected to demonstrate strong values and work with all stakeholders to lead sustainable organisations. In an era of fast changes, globalisation, technology and social media, the business leadership challenges are greater than ever and yet there are not enough guidelines and tools to show leaders how to balance the different (and sometimes contradicting) expectations.

It is therefore the aim of this chapter to discuss responsible leadership, what role such leaders play in advancing CSR and how to use existing knowledge and frameworks of leadership to achieve this. There are various leadership concepts and frameworks that can assist existing and potential leaders in finding the leadership style that is suitable for the individual leader and for the organisation. We will start by examining the most relevant concepts of responsible, sustainable and ethical leadership and then move on to other leadership perspectives that can be applied to CSR: purpose-driven and value-based leadership, transformational leadership, servant leadership, authentic leadership and conscious leadership. We will also discuss shared leadership and offer a holistic definition of strategic CSR leadership.

Before we do this, it should be noted that strategic CSR and responsible organisations do not have to be led from the top down and there is an increasingly important role for everyone in the organisation to enhance CSR. However, when a CEO of a company or a leader of an organisation strongly believes in sustainability or CSR and holds dear values that help to achieve higher levels of CSR, the organisation is more likely to achieve these results. This does not mean that the lack of responsible leadership will always lead to irresponsible organisations (as there are other mechanisms that can be used to achieve this goal), but it definitely makes it more challenging. The most effective way of reaching strategic CSR is when it is embedded throughout the company and the vision for it is shared by both the formal leader of the organisation (e.g. CEO or founder) and informal leaders, who can be found among all employees and other stakeholders.

Sustainable, responsible and ethical leadership

A leader is someone who crafts a vision and inspires people to act collectively to make it happen, responding to whatever changes and challenges arise along the way. A sustainability leader is someone who inspires and supports action towards a better world. (Polly Courtice, Director, Cambridge Institute for Sustainable Leadership)

Just as there are many definitions of sustainability, there are many definitions of sustainable leadership. Is it about a leader that cares about environmental sustainability? Is it about making a difference and a better world? Or is it about financial sustainability, in which case sustainable leadership is about making profit?

Sustainable leadership

The *Financial Times* Business Lexicon (2017b) defines sustainable leadership in environmental terms, emphasising the role that business leaders play in addressing urgent issues that human society faces, such as climate change. It also explains that sustainable leadership cannot be a one-person show, and that many change agents are required to achieve this goal (this will be further discussed in the section on shared leadership below).

The Cambridge Institute for Sustainable Leadership lists the following seven key characteristic traits and styles as important in distinguishing the leadership approach taken by individuals tackling sustainability issues (Fistis et al., 2014):

- systemic, interdisciplinary understanding
- emotional intelligence and a caring attitude
- a values orientation that shapes culture
- a strong vision for making a significant difference
- an inclusive style that engenders trust
- a willingness to innovate and be radical
- a long-term perspective on impacts.

This list emphasises the importance of purpose and values and focuses on making a difference. This includes both the natural environment and society at large.

Avery and Bergsteiner (2010) used the metaphor of honeybees to describe sustainable leadership and one of the locusts to portray unsustainable business and leadership. The main difference between the two groups is their answer to the question: 'Who is this business for and what is our purpose?' The authors define sustainable leadership as taking a long-term perspective in making decisions; fostering systemic innovation aimed at increasing customer value; developing a skilled, loyal and highly engaged workforce; and offering quality products, services and solutions. While the honeybees create something that is long lasting and can be sustained for many years, the locusts leave nothing but destruction.

Szekely and Knirsch (2005) argued that sustainability takes place only when there is an active leader/manager within the company who champions this approach. Their research showed that it always takes a leader to transform a company into a sustainable, socially responsible enterprise. Sustainable leadership starts by carefully examining all the factors that determine the sustainability performance of the company and its suppliers. These factors can be internal (mainly managerial and organisational) or external (stakeholders' demands), which can be challenging. However, it should be noted that the approach of this book is that CSR can also be created bottom-up through the leadership of employees who do not necessarily hold executive positions in the company.

Yvon Chouinard, Patagonia's founder, is a well-known example of sustainable leadership. Chouinard believes that we have turned from citizens of the world to consumers of the world, and that until we acknowledge our obsession with consumption and addiction, we will not be able to save our planet. He does not like the word 'sustainability' because the actions that are attached to it are not enough. Chouinard is dedicated to constantly improving Patagonia so it can become the most sustainable company possible (see the opening case study in Chapter 5).

Responsible leadership

Very similar to the concept of sustainable leadership is the notion of responsible leadership. According to the *Financial Times* Business Lexicon (2017a), responsible leadership is about making business decisions that, next to the interests of the shareholders, also take into account all the other stakeholders, such as workers, clients, suppliers, the environment, the community and future generations. Responsible leaders consider whether their business activities are sustainable and are not polluting the surrounding environment. Such leaders identify systemic risks that the business activities might contribute to, instead of taking short-term risks for quick profits that could endanger the reputation of the company. Responsible leaders care about the welfare of the people in their workforce and ensure sustainability throughout the entire supply chain.

Maak (2007: 331) defined responsible leadership as 'the art and ability involved in building, cultivating and sustaining trustful relationships to different stakeholders, both inside and outside the organisation, and in co-ordinating responsible action to achieve a meaningful, commonly shared business vision.' This definition does not only specify what responsible leaders do, but also defines the impact of such a leadership style on the relationship with all stakeholders and on achieving a *meaningful* vision.

The UN Global Compact also offered a working definition of responsible leadership in 2008, referring to it as 'The art of motivating, communicating, empowering and convincing people to engage in a new vision of sustainable development and the necessary change' (GRLI Foundation, 2008: 11). The first part of the definition examines the actions that are required of responsible leaders, while the second part examines the goal of such leadership, which is sustainable development for the world.

Northouse (2012) listed five principles of responsible leadership:

1. *Respect*: Respect others to allow them to be themselves, with creative wants and desires.
2. *Service*: Place followers' welfare foremost in plans.
3. *Justice*: Impose fair treatment.
4. *Honesty*: Act truthfully.
5. *Community*: Take into account own and followers' purposes whilst working towards common goals.

Ethical leadership

Another related term that has been used in this context is ethical leadership. Ethical leaders display behaviours that indicate they seek to do the right thing, are consistent in their pursuit of their ethical standards and do not compromise even when others pressurise them. Ethical leaders are characterised by honesty, openness and integrity as well as by a desire to do what is right (Brown and Treviño, 2006).

In summary, we can see that the ever-growing discourse on business leadership now has an emerging new perspective, in the form of sustainable, responsible and ethical leadership. While this conversation is only in its early days, we already have some definitions and principles that can assist women and men who want to make a difference and create a business that is not just best in the world, but also best *for* the world. Adopting such a leadership style should increase the level of CSR and the positive impact of the organisation on society and the environment, as well as create a long-lasting and successful organisation in which employees, consumers and shareholders are satisfied.

Leading responsibly therefore means leaders opening up to a broader set of stakeholders, with the goal of securing the legitimacy of the organisation in a given society and establishing and maintaining mutually beneficial stakeholder relations. This implies that such leaders need to balance different and sometimes contradicting expectations, be involved in conflict resolutions and offer a vision that is about a positive impact for society.

Question for reflection and discussion

Re-read the case study of Unilever's Paul Polman. How does he demonstrate in his philosophy and actions responsible, sustainable and ethical leadership?

Purpose-driven leadership

In 2009, Simon Sinek delivered a TED talk on how great leaders inspire action. This video has become one of the most viewed TED talks of all time, with approximately 30 million views to date. His books on leadership (Sinek, 2011, 2014) are on the best-selling lists. What was the idea he presented that became so popular? As Sinek himself says, it was the simplest idea and all he did was codify it. This ground-breaking idea was that all inspirational and successful leaders (and organisations) work in the same way, which is the complete opposite to everyone else.

Using what he calls 'the golden circle' (Figure 6.1), Sinek (2011) presents three levels of analysis: why, how and what. Every organisation in the world knows what they do – what they produce, sell and deliver. They also usually know how they do it – designing, manufacturing, marketing, and so on. However, only great organisations and leaders know *why* they do what they do.

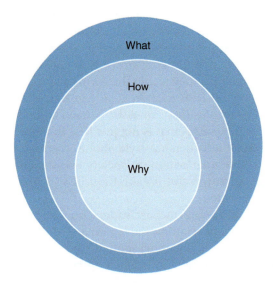

Figure 6.1   **The golden circle (based on Sinek, 2011)**

Sinek demonstrates how the golden circle works using the example of Apple as an inspirational company. Here is how almost every computer company in the world operates:

- What? – We make great computers.
- How? – They are beautifully designed and user-friendly.
- Why? – To make money.

This is not inspirational and it does not create emotional attachment to the company, brand or leader. Here is how Apple works instead:

- Why? – In everything we do, we believe in challenging the status quo; we believe in thinking differently (Steve Jobs often spoke about making a dent in the universe and Apple's slogan for years was 'think differently').
- How? – The way we challenge the status quo is by making products that are beautifully designed, innovative and user-friendly.
- What? – We just happen to make computers; do you want to buy one?

For years, Apple used its marketing campaigns to feature concepts and innovation instead of products. While Apple was not a great example of a socially responsible company for many years, it is often used as an outstanding case of innovation, leadership and a purpose-driven organisation. Sinek demonstrates that our decision making is emotional, not rational, and that people don't buy what you do, they buy why you do it. Having a purpose that is aligned with making significant positive impact on the world should therefore create emotional commitment in employees, consumers and other stakeholders.

Part of the reason why it is so difficult for many organisations to identify their purpose is the dominance of profit motive, as this CSR book argues, which also diverts the focus from the 'why' to the result – making money. As such, too many organisations and leaders believe their 'why' is to maximise profit, improve results or outperform their competitors (e.g. Jack Welch, CEO of General Electric, always spoke about being number one and being second to no one). But as Sinek explains, this is the *result*, not the reason for existing (*raison d'être*). It is the means to an end – but what is the end?

When people and organisations have a strong purpose, they inspire action, create trust and perform better than everyone else. That is because we are not just profit-driven creatures, instead we are purpose-driven humans. For millennia, humans were engaged in philosophy and religion trying to find their 'why'. It is only in the last few decades that money has seemed to be the answer, but that answer might be a false one. Dan Pink (2009) explains that when we try to use money as a motivator, not only is it ineffective in the long term, but it also results in unethical behaviour. The three drives that really motivate people are *mastery*, *autonomy* and *purpose*.

As such, it is essential for organisations and leaders to define a higher-level purpose for what they do. One of the ways to do this is to look at the *long-term social impact* the company has over a large number of people. Take, for example, a telecoms company that sells mobile phones. If its golden circle is outside in, it will tell us about what it sells – mobile phones, plans, reception range, and for what prices. This is not inspiring or engaging for employees, consumers and other stakeholders. On the other hand, if the company starts with the 'why', it would consider, measure and talk about the impact it has on people's lives every day: that is, how it helps people connect, keep in touch and assist each other in times of need. This purpose will also feed into the company's strategic CSR, as it can use its resources, knowledge and core competencies to help the community.

Mark Zuckerberg, the founder and CEO of Facebook, is emerging as a purpose-driven leader. In the last few years, Zuckerberg not only started a large philanthropic foundation together with his wife, but also shifted Facebook to benefit society. In his commencement speech at Harvard University in May 2017, Zuckerberg said:

> Today I want to talk about purpose. But I'm not here to give you the standard commencement about finding your purpose. We're millennials. We'll try to do that instinctively. Instead, I'm here to tell you finding your purpose isn't enough. The challenge for our generation is creating a world where everyone has a sense of purpose. [...] Purpose is that sense that we are part of something bigger than ourselves, that we are needed, that we have something better ahead to work for. Purpose is what creates true happiness. [...] But it's not enough to have purpose yourself. You have to create a sense of purpose for others. I found that out the hard way. You see, my hope was never to build a company, but to make an impact. And as all these people started joining us, I just assumed that's what they cared about too, so I never explained what I hoped we'd build.

EXERCISE

1. Apply the golden circle to a company you work(ed) in or a company that you know. What is the what, how and why of this company?
2. Is the why clear and known by all stakeholders?
3. Does the company work from the centre of the circle out or vice versa? How can it improve its work based on this framework?

Value-based leadership

Another important way to create purpose-driven leadership and discover your 'why' is by going back to your basic values, which were discussed in Chapter 4. As you may recall, values are stable, evaluative beliefs that guide our preferences and behaviour. They are trans-situational goals that vary in importance as guiding principles in people's lives. One definition of responsible leadership sees it as a 'value-based and through ethical principles driven relationship between leaders and stakeholders' (Pless, 2007: 438) and, as such, value-based leadership is another important part of this chapter.

Every person has values, including CEOs and organisational leaders, but some might feel they need to leave their values at the door when they put on the hat of a CEO, who needs to ensure financial sustainability for the company. However, research shows (see below) that CEOs and leaders with a strong value base, who work and live by their values, create a strong organisational culture, trust and socially responsible companies. Leaders with high levels of benevolence and universalism values, who act according to their values, are in a better position to lead strategic CSR.

For example, one study (Waldman et al., 2006b) examined the values of 500 CEOs in 17 countries. The results demonstrated that leaders with strong stakeholder values were viewed as visionary and not authoritarian, while leaders with strong economic values were the exact opposite. Interestingly, this study demonstrated that visionary leaders with strong stakeholder values (instead of economic values) were at the most financially successful companies. Ethical leadership has been positively linked to other elements of organisational effectiveness: when employees perceived the leadership to hold 'morality and fairness' values, they were more optimistic about the future and perceived the top management as effective.

By now, you can see how virtue ethics is strongly related to CSR leadership. Values and traits that were considered virtuous over 2000 years ago by Greek philosophers, including courage, justice, truthfulness and loyalty, can serve both the leaders and the organisations they lead in creating a company that has a positive impact on society. As such, it is essential to know one's values and positive traits and to apply them in leading a socially responsible company.

Indra Nooyi has been the CEO of PepsiCo, the second largest food and beverage business in the world by net revenue, since 2006. She often discusses her own personal values and how they impact her leadership. Growing up in India, she learned from her father to trust people, assume they have good intentions and see the best in everyone. Her values drove her leadership style and impacted her decision to frame PepsiCo's mission around 'performance with purpose'. Her international background, her years of living in poverty and her being one of the most powerful women in the world (for many years, according to Forbes) impact her passion for diversity and inclusion.

Transformational leadership

Transformational leadership is a very popular perspective of leadership that emerged in the 1970s. While transformational leadership has been vastly used to create effective organisations in general, some of its components can be applied to CSR and to leaders who makes a genuine difference in the world (Groves and LaRocca, 2011).

Transformational leadership explains how leaders change organisations by creating, communicating and modelling a vision for the organisation and inspiring employees to strive towards this vision (Burns, 1978; Bass, 1985). Transformational leaders work by tapping into and inspiring the higher motivations of followers, not by offering monetary rewards and other resource exchanges but by understanding that people are also purpose and vision driven. In addition, transformational leadership has been defined in terms of how such leaders stress self-sacrifice for the long-term good of the larger group or collective.

Transformational leadership is associated with being a moral agent, raising followers to higher levels of moral consciousness, which makes it highly relevant to the context of responsibility and sustainability. Transformational leaders are perceived as agents of change and if the change is a more responsible organisation, a more sustainable company or a better world, transformational leadership provides a pathway to achieve these goals. Although such leaders are not necessarily described as ethical or socially responsible, the transformational leadership theory requires that such leaders are trusted, which indicates a potential link to integrity through congruous behaviours (Angus-Leppan et al., 2010).

Firstly, we need to differentiate between transformational leadership and transactional leadership. James Burns (1978), who coined both terms in the 1970s, defined transactional leaders as people in positions of power who gain compliance by using rewards and penalties. Transformational leadership, on the other hand, engages employees by appealing to their values and aspirations via a meaningful vision. This difference is similar to the one often made between managers and leaders.

Several descriptions and models of transformational leadership exist and most include the following four elements: creating a strategic vision, communicating the vision, modelling the vision and building commitment towards the vision (Burns, 1978). These are shown in Figure 6.2 and described next:

Figure 6.2   The transformational leadership model (based on Bass, 1985)

1. *Develop a vision to benefit the society*: transformational leadership establishes a vision that engages employees with objectives they did not think possible. These leaders outline a strategic vision of a realistic and attractive future that bonds employees together and focuses their energy towards achieving this future. Strategic vision creates a 'higher purpose' that energises and unifies employees, such as for a more just society or a world in which the environment is well looked after. Transformational leaders of responsible companies can portray a vision in which the business is used to address climate change, poverty and hunger, conflict and war. It should be noted that such a vision could originate from employees, or even clients, suppliers and other stakeholders. A shared strategic vision plays an important role in organisational effectiveness.

2. *Communicate the CSR vision*: if vision is the substance of transformational leadership, communicating that vision is the process through which it is manifested and achieved. Transformational leaders communicate meaning and frame messages around a higher-level purpose with an emotional appeal that captivates employees and other corporate stakeholders. The vision is brought to life through metaphors, stories and other vehicles that engage people's emotions. When Martin Luther King made his famous speech, 'I have a dream', he managed to do it so clearly that everyone could share the same dream. He did not say 'I have a plan', but used words and metaphors that were engaging and inspiring.

3. *Create commitment towards the vision among all stakeholders*: transformational leaders do not only communicate a vision; they enact it. They 'walk the talk' and lead by example. Such behaviour builds trust in the leader and shows people what needs to be done to achieve the vision. Ben Cohen and Jerry Greenfield used to walk out of their offices and march with their employees for causes that were important to them (they still do it today, although they are no longer in the Ben & Jerry's CEO position). John Mackey, the CEO of Whole Foods Market, is vegan and promotes animal rights. These responsible transformational leaders and many others walk the talk and thus create trust and commitment.

4. *Walk the talk and model the CSR vision*: to transform the vision into reality, transformational leaders create employee commitment towards it. They do so by using their rhetoric talent and charisma and by building a contagious enthusiasm that revitalises people to adopt the vision and work hard to achieve it. They use positive psychology to achieve this, focusing on what can be instead of focusing on problems. In the case of CSR, transformational leaders involve employees in creating the vision of a more sustainable future and involve them through volunteering and contribution.

Research shows that transformational leadership can help make a difference, lead change, motivate employees and create emotional attachment to the organisation that is led by such a leader. According to Waldman et al. (2006a, 2006b), transformational leaders inspire people by shifting the focus from the individual to the collective, thus inspiring employees by having a vision for a greater purpose, just like Paul Polman does in the opening case study. Their research examined the role of CEOs in determining the extent to which their firms engage in CSR and showed that CEO intellectual stimulation (but not CEO charismatic leadership) is significantly associated with the propensity of the firm to engage in strategic CSR.

EXERCISE

Find an example of a transformational leader, who is also responsible and ethical. How does this leader apply responsibility and sustainability to the four aspects/stages of transformational leadership?

Servant leadership

Another leadership style that is closely related to CSR is servant leadership. It has been gaining popularity in the last few decades, although the idea of servant leadership is rooted in ancient Chinese philosophy, religious scriptures and other sources. Being both a philosophy and a practice, servant leadership is defined as leadership that focuses on serving others due to a sense of calling and higher purpose.

Robert Greenleaf (1970) coined the phrase 'servant leadership' in his book *The Servant as Leader*, in which he explains:

> The servant-leader is servant first … It begins with the natural feeling that one wants to serve, to serve first. Then conscious choice brings one to aspire to lead. That person is sharply different from one who is leader first, perhaps because of the need to assuage an unusual power drive or to acquire material possessions. The leader-first and the servant-first are two extreme types. Between them there are shadings and blends that are part of the infinite variety of human nature. (Greenleaf, 1970: 7)

Servant leadership is based on the view that leaders serve followers, rather than vice versa: leaders help employees fulfil their needs and are coaches, stewards and facilitators of employee development. Traditional leadership generally involves the accumulation and exercise of power by one at the 'top of the pyramid'. In contrast, the servant-leader shares power, puts the needs of others first and helps people develop and perform as highly as possible.

Larry Spears, CEO of the Greenleaf Center for Servant Leadership, identified 12 characteristics of servant leadership (Spears, 2017):

1. *Calling*: servant leaders have a strong sense of purpose and are willing to sacrifice themselves for the good of others. This calling to serve is deeply rooted and values-based, and these leaders desire to make a difference for others and will pursue opportunities to make a difference and to impact the lives of employees, the organisation and the community, never for their own gain.

2. *Listening*: servant leaders use active listening skills to understand the feelings and the will of others. They listen with empathy to other people's ideas and value them.

3. *Empathy*: with high emotional intelligence, servant leaders are able to identify other people's emotions and relate to them.

4. *Healing*: one of the great strengths of servant leadership is the potential for healing oneself and others. The positive relationship between servant leaders and the people around them has a healing effect.

5. *Awareness*: general awareness, and especially self-awareness, strengthens the servant leader. Such leaders know what is going on and do not ignore reality and other people's perspectives.

6. *Persuasion*: persuasion is considered a 'soft' influence tactic rather than a hard one, resulting in commitment rather than in compliance or resistance. Servant leaders seek to convince others, rather than coerce them.

7. *Conceptualisation*: servant leaders seek to nurture their abilities to 'dream great dreams'. They can conceptualise and communicate a great vision while finding the balance with everyday operations.

8. *Foresight*: foresight enables servant leaders to understand lessons from the past, the realities of the present and the likely consequences of a decision in the future.

9. *Stewardship*: servant leaders are responsible for and are capable of preparing the organisation for its destiny, usually for the betterment of society. Stewardship is the desire to prepare the organisation to contribute to the greater good of society.

10. *Growth*: servant leaders are committed to helping employees develop and grow.

11. *Building community*: servant leaders have a strong sense of community spirit and work hard to foster it in an organisation so that it is shared by all employees.

12. *Nurturing the spirit (joy)*: working in an organisation led by a servant leader will lead to employee happiness and meaningfulness, which is constantly nurtured and celebrated. The servant leader reminds employees to reflect on the importance of both their struggles and successes and to learn from both.

EXERCISE

Go back to the opening case study of this chapter about Paul Polman. Which of the 12 aspects of servant leadership are demonstrated in the case? Can you find examples of the other aspects using additional sources?

Research shows (Greenleaf and Spears, 2002) that servant leadership can help create positive workplace outcomes such as employee engagement, trust in the leader, performance and commitment. Servant leaders are likely to engage individuals to be more motivated, empowered and action-oriented in environments that sustain hope and trust. Showing concern and making the needs and interests of others a priority demonstrate empathy and elicit trust. As Sendjaya and Pekerti (2010: 647) state:

> When servant leaders put followers' needs and interests above those of themselves, maintain consistency between words and deeds, engage in moral dialogue with followers, and instil a sense of purpose and meaning in followers, they accumulate the trust of their followers.

While there are some similarities between transformational leadership and servant leadership, they are quite different, particularly around the focus of the leader (Stone et al., 2004). The transformational leader's focus is directed towards the organisation and building commitment for organisational objectives, while the servant leader's focus is on the followers and the organisation comes second. However, both transformational leadership and servant leadership offer the conceptual framework for dynamic leadership that can be applied well to the context of CSR and hyper goals and when served for a CSR purpose, these leadership styles become more similar.

The framework of servant leadership is very relevant to CSR and it is often used in this context. The sense of a calling to serve society and the environment, as in the opening case study of Paul Polman, is vital for leading a sustainable and responsible organisation. The state of mind of a CEO that is there to serve others instead of being self-serving is essential for a genuine concern about all stakeholders. Such servant leaders are not there for the power and the money but see their role as an opportunity to serve. Moreover, empathy and listening skills are crucial for those leaders who, as required in strategic CSR, want to work with a broad set of stakeholders, listen to their opinion and try to find a balance between them all.

Authentic leadership

Authentic leadership is defined as leadership that displays leader behaviour true to the inherent moral values of the leader (Avolio and Gardner, 2005) and, as such, it is related to value-based leadership while incorporating other aspects of responsible leadership. The basic assumption underlying the authentic leadership approach is that the more people learn about themselves, the greater understanding they gain of their inner purpose and the better leaders they can become. Putting it simply, authentic leaders know who they are and behave in full alignment with their true self. As such, authentic leadership is often seen as a journey in which the leader constantly discovers who she or he is and finds ways to lead her or his life and the organisation accordingly.

Authentic leaders demonstrate a passion for their purpose, practise their values consistently and lead with their hearts as well as their heads. The leader's behaviour keeps its integrity with the leader's personal values. Such leaders establish long-term, meaningful relationships and have the self-discipline to get results.

Walumbwa et al. (2008) found that authentic leadership has strong correlations with specific job outcomes. These authors referred to authentic leadership as a pattern of leader behaviour that draws upon and promotes both positive psychological capacities and a positive ethical climate in order to foster greater self-awareness, an internalised moral perspective and a transparent relationship with followers. Their research found authentic leadership to correlate positively with job performance, job satisfaction and organisational climate. Similarly, Thomas et al. (2004) found that authentic leadership is associated with several positive business outcomes including revenue.

According to *Forbes Magazine*, 'doing good requires authentic leadership' and there is growing expectation of authentic leadership from stakeholders, socially conscious consumers and purpose-driven employees who want to work for companies that have a greater mission (Sinha, 2013). Let us state it clearly: the positive outcomes of strategic CSR that are detailed throughout this book will only emerge when the leadership and the company are authentic about their desire to contribute to humanity. Being a responsible and ethical leader demands a strong self-concept and values that can be aligned with taking such a direction for the firm. As such, authentic leadership is an essential part of strategic CSR.

Shared leadership

While the previous sections of this chapter emphasised the roles and leadership style of people in formal positions, it was also stated in the introduction that leadership, particularly CSR leadership, can emerge from all people at all levels of the organisation, and sometimes from people outside the organisation as well, thus creating a 'leaderful organisation'. Shared leadership is based on the notion that nearly every person is capable of sharing the burden and responsibility of leading, at least to some extent, in nearly all types of organisational circumstances (Pearce and Conger, 2003).

Shared leadership entails the serial emergence of both formal and informal leaders as part of a simultaneous, ongoing and mutual influence process. According to Pearce et al. (2014), all leadership is shared leadership; it is simply a matter of degree – sometimes it is shared completely while at other times it is not shared at all. At its most extreme, shared leadership is just what it sounds like: all social actors in an organisation or a team are involved in the process of leading one another towards a productive goal.

Shared leadership suggests that leadership is plural, not singular: any organisation, department or team may have several leaders at the same time, with each person leading on a different area. Shared leadership flourishes in organisations where the formal leaders are willing to delegate power and encourage employees to take initiative and risks without fear of failure. It calls for a collaborative rather than an internally competitive culture because employees take on shared leadership roles when co-workers support them in their initiative (Pearce et al., 2014).

Shared leadership is based on the idea that leadership is a role, not a job, and does not belong to one individual in the organisation. Dennis Donovan was such a leader at Home Depot and the recipient of the HR Executive of the Year Award in 2003. He stated his shared leadership view: 'I start with the premise that the function of leadership is to produce more leaders, not more followers. You get a more intelligent, responsible followership if the followers themselves have experience with leadership' (Mackey and Sisodia, 2014).

Employees are leaders when they envision (or share someone else's vision of) a better future for the organisation and work bottom up to make this vision come true. They become powerful change agents and help lead and facilitate this change by working with all stakeholders to achieve the vision and goals. This includes a CSR vision of better humanity, the community or the environment. Also related to CSR, shared leadership exists when employees engage in organisational citizenship behaviours that improve the performance and wellbeing of their peers, such as through mentoring and volunteering.

In organisations with both strategic CSR and shared leadership, any employee can have a vision of how to use the company's resources, core operations and competencies to create a positive social impact. This could be aligned with the overall mission and vision of the organisation and may strengthen them. Shared CSR leadership is the essence of employee-led CSR, which will be discussed in the next chapter. It means that employees can choose which charity organisations to support, initiate CSR programmes or even start a social enterprise that is supported by their employer. Furthermore, employees play an active part in socially responsible companies that support shared leadership, champion their company's CSR and become a change agent to enhance it.

Conscious leadership

As you will recall, conscious leadership is one of the four tenets of a conscious business, which is a business galvanised by higher purposes that serve and align the interest of all major stakeholders. As can be seen in Figure 6.3, the four tenets are: higher purpose and core values; stakeholder integration (which has already been discussed in Chapter 3); conscious culture and management; and *conscious leadership*, which is the focus of this section. However, all four tenets are important for conscious leadership, as it is purpose- and value-driven and focused on a broad set of stakeholders.

Figure 6.3   Conscious leadership is one of the four tenets of conscious capitalism (based on Mackey and Sisodia, 2014)

According to Mackey and Sisodia, conscious leaders seek to make a positive impact on the world through their organisations. Such leaders *serve* from a higher *purpose* and inspire a *vision*, are self-aware and introspective. As such, conscious leadership can be seen as an integration of transformational leadership, responsible leadership, purpose-driven leadership, servant leadership and authentic leadership.

Similar to servant leaders, conscious leaders transcend ego for the greater good of the organisation and humanity. Furthermore, conscious leaders have a genuine curiosity to understand others and create a deeper connection. They lead and create organisational cultures in which everyone can flourish, feel empowered and realise their potential because they lead with an emphasis on what the 'whole' needs – employees, customers, stakeholders and the organisation. Connecting with the whole and aligning purposes create win–win–wins, sustained results and better futures.

Examining the traits and virtues of conscious leaders, they are confident, compassionate, courageous and can make tough decisions while taking full responsibility for those decisions. They practise humility and authentic power. This is power from within rather than an external power based on the trappings of titles and prestige. Such leaders live life from a place of integrity and wholeness and are grounded in values, family, community and work.

Serve from a higher *purpose* and inspire a vision

Are *self-aware* and introspective

Have a genuine *curiosity* to understand others and create a deeper connection

Create *cultures* where others can flourish, feel empowered and realise their potential

Lead with an emphasis on the *whole*

Can make tough decisions while taking full *responsibility* for their decisions

Practise *humility* and authentic power

Figure 6.4   **The seven components of conscious leadership (based on Mackey and Sisodia, 2014)**

Figure 6.4 summarises the seven components of conscious leadership. It shows how this approach incorporates ideas from other leadership perspectives that have been discussed in this chapter and how applying it can assist in developing strategic CSR.

Holistic approach to CSR leadership

This chapter has detailed several approaches to leadership that can be applied and implemented in the context of CSR. The obvious ones are sustainable, responsible and ethical leadership, but other leadership styles can be applied here as well. Transformational leadership offers four stages of creating a vision, communicating and modelling it to create an overall commitment to this vision. It is easy to apply to the CSR context – all we need is for the vision to be about a courageous contribution to humanity. Servant leadership is also highly relevant for organisations and leaders who want to serve society instead of just utilise society to maximise profits. It is essential that CSR leadership be authentic, and as such, authentic leadership is essential. And yet, CSR leadership is never about the one person at the top – it needs to be shared with all employees in order to be as holistic as strategic CSR requires it to be. Finally, conscious leadership adopts almost all of these approaches to offer a leadership style that is responsible, sustainable, purpose-based, value-based, servant and authentic.

It might be overwhelming to see so many leadership frameworks and styles, each one with such a long list of traits and behaviours which might seem unachievable. However, the goal of this chapter was not to overwhelm but to offer a range of leadership styles that can serve strategic CSR and to shed light on what each of these means, so that CSR leaders can use whatever they find suitable for their personal and organisational purposes. Eventually, CSR leadership needs to be authentic and it is about adopting one's values, purpose and personality to embed CSR in the organisation one leads, be it in a formal position or not.

To end this chapter, we would also like to offer a CSR leadership concept that is based on the definition of strategic CSR. As such, we define strategic CSR leaders as people (in any position) with a strong purpose and a vision to better human-ity, who incorporate a holistic CSR perspective within a firm's strategic planning and core operations, work to meet the interests of a broad set of stakeholders, and strive to achieve maximum economic and social value over the medium to long term. They do so based on a strong purpose and values, while being true to the self and with the aim to serve others. They share the leadership with others in the organisation in order to achieve these goals.

Summary

Strategic CSR is about tying the company's strategy to a holistic CSR approach that is embedded in the entire organisation. As such, there is a vital role for the leader at the top of the organisation in making it happen. However, our knowledge of CSR leadership and of which leadership styles are more relevant to CSR is very limited. It was therefore the aim of this chapter to shed light on CSR leadership, detail sev-eral leadership approaches and show how they can be applied in the context of strategic CSR.

The leadership styles that are naturally related to CSR are sustainable, responsi-ble and ethical leadership. Such leaders inspire and support action towards a better world and work with all stakeholders in order to achieve a meaningful and com-monly shared business vision. Ethical leaders are also deeply engaged in doing the right thing and making business decisions that are moral.

Similarly, using concepts of purpose and values that were already discussed earlier in this book can help shape a leadership style that is relevant to CSR. Purpose-driven leadership is about starting with a strong 'why', and when this 'why' is about making a positive impact on society and the environment it becomes a CSR leadership style. Having strong values such as benevolence and universalism and acting according to these values can help people become strong CSR leaders.

Other leadership styles and approaches can also be highly relevant to the context of CSR. For example, transformational leadership can become CSR leadership if the vision that such a leader creates, communicates, models and builds commitment towards is focused on being 'best *for* the world'. Servant leadership is strongly focused on serving others. While servant leadership is often about serving employees, it can be applied to serving other stakeholders and society at large and, as such, to strategic CSR. Finally, authentic leadership implies that the leader is true to her/himself and her/his values and purpose. It can be argued that authentic CSR leadership is the only way to achieve trust in and commitment for the CSR vision.

It is important to note that CSR leadership does not have to derive from the CEO of the company. In fact, CSR may be more effective if its leadership is to be shared throughout the organisation. Any employee can lead a CSR vision (be it her/his own vision or another person's vision) and create commitment around it.

The concept of conscious leadership offers a combination of all the aforementioned leadership styles. Conscious leaders serve from a higher purpose and values, inspire a vision and are self-aware and introspective. Their goal is to make a positive impact on the world instead of gaining power.

These leadership styles and approaches demonstrate that when the leader of the company is authentically passionate about making a difference and develops a vision that is about higher purpose, people will be more inspired to follow. It does not really matter which leadership style you adopt. What is important is the focus of your leadership and how it is used to serve.

General questions

1. This chapter listed several leadership styles. Which one did you find most relevant to CSR? Which was more appealing on a personal level? Why?
2. Examine the definitions of sustainable, responsible and ethical leadership. Where do they overlap? What are the unique aspects of each? What is still missing when all three are combined?
3. Transformational leadership is one of the most popular approaches but it does have some limitations. What do you think these limitations are and what are their implications for CSR?
4. In your opinion, why does CSR leadership have to be authentic? What are the possible consequences of CSR leadership that is not true to self?
5. Provide three strong advantages of shared CSR leadership and three risks/disadvantages. Do you still think it is important that CSR leadership will be shared throughout the organisation? Why?

Key definitions

- A sustainable leader is someone who inspires and supports action towards a better world (Fistis et al., 2014).
- Responsible leadership is about making business decisions that, next to the interests of the shareholders, also take into account all the other stakeholders, such as workers, clients, suppliers, the environment, the community and future generations (*Financial Times*, 2017a).
- Responsible leadership is the art of and ability involved in building, cultivating and sustaining trustful relationships with different stakeholders, both inside and outside the organisation, and in co-ordinating responsible action to achieve a meaningful, commonly shared business vision (Maak, 2007).

- Transformational leaders work by tapping into and inspiring the higher motivations of followers as well as by understanding that people are also purpose and vision driven. They create a strategic vision, communicate the vision, model the vision and build commitment towards the vision (Burns, 1978; Bass, 1985).
- Servant leadership is defined as leadership that focuses on serving others, mainly employees, due to a sense of calling and higher purpose (Greenleaf and Spears, 2002).
- Authentic leadership is defined as leadership that displays leader behaviour true to the inherent moral values of the leader (Avolio and Gardner, 2005).
- Shared leadership is the view that leadership is plural, not singular: any person can be a leader of certain aspects in any organisation, group or team. It is based on the idea that leadership is a role, not a job, and does not belong to one individual in the organisation (Pearce et al., 2014).
- Conscious leadership seeks to make a positive impact on the world through companies and organisations. Such leaders *serve* from a higher *purpose* and inspire a *vision*, are self-aware and introspective (Mackey and Sisodia, 2014).
- Strategic CSR leaders are people (in any position) with a strong purpose and a vision to better humanity, who incorporate a holistic CSR perspective within a firm's strategic planning and core operations, work to meet the interests of a broad set of stakeholders and strive to achieve maximum economic and social value over the medium to long term.

References

Angus-Leppan, T., Metcalf, L. and Benn, S. (2010) 'Leadership styles and CSR practice: An examination of sensemaking, institutional drivers and CSR leadership', *Journal of Business Ethics*, 93(2): 189–213.

Avery, G. C. and Bergsteiner, H. (2010) *Honeybees and locusts: The business case for sustainable leadership*. Sydney: Allen & Unwin.

Avolio, B. J. and Gardner, W. L. (2005) 'Authentic leadership development: Getting to the root of positive forms of leadership', *The Leadership Quarterly*, 16(3): 315–38.

Bass, B. M. (1985) *Leadership and performance beyond expectations*. New York: Free Press.

Brown, M. E. and Treviño, L. K. (2006) 'Ethical leadership: A review and future directions', *The Leadership Quarterly*, 17(6): 595–616.

Burns, J. M. (1978) *Leadership*. New York: Harper & Row.

Cooperrider, D. and Fry, R. (2009) 'A Peter Drucker moment: Harnessing the innovation-generating potential of a shareholder and stakeholder theory of the firm', *The Journal of Corporate Citizenship*, 36: 3–7.

Financial Times (2017a) Responsible leadership. Available at: http://lexicon.ft.com/Term?term=responsible-leadership (Accessed: 14 May 2017)

Financial Times (2017b) Sustainability leaders. Available at: http://lexicon.ft.com/Term?term=sustainability-leaders (Accessed: 14 May 2017)

Fistis, G., Rozman, T., Riel, A. and Messnarz, R. (2014) 'Leadership in sustainability', in B. Barafort (ed.), *European Conference on Software Process Improvement*. Berlin: Springer.

Greenleaf, R. (1970) *The servant as leader*. Indianapolis, IN: Robert K. Greenleaf Center.

Greenleaf, R. K. and Spears, L. C. (2002) *Servant leadership: A journey into the nature of legitimate power and greatness*. New York: Paulist Press.

GRLI Foundation (2008) The globally responsible leader: A call for action. Available at: www.oasishumanrelations.org.uk/content/uploads/2015/01/GRLI-Call-to-Action.pdf (Accessed: 19 May 2017)

Groves, K. S. and LaRocca, M. A. (2011) 'Responsible leadership outcomes via stakeholder CSR values: Testing a values-centered model of transformational leadership', *Journal of Business Ethics*, 98(1): 37–55.

House, R., Hanges, P., Javidan, M., Dorfman, P. and Gupta, V. (2004) *Culture, leadership, and organizations: The GLOBE study of 62 societies*. Beverly Hills, CA: Sage.

Maak, T. (2007) 'Responsible leadership, stakeholder engagement, and the emergence of social capital', *Journal of Business Ethics*, 74(4): 329–43.

Mackey, J. and Sisodia, R. (2014) *Conscious capitalism*. Boston, MA: Harvard Business Review Press.

Northouse, P. G (2012) *Leadership: Theory and practice*. Thousand Oaks, CA: Sage.

Pearce, C. L. and Conger, J. A. (2003) *Shared leadership: Reframing the hows and whys of leadership*. Thousand Oaks, CA: Sage.

Pearce, C. L., Wassenaar, C. L. and Manz, C. C. (2014) 'Is shared leadership the key to responsible leadership?', *The Academy of Management Perspectives*, 28(3): 275–88.

Pink, D. (2009) *Drive: The surprising truth about what motivates us*. New York: Penguin.

Pless, N. M. (2007) 'Understanding responsible leadership: Role identity and motivational drivers', *Journal of Business Ethics*, 74(4): 437–56.

Sendjaya, S. and Pekerti, A. (2010) 'Servant leadership as antecedent of trust in organizations', *Leadership & Organization Development Journal*, 31(7): 643–63.

Sinek, S. (2011) *Start with why: How great leaders inspire everyone to take action*. London: Penguin.

Sinek, S. (2014) *Leaders eat last: Why some teams pull together and others don't*. London: Penguin.

Sinha, P. (2013) Doing GOOD requires authentic leadership. Available at: www.forbes.com/sites/prernasinha/2013/12/20/43/#4168fe8c7cf8 (Accessed: 19 May 2017)

Spears, L. (2017) 12 principles of servant leadership. Available at: http://csdaca.org/wp-content/uploads/2016/08/Handout-12-Principles-of-Servant-Leadership.pdf (Accessed: 14 May 2017)

Stone, G. A., Russell, R. F. and Patterson, K. (2004) 'Transformational versus servant leadership: A difference in leader focus', *Leadership & Organization Development Journal*, 25(4): 349–61.

Szekely, F. and Knirsch, M. (2005) 'Responsible leadership and corporate social responsibility: Metrics for sustainable performance', *European Management Journal*, 23(6): 628–47.

Thomas, T., Schermerhorn, J. R. and Dienhart, J. W. (2004) 'Strategic leadership of ethical behavior in business', *Academy of Management Executive*, 18(2): 56–66.

Waldman, D. A., De Luque, M. S., Washburn, N., House, R. J., Adetoun, B., Barrasa, A., Bobina, M., Bodur, M., Chen, Y. J., Debbarma, S. and Dorfman, P. (2006a) 'Cultural and leadership predictors of corporate social responsibility values of top management: A GLOBE study of 15 countries', *Journal of International Business Studies*, 37(6): 823–37.

Waldman, D. A., Siegel, D. S. and Javidan, M. (2006b) 'Components of CEO transformational leadership and corporate social responsibility', *Journal of Management Studies*, 43(8): 1703–725.

Walumbwa, F. O., Avolio, B. J., Gardner, W. L., Wernsing, T. S. and Peterson, S. J. (2008) 'Authentic leadership: Development and validation of a theory-based measure', *Journal of Management*, 34(1): 89–126.

Zuckerberg, M. (2017) 'Building global community', *Facebook*, 16 February. Available at: www.facebook.com/notes/mark-zuckerberg/building-global-community/10103508221158471 (Accessed: 1 June 2017)

Further reading and links

Bass, B. M. and Riggio, R. E. (2006) *Transformational leadership*. Hove: Psychology Press.

Greenleaf, R. K. (1977) Servant leadership. Available at: www.american.edu/spa/leadership/application/upload/Greenleaf,%20Servant%20Leadership.pdf (Accessed: 19 May 2017)

Hargett, T. R. and Williams, M. F. (2009) 'Wilhelmsen Shipping Company: Moving from CSR tradition to CSR leadership', *Corporate Governance: The International Journal of Business in Society*, 9(1): 73–82.

Hargreaves, A. and Fink, D. (2012) *Sustainable leadership*. San Francisco, CA: Wiley.

Luthans, F., Norman, S. and Hughes, L. (2006) 'Authentic leadership: A new approach for a new time', in R. J. Burke and C. Y. Cooper (eds), *Inspiring Leaders*, pp. 84–104. Abingdon: Routledge.

RSAnimate (2010) Drive: The surprising truth about what motivates us. Available at: www.youtube.com/watch?v=u6XAPnuFjJc (Accessed: 19 May 2017)

Russell, R. F. and Gregory Stone, A. (2002) 'A review of servant leadership attributes: Developing a practical model', *Leadership & Organization Development Journal*, 23(3): 145–57.

Shamir, B. and Eilam, G. (2005) '"What's your story?": A life-stories approach to authentic leadership development', *The Leadership Quarterly*, 16(3): 395–417.

Spears, L. (2017) 12 principles of servant leadership. Available at: http://csdaca.org/wp-content/uploads/2016/08/Handout-12-Principles-of-Servant-Leadership.pdf (Accessed: 14 May 2017)

TED (2009) Simon Sinek: How great leaders inspire action. Available at: www.ted.com/talks/simon_sinek_how_great_leaders_inspire_action (Accessed: 14 May 2017)

Voegtlin, C., Patzer, M. and Scherer, A. G. (2012) 'Responsible leadership in global business: A new approach to leadership and its multi-level outcomes', *Journal of Business Ethics*, 105(1): 1–16.

All Aboard: Involving Stakeholders in CSR   7

Learning outcomes

By the end of this chapter, students should be able to:

- explain the importance of stakeholder involvement in CSR
- detail several ways in which employees can be involved in CSR (including corporate volunteering, payroll giving and sustainability) and the rationale and manner for doing it effectively

- list the benefits and ways of involving consumers in CSR and understand the limitations of doing so
- define socially responsible investment with its three main components and describe ways of involving investors in CSR.

Case study   Singtel and Optus – Holistic stakeholder engagement in CSR

Singtel (Singapore Telecommunications Limited) is a Singaporean telecommunications company, with over 640 million customers in 25 countries. It is the largest mobile network operator in Singapore and, in terms of subscribers, it is the second largest in the world. With S\$16.7 billion in revenue and S\$3.9 billion in profit as at March 2017, Singtel has a strong focus on sustainability, CSR and stakeholder engagement.

Singtel's approach to CSR seeks to actively contribute to society. Singtel aims to make a lasting positive impact on its stakeholders, acknowledging that the industry it operates in can have unintended impact on society and the environment. Singtel's sustainability strategy seeks to create shared value and mitigate the risks to the company, its stakeholders and the environment. The company is committed to being a responsible corporate citizen and strives to build a sustainable future for its stakeholders in four key areas: marketplace, people, environment and community.

When it comes to engaging its stakeholders, Singtel combines proactive and responsive approaches. Every three years, Singtel proactively performs a formal stakeholder engagement exercise, surveying a whole range of stakeholders: employees, senior management, customers, suppliers, not-for-profit and community partners. The survey examines what issues of sustainability and responsibility are important to the stakeholders; what issues they believe Singtel can play a role in; and what areas have the greatest impact on the company. This proactive approach results in themes that help Singtel shape its focus on sustainability, its operations and communication with its stakeholders.

Singtel's employees are engaged in CSR either as part of the corporate, as teams or as individuals. Corporate programmes provide employees with an opportunity to be part of social change initiatives and Singtel also encourages VolunTeaming: volunteering of business units. For example, Optus, the Australian subsidiary of

(Continued)

Singtel, is a founding member of the Australian Business and Community Network – a group of business leaders who desire to create positive social change by engaging with high-school students and educators. The programme aims to provide students with the skills and work experience they require to make sound personal, educational and vocational choices. In this programme, Optus employees actively mentor students from disadvantaged backgrounds and provide them with work experience opportunities at Optus.

In addition to corporate volunteering opportunities, Singtel employees can volunteer for any cause that they are passionate about and receive paid leave to do so, while some CSR initiatives even originate from the employees. For example, one Optus employee came up with an idea to use an existing service package to help homeless people. The employee noticed that many homeless people were purchasing a '$2 per day' plan, which was originally aimed at students who cannot commit to a regular phone plan. The employee suggested that homeless people have a similar package, where they are also not charged for any calls to social services and welfare agencies. That way, their basic needs of contact with authorities responsible for their welfare can be guaranteed. Employee surveys show that CSR is now seen as the most important factor in employee engagement in Singtel, leading to pride and commitment.

Helping those in need is also a way Singtel involves consumers. Optus has a pilot programme of 'donate your data', where customers pledge to donate their unused data (rather than just letting it expire). The data quota donated gets pooled, matched by Optus and transferred to mobile plans for Optus' charity partners, such as The Smith Family, who then distribute phone plans to people in need. Business customers are also engaged in Singtel's CSR efforts, some of which explicitly require that Singtel (being their supplier) be socially responsible in various areas (health and safety, environmental sustainability, equity and diversity, etc.). Singtel reports to them on its actions and approach in these areas. Singtel initiates engagement with business customers and business round tables and reports on its own social responsibility actions and achievements, with the intention of inspiring a similar focus or collaboration on issues.

Regarding its own *suppliers*, Singtel requires high CSR standards. Prior to bidding for work with Singtel, potential suppliers are informed of Singtel's approach to social and environmental issues. To become a supplier for Singtel, the company must commit to adhere to Singtel's code of conduct, which covers comprehensive CSR issues, such as health and safety, equity and diversity, environmental sustainability, honesty and accountability. Singtel requires periodic reports from its suppliers and, if there are any concerns, Singtel engages with them in various ways to resolve these issues.

Finally, Singtel's *investors* are engaged with the company's CSR by periodic reporting on Singtel's CSR initiatives, actions and achievements through its sustainability reports. Should investors seek further information, it is provided through face-to-face consultation.

Singtel's CSR initiatives often simultaneously involve multiple stakeholders. For example, Singtel chose to address cyber security and online safety by linking with several organisations, such as iZ HERO Lab in Singapore (a programme designed to educate and prepare children to engage with the digital world). Optus developed the Digital Thumbprint programme together with leading education experts, currently delivered free of cost to secondary schools in Australia. Singtel's work in this area of cyber security and online safety supports customer satisfaction with their use of Singtel's services, as well as the consumers' health and safety.

Questions

1   Why do you think it is important for Singtel to engage its stakeholders in its CSR activities?
2   How does Singtel's stakeholders' engagement guide its CSR strategy?
3   How does Singtel's engagement differ across stakeholders?
4   Explain why this is a good example of strategic CSR.
5   What are the risks of Singtel's stakeholders' engagement strategy?
6   Design a new ambitious plan for stakeholder engagement for Singtel or its subsidiary in your home country. Who would benefit from such an initiative? What risks and difficulties can you identify in this plan?
7   What is required to allow other multi-national companies to engage stakeholders in a similar way to that of Singtel's?

Bibliography

Tongzon, J. L. (2004) 'Singapore Telecom's touching lives fund: A corporate-government-community partnership', *Corporate Social Responsibility in the Promotion of Social Development*, 93.

Links

Sustainability at Singtel (2017) Available at: www.singtel.com/about-us/sustainability/sustainability-at-singtel (Accessed: 28 May 2017)
Optus Sustainability Reports (2017) Available at: www.optus.com.au/about/sustainability/reports (Accessed: 28 May 2017)

(Continued)

Optus Donate Your Data (2017) Available at: https://theyeslab.com.au/projects/donate-your-data (Accessed: 28 May 2017)

Optus Community Programmes (2017) Available at: www.optus.com.au/about/sustainability/community (Accessed: 28 May 2017)

Optus Customer Engagement (2017) Available at: www.optus.com.au/about/sustainability/responsibility/customers (Accessed: 28 May 2017)

Introduction: Moving from stakeholder management to involvement

Chapter 3 covered the various stakeholders of companies and explained how important it is to be responsible towards each stakeholder group as part of strategic CSR. The concept of stakeholders shifted the focus from shareholders only to many other groups that affect or are being affected by the company and the ways in which it achieves its goals. As you will recall, stakeholders include many groups that affect or are being affected by the company, such as employees, consumers, investors and suppliers. The way that a company manages its relationship with its stakeholders is a strong indicator of its CSR level.

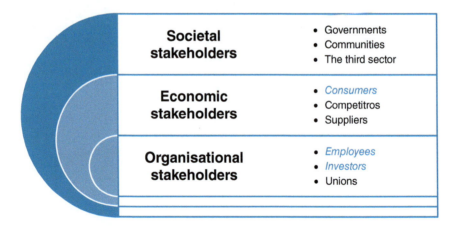

Figure 7.1   Stakeholders that can be involved in any company's CSR

In this chapter we will focus on three stakeholder groups that were mentioned in Chapter 3 (shown in italics in Figure 7.1) and examine ways in which a company can engage and involve these stakeholders in contributing to its CSR: employees, consumers and investors (although the lion's share of this chapter will be focused on employees' involvement in CSR). Naturally, all stakeholder groups can be involved in CSR; however, due to the current focus of research and knowledge as well as due to space limitations, we will only elaborate on three stakeholder groups. Involving organisational stakeholders such as employees and investors and economic stakeholders such as consumers can help the company maintain high levels of CSR and sustainability throughout its value chain and achieve much higher levels of sustainability, responsibility and philanthropy compared to corporate initiatives that are only focused on the company's direct actions.

Employee involvement in CSR

We now know that employees are a major stakeholder group of any organisation and the principal asset of any company. Without engaged employees, no organisation can achieve its goals of high performance. However, many surveys show that employee engagement is declining and it therefore has become the 'holy grail' of many companies to attempt to find innovative ways in which to create an emotional attachment between the organisation and its people. Employee engagement is a growing strategy for driving performance and building a competitive advantage. It is a desirable condition that has an organisational purpose and which indicates employee involvement, commitment, enthusiasm, focused effort and energy. Employee engagement is often perceived as both a state of mind and a behaviour that links employees and employers beyond formalised role requirements.

Some organisations attempt to achieve employee engagement through generous remuneration and pampering employees, aiming to be on the 'best companies to work for' list. However, research shows that pampering employees can only achieve high satisfaction in the short term; after a couple of years it is often replaced by a sense of entitlement. As such, other organisations strive to develop employee engagement by creating a purpose-driven company that is socially responsible and in which employees are proud to work.

Specifically, many organisations strive to increase employee engagement and performance by directly involving their people in their CSR efforts. By doing so, they expose employees to what the company does in this area and increase employee awareness and pride. They also leverage the valuable human capital, talents and skills of their employees to increase their levels of giving and community involvement as well as the visibility of these efforts. This can be done in many ways, including employee-led CSR, corporate volunteering and payroll giving, all of which will be covered next.

It is important to note that employees have their own set of values, personality, self-concept and life goals and that they may care about CSR more than some companies realise. In 2015, nine different surveys showed that an increasing percentage of employees care about the role their employer plays in society, would like to see more emphasis on CSR and sustainability and feel proud to work in a sustainable company. In the survey I conducted with the UN PRME, over 90 per cent of business students said it was very important for them to work for a responsible employer and that they would even agree to a reduction in their initial salary to work for a responsible company.

As such, we need to refer to employee social responsibility (ESR), which was defined as the combination of an employee's socially responsible identity and socially responsible behaviour aimed at the promotion of some social good (Haski-Leventhal et al., 2017). ESR is one of the most important factors in creating a constant, devoted and genuine employee engagement in CSR.

Employee engagement and CSR – two aspects

When discussing employee engagement and CSR, we need to bear in mind that there are two main aspects to it. The first is employee engagement *through* CSR – when companies use CSR to involve their employees and increase their enthusiasm for the organisation, their pride in working for this organisation and their affective commitment. Surveys by Cone Inc. found that three out of four millennials want to work for a company that 'cares about how it impacts and contributes to society'. Furthermore, 70 per cent of millennials who are already employed are aware of their employer's CSR and 65 per cent report that CSR makes them feel loyal to their company (see Meister, 2012).

Figure 7.2   Employee engagement and CSR

The other aspect is employee engagement *in* CSR, which translates to levels of employee participation in CSR efforts, from leading it to taking part in existing programmes. The relationship between these two aspects is reciprocal (see Figure 7.2). Employees who are more engaged in the workplace tend to engage in extra role behaviour, including CSR and corporate volunteering. On the other hand, employee participation in CSR and corporate volunteering may lead to higher levels of satisfaction, commitment and engagement (Brammer et al., 2007).

Involving employees in CSR: Motivations and benefits

There are many good reasons for involving employees in CSR. Firstly, if the organisation adopts strategic CSR, then it follows that a holistic approach is implemented with a broad set of stakeholders. Organisations cannot be holistic about their CSR and apply it in every aspect of the organisation without a full involvement of their employees. In addition, employee involvement in CSR (e.g. in corporate volunteering) makes it more visible and thus can help improve the public perception of the company and the positive image of the brand. Furthermore, CSR can be done both externally (with external stakeholders) and internally. Internal CSR means that employees are treated fairly and ethically, but it also means that employees are given opportunities to thrive and do the things they love. Internal CSR may therefore have implications for employee engagement in CSR.

In the last 20 years, research has shown that employee engagement in CSR is related to many positive workplace outcomes. It was found to be related to employee organisational commitment, which is the bond employees experience with their organisation. For example, a large international survey found that employees who approved of their employer's CSR were far more engaged and believed their employer was interested in their wellbeing, compared to those who did not approve of the employer's CSR. Committed employees feel a connection with their organisation – that they fit in and that they understand the goals of the organisation (Mirvis, 2012). The strongest type of organisational commitment is affective commitment, defined as an emotional attachment to an organisation characterised by identifying with it and wanting to care for it (Allen and Meyer, 1996). CSR and employee engagement in CSR were also found to be related to job satisfaction, which is the 'pleasurable emotional state resulting from the appraisal of one's job as achieving or facilitating the achievement of one's job values' (Locke, 1969: 316). When employees are satisfied and committed, they perform better and turnover declines; both results are also related to the financial performance of the company.

Furthermore, by involving employees in CSR, the company creates an organisational culture of CSR. Organisational culture is a system of shared assumptions, values and beliefs, which governs how people behave in organisations (Schein, 1996). These shared values have a strong influence on the people in the organisation and impact the way in which employees behave, think, feel, dress, act and perform their jobs. It is the DNA of the company, determining who we are and what we stand for. To apply strategic CSR, it is essential to build a strong and shared culture of caring, giving, responsibility and sustainability, and this cannot be achieved without the involvement of employees.

In addition, employees can serve as a link between the company and the community. If a company wants to be fully involved in the community in which it operates, what better way of doing it than by involving the people in the community that work for this company. Employees have families and friends; they volunteer, they know and care about certain charities and causes and they can help their employers find excellent partners to ensure that their giving is strategic and effective. Employees can be the voice of the local community and assist the company in choosing its CSR targets.

Finally, by involving the employees, a lot more can be done. The more human and other resources used, the more talents and skills are channelled towards the company's CSR, further resulting in a stronger social impact. We will further discuss what social impact is and how to measure and report on it in Chapter 8, but it is clear that the more employees who are involved in CSR, either within or outside their working hours, the more that can be achieved.

Three models of employee engagement in CSR

Mirvis (2012) offered a framework of employee engagement in CSR that includes three different approaches to involving the company's people in its social responsibility (see Figure 7.3). The three approaches differ mainly by whose interests CSR aimed to serve and for what motivation. The model is based on the psychological contract theory, according to which employees and employers develop mutual expectations based on interviews, past experience, current experience and so on, and meeting these expectations is an essential part of being satisfied with this relationship.

The first approach is the *transactional approach*, where programmes are undertaken to meet the needs and interests of employees who want to take part in the CSR efforts of a company. From the company's perspective, engaging employees in CSR is done for instrumental reasons – recruitment, engagement and performance – so it can serve the organisational performance and increase profit. From the employee perspective, CSR participation is something they expect of the employer, together with other benefits such as teambuilding and workplace 'fun'. The CSR is reactive and is based on the notion of *homo economicus* (economic man, a person who makes rational choices based on self-interest).

The second approach, *the relational approach*, occurs when the organisation and its employees make a joint commitment towards social responsibility. This joint obligation helps to build a culture of CSR and the brand of the company as a caring organisation. The employees are interested in building a self-concept of a giving person and a social identity as being part of a responsible organisation. While this is somewhat more focused on others, the motivations (of both individuals and the organisation) are still quite self-centred. In this approach, CSR is integrated into the organisation and it is more proactive. It is based on the perception of humans as *homo reciprocans* (reciprocating humans – humans as cooperative actors who are motivated by improving their environment).

	Transactional	Relational	Developmental
Corporate motivation	To improve HR practices and workplace outcomes.	To create an organisational culture of CSR.	To impact society and to make a real difference.
Employee motivation	To have fun, to get opportunities to volunteer while working.	To be part of something greater, to change self-concept and social identity.	To make a difference.
Perception	*Homo economicus*	*Homo reciprocans*	*Homo communicans*

Figure 7.3 **The three approaches to employee engagement in CSR (based on Mirvis, 2012)**

Thirdly, there is *a developmental approach*, in which a company aims to fully activate and develop its employees and the firm itself to produce greater value for business and society. The main motivation of both employees and employers is to make a difference and create a greater social impact. This suits well purpose-driven organisations and people and can create a meaningful contribution to the community. CSR in this case is transformative and goes beyond proactive into CSR leadership. It is based on the perception of employees as *homo communicans* (connected humans – people prefer to stay in contact with and connected to the surrounding world in their economic and social life).

These approaches define the 'why' of CSR and the motivation of engaging employees in CSR. Consequently, it also impacts the 'how'. For example, in the developmental approach, the main motivation is to benefit society. This would impact which not-for-profit organisations the company works with, how often and in what way. If the aim is to make a difference, the company will aim to find the pathway in which its CSR will make the biggest contribution. This is often aligned with the company's mission and the employees' skills, as this is where the contribution can be really essential.

Quick question

Reflect on the Singtel case. In your opinion, is the way in which the company engages its employees in CSR transactional, relational or developmental?

CSR congruence model

In Chapter 2, we presented the CSR congruence model (Haski-Leventhal et al., 2017), showing that companies and employees can be placed on a social responsibility engagement matrix, based on both their behaviour and their identity. This analysis leads to four types of CSR/ESR: low CSR/ESR, behaviour-based CSR/ESR, identity-based CSR/ESR and intertwined CSR/ESR. What is presented in this chapter is the result of the combination of the employer's CSR type and the employee's ESR type. The proximity between the two (or lack thereof) can lead to positive workplace outcomes or to challenges that need to be addressed.

Figure 7.4 shows the 16 possible results of the combination of four CSR patterns with four ESR patterns. These combinations can result in full congruence, no congruence or single-dimensional congruence (when the employer and employee match on either socially responsible identity *or* behaviour, but not on both). Each combination of specific CSR and ESR patterns has different levels of congruence, outcomes and action required to achieve better results.

According to this model, the optimum results will occur when employees with an intertwined social responsibility pattern work for employers with the very same pattern. In this case, employees who have strong socially responsible identity and behaviour work for a similar organisation, resulting in positive outcomes for the employee, the company and the community. However, when employees with very strong ESR work for a company that has low CSR, the result could be disengagement and withdrawal behaviour, with a risk of turnover and low performance. While companies with low CSR may have thrived in the past, with the current ESR level of millennials this could change very quickly, and companies that are not going to adapt accordingly will find it difficult to win the war on talent.

What the CSR congruence model strives to do is to offer an explanation for why CSR leads to employee engagement but not in all companies and not for all employees. It offers a way of understanding the underlying psychological mechanisms of CSR and employee engagement. To do so, we need to analyse and understand both the behaviour and the identity of the employers and employees to understand these processes and predict their results. As can be seen in Figure 7.4, many of the actions involve changing the behaviour of employees, socialising them into social responsibility and involving them in the CSR efforts of the company. These can be done in the following ways: employee-led CSR, corporate volunteering, employee giving and sustainability. These four approaches will be discussed next.

Employer \ Employee	Entwined ESR	Behaviour-based ESR	Identity-based ESR	Low ESR
Entwined CSR	*Full congruence* *outcomes*: P-O fit, attraction, commitment and retention. *Action*: sustaining high levels of CSR engagement and congruence.	*Single-dimensional congruence* *outcomes*: organisational citizenship behaviour and performance. *Action*: socialising employees into socially responsible identity.	*Single-dimensional congruence* *outcomes*: possibly positive HR outcomes. *Action*: creating opportunities for active participation.	*No congruence* *outcomes*: employee indifference. *Action*: engaging employees in CSR identity and behaviour.
Behaviour-based CSR	*Single-dimensional congruence* *outcomes*: employee participation in CSR. *Action*: influencing organisational values.	*Full congruence* *outcomes*: employee participation in CSR. *Action*: building CSR identity.	*No congruence* *outcomes*: employee disengagement and withdrawal. *Action*: aligning interests, values and actions.	*Single-dimensional congruence* *outcomes*: indifference. *Action*: increasing participation through policy.
Identity-based CSR	*Single-dimensional congruence* *outcomes*: possibly positive HR outcomes with risk of disengagement due to the lack of action. *Action*: employee-led CSR.	*No congruence* *outcomes*: employee resentment, lack of trust. *Action*: aligning interests, values and actions.	*Full congruence* *outcomes*: person–organisation fit; attraction, retention and commitment. *Action*: aligning identity and behaviour.	*Single-dimensional congruence* *outcomes*: employee indifference, lack of trust. *Action*: socialising employees into company's CSR values.
Low CSR	*No congruence* *outcomes*: employee disengagement and organisational withdrawal. *Action*: employee-led CSR.	*Single-dimensional congruence* *outcomes*: HR outcomes not related to E-CSR. *Action*: employee-led CSR to increase corporate behaviour.	*Single-dimensional congruence* *outcomes*: disengaged employees; lack of trust. *Action*: employee-led CSR to change the CSR identity and values.	*Full congruence* *outcomes*: indifferent employees. *Action*: stakeholder pressure, possible social and environmental challenges.

Figure 7.4 The CSR congruence model (based on Haski-Leventhal et al., 2017)

EXERCISE

- If you were a socially responsible employee working for a large company that does not have any CSR values or activities, what would you do?
- What would you do if the company did give a lot to charity, but you felt that it does not really hold the values and identity to match?

Employee-led CSR and champions

The opening case of Singtel provided an example of one employee who identified a social issue (homelessness) and found a way in which the company can assist using its core operations. This is an example of an employee-led CSR initiative in a company that also has employer-led CSR. Another example comes from Westpac, one of the four largest banks in Australia. Westpac allows teams and departments to choose the targets of their corporate volunteering and giving. One of the company's employees, Daniel Heycox, an ER Consultant, Employee Relations and Policy at Westpac, also started his own not-for-profit, called *I am a Boat Person Inc.* This organisation aims to help refugees who come to Australia in boats and who are often referred to by the government and the public as 'boat people'. *I am a Boat Person Inc.* delivers financial literacy to refugees and, as such, it is very much aligned with what the bank does and can be seen as an example of strategic CSR. Daniel, who is also the co-founder and the managing director of the not-for-profit, managed to get his entire team to support this organisation, through a donation of time, skills, money and other resources, and to get the support of the bank behind him. If you visit the company's website (www.iamaboatperson.org.au) you will see that Westpac HR Employee Shared Services is one of its major supporters.

There are three main approaches to employee engagement in CSR: employee-led, employer-led and joint involvement, which can be seen as part of a continuum (see Figure 7.5). These approaches differ in the question of who is dominant in the decision making on CSR strategy, tactics and direction, including the process and goals. In the *employee-led approach*, employees lead the CSR and sustainability of the company from bottom up. People who are passionate about these issues collaborate with their peers and often influence the company to support their efforts. Employee-led CSR means that employees push for an increase in their employer's CSR behaviour and identity; that they create opportunities for their own engagement and involvement; and that they choose where to volunteer and how.

On the other end of the spectrum there is *the employer-led approach*, in which all CSR initiatives derive from the organisational leadership (including CSR managers). The executive management is in charge of CSR, decides on the strategy, selects the targets of philanthropy and might encourage employees to participate. In many companies, there is now a combination of the two approaches (joint involvement in CSR) where the employer has a strong CSR and supports the endeavours of employees, sometimes allowing them to choose which charities to volunteer for. Joint CSR efforts can be closer to employee-led or employer-led, depending on the autonomy and involvement of the employees.

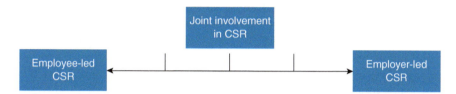

Figure 7.5   Employee-led/employer-led CSR continuum

One question that is very relevant to the topic of this book is: which one tends to be more strategic? Does CSR tend to be more aligned with the company strategy and mission and with its core operations and decision making when it comes from the top? Or is it more holistic and involving a broad set of stakeholders when it is a bottom-up approach, led by the employees and other stakeholders? Unfortunately, we do not have enough data and evidence to answer this question yet. On the one hand, Porter and Kramer (2002, 2006 and 2011) speak about strategic philanthropy and creating shared value mainly in an employer-led approach, striving to convince us that we need a steering hand for CSR to be more strategic. This approach is dominated by the assumption that such initiatives need a certain degree of fit between the strategy of the firm and the mission of the charity in order to maximise the effects of the partnership. According to these writers and some others (e.g. Werther and Chandler, 2011), the company needs to pre-determine its overall CSR strategy and decide which benefits it seeks to achieve for the community, the company and its employees (Werther and Chandler, 2011). Some scholars (Kim et al., 2010) have argued that companies with well-known brands should work with well-known charities as this creates a familiarity fit and is more favourably perceived by the general public.

However, the aforementioned example of employee-led CSR at Westpac and the financial literacy for refugees demonstrate that even when CSR initiatives come from employees, they may still be strategic and aligned with what the company stands for and does best. It might require some guidance, but employee-led CSR can be just as strategic as employer-led. In addition, the benefit of this approach is that it provides employees with a sense of autonomy, purpose and control and can motivate them even further than just offering them opportunities to participate. The ability to choose the charity one gives to through the workplace was found to affect participation rates and giving levels (Grant, 2012; Haski-Leventhal, 2013).

Another way of finding a balance between employer-led and employee-led CSR is to involve employees as change agents and champions of CSR. In the organisational change literature, a change agent is anyone with enough knowledge and enthusiasm to be able to help promote the change the company is trying to implement. We will expend more time on involving employees as change agents in Chapter 12, but for now, it is important to note that even when the CSR is planned and implemented by the company, employees can do more than just participate. Some employees have high levels of ESR and a strong socially responsible identity and behaviour (therefore an intertwined ESR) and are looking for ways to support the CSR of the company they work for. By mapping the CSR champions in the company and involving them in championing the CSR, champions can inform, recruit and engage their peers in CSR in order to increase involvement and impact. People are four times more likely to volunteer if they are asked directly by a friend or a peer than if they just get a general email addressed to everyone. Word of mouth is a much more effective way of 'selling', including CSR to employees. Furthermore, many employees see being tagged as a CSR champion as a way of recognition and support for their values and efforts, and often find it highly motivating. Therefore, involving employees as CSR champions is an effective way of balancing employee-led and employer-led CSR.

Corporate volunteering

Volunteering is any activity in which time is given freely to benefit another person, group or organisation (Wilson, 2012). Corporate volunteering (also known as employee volunteering or employer-supported volunteering) is defined as 'employed individuals giving time, knowledge, effort and money on company time during a planned activity for an external non-profit or charitable group or organisation' (Rodell and Lynch, 2016: 611). It occurs when employer organisations demonstrate commitment towards their employees' volunteering by enabling, organising and allowing employees to volunteer as part of their work commitment. Corporate volunteering makes people more able and available to volunteer as it combines volunteering with another life demand, in this case work. It increases the impact and levels of CSR and offers a great opportunity to involve employees in CSR while also building team spirit, creating a strong sense of affiliation to the workplace and offering meaningful leisure activities.

Corporate volunteering can be paid or unpaid. By 'paid' we do not mean that people get money for participating in these activities, but rather that they get paid leave to volunteer or that volunteering is done during paid working hours. Many companies offer 2–5 annual paid leave days that employees can use to volunteer. In some cases, employees can use this leave time to volunteer for any (recognised/ registered) organisation of their own chosing, and in other cases the company lists charities that employees can volunteer for. For example, the National Australia Bank (NAB) realised that offering two days a year is not an effective way to encourage volunteering, since most people do not volunteer in a full-day time block and most charities require 2–4 hours per week of volunteering to meet their needs. As such, NAB changed this to 16 hours, which can be taken in as many time slots as needed. Still, even in companies with paid leave to volunteer, the participation rate is not very high, and only 10–20 per cent of employees take advantage of this opportunity. While some people argue that if you pay people it is not really volunteering, it can also be said that it is not direct pay but rather providing people with the time to volunteer. Employees can still choose voluntarily to participate and can sometimes choose the recipients of their voluntary work.

Corporate volunteering can be done on an *individual* basis, in which one employee volunteers for an organisation (again, either during or after working hours, or while receiving paid leave to volunteer). It can also be a *team* effort, in which a group of people, be it from the same department or across the organisation, volunteer together. Research shows that volunteering together can create a meaningful experience and a bond between employees (Haski-Leventhal and Cnaan, 2009). Some companies use corporate volunteering as a team-building exercise, and sometimes by doing so they seem to miss the real target of volunteering, which is helping the not-for-profit/community. Next, corporate volunteering can occur at the organisational level, in which the whole organisation volunteers together in *one annual day* of volunteering. For example, Kraft Foods, Unilever and Lendlease are all companies that offer an annual day of volunteering. In the case of Lendlease it is called Community Day, but many employees have provided feedback that one day in a year is not enough to meet the needs of the community. The company therefore implemented its Community 365™ programme to allow employees to volunteer outside the annual day while getting paid leave to volunteer and having volunteering opportunities being organised for them.

Another important typology of corporate volunteering refers to what kinds of skills employees use when they volunteer through their workplace. *Skill-based volunteering* is on the rise and it implies using the same skills in employees' paid roles as in their volunteering. This allows the company and employees to not only be more effective in their giving but also to be more strategic in their CSR. In skill-based volunteering, employee engagement in CSR is usually aligned with what the company stands for and its core operations. For example, NAB, like many other companies, engaged its employees in planting trees, painting walls and delivering meals to people and organisations in need, until they realised this was not strategic CSR and it was not the most effective and efficient way to give. After all, the company employs bankers who know about money, not gardeners or decorators. The focus of the company's corporate volunteering programmes has now shifted to be more aligned with a financial institute, such as financial literacy and assisting Indigenous Australian small businesses.

The benefits of corporate volunteering to companies, employees and the community

There are many benefits of corporate volunteering to all three groups of players. For the *company*, corporate volunteering can improve its brand and reputation, as volunteers are visible and make a good image for the company. As was discussed above, corporate volunteering can enhance employee morale and retention and consequently performance and result in a lower turnover. It also allows the company to network more efficiently with the community and many other organisations, be it not-for-profits, other businesses or the government.

Employees also gain many benefits from corporate volunteering and it is good to communicate these benefits to employees to increase participation in CSR. Employees receive the opportunity to volunteer without taking time off their leisure activities, as corporate volunteering usually combines volunteering with work. It is also more convenient to participate in a volunteering activity that is being organised for you and to do so with your peers (which helps overcome the social anxiety some people experience when starting to volunteer). By doing so, the volunteer gains all the known benefits of volunteering without conceding as much time: volunteers gain emotional (feeling great about myself), social (connecting with other volunteers and service recipients), career (learning new skills) and network benefits, to mention just a few. In addition, the volunteers become better acquainted with their peers, bosses and subordinates as well as with the organisation they work for.

Finally, the *community* benefits from the much-needed human resources that can help deliver required services. Volunteering, including corporate volunteering, increases the social capital in the community and the level of trust. Research shows that many people prefer receiving services from volunteers rather than paid employees as they perceive them to be more altruistic. Corporate volunteering is a great example of multi-sectoral collaboration in which the networks of all participants grow and strengthen. The not-for-profits often receive additional resources from the companies that send their employees to volunteer, such as financial support, in-kind donation and partnerships.

Mini case study   Motivation and benefits of corporate volunteering in Australia

I initiated a CSR partnership network in Australia to create and share knowledge on CSR and our first study was on corporate volunteering. We found that the strongest motivations of employees to participate were: 'It makes work more meaningful to me.' As such, in a spill-over effect, corporate volunteering can help enhance the

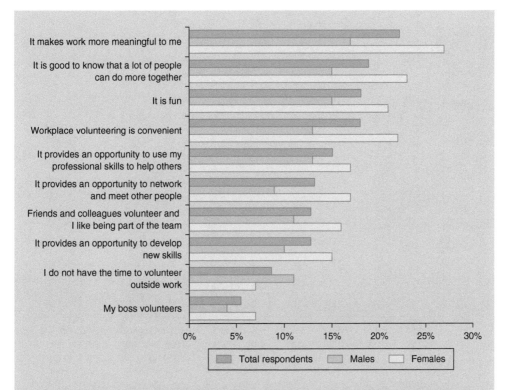

Figure 7.6   Motivation of Australian employees to participate in corporate volunteering

meaningfulness and purposefulness of one's work. The second strongest motivation was: 'It is good to know that a lot of people can do more together.' People choose to volunteer through the workplace rather than on their own, knowing that with their peers they create a stronger collective impact. Figure 7.6 shows how females' motivations were higher than those of males in almost every category.

In addition, as can be seen in Figure 7.7, we found that employees who participated in corporate volunteering demonstrated a higher level of affective commitment, which is the emotional attachment to the workplace. Corporate volunteering participants were significantly more willing than non-participants to spend the rest of their career in the organisation and felt a sense of ownership of what was going on in the organisation (see Figure 7.7).

(Continued)

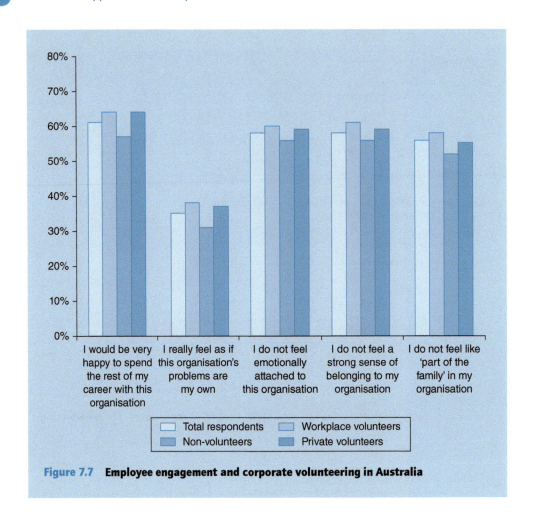

Figure 7.7   Employee engagement and corporate volunteering in Australia

Costs and challenges of corporate volunteering

While corporate volunteering has many benefits to all three major players, it also poses some costs and challenges that need to be addressed in order to maximise the benefits.

For the *company*, corporate volunteering costs include paid leave, working hours, lost opportunity and reduced productivity. Some companies address this by organising corporate volunteering on weekends or instead of other employee leisure activities. However, it should also be acknowledged that if done correctly, corporate volunteering can increase engagement and productivity, compensating for the lost time. It can also be challenging for big corporations to work with not-for-profits and partner with them. The organisations need to align in values and work cultures for the partnerships to work well.

Employees who volunteer lose time and productivity, which could imply having to work harder after volunteering to make up for the lost work (particularly if employees are managed by results and not by the hours they do). In addition, employees who volunteer face all the known difficulties of volunteering in general, such as the emotional burden of being exposed to other people's troubles (including secondary trauma in some cases), social anxiety when starting to volunteer and the challenge of doing unfamiliar tasks. Training new volunteers through the company and preparation for some types of volunteering can help to overcome these challenges.

As for the *community*, corporate volunteering can sometimes serve the company rather than the not-for-profits or the service recipients. When the company focuses on team building and employee engagement and not on the needs of the recipients, then corporate volunteering does not serve well. Often, corporate volunteering is done as an episodic (one-off) activity and in a large group, whereas many not-for-profit organisations require ongoing individual help. In addition, it can be very challenging for some small charities to work with large corporations and it requires setting expectations clearly and working on the relationship between the two organisations. However, one of the largest challenges for not-for-profits is that although volunteers do not earn money, they do cost money: it is a burden on the not-for-profit's (human and financial) resources to work with so many volunteers and the corporations do not always compensate them for these costs. Adding to these that they have a limited relationship with the volunteers, cannot train them or manage their behaviour, it is a challenge. In the next section, we will discuss how strategic corporate volunteering can overcome these issues.

Questions for reflection and discussion

1. Can you think of any additional benefits and costs of corporate volunteering for each of the three groups of players?
2. Do you think the benefits outweigh the costs or *vice versa*?
3. How can corporate volunteering be done better?

Strategic CSR and strategic corporate volunteering

We now know that strategic CSR is the incorporation of a holistic CSR perspective within a firm's strategic planning and core operations so that the firm is managed in the interest of a broad set of stakeholders to achieve maximum economic and social value over the medium to long term. Similarly, strategic corporate volunteering programmes align with this approach if they are based on the company's strategy and core operations, planned and executed through the collaboration of all relevant stakeholders in order to achieve maximum impact for all.

Therefore, it is clear that 'random acts of charity' in corporate volunteering are not strategic. If a bank sends its employees to plant trees, it is not aligned with the bank's strategy and core operations. If corporate volunteering is only done as a team-building exercise, it does not maximise the impact for all players. And if the broader set of stakeholders is not involved in planning and designing corporate volunteering, it is not going to serve them well. Furthermore, an annual day of volunteering that is focused more on the corporation than on community needs is not strategic.

Some not-for-profits have started to put their foot down in recent years and decline offers from big corporations to have employees volunteer for them. Some organisations in the community sector complain that corporate volunteering uses their resources and yet does not meet their needs through these initiatives (Lee, 2010). The Salvation Army and many other organisations now accept corporate volunteers only if a partnership is created with the corporate, with a long-lasting relationship and an involvement in the design and execution of corporate volunteering. As such, it is important to follow the 'three Ps' of strategic corporate volunteering – perspective, purpose and partnership – as detailed in Figure 7.8.

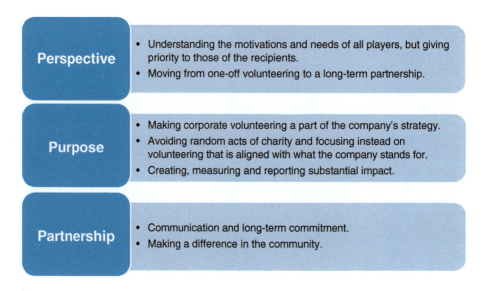

Perspective
- Understanding the motivations and needs of all players, but giving priority to those of the recipients.
- Moving from one-off volunteering to a long-term partnership.

Purpose
- Making corporate volunteering a part of the company's strategy.
- Avoiding random acts of charity and focusing instead on volunteering that is aligned with what the company stands for.
- Creating, measuring and reporting substantial impact.

Partnership
- Communication and long-term commitment.
- Making a difference in the community.

Figure 7.8   The 'three Ps' of strategic corporate volunteering

Effectively engaging employees in corporate volunteering

In order to attract employees to corporate volunteering, the first issue is ensuring an awareness of the volunteering opportunities and what is involved in participating, including highlighting the benefits. Whether the programme includes groups of employees volunteering together at the same time and place, or just introducing employees to volunteering opportunities and providing them with the leave days required, employers first have to understand the motivations and needs which are to be met. The most important motivation and benefit to volunteers (including corporate volunteers) is knowing that they made a difference. Introducing them correctly to the recipient organisation and allowing them to see results may lead to better satisfaction with the programme as well as with the organisation they work in.

Employees need to be connected to the cause and the impact of corporate volunteering, not just to the activity. It is important to share with employees the stories of the not-for-profits they will be working with. In addition, employees are more likely to participate in corporate volunteering if they are asked directly by a friend as opposed to receiving a mass email. As such, it is important to map the CSR and corporate volunteering champions in the organisation and ask them to recruit more volunteers. In addition, it is important to create a sense of necessity and urgency – people are more likely to volunteer if they feel that they really are needed. Next, it is essential to create a culture of giving and to have the organisational leadership model this behaviour by volunteering themselves. Employees who participate in corporate volunteering should be celebrated and rewarded, but through words, not tangible gifts. Finally, it is important to understand why employees in each organisation tend to volunteer and to ensure that the corporate volunteering created in the organisation meets employees' expectations.

Employee giving

In addition to corporate volunteering, one of the more common ways of involving employees in CSR is through the company's philanthropic giving. Many companies give money to charity for various reasons, from a desire to give back to the community and make a difference to public relations and tax deduction.

Employees are often encouraged to be part of their employer's donations, either in a one-off fundraising effort or in an ongoing giving. One-off fundraising in the workplace often happens when there is an urgent need in the community, including the global community, such as in the aftermath of a mega natural disaster. Ongoing giving occurs when employees continuously give money to charity through their workplace, often through what is known as payroll giving, which we will elaborate upon next. In some cases, employees lead fund-raising events to raise money or sponsorship for a charity they are involved with.

In addition, employees can give monetary donations or in-kind donations, such as food, toys and blankets, which are collected by their employers and given to a charity organisation. This is also generally more common in the case of disasters. However, it should be noted that, in these cases, a financial donation is a lot more efficient and sustainable, since it is a big strain on the not-for-profit's resources to collect, store, transfer and distribute goods when their focus is on helping people in emergency situations. Money is easier to transfer than goods and can help ensure that people who were affected by the disaster get exactly what they need.

Workplace giving varies by tax deduction, matching by the employer and donor choice. In many workplaces, but not all, there is an option of giving to charity and receiving a tax deduction as a result. This is particularly the case with payroll giving, as it allows the company to ensure that the tax is deducted from the employee's salary. This also varies by country, as in some countries charitable giving is tax deductible in certain conditions (and these legal conditions also change from one country/state to another) while in others it is not. Secondly, in some organisations, the employer matches the donations of the employees. This could be through payroll giving, in which the employer matches the total revenue raised by employee giving (sometimes to a certain maximum level) or in a one-off fundraising event. Finally, workplaces differ in the level of donor choice – in some companies employees can choose any charitable organisation to donate to, while in others they can choose from a prepared list of organisations chosen by the company, or give only to organisations that are listed on governmental listings or that offer tax deduction, and so on.

Payroll giving

'Payroll giving' refers to ongoing donations made by employees through continuous salary deductions. Employers automatically deduct authorised donations from salaries, which are then given to the local third party (such as United Way or other agencies) and distributed to not-for-profits. The givers usually benefit from immediate tax relief at their entire marginal rate on an unlimited donation as it is deducted (Potter and Scales, 2008). The most successful payroll-giving programmes have been found in the US, where about 26 per cent of employees participate in some form of payroll giving (Wright, 2002), and in the UK (Romney-Alexander, 2002). It is one of the most powerful and efficient institutional mechanisms for generating significant donations across income levels.

The reason many employees prefer to give through their workplace is that they can give more to the charity for less. To illustrate, an employee can give $5 to charity out of their monthly salary, getting $1 back due to tax deduction and this $5 is then matched by the employer. In our imaginary example, the charity organisation gets $10 when the employee only gave $4. In addition, collective contribution by employees increases the overall impact on the charity organisation.

For companies, payroll giving is an efficient way to involve employees in CSR and to align the giving of the company with the giving of the people who work for it. It creates a greater collective impact and creates a convenient way for employees to give, making it seem like another benefit for employees.

Engaging employees in payroll giving

A study of 750 employers in the UK, which aimed to understand how some companies achieve higher levels of employee participation (The Giving Campaign, 2009), found that strategic communication, management support, recognition of business benefits and matching employee donations all led to higher participation levels. This study also identified two barriers to payroll-giving participation: a lack of staff interest and concerns of employee preference to private forms of giving.

Another study (Haski-Leventhal, 2013) found that the two main employee motivations to participate in payroll giving were the matching of donations by the employer and the convenience of giving when it is done through the workplace. It was further reported that employees who knew that their employer matched their donations tended to give more than others, but that many employees did not actually know whether such matching happened. Therefore, it is essential that employers offer donation matching and communicate it clearly to all employees in order to increase and maintain high levels of participation.

There are a few other important practices that can increase employee giving of money and in-kind donations through the workplace. It is highly important to connect employees to the causes and charities and to the impact their donations make. People do not want to give for the sake of giving, instead they want to give to make a difference and this must be communicated back to the employees, not only to increase participation but also as an ethical responsibility and for accountability. It is also important to explain to employees how and why the target organisations were chosen and, if possible, to involve employees in the selection process. In addition, the company needs to inform employees about the tax benefits and to demonstrate how they can give more to the not-for-profit through their workplace compared to personally donating money directly to them. Using the champion networks, asking people personally to donate and sharing real-life stories about the impact that donations make can also create engagement.

Involving employees in sustainability

In Chapter 5 we covered environmental sustainability and explained what it is and how to involve employees in the company's sustainability efforts. To transform the company's value chain into a sustainable one and to reduce the negative environmental impact, employees need to be involved. It is important that they understand that they have an important role to play, both as employees and as private citizens, in protecting the environment. As Robert Swan (a British historian, explorer and activist, who was the first person to walk to both Poles) said: 'The greatest threat to our planet is the belief that someone else will save it' (Stevenson, 2012).

Here are a few key ways to involve employees in the sustainability journey of the company:

- *Research*: look at the big picture and identify the company's greatest impacts across the value chain. Get employees to help in this research and involve them in finding solutions to address your key issues.
- *Educatation*: involve and educate staff in sustainability on multiple levels, both at work and at home. When employees are committed to sustainability, they will want to reduce their carbon footprint both when working and when coming home after work. By doing so, the overall contribution of the company to sustainable development increases. For example, Arup, Genentech, Salesforce, the San Francisco Unified School District, the University of California at San Francisco, United Airlines and Virgin America have all offered their employees in California solar energy programmes for their private homes.
- *Green transportation*: encouraging employees to use public transportation, car-pooling, cycling and other 'green' transportation options rather than taking their cars to work can help reduce the company's impact on the environment. For example, at Optus Australia (see opening case study) there are only 2,000 car spaces for 7,000 employees. Employees get special buses to take them to and from work, they have access to a train station next to the offices and they are encouraged to use bicycles and car sharing.
- *Reducing waste*: some companies involve their employees in their efforts to reduce waste as much as possible, going far beyond recycling paper. For example, Google is committed to creating zero waste and six Google data centres are diverting 100 per cent of waste from landfill. The company has strived to find 'projects that do double duty' that not only reduce or divert waste but also have an added benefit, like energy savings or improved process efficiency. Employees are involved and understand why they are served 'ugly fruit' (fruit that usually goes to waste because it is not 'pretty' enough to be sold in supermarkets) in the many cafés and restaurants at Google (also see Chapter 12 case study).
- *Reducing energy consumption*: encouraging employees to reduce their energy consumption is one of the first things that companies did when sustainability became a popular business goal. Employees were asked to turn off lights, computers and screens when they left their offices even back in the 1980s. However, now that technology can take care of this, employees are encouraged to sustain their energy consumption at home as well and to divert to a more sustainable energy.
- *Innovative design*: employees design, manufacture and sell the company's products. It is possible to involve employees in sustainable design thinking and encourage them to come up with innovative solutions, products and packaging to reduce waste and the environmental impact across the entire value chain.

- *Food choices*: one-third of employees' (and all humans') carbon emissions are related to the food they eat. eBay employees get to eat food that is not only tasty and healthy but is also good for the planet. eBay and other companies have partnered with Bon Appetit, a catering company that emphasises food choices that are good for people and the planet with its low-carbon diet. For example, it uses locally grown produce, reduces the use of meat and cheese, eliminates airfreighted food and focuses on zero food waste. It uses corporate gardens in which employees can also be involved.

Green teams

Green teams are groups of people from one organisation (but usually across departments) who come together to identify and implement specific solutions to help their employer operate in a more environmentally sustainable manner. While green teams are usually an example of employee-led CSR and a bottom-up initiative, they are sometimes mandated or encouraged by the organisational leadership.

A few years ago, two associate consultants in the New York office of Bain & Company consultancy firm proposed creating a green team to help the company set an example of sustainable business practices. The office took the idea and ran with it, and so did the firm as a whole by achieving CarbonNeutral® certification in 2012. According to Bain & Company, its green teams helped to identify and implement environmentally-sustainable practices across its offices, including third-party energy-efficiency audits of Bain offices, double-sided printing, use of recycled paper, fluorescent lightbulbs, magazine exchanges and junk-mail cancellation, video conferencing where possible instead of travel, along with plenty of fun things like the Ugly Mug contest (bring in your ugliest coffee mug from home and use it instead of disposable cups).

Consumers: Sustainable and ethical consumerism and consumer philanthropy

Consumers who buy and use the products and services of the company are also people with values, ethos and their own levels of social responsibility. We are all consumers of various products and buy from various companies, and our consumer behaviour can make a difference to this planet and the animals and humans that inhabit it. As companies dealing with CSR issues, consumer social responsibility and behaviour offer great roles and opportunities. It is hard to talk about CSR without discussing the individual level of social responsibility, particularly among consumers.

Consumer social responsibility focuses on the fact that the individual makes social choices through consumption activity, thus revealing their social values and preferences (Devinney et al., 2006).

Various polls show us that consumers care more deeply than ever before about the CSR and sustainability of the companies they purchase from. As was mentioned in Chapter 3, 88 per cent of consumers believe companies should achieve their business goals while improving society and the environment, and 83 per cent think companies should support charities and non-profit organisations with financial donations. An international study conducted in 2015 with over 10,000 citizens showed that 81 per cent of consumers would make personal sacrifices to address social, environmental issues and 90 per cent expect companies to operate responsibly. However, it is also clear that while many consumers report that they care about these issues, it does not necessarily translate into actual consumer behaviour and consumption. Often, people buy what is on sale rather than what is ethical and sustainable.

Devinney et al. (2006) define consumer social responsibility (or as they refer to it, C_NSR) as the conscious and deliberate choice to make consumption choices based on personal and moral preferences and beliefs. C_NSR includes two basic components: (1) an 'ethical' component relating to the underlying importance of the non-traditional and social components of a company's products and business processes; and (2) a 'consumerism' component that implies that the preferences and desires of consumer segments are partially responsible for the increasing influence of ethical or social factors.

Consumers are constantly informed (e.g. via traditional and social media and through articles and books like the one you are reading now) about corporate behaviour, both positive and negative, and can decide whether to buy/avoid buying from a company based on this behaviour or to ignore this information. When companies create a product to use the profit from its sales to donate to charity (e.g. Gap created the Red label apparel and the profits from sales went to Aids funds), it may encourage some consumers to buy from them. On the other hand, when companies are scrutinised in the media about their corporate irresponsibility, some consumers may boycott the company, as was the case with Nike and Nestlé in the past, to name just two examples of many.

These choices (buying from a responsible company, avoiding buying from an irresponsible company or ignoring this information altogether) are based on consumer awareness, values, interest and capability. We must remember that in many cases there is not enough information available for the consumer, or not enough choice, to make such a decision.

Based on all of the above, we can offer the model of consumer decision making and CSR shown in Figure 7.9.

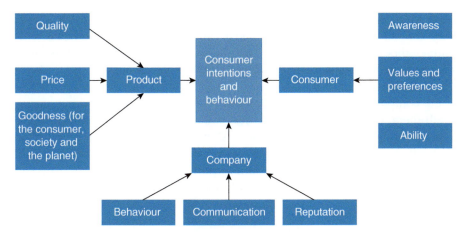

Figure 7.9   **Consumer social responsibility and behaviour**

Questions for reflection and discussion

1. As a consumer, what drives you to buy from a certain company?
2. Examine the model in Figure 7.9. Which factors influence your decision the most?
3. What are the consequences for consumer involvement in CSR?

Consumer responsibility and behaviour present a great opportunity for companies to create an emotional attachment to the brand and to involve more people in making a positive impact. Companies have only just started to realise that people might prefer buying products that are not only better for them but also genuinely good for the planet and for society. Many companies now offer more sustainable products to meet the growing demand, and some companies are entirely driven by a social and/or environmental purpose in the way they appeal to consumers.

Another fast-growing trend is consumer-based philanthropy. It is now understood that donations alone cannot address societal needs and some people are reluctant to just give donations. As such, many not-for-profit organisations partner with big corporations to sell products and donate some of the proceeds of the sales to charity. For example, many 'pink' products are available and some percentage of the profits will go to breast cancer research funds or other not-for-profits. In the last two decades, many social enterprises have started to sell products to raise money for societal and environment needs. In order to so, it is important for the product to be of good quality, priced fairly and genuinely good for the consumer, society and the planet. The product itself can be used to communicate with the consumer about the problem that the company is trying to solve and the consumer can be involved in the process of addressing the issue, as we will see in the opening case study in Chapter 8.

Some companies involve their consumers in volunteering and donating money through them. Optus, in the opening case study, offers consumers an opportunity to donate money through their phones. Consumer volunteering is an untapped resource that not many companies are using yet, but this may change quickly in the near future. Creating and organising opportunities for consumers to volunteer through the company they buy from could have an immense impact.

Mindful and sustainable consumption

Every time someone makes a decision about whether or not to purchase a product or service, there is the potential for that decision to contribute to a more or less sustainable pattern of consumption (Young et al., 2010). As such, there is a growing awareness of responsible consumption and a movement towards mindful and sustainable consumerism.

Customer-centric sustainability refers to the consumption-mediated impact of marketing actions on the environmental, personal and economic wellbeing of the consumer (Sheth et al., 2011). Mindful consumption implies consumers restraining themselves in acquisitive, repetitive and aspirational consumption. *Mindful consumption* is reinforced by a mindset that reflects a sense of caring toward self, community and nature. *Sustainable consumption* refers to consumers who prefer products or services which do least damage to the environment as well as those who support forms of social justice (Young et al., 2010).

An emerging concept in the area of consumer responsibility is *mindful consumption*, which can address the negative results of overconsumption. As the desire for consumption-based (temporary) happiness has led to mindless consumption with an enormous impact on people's lives and the environment, mindful consumption aims to fix this (Sheth et al., 2011). Mindfulness is a form of meditative practice that encourages people to become attentive to and aware of their thoughts, behaviours and actions in everyday life, and mindful consumption aims to inculcate this mindset in our approach to consumption, manufacturing and marketing (Pusaksrikit et al., 2013). It is designed to help people consider the consequences of their consumption and is based on the assumption that consumers have the power to choose what and how much to consume. Mindful consumption involves training the mind and altering one's behaviour by encouraging consumers to care about their own wellbeing and that of their community as well as nature, and it calls on both consumers and businesses to adopt a sense of moderation in their activities and decisions (Sheth et al., 2011).

Before we finish this section on consumer social responsibility, it is important to note that while consumers should be responsible for their own choices and need to ensure that the products they buy are not harmful, it is still the responsibility of businesses and business regulators to assure consumers that harmful products are not being sold. To say that the harm done to people's health because of fast food companies is the sole responsibility of the consumers who buy this food is unfair. Consumers do not always have the information required, the capability or even the funds to always make informed and smart choices. Companies manufacture demand, market directly to children and use unethical ways of marketing (also see Chapter 11) and then blame the consumers for their consumption choices. As was said by the American novelist, Jonathan Safran Foer, in his 2009 book *Eating Animals* (p. 154):

> It shouldn't be the consumer's responsibility to figure out what's cruel and what's kind, what's environmentally destructive and what's sustainable. Cruel and destructive food products should be illegal. We don't need the option of buying children's toys made with lead paint, or aerosols with chlorofluorocarbons, or medicines with unlabeled side effects. And we don't need the option of buying factory-farmed animals.

Key points for consideration

- Pay attention to customer perceptions of your CSR.
- Prioritise CSR initiatives that involve the customer experience.
- Target your CSR communications to customer segments.
- Emphasise the customer experience benefit as well as the 'greater good' of your CSR efforts.
- Don't expect customers to pay more for CSR although some would be willing to do so.
- Recognise the difference between the cost and the value of CSR.

Involving investors and shareholders

Socially responsible investment (SRI)

Just like employees and consumers, investors and shareholders are people with values who might care about issues other than maximising their share value. When we talk about investors, we are not only speaking about the multi-billionaires who invest heavily in a business, but also about the many people who buy shares and even people who invest indirectly through their pension and superannuation funds.

Among these shareholders and investors, there is a fast-growing interest in socially responsible investing.

Milton Friedman said that the only social responsibility of a company is to its shareholders, but what if the shareholders themselves start to demand wider responsibility and sustainability? Even from the narrow view of making profit, many investors now understand that if they want their investment to yield profit in the long term, they might as well invest in something that will last into the next decades, and perhaps tobacco, coal and oil companies do not have a bright future if we want to keep this planet and maintain people's health. After the impact of Enron's collapse, it was understood that unethical and irresponsible corporate behaviour is not good for investors either.

In the last few years, we have seen more and more examples of shareholders pushing companies to have higher levels of CSR. Here are some examples: Amazon shareholders demanded that the company produce a sustainability report; Netflix, Inc. was pushed by shareholders on indigenous people's rights; and at HD Supply, shareholders wanted greenhouse gas emission reductions. In all these examples, and many others, it was the shareholders who cared about issues beyond just maximising profit.

Socially responsible investing (SRI) – also known as sustainable, socially conscious, green or ethical investing – is any investment strategy which seeks to consider both financial return and social and environmental and/or societal good. In general, socially responsible investors encourage corporate practices that promote environmental stewardship, consumer protection, human rights and diversity. In other words, SRI can promote CSR and sustainability beyond what is currently happening in the business sector. SRI is an investment approach that uses both financial and non-financial criteria to determine which assets to purchase but whose distinguishing characteristic is the latter (Guay et al., 2004).

SRI is captured in many of the recent changes around investment. Firstly, many shareholders want to know how companies are ranked compared to others before they invest in the company. For these reasons, stock markets and stock market indices, such as Dow Jones or Nasdaq, started two decades ago to offer sustainability indices of public companies to inform investors but also to change corporate behaviour. These indices will be discussed in Chapter 9.

In addition, we witness the shift of sustainable investment in many pension funds. For example, in Australia there is the Australian Ethical Super, which invests pension funds in renewable energy, sustainable products, medical solutions and education and avoids investment in coal, oil, tobacco, weapons and gambling (www.australianethical.com.au). In addition, many other pension funds offer employees a 'green investment' option in which their money will be invested in responsible and sustainable companies. Interestingly, often sustainable investment yields better results than other share options, for reasons outlined here amongst others.

Social screening, community investment and shareholder activism

SRI usually includes three types of shareholder activities: social screening, shareholder activism and community investment, all three of which will be detailed next.

Social screening means that shareholders and investors try to choose where to put their money based on one of the two possible screening methods: positive and negative. Positive screening means specifically looking to invest in companies that are more sustainable or serve the vision of a more sustainable planet and the wellbeing of society. Negative screening implies investment in all companies but the ones that do the most harm. The Australia Ethical 'Super' example above demonstrates both positive and negative screening.

In addition, SRI includes *shareholder activism*, which is the effort and attempt of shareholders to positively influence corporate behaviour and demand that the companies they invest in be more sustainable in every aspect of sustainability. People use their rights as shareholders and their voting power to address environmental, social and corporate governance issues. There are several ways a shareholder can make changes: by vote of proxies, writing letters to the company's investor relations department, filing resolutions, requesting in-person meetings and, if all of the above do not work, they can divest their funds elsewhere. Guay et al. (2004) explained that activists often file shareholder resolutions related to social or environmental issues at corporate annual meetings, or use other measures including SRI and the media to try to shape corporate actions.

Finally, SRI includes *community investment*. This type of socially responsible investment is the a priori decision to invest in social business, not-for-profits and organisations that benefit society and the community. As such, this investment is not done by purchasing stocks but instead by putting money directly into for-benefit organisations, with the emphasis being more on social rather than financial return on investment (or SROI, see Chapter 8). Community investing creates social impact and the money is directly put to work to increase the wellbeing of people, animals or their environment. An example is the UK Social Impact Bonds in which investors invest in social enterprises and not-for-profits and get a financial return on their investment from the government if the social enterprise/not-for-profit manages to create a measurable impact on society.

How to involve shareholders in CSR

Firstly, it is essential to communicate the company's values and CSR to all stakeholders and particularly to shareholders. This can be done in annual reports that will be discussed in Chapter 10. Since many shareholders read the company's financial reports, many companies have moved to integrated reporting so sustainability reports and financial reports are developed together.

Secondly, if shareholders demonstrate shareholder activism, it is best not to withdraw into defensive mechanisms but rather to see it as a great opportunity to improve the company and its positive reputation. The examples of shareholder activism detailed above all seem reasonable and beneficial to the company and the community. If shareholders request that CSR items be put on the agenda for the annual general meeting, it could be a valuable input for the company: work with socially responsible shareholders, engage in meaningful conversation and work together to improve the CSR of your company.

Finally, it is important to attract shareholders who understand that CSR and sustainability are important for the company. You may recall the case study in Chapter 6 of Paul Polman who, when made CEO, approached the shareholders and encouraged shareholders who are only focused on short-term profit to invest elsewhere. A good alignment between the values of the company and those of the people who invest money in it can help all parties to be satisfied.

Summary

Based on the strategic CSR approach, it is clear that to be strategic, companies need to involve their major stakeholders in their CSR and that there are many benefits of doing so. In this chapter, we focused on three stakeholder groups, namely employees, consumers and investors, and discussed why and how to involve them in the company's efforts to be more responsible and sustainable.

Employee involvement in CSR is a fast-growing trend, as it can create a great social impact, engage employees, increase performance and help the community. Three main ways of doing so were examined in this chapter: corporate volunteering, payroll giving and employee involvement in environmental sustainability. Corporate volunteering occurs when employers support the volunteering efforts of their employees by organising opportunities for employees to give time to the community while working. There are great benefits of corporate volunteering to all the involved parties, particularly when corporate volunteering is strategic and effective methods for involving the employees are used.

In addition, employees can be involved in workplace giving, be it fund-raising events or payroll giving, in which employees donate money directly from their salary. Here too, there can be good benefits for the company, its employees and the community, but payroll giving is not as engaging and as visible as corporate volunteering.

Finally, employees can be involved in their employer's efforts to be more environmentally sustainable. It was argued here that overall sustainability couldn't be achieved without the full involvement of employees. Many examples of the ways in which corporations involve their employees in sustainability, from sustainable transportation to energy consumption, were detailed.

In addition to employees, consumers may also have high levels of social responsibility and involving consumers in the company's CSR efforts can help achieve a great social impact while also creating attachment to the brand. Consumers need to be informed about the social responsibility of the company they buy from and about the sustainability of the products they purchase, and some companies find creative ways to communicate with consumers and involve them in their CSR.

Finally, investors care more than ever before about the sustainability and responsibility of the companies in which they invest. As such, we see the rise of socially responsible investment, which seeks to consider both financial return and social, environmental and societal good. The three main components of SRI are social screening, community investment and shareholder activism, all of which were detailed and explained in this chapter.

Involving these three groups of stakeholders as well as other stakeholders in the company's CSR can have an immense positive impact on the community, the company and the involved stakeholder group. People now start to expect that the company they work for, buy from or invest in will offer them ways to give and be responsible. It is not only part of strategic CSR but in the future could be an essential part of maintaining competitive advantage, attracting talent, money and maintaining brand loyalty.

General questions

1. This chapter details the rationale and the manner in which employees, consumers and investors can be involved in CSR. Which other stakeholders can be involved in CSR? How? Find some examples of companies that involve such stakeholders and evaluate if they do it well.
2. Stakeholder involvement in CSR leads to positive results for the community, the company and the involved stakeholder. What are the disadvantages of stakeholder involvement in CSR? How can companies address these challenges?
3. Find a company that has an ongoing partnership with a not-for-profit. How does the company currently involve its stakeholders in this relationship (if at all)? Suggest three ways of involving stakeholders in this relationship and consider the benefits and challenges of this approach.
4. As a current/future/past employee and consumer (and perhaps as an investor as well), how would you like companies to involve you in their CSR efforts (if at all)? Why? Can you impact the business you are involved in as a stakeholder and change their CSR?

Key definitions

- Employee social responsibility (ESR) is the combination of an employee's socially responsible identity and socially responsible behaviour aimed at the promotion of some social good (Haski-Leventhal et al., 2017).
- Corporate volunteering (also known as employee volunteering or employer-supported volunteering) is defined as 'employed individuals giving time, knowledge, effort and money in company time during a planned activity for an external non-profit or charitable group or organisation' (Rodell and Lynch, 2016).
- Strategic corporate volunteering programmes are based on the company's strategy and core operations, planned and executed through the collaboration of all relevant stakeholders in order to achieve maximum impact for all.
- 'Payroll giving' refers to ongoing donations made by employees through continuous salary deduction.
- Consumer social responsibility (or C_NSR) is the conscious and deliberate choice to make consumption choices based on personal and moral preferences and beliefs (Devinney et al., 2006).
- Mindful consumption aims to inculcate a mindfulness mindset in people's approach to consumption, manufacturing and marketing (Pusaksrikit et al., 2013).
- Socially responsible investing (SRI), also known as sustainable, socially conscious, green or ethical investing, is any investment strategy which seeks to consider both financial return and social and environmental and/or societal good. SRI is an investment approach that uses both financial and non-financial criteria to determine which assets to purchase, but whose distinguishing characteristic is the latter (Guay et al., 2004).
- Shareholder activism is the effort and attempt of shareholders to positively influence corporate behaviour and demand that the companies they invest in will be more sustainable in every aspect of sustainability.
- SROI is a principles-based method for measuring extra-financial value (such as environmental and social value) relative to the resources invested.

References

Allen, N. J. and Meyer, J. P. (1996) 'Affective, continuance, and normative commitment to the organization: An examination of construct validity', *Journal of Vocational Behavior*, 49(3): 252–76.

Brammer, S., Millington, A. and Rayton, B. (2007) 'The contribution of corporate social responsibility to organizational commitment', *The International Journal of Human Resource Management*, 18(10): 1701–719.

Devinney, T. M., Auger, P., Eckhardt, G. and Birtchnell, T. (2006) The other CSR: Consumer social responsibility. Available at: www.researchgate.net/profile/Timothy_Devinney/publication/228136634_The_Other_CSR_Consumer_Social_Responsibility/links/0fcfd5080dcfc8cc68000000.pdf (Accessed: 28 May 2017)

Foer, J. S. (2009) *Eating animals*. New York: Little, Brown.

Grant, A. M. (2012) 'Giving time, time after time: Work design and sustained employee participation in corporate volunteering', *Academy of Management Review*, 37(4): 589–615.

Guay, T., Doh, J. P. and Sinclair, G. (2004) 'Non-governmental organizations, shareholder activism, and socially responsible investments: Ethical, strategic, and governance implications', *Journal of Business Ethics*, 52(1): 125–39.

Haski-Leventhal, D. (2013) 'Employee engagement in CSR: The case of payroll giving in Australia', *Corporate Social Responsibility and Environmental Management*, 20(2): 113–28.

Haski-Leventhal, D. and Cnaan, R. A. (2009) 'Group processes and volunteering: Using groups to enhance volunteerism', *Administration in Social Work*, 33(1): 61–80.

Haski-Leventhal, D., Roza, L. and Meijs, L. C. (2017) 'Congruence in corporate social responsibility: Connecting the identity and behaviour of employers and employees', *Journal of Business Ethics*, 143(1): 35–51.

Kim, H. R., Lee, M., Lee, H. T. and Kim, N. M. (2010) 'Corporate social responsibility and employee–company identification', *Journal of Business Ethics*, 95(4): 557–69.

Lee, L. (2010) 'Corporate volunteering: Considering multiple stakeholders', *Third Sector Review*, 16(1): 87–104.

Locke, E. A. (1969) 'What is job satisfaction?', *Organizational Behavior and Human Performance*, 4(4): 309–36.

Meister, M. (2012) 'The future of work: Corporate social responsibility attracts top talent', 7 June. Available at: www.forbes.com/sites/jeannemeister/2012/06/07/the-future-of-work-corporate-social-responsiblity-attracts-top-talent/2/#77ebe58a40bc (Accessed: 28 May 2017)

Mirvis, P. (2012) 'Employee engagement and CSR', *California Management Review*, 54(4): 93–117.

Porter, M. E. and Kramer, M. R. (2002) 'The competitive advantage of corporate philanthropy', *Harvard Business Review*, 80(12): 56–68.

Porter, M. E. and Kramer, M. R. (2006) 'Strategy and society: The link between corporate social responsibility and competitive advantage', *Harvard Business Review*, 84(12): 78–92.

Porter, M. E. and Kramer, M. R. (2011) 'Creating shared value', *Harvard Business Review*, 89(1/2): 62–77.

Potter, V. and Scales, J. (2008) Review of payroll giving. Available at: www.giveall.org/Repository/90/Documents/PG_Rep_Strategy.pdf (Accessed: 28 May 2017)

Pusaksrikit, T., Pongsakornrungsilp, S. and Pongsakornrungsilp, P. (2013) 'The development of the mindful consumption process through the sufficiency economy', *Advances in Consumer Research*, 41: 332–5.

Rodell, J. B. and Lynch, J. W. (2016) 'Perceptions of employee volunteering: Is it "credited" or "stigmatized" by colleagues?', *Academy of Management Journal*, 59(2): 611–35.

Romney-Alexander, D. (2002) 'Payroll giving in the UK: Donor incentives and influences on giving behaviour', *International Journal of Nonprofit and Voluntary Sector Marketing*, 7(1): 84–92.

Schein, E. H. (1996) 'Culture: The missing concept in organization studies', *Administrative Science Quarterly*, 41(2): 229–40.

Sheth, J. N., Sethia, N. K. and Srinivas, S. (2011) 'Mindful consumption: A customer-centric approach to sustainability', *Journal of the Academy of Marketing Science*, 39(1): 21–39.

Stevenson, A. (2012) Robert Swan OBE: 'The greatest threat to our planet is the belief that someone else will save it'. Available at: www.huffingtonpost.com/aiko-stevenson/robert-swan-antarctica_b_1315047.html (Accessed: 2 October 2017)

The Giving Campaign (2009) *The business of giving: A summary report of the business benefits of payroll giving*. London: The Giving Campaign.

Werther, W. B. and Chandler, D. (2011) *Strategic corporate social responsibility: Stakeholders in a global environment* (2nd edn). Thousand Oaks, CA: Sage.

Wilson, J. (2012) 'Volunteerism research: A review essay', *Nonprofit and Voluntary Sector Quarterly*, 41(2): 176–212.

Wright, K. (2002) *Generosity versus altruism: Philanthropy and charity in the US and UK*. London: Centre for Civil Society, London School of Economics and Political Science.

Young, W., Hwang, K., McDonald, S. and Oates, C. J. (2010) 'Sustainable consumption: Green consumer behaviour when purchasing products', *Sustainable Development*, 18(1): 20–31.

Further reading

Bain (2017) Bain social impact. Available at: www.socialimpactatbain.com/pursue-your-passions/green-teams.aspx (Accessed: 28 May 2017)

Becker-Olsen, K. L., Cudmore, B. A. and Hill, R. P. (2006) 'The impact of perceived corporate social responsibility on consumer behavior', *Journal of Business Research*, 59(1): 46–53.

Seth, S. and Khan, M. S. (2015) 'Green marketing: Solving dual purpose of marketing and corporate social responsibility', *Management Studies and Economic Systems*, 1(3): 181–8.

Part III
CSR measurement and communication

CSR Impact: Creating, Measuring and Communicating the Impact

8

Learning outcomes

By the end of this chapter, students should be able to:

- define social impact
- explain the importance of measuring it
- detail some of the currently available tools and frameworks
- discuss the related challenges and how to overcome them.

Case study   Thankyou – Innovative social impact assessment and communication

The social enterprise Thankyou is an example of how a few young adults with a passion for a cause can question and change existing systems and have a positive impact on the lives of many. Thankyou Water was established in 2008 by three young Australians (Daniel Flynn, Justine Flynn and Jarryd Burns) to address the global water crisis. The idea was born when Daniel Flynn discovered through a university assignment that almost 900 million people across the world do not have access to safe drinking water, while the Australian bottled water industry is worth approximately AU\$600 million. Together with a group of friends, Flynn decided to launch a bottled water company with the aim of donating 100 per cent of its profits to funding water provision and projects in developing countries.

After a few difficult years, Thankyou Water managed to get on the shelves of all the big supermarkets in Australia. In 2013, the social enterprise rebranded itself as Thankyou and expanded its product range to include food (to address food insecurity) and bodycare products (to address sanitation and hygiene in the developing world). Today, Thankyou's product range comprises over 50 products available for purchase on its website as well as in retail stores, including all the leading supermarkets in Australia. In 2016, Thankyou launched a babycare range (Thankyou Baby) to address child and maternal health issues and started work to set up Thankyou in New Zealand. To fund the new goals and product lines, Daniel Flynn wrote a book (*Chapter One*), and launched a 'pay what you want' campaign for the book. Thankyou managed to raise over AU\$1.4m in 28 days due to high consumer loyalty and a reliable network, and as of February 2017 the company had sold over 93,000 books.

Thankyou is owned by a registered charitable entity, the Thankyou Charitable Trust, and employs 55 people. After accounting for the enterprise's operating costs, the company gives 100 per cent of its profits to the Trust to fund the various programmes being implemented by its project partners. The company works with a number of significant organisations, including Oxfam, World Vision, UNICEF, Splash and One Heart World-Wide.

Thankyou had to compete with established water, food, bodycare and baby product brands and overcome various tests and challenges to become one of the most awarded and celebrated enterprises in Australia. Its aim is in alignment with the first UN SDG to eliminate global poverty by 2030. Thankyou has harnessed the use of social media to involve its consumers in its efforts to make a difference. Thankyou is transparent in its operations and provides its customers with easy access to information on its financials, successes and struggles. This social enterprise has received a number of awards such as the Westpac 200 Businesses of Tomorrow 2017 and the Anthill Cool Company Awards 2016. Daniel Flynn has also won the 2015 EY Entrepreneur of the Year Award and has been an Australian of the Year Award finalist.

Thankyou takes its social impact measurement very seriously. The social enterprise currently funds projects in India, Vietnam, Cambodia, Laos, Nepal, Bangladesh, Myanmar, Sri Lanka, Papua New Guinea, Timor-Leste, Vanuatu and Australia. According to the company's social impact reports in 2017, Thankyou has given over AU$5.5 million to people in need and funded water and sanitation services for 545,360 people, food provision for 132,664 people, with over 28.7 million days of food, as well as maternal health services for 77,314 people within just the first eight months of the launch of Thankyou Baby. The company's work has helped families in developing countries avoid disease and sickness by providing access to clean, safe drinking water.

Thankyou measures and communicates its social impact to its loyal customers and other stakeholders and, like everything it does, this too is unique and innovative. The company developed an 'impact tracker' (Track Your Impact) so every Thankyou product has a unique code used to inform customers of the exact GPS coordinates of the area they are impacting along with details of the project. Customers can also create a profile with all their tracking codes and, once a project is completed, the customer receives a social impact report.

In addition to the company's intended positive impact (e.g. providing clean water), its work has created unintended positive impacts as people are no longer sick and are able to attend school, get a job and come out of poverty. The company has empowered people to use their limited financial resources for business and economic purposes as opposed to spending money on water or medical treatment.

(Continued)

This has enabled families to lift themselves out of poverty and send their children to school, giving them the opportunity to have careers and improve their standard of living. However, Thankyou also creates an unintended negative impact. As its water bottles and product packaging involve a significant use of plastic, the company appears to be contributing to the issue of waste generation.

Through its simple messaging, sleek product design and packaging and honest interaction with consumers, Thankyou has made giving 'cool' and impact measurement a concept for all to understand and appreciate. As Daniel Flynn stated in his book, *Chapter One*, Thankyou is a social enterprise that high-fived the status quo, with a chair. The operating model of the enterprise is disruptive – it challenged every rule in the book and has attempted to change the way things are done. This enterprise is a testament to how if people push through challenges and keep reminding themselves of their 'why,' their purpose, they can change the way the game is played.

Questions

1. Why do you think so many people find Thankyou to be an inspiring organisation? Why has the enterprise won so many awards?
2. Why is it important for a company like Thankyou to be transparent and report on its social impact to all its stakeholders all the time?
3. Although it is only a small social enterprise in Australia, what can the big corporations learn from Thankyou about measuring and reporting on impact?
4. Examine the social impact reported in this case and organise it according to input (what they give), output (what comes out of it) or long-term societal impact. What did you learn from this?
5. How can big corporates work better with social enterprises to increase their social impact?

Bibliography

Flynn, D. (2016) *Chapter One: You have the power to change stuff.* Sydney: The Messenger Group.
Kimmorley, S. (2015) 'In good company: How Thankyou water got the attention of Australia's biggest retailers', *Business Insider*, 5 May.

Links

Chapter One (2017) Available at: https://chapterone.thankyou.co (Accessed: 23 April 2017)
Chapter One (2017) Available at: www.youtube.com/watch?v=Yx44cXeKC7s (Accessed: 23 April 2017)
Daniel Flynn at TEDxBrisbane (2017) Available at: www.youtube.com/watch?v=RTZC6PmsqGI (Accessed: 23 April 2017)
Justine Flynn at TEDxSouthBankWomen (2017) Available at: www.youtube.com/watch?v=5oeRbwS 6NaE (Accessed: 23 April 2017)

Thankyou (2017) Available at: www.thankyou.co (Accessed: 23 April 2017)

Thankyou Social Impact Report (2017) Available at: https://thankyou.co/impact (Accessed: 23 April 2017)

Thankyou, Our Story (2017) Available at: https://thankyou.co (Accessed: 23 April 2017)

The Coles and Woolworths Campaign (2017) Available at: www.youtube.com/watch?v=xsvzYq2melM (Accessed: 23 April 2017)

The Thankyou Model (2017) Available at: https://thankyou.co/structure (Accessed: 23 April 2017)

Introduction: What gets measured gets managed

Since the early 1990s, there has been an increasing demand from funders, tax-payers and citizens regarding the accountability and responsibility of not-for-profits to demonstrate the impact they create using donations and grants. Emphasis has been placed on the impact and long-term outcomes that not-for-profits have been able to create and the extent to which they have been successful in addressing complex social problems such as poverty and inequality (Ebrahim and Rangan, 2010). As such, the concept of social impact was discussed and developed, with appropriate tools and frameworks to allow such organisations to measure the impact they create.

In recent years, similar expectations have started to emerge in regard to companies' CSR and social businesses. If companies receive tax benefits when they give to charity, utilise employees' money and time to benefit the community and claim that they benefit society, shouldn't they be held accountable and demonstrate the impact they claim to create? Measuring impact allows companies to prove that they really are making a difference, to measure their progress and to allow others to compare the impact made by their company to other companies.

Furthermore, the lines between investors and funders have recently begun to blur, giving rise to concepts such as 'social accountability' or 'social return on investment' and the discussion on corporate social impact has started to penetrate the corporations' boardrooms. There has also been a rise in the formalisation of social impact, particularly in the developed world, which has seen the creation of tools and frameworks to measure social impact as well as the emergence of experts (including auditors and evaluators) around impact measurement. These developments create a great opportunity for corporations to start measuring their impact and engage stakeholders in their story of change.

However, often, too often perhaps, CSR reports tend to focus on input, that is what the company has invested in contributing to society, such as the amount of money given or the number of employees who volunteered in the previous year for so many hours. Some companies also report on the activities that took place, but it is still rare to find reports that measure and communicate the long-term outcomes their CSR had on society and the planet. However, social impact assessment indicates a focus on the results of an activity and not on the activity itself. In other words, we need to focus on the outcomes of an activity and not on the processes, inputs or outputs that make up an activity.

In addition, impact is sometimes communicated in qualitative terms such as 'we are saving lives' or 'our organisation has made a difference in the education of many children'. However, these statements do not assess the measureable impact or effectiveness of an organisation, demonstrate progress over time or allow for comparisons. Companies need to measure their impact and report it, showing the actual difference that was made to whom over a certain period of time.

As such, in this chapter we will offer definitions of social impact, explain the importance of measuring it, detail some of the current tools and frameworks to allow more systematic measurement and comparisons, and discuss the related challenges and how to overcome them.

Social impact, collective impact and social impact assessment

Social impact (or mission-related impact) has many definitions and frameworks, and while there is no one agreed-upon definition, most of the existing ones include the aspects of positive change due to intervention. One such definition is offered by the International Association for Impact Assessment (IAIA), which defines impact as change to one or more of the following: 'people's way of life, their culture, community, political systems, environment, health and wellbeing, personal property and rights and their fears and aspirations' (Vanclay, 2003: 8). In this definition, the focus is on the object of change. The definition provides a relatively narrow list of items that, when changed for the better, social impact is created. While we can think of items that are not on the list (e.g. education), some of the items listed are broad enough to include almost anything. As such, we can include education and most of the other items on the list under 'wellbeing'.

Another definition, offered by Auerswald (2009: 52), describes social impact as 'the creation of benefits or reductions of costs for society – through efforts to address societal needs and problems – in ways that go beyond the private gains and general benefits of market activity'. This definition is quite different from the first one and examines the 'what' (benefits or reduction in costs), the 'how' (efforts to address problems) and the 'why' (the desire to go beyond maximising profits) of social impact.

While most definitions of social impact usually focus on the creation of benefits to some group of people/animals or the environment, it should be noted that social impact could also prevent negative results, such as mortality, illness or crime, while also reducing costs for governments and society. If a company is involved in enhancing people's physical and psychological wellbeing as part of its CSR, it may indirectly reduce mortality rates, stress and suicide attempts while also saving taxpayer money in the long run, with a reduced need for healthcare and a reduction in healthcare costs. For example, Meals on Wheels America, due to its safety checks in elderly people's homes, helps to prevent falls which cost the nation US$34 billion each year. By helping to reduce the number of falls, the organisation helps to further reduce illnesses, injuries and mental disorders while also saving money.

Collective impact is the commitment of a group of actors from different sectors to a common agenda for solving a specific social problem, using a structured form of collaboration (Kania and Kramer, 2011). According to Kania and Kramer, the concept of collective impact is based on the idea that for organisations (be it not-for-profits or companies) to create long-lasting and sustainable solutions to social and environmental problems on a large scale, they need to co-ordinate their efforts, create cross-sector coalitions and work together around clearly defined goals. This is opposed to what these authors call 'isolated impact', an approach oriented towards finding and funding a solution embodied within a single organisation, with the hope of growing or replicating the programme to extend their impact more widely.

Social impact assessment (SIA) or measurement includes the 'processes of analysing, monitoring and managing the intended and unintended social consequences, both positive and negative, of planned interventions' (Vanclay, 2003: 5). Based on this definition, SIA comprises three main activities: analysis (including qualitative and quantitative data analysis), monitoring (which may include auditing, comparisons to other organisations or to previous performance) and managing the impact created by the company (including setting direction, goals and objectives and ensuring the achievement of the same).

Interestingly, this definition includes unintended and negative impact, while most companies tend to measure intended and positive impact. By measuring the unintended negative impact a company might have, it can help monitor, control and reduce it or even find alternative ways of contributing to society that might avoid the negative impact altogether. For example, our opening case of Thankyou might have a negative impact on the environment due to the plastic bottles it sells. Measuring the negative impact and finding ways to reduce it (e.g. using recyclable plastic) might help the company to be and be perceived as being 'more holistically good'.

Another example is TOMS Shoes (www.toms.com). TOMS was established in 2006 with CSR as its main purpose. TOMS is often seen as a social business, because for every pair of shoes TOMS sells in the developed world, it gives a free pair of shoes to a child in need. From the company's early days, founder Blake Mycoskie, who was motivated by the poverty he encountered in Argentina, has worked to holistically integrate sustainable and responsible practices, from the materials used to make the shoes (natural hemp, organic cotton and recycled polyester) to the packaging used for the shoes (made from 80 per cent recycled post-consumer waste and printed with soy ink). Obviously, the company has tremendous positive outcomes (children receiving shoes) and long-term impact.

Shoes give children a mode of transportation, health and safety. For some children, having shoes means the ability to walk to school and get an education, while for others it means staying healthy and safe, the ability to help their family, and so on. It is also an example of strategic CSR, as the company's giving is fully aligned with its core operations. However, TOMS has been criticised for having (unintended) negative impact on local markets, including shoemakers and retailers running out of business in areas where the company donates its shoes (Wydick, 2015). In 2010, TOMS was involved in measuring its social impact and the team working on it measured the impact on local markets in El Salvador, discovering that while it was not significant, TOMS still had some negative impact on local markets. Measuring this allowed the company to be more aware of the negative impact, monitor it and strive to reduce it.

The importance of measuring impact

Social impact assessment takes time, effort and money and social impact can be very difficult to quantify and measure accurately. Some companies argue that instead of putting all these resources into measuring social impact, they might as well just focus on creating it. However, measuring social impact can help improve the benefits to society, the same way that conducting quality control on products the company sells helps to improve the product and ensure market satisfaction. It is therefore highly essential to measure the social impact of CSR and corporate giving, for several reasons, detailed below:

Constant benchmarking and improvement: According to McKinsey & Company (2017a, 2017b), the goal of social impact assessment is to drive improvements that increase the value of programmes to the people they serve. Social impact assessment helps organisations to plan better, implement more effectively and successfully bring initiatives to scale. Indeed, social impact assessment can improve the impact made, as what gets measured gets done. If a company gives millions of dollars to charity without social impact assessment, how does it know that the money was invested in the best way possible? How does it know that the money, taken from shareholders, governments and other stakeholders, really served society? And how can it improve on what it does without benchmarking and comparing its impact to others?

Accountability: Assessment also facilitates accountability, which is the obligation on the company to account for its activities, accept responsibility for them and disclose the results in a transparent manner. It also includes the responsibility for money or other entrusted property. The same accountability and transparency that a company should have in regard to the use of shareholder money need to apply to corporate giving. Being accountable about the company's CSR and philanthropy can help guide the allocation of scarce resources in the most effective way.

Stakeholder management: Social impact assessment is part of good corporate stakeholder responsibility and stakeholder integration. There are many stakeholders who affect or who are affected by the company's giving, from shareholders whose money is used for CSR activities to employees who give time for these activities, but most of all, the community and the recipients (both direct and indirect) of CSR. Responsibility to these stakeholders and constant communication with them is also translated into disclosing the positive and negative impacts of the company.

Inspiring others: By measuring and reporting on their social impact, companies can inspire others to be involved (as will be further discussed in Chapter 9). This is not about the company raving about its performance, rather it is about the company becoming a CSR leader to inspire and encourage others to do the same, even its competitors. When other companies see the scale of the impact that was made and how CSR can make a difference to society and to the environment, they might be encouraged to be part of the movement for change. If others replicate the CSR programmes of a certain company, this actually contributes to a higher level of (collective) impact.

Clear goals: Measuring social impact can also help companies to identify and articulate their CSR goals and objectives. When objectives are made in quantifiable and measurable terms, not only is it easier to measure their achievement but it can also clarify the pathways to achieve these goals. While it might be tempting to keep goals obscure so that we do not fail, measurable objectives are the only way to really know whether we have succeeded.

Social impact measurement tools and methods

With more and more companies beginning to talk about the need to create and measure social impact and with the benefits of social impact assessment receiving more attention, the applications of existing social impact assessment tools started to emerge and new tools and methods were further developed. These developments made social impact assessment more accessible and further contributed to the constant need and desire to measure.

There are many (possibly over 20) social impact assessment tools and frameworks, which differ by their level of sophistication, the knowledge required to use them, their target audience and whether they are more quantitative or qualitative. This chapter will not provide information on all of these tools and frameworks, but will detail several of these and offer a starting point for those interested in perusing more information on social impact assessment. Some of these tools were used for many

Method	What it is	Benefits	Limitations
Logic models	A graphic display of the relationship between inputs, activities and results (outcomes and long-term impact).	• Easy to develop and comprehend. • Establishes a clear link between inputs/activities and results. • Differentiates between input, short-term and long-term results.	• No monetisation. • Comparison issues. • Difficult for collective impact measurement. • Weak analytical tests of causal links in the model.
Theory of change	A framework that suggests starting with the desired impact and working backwards to activities and input.	• Similar to the benefits of logic models. • Focuses on the end results. • Ensures that activities serve results.	• Similar to the limitations of logic models. • Risk of not measuring impact, only aiming towards it.
Social return on investment	A framework for measuring and accounting for value; incorporating social, environmental and economic costs and benefits.	• Different stakeholder perspectives. • Measures both financial and social values. • Converts social impact into financial language. • Can both forecast and evaluate.	• Time-consuming. • Too much focus on monetary results. • An outcome rather than a process evaluation. • Requires a diverse skill set and accreditation.
Social audit and accounting	A framework for the ongoing monitoring and evaluating of impact as part of the company's accountability to internal and external stakeholders.	• Offers a holistic and easy-to-follow process of examining impact. • Takes into account external stakeholders' perspective. • Provides a rich source of information.	• Can be labour-intensive. • Not explicitly recognised by funders and lenders. • Lack of empirical research.
SIMPLE (Social IMPact measurement for Local Economies)	A framework that involves an internal strategic review, alongside an outcomes-based assessment.	• Universally applicable to all socially motivated businesses across different sectors and contexts. • Effective in start-ups and strategic planning. • Helps procurement and funding opportunities. • Assists in identifying key areas of performance.	• Stages are not all clear. • Difficult to implement the 'embed it' stage. • Not enough support and evidence on its effectiveness.

Figure 8.1 **Several social impact assessment tools, their benefits and limitations**

years among not-for-profits and social enterprises, while others are more tailored to the needs of corporations. In this chapter, we will focus mainly on logic models, theory of change, social return on investment (SROI), social accounting and audit (SAA) and SIMPLE. Each of these tools will be discussed next, with the benefits and limitations of the various tools and methods listed in Figure 8.1.

Logic models

Logic models are frameworks used for programme planning, management and evaluation. A logic model (also known as a 'logical framework', 'programme logic' and 'programme theory' or 'impact value chain') is an easy to understand graphic display of the relationship between the programme's resources (inputs), activities and intended or actual results, both short term (often referred to as outcomes) and long term (impact) (Kaplan and Garrett, 2005).

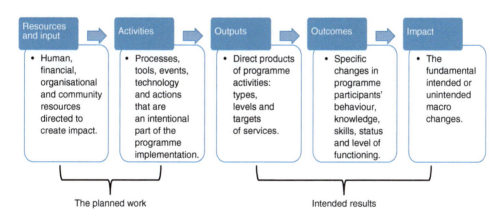

Figure 8.2 The basic logic model

Logic models include several components that are read from left to right and follow a chain of reasoning or 'If x then y' statements, which connect the programme's parts (see Figure 8.2). These components are often mistakenly used interchangeably. Some companies declare to report their impact but only report on input and activities, as it is a lot harder to measure the long-term macro-level impacts an organisation has had on society. Figure 8.2 summarises these five components and defines them to assist in clearly differentiating the various stages of impact creation.

To illustrate, let us use a well-known international not-for-profit, Meals on Wheels America. On its website it declares (italics for emphasis, not in original):

Meals on Wheels America is the oldest and largest national organization supporting the more than 5,000 community-based senior nutrition programs across the country that are dedicated *to addressing senior hunger and isolation*. This network exists in virtually every community in America and, along with more than *two million volunteers*, delivers the *nutritious meals, friendly visits and safety checks* that enable America's seniors to live *nourished lives with independence and dignity*. By providing funding, leadership, research, education and advocacy support, Meals on Wheels America empowers its local member programs to *strengthen their communities*, one senior at a time.

Let's apply this statement to a logic model. By examining this quote (without even delving into the company's annual reports) we can see some of the *resources/inputs* used. The human resources include many paid staff and two million volunteers (assuming each one gives at least two hours per week, the time resources = four million hours). There is also the food, the money, the physical buildings and venues, the cars, the petrol, and so on and so forth. With additional work, one can actually assign a dollar value to all these inputs.

Then there are the *activities*. In this case the main activity is the preparation and delivery of meals. Volunteers collect the meals that someone else has prepared and deliver them to senior people in need. In activities, we can also include the operation management and the facilitation of all these millions of meal deliveries that take place all over the country every year. In the above statement, the organisation further states that it has additional activities 'providing funding, leadership, research, education and advocacy support'.

The *outputs* are the direct products of this programme. While the original main output was to deliver 'nutritious meals' to senior citizens, over time it was realised that by visiting the elderly, volunteers can also check that they are safe and healthy, and offer them some social connections as well: 'nutritious meals, friendly visits and safety checks.' Some volunteers take their children with them when delivering the meals and it can be a real joy for lonely older people.

The *outcomes* are changes to the lives and wellbeing of the service recipients and other stakeholders, or, as stated above, 'addressing senior hunger and isolation' and 'nourished lives with independence and dignity'. People's physical wellbeing should increase as a result of receiving nutritious meals, avoiding the consequences of food insecurity and having someone check if they are injured or ill. Their psychological wellbeing should increase as a result of social interactions, increased dignity and reduced stress.

Finally, the macro long-term *impact* is also stated in the above: 'empowering local member programmes to strengthen their communities.' When people volunteer and connect with one another, the social capital in the community increases. Social capital has many definitions but can be perceived as the social connections and connectedness in the community, resulting in co-operation, mutual benefits, trust and resilience. When communities have high levels of social capital, their overall wellbeing is increased and they are more resilient when facing difficulties. Think, for example, of how a well-connected community would face a natural disaster compared to one in which everyone is isolated. Such a long-term macro-level impact has many benefits, in addition to the overall increase in food security and people's wellbeing, which in turn can also prevent other negative impacts and save resources for society and the government.

When measuring impact, the organisation could/should quantify all these measures. Setting clear and measurable objectives for a programme means using numbers and a timeline and providing evidence that the impact has been achieved. For example, Meals on Wheels America might set objectives as follows: in 12 months, service recipients will report on higher levels of health and sense of security. Indeed, on the company's website, it is reported that 83 per cent of recipients say they have improved health, 92 per cent say the service enables them to stay at home, while 87 per cent say it allows them to stay at home. There are measures and indicators to many of the above outputs, outcomes and impacts, which can assist CSR programmes in measuring their social impact. Setting goals, collecting data, measuring results in comparison to these goals and reporting on all of the above are at the essence of social impact assessment.

The logic model is relatively easy to develop and comprehend, and it does not take advanced knowledge and many resources to put into practice. The model establishes a clear link between inputs/activities and results and therefore can help improve any of these components. It helps to differentiate between input, short-term and long-term results, which is a well-known pitfall of social impact assessment. Logic models can be used as a planning tool when developing a policy or a programme strategy as well as an assessment tool.

On the other hand, it does not necessarily offer a quantitative measure of impact; in particular, it does not help understand the impact in monetary terms. It poses some comparison issues, as each organisation might develop its own story using the logic models. Furthermore, it is difficult (but not impossible) to use logic models for collective impact measurement, and the analytical tests of causal links in the model are weak.

EXERCISE

1. Examine the opening case of Thankyou. What are the inputs, activities, outputs, outcomes and impact the organisation achieves?
2. Look for an annual report of a large corporation and examine the way it reports on its social impact. What is measured? What is reported and not reported upon? What can you learn from this?

Theory of change

Theory of change is similar to the logic model as it also uses the same components, namely input, activities, outputs and outcomes. However, it is different in the sense that it works from the end backwards. Theory of change is a framework that suggests to start with the desired impact and work from there all the way to activities and input. Instead of trying to measure the impact of what it is that we are already doing, we plan the activities based on the impact we want to achieve.

Theory of change is an approach to planning and evaluating activities, projects, services or communities of service to deliver identified long-term changes, or outcomes (Connell and Kubisch, 1998). The approach involves the identification of desired outcomes, and uses a 'backwards planning' approach to map the intermediate outcomes and activities, or interventions, required to deliver these long-term changes. As such, theory of change requires the following five steps in the following order (see also Figure 8.3):

1. *Identify the desired impact* (or long-term outcomes) and articulate the assumptions associated with these outcomes. What is it that your organisation desires to achieve? In the case of Thankyou, Daniel Flynn and other co-founders were deeply moved by the fact that 900 million people today do not have access to safe water. Their goal was to change that, and this is how they started. Other organisations will have other large-scale and long-term goals such as gender equity, addressing poverty or building strong and resilient communities, just to name a few.

2. Use a 'backwards mapping' technique to understand the pathway to change. What *intermediate outcomes* are required to deliver the desired long-term impact? In the case of Thankyou, the founders thought about what was required to start building sustainable water sources in developing and under-privileged communities.

3. Develop *indicators for outcomes* so that progress towards long-term outcomes can be measured and evidenced. As mentioned above, this is the stage at which large-scale and sometimes obscure goals need to be translated into measurable objectives. Thankyou could, for example, set a goal of building 100 wells in seven countries in the next ten years. It could also count how many people now have access to clean water as a result of its new well (on its website it reports that, as of February 2017, it had assisted over 500,000 people to gain access to safe water, sanitation and hygiene services). However, over time, using additional indicators and outcomes, the company may demonstrate how it also created impact around education (children who are no longer sick due to unsafe water can now attend school), work opportunities and stronger communities.

4. *Identify interventions or activities required to deliver the identified outcomes.* This is when the organisation starts to understand what is required to achieve

the above outcomes and impact and to aim for the input, resources and activities that would allow it to achieve the impact. In the case of Thankyou, the company realised that starting a water company and selling bottled water could help the company raise the funds needed to build the wells. It later started setting new goals for impact and outcomes and developed new resources and activities to achieve these as well.

5. *Write a narrative account of the change made.* This part is shifting away from the mere four or five stages we saw in the logic models, to move into reporting. In this case, the theory of change model suggests writing (or sharing in other forms, such as the TED talk by Thankyou) a compelling story about the impact, outcomes and activities conducted by the organisation. The narrative allows the organisation to not only share its story and provide evidence of impact but also to gain further support and resources and reflect on what was achieved. As such, this can be seen as a cycle, and after stage 5 the organisation goes back to stage 1 and the cycle continues.

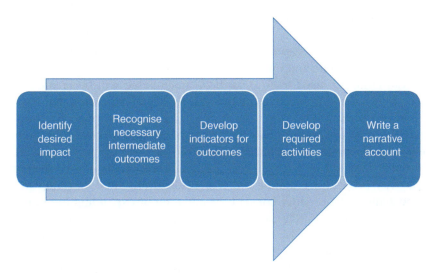

Figure 8.3   The five steps of theory of change

Theory of change shares some of the benefits and limitations of logic models but also has some unique ones. Focusing on the desired impact and end results from the very beginning can help ensure focus on the achievement of long-term outcomes. The inputs, activities and outputs are all designed with this end result in mind. It also encourages the organisation to share the story of change, how it was achieved and what impact was created so that other organisations can learn from it. However, since the desired impact is set at the start, it is possible that it will not be measured adequately.

Social return on investment (SROI)

The social return on investment (SROI) method was developed in 1996 by the Roberts Enterprise Development Fund (REDF), a philanthropic organisation that creates employment opportunities for people facing the biggest barriers to work (Rosenzweig, 2004). Built on the basic idea of financial return on investment (ROI), SROI attempts to quantify both economic and social impacts of social enterprises by applying a monetary value to ventures or activities with social objectives and examining the ratio between money (and other resources) invested in a programme and its social value (including money saved). As such, a calculation of SROI could result in a conclusion that for every $1 invested in a certain social programme, $7 were saved, or a ratio of 1:7.

SROI is a framework for measuring and accounting for a broader concept of value; it seeks to reduce inequality and environmental degradation and improve wellbeing by incorporating social, environmental and economic costs and benefits. It monetises a variety of outcomes and provides an idea of how much social value will be created through every dollar of investment. According to EY (2017), SROI is an alternative accounting and economic analysis that is capable of measuring the wider concept of value generated through social investments, which takes into account social, economic and environmental factors.

SROI can either be used to *forecast* how much value will be created if activities meet their intended objectives or to *evaluate* actual outcomes that have taken place. For forecasting, SROI can help in making a more informed decision of the CSR activities/projects/programmes that a company should select to implement. It can help decision makers see which programme will yield the highest social return on investment, instead of focusing on costs alone. In highlighting the potential of the activity/project/programme under consideration, SROI can help in raising funds and achieving a broader consent for initiating or expanding the same.

As for evaluation, a SROI can assess the efficiency with which a CSR programme/activity has been planned and delivered. A sensitivity analysis of the SROI against the cost of the initiative can provide a broad direction towards streamlining in the future. The process of deriving the SROI, the project costs and the key financial and social value can be used to evaluate a CSR programme and so plan it better in the years to come. It can also be used to communicate with a broad set of stakeholders who need to be informed about the company's CSR activities and impact.

SROI can be calculated by identifying the following metrics (see Brooks, 2009):

- *Enterprise value*: the net revenues from the business side of a social venture.
- *Social purpose value*: the value that the enterprise creates for society.
- *Blended value*: the enterprise and social purpose values minus the long-term debt.

SROI is complicated to calculate and requires knowledge of each metric and how to calculate it. There are webinars and workshops to assist people who want to learn how to do this. In addition, there are many firms and organisations that can assist companies, not-for-profits and social enterprises to calculate their SROI.

The advantages of SROI are that, in accordance with strategic CSR, it includes and communicates with a broad set of stakeholders and takes into account their various perspectives. It measures both financial and social value, but by using a dollar value to assess a social impact, it allows for a good comparison between programmes and organisations. By using financial language, it may be easier to communicate with profit-minded executives and build a business case for CSR. As for the limitations, SROI is time-consuming and requires specific skills, knowledge and accreditation. The evaluation is focused on money and outcomes, rather than on the process. There is a risk that the focus is too much on the dollar value, and some outcomes cannot be easily translated into a monetary outcome.

Social accounting and audit (SAA)

In 1972, Charles Medawar developed the social audit, also known as social accounting and audit (SAA) (Belal, 2002). The SAA is a framework for ongoing monitoring and evaluating of impact as part of the company's accountability to internal and external stakeholders. The framework can assist organisations, including companies with CSR, in evaluating their social, environmental and economic objectives and ensure that these are functioning in line with the values of the organisation. SAA can help companies to prove, improve and account for (see Figure 8.4) the difference they are making. It can also assist in planning and managing the organisation, as well as demonstrate impact.

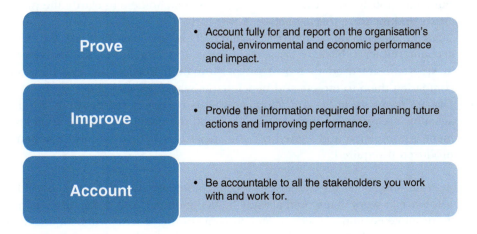

Prove
- Account fully for and report on the organisation's social, environmental and economic performance and impact.

Improve
- Provide the information required for planning future actions and improving performance.

Account
- Be accountable to all the stakeholders you work with and work for.

Figure 8.4   The three components of SAA

SAA can help understand and report on the impact the organisation has on people, the planet and the way it uses resources. It also helps to manage the organisation and improve its effectiveness. It can be used by any organisation, whether not-for-profit, public or private sector and of any size or scale. It uses eight key principles to underpin its process, ensure that verification is effective and deliver continuous improvement. These are:

1. Clarify purpose
2. Define scope
3. Engage stakeholders
4. Determine materiality
5. Make comparisons (benchmarking)
6. Be transparent
7. Verify accounts
8. Embed the process.

In addition, there are four main stages of SAA:

1. *What difference do we want to make? Clarify the desired impact.* Similar to the theory of change, in this step the company needs to have a clear CSR vision and clarify what kind of impact it wants to create and for whom. At this stage, the company also needs to identify all the relevant stakeholders.
2. *How do we know we are making a difference? Impact assessment plan.* At this stage, it is important to understand and identify indicators and outcomes. As mentioned above, there are indicators and measures of many social impact goals and it is important to find and utilise them. At this stage, the company can continuously collect data and engage its stakeholders to clarify the plan to create and measure the impact.
3. *What is the difference we are making?* This involves drafting the social accounts, either in basic or advanced format. The data and indicators collected in step two are used to report on performance, impact and key outcomes, comparing them to targets and benchmarks where appropriate.
4. *Can we prove we made a difference?* This is the audit stage where the draft accounts are tested by the social auditor and the panel. The social audit statement is completed and signed off, the social report finalised and a summary produced if required.

Throughout, the social impact assessment includes the use of concise checklists and reference to work that would already be being undertaken within the organisation to promote economy of effort. The outcome of the process will be a document that staff, board and external stakeholders can use to see the value of the activities covered.

SAA has many advantages: it offers a holistic and easy-to-follow process of examining impact, takes into account external stakeholders' perspective and provides a rich source of information. On the other hand, it can be labour-intensive and takes a lot of time and effort. It is not yet explicitly recognised by funders and lenders and we lack academic research on it.

SIMPLE: Social IMPact measurement for Local Economies

SIMPLE (Social IMPact measurement for Local Economies) is a social impact assessment framework that combines an internal strategic review with an outcomes-based assessment to help managers of socially motivated businesses to visualise where and how they make positive contributions to society. SIMPLE can be used by organisations, including companies, to communicate the social benefits and added social value created by their (CSR) activities.

SIMPLE was developed by Social Enterprise London (SEL) together with the University of Brighton. It includes five stages:

1. *Scope it*: By carrying out a strategic review, boundaries of scope can be set. This requires the company to select the relevant area(s) or scope(s) to be explored. Whilst considering the scope, organisations can take into account the aims and activities of the company, its stakeholders' priorities and needs, the environment and the company's internal drivers.
2. *Map it*: At this stage, the company needs to map out the effects of daily work activities. Part of this mapping requires the exploration of relationships between the work/activities that are being carried out by the organisation and the short-, medium- and long-term effects of doing so. This can also be used to map out where impact is likely to occur in the future, taking into account the data that should be collected to evidence such impact.
3. *Track it*: At this stage, the company tracks outcomes by assigning appropriate indicators. The continuation of data collection processes enables the generation of a representation of the impact being measured.
4. *Tell it*: This stage includes exploring and discussing the social impacts that were measured in the previous stages, and contextualising them for a range of stakeholders and audiences.
5. *Embed it*: This is an ongoing stage in which the previous stages of collecting data and measuring impact are continuously embedded into the organisation.

By selecting suitable indicators, organisations can evidence their social impact based on the systems they have put in place in order to gather appropriate information. This can help organisations visualise how they are creating positive social change and in turn collect supporting evidence for the outcomes being created, as a result of the project/activity being measured. The framework can be useful for identifying information that is not currently being measured for the future, to demonstrate the organisation's level of social impact.

The benefits of using the SIMPLE framework include improving an organisation's performance through strategic analysis and maintaining adaptability for different circumstances within diverse types of organisations. Research shows that while the SIMPLE framework delivers positive learning experiences on impact measurement, there is not enough knowledge and support on embedding social impact assessment in an organisation.

Impact measurement challenges

While social impact assessment has many benefits for the companies that try to assess it, for the CSR beneficiaries and for the company's stakeholders – it can also be quite challenging to implement. Social impact assessment is costly, difficult and ambiguous. It takes time, effort and knowledge. And while there are many tools and frameworks, as was shown above, it can be overwhelming and confusing. As such, it is little wonder that many companies don't manage to successfully measure social impact and report on it, and focus instead on inputs and activities. In this section, several such challenges will be discussed with some pathways to overcome or address them.

Firstly, *the nature of social impact* makes it difficult to measure. Social impact is hard to assess in a short time frame. Outcomes, particularly long-term macro-level outcomes, are not as easily quantified as outputs. They can be the ambiguous results of numerous variables. It is easier to discuss how many employees volunteered last year and explain what they did, rather than try to show what long-term effects their volunteering had. However, it is not impossible. There are macro-level indicators that can be cautiously used to discuss the company's contribution to society while acknowledging that it only played a part in this achievement.

Secondly, social impact assessment can be *difficult and costly*. Doing it properly takes a large amount of time, money and knowledge. Not every company that contributes to society has the skills or resources to measure impact. Some frameworks and tools, such as SROI, require an advanced set of skills and knowledge to implement. This is particularly the case with smaller companies (SMEs) that do not have the human and financial resources to deal with this. In order to address this challenge, companies could collaborate with others to measure and create impact. There are supportive organisations that can help companies with this difficult task. Furthermore, companies can work together to create collective social impact and measure it together as well. In addition, many companies that contribute to not-for-profits ask that the recipient organisation helps to measure the impact created.

Thirdly, there is the *attribution* challenge. The measurement challenge that many organisations face is to demonstrate a connection between output (e.g. number of meals delivered to elderly people) and outcome (e.g. increased food security, decreased illness and injuries) and to describe that connection quantitatively (i.e. 'Our operations lowered falls by 15 per cent of elderly people in their homes in the last 12 months'). Quantifying and tracking this relationship is costly and it is almost impossible to demonstrate. Even if the organisation manages to collect all the required data before and after the intervention, it is still hard to show that no other factors were involved in the results. To achieve this, organisations can use control groups and measure the results using valid indicators before and after. It is also possible to partner with academics who are keen to get access to the data and analyse it so they can publish academic articles based on the same.

Fourthly, social impact assessment *consumes resources* that could be directly invested in the programme and service recipients. Even if social impact assessment is outsourced, it still costs money and there can be an objection from investors or the executive leadership to invest so much money and divert it from the programme. A perception exists that outcomes and impacts are too costly and time-consuming to measure systematically (McCreless et al., 2013). However, as was explained earlier in this chapter, social impact assessment can also save a lot of resources by facilitating a comparison of programmes and ensuring the programmes are as cost-effective as they can possibly be. There are also ways of reducing costs, such as training the company's CSR champions and stakeholders to take an active part in this process, develop the required knowledge and skills, and assist.

Fifthly, companies that want to measure their social impact face a lack of standardised measures for impact measurements. Presently there are no standardised measures to assess social impact, although best practices are emerging (Rosenzweig, 2004). The primary reason behind the lack of standardisation of a tool to measure social impact is the diverse nature of impact created by companies, not-for-profits and social enterprises, which also makes it difficult to compare the effectiveness of a programme or an organisation. The variety of frameworks and tools, however, also implies that each organisation can use the ones that best suit its needs, abilities and resources.

Summary

A growing number of companies began to measure and report on the social impact of their CSR as expectations emerged together with many tools and frameworks. Social impact is about the changes that occur in people's lives, in the community and in the environment as a (direct or indirect) result of certain intervention (in the context of this book, through CSR). There are several definitions of social impact, some of which also include unintended impact or negative impact. In addition, there is now a shift toward collective impact in which several organisations and stakeholders work together to increase the breadth and depth of the impact.

Companies have now started to understand that measuring impact is important, as part of their accountability to their stakeholders, in their communication and in engaging employees and consumers. Social impact assessment (which is processes of analysing, monitoring and managing the intended and unintended social consequences) also provides vital information that allows a company to assess the effectiveness and efficiency of its CSR compared to other companies, to what it has done in the past and to what it could do in the future. It therefore creates a pathway for improvement and a strong impact in the future.

In the last few decades, over 20 different tools and frameworks have emerged, with some being more prominent and commonly used than others. We have looked at logic models, which are a graphic display or map of the relationship between a programme's inputs, activities, outputs, outcomes and impact. Similarly, the theory of change uses the same four or five components, but suggests starting with the end result in mind and working back to what is required to achieve this. SROI is a little different, being a more quantitative and systematic tool to measure impact, while considering all stakeholders. Similarly, the social accounting and audit (SAA) tool is a framework for ongoing monitoring, evaluation and accountability to internal and external stakeholders of the organisation. Finally, SIMPLE uses five stages from mapping impact to embedding it in the organisation. There are many other tools and frameworks that can be examined. While it can be overwhelming, it is important to make your organisation familiar with the various options and apply the one most suitable to you.

Social impact assessment is far from easy. It requires time, knowledge and resources. Not all organisations have these resources and some argue that by diverting resources towards social impact assessment, organisations do not maximise their contribution. It is important to acknowledge these and other challenges and find creative ways to address them, as social impact assessment is going to become an essential part of CSR.

General questions

1. There are presently many measures and tools offered for companies that want to measure the social impact of their CSR. Why is it important to choose the right tool for the company?
2. Examine the various social impact tools presented in this chapter. Think about three kinds of organisations: not-for-profits, social enterprises and large corporations. Which tool would you offer to each kind of organisation?
3. What could be the right tool for Thankyou and TOMS Shoes? Why?

4. If you were a consultant helping companies to measure their social impact, how would you convince them to measure both the positive and the negative impact they create? How would you get over the fears that an organisation may face in measuring and reporting negative impact?

Key definitions

- Social impact (or mission-related impact) is the changes to people's way of life, their culture, community, political systems, environment, health and wellbeing, personal property or rights and their fears and aspirations (Vanclay, 2003).
- Social impact is the creation of benefits or reductions of costs for society – through efforts to address societal needs and problems – in ways that go beyond the private gains and general benefits of market activity (Auerswald, 2009).
- Social impact assessment is the 'processes of analysing, monitoring and managing the intended and unintended social consequences, both positive and negative, of planned interventions' (Vanclay, 2003).
- Collective impact is the commitment of a group of actors from different sectors to a common agenda for solving a specific social problem, using a structured form of collaboration (Kania and Kramer, 2011).
- Logic models are a graphic display or map of the relationship between a programme's resources, activities and intended/actual results (Kaplan and Garrett, 2005).
- Social return on investment (SROI) is a stakeholder-driven evaluation tool that applies a monetary value to ventures with social objectives by identifying a set of six metrics including enterprise value, social purpose value, blended value, enterprise index of return, social purpose index of return and blended index of return (Ryan and Lyne, 2008).
- The social accounting and audit (SAA) tool is a framework for continuous monitoring, evaluation and accountability to internal and external stakeholders of the organisation.

References

Auerswald, P. (2009) 'Creating social value', *Stanford Social Innovation Review*, 7(2): 51–5.

Belal, A. R. (2002) 'Stakeholder accountability or stakeholder management: a review of UK firms' social and ethical accounting, auditing and reporting (SEAAR) practices', *Corporate Social Responsibility and Environmental Management*, 9(1): 8–25.

Brooks, A. C. (2009) *Social entrepreneurship: A modern approach to social value creation*. Englewood Cliffs, NJ: Prentice Hall.

Connell, J. P. and Kubisch, A. C. (1998) 'Applying a theory of change approach to the evaluation of comprehensive community initiatives: Progress, prospects, and problems', *New Approaches to Evaluating Community Initiatives*, 2(15–44): 1–16.

Ebrahim, A. S. and Rangan, V. K. (2010) 'The limits of nonprofit impact: A contingency framework for measuring social performance', *Harvard Business School General Management Unit Working Paper no. 10–099*. Available at: https://papers.ssrn.com/sol3/papers.cfm?abstract_id=1611810 (Accessed: 23 April 2017)

EY (2017) Social return on investment: Defining the impact of social sector initiatives. Available at: www.ey.com/Publication/vwLUAssets/EY-Government-and-Public-Sector-Social-Return-on-Investment/$File/EY-Social-Return-on-Investment.pdf (Accessed: 23 April 2017)

Kania, J. and Kramer, M. (2011) 'Collective impact', *Stanford Social Innovation Review*, 9: 36–41.

Kaplan, S. A. and Garrett, K. E. (2005) 'The use of logic models by community-based initiatives', *Evaluation and Program Planning*, 28(2): 167–72.

McCreless, E., Visconti, P., Carwardine, J., Wilcox, C. and Smith, R. J. (2013) 'Cheap and nasty? The potential perils of using management costs to identify global conservation priorities', *PloS one*, 8(11): e80893.

McKinsey & Company (2017a) What is social impact assessment? Available at: http://mckinseyonsociety.com/social-impact-assessment/what-is-social-impact-assessment (Accessed: 23 April 2017)

McKinsey & Company (2017b) The history of social impact assessment. Available at: http://mckinseyonsociety.com/downloads/tools/LSI/The-history-of-social-impact-assessment.pdf (Accessed: 23 April 2017)

Rosenzweig, W. (2004) Double bottom line project report: Assessing social impact in double bottom line ventures. Available at: http://escholarship.org/uc/item/80n4f1mf (Accessed: 23 April 2017)

Ryan, P. W. and Lyne, I. (2008) 'Social enterprise and the measurement of social value: Methodological issues with the calculation and application of the social return on investment', *Education, Knowledge & Economy*, 2(3): 223–37.

Vanclay, F. (2003) 'International principles for social impact assessment', *Impact Assessment and Project Appraisal*, 21(1): 5–12.

Wydick, B. (2015) 'The impact of TOMS Shoes', *Across Two Worlds*, 16 March. Available at: www.acrosstwoworlds.net/?p=292 (Accessed: 28 May 2017)

Further reading and links

Center for Theory of Change (2017) Available at: www.theoryofchange.org (Accessed: 23 April 2017)

Davenport, K. (2000) 'Corporate citizenship: A stakeholder approach for defining corporate social performance and identifying measures for assessing it', *Business & Society*, 39(2): 210–19.

Du, S., Bhattacharya, C. B. and Sen, S. (2010) 'Maximizing business returns to corporate social responsibility (CSR): The role of CSR communication', *International Journal of Management Reviews*: 12(1): 8–19.

McKinsey (2017) LSI: Why is SIA important? Available at: www.youtube.com/watch?time_continue=18&v=RB1Z5_xr6F0 (Accessed: 3 April 2017)

McKinsey on Society (2017) The history of social impact assessment. Available at: http://mckinseyonsociety.com/downloads/tools/LSI/The-history-of-social-impact-assessment.pdf (Accessed: 16 March 2017)

McKinsey on Society (2017) What is social impact assessment? Available at: http://mckinseyonsociety.com/social-impact-assessment/what-is-social-impact-assessment (Accessed: 23 April 2017)

Meals on Wheels America (2017) Available at: www.mealsonwheelsamerica.org (Accessed: 16 April 2017)

Nowak, A., Szamrej, J. and Latané, B. (1990) 'From private attitude to public opinion: A dynamic theory of social impact', *Psychological Review*, 97(3): 362.

SAA (2017) Overall process of social accounting and audit. Available at: http://1068899683.n263075.test.prositehosting.co.uk/wp-content/uploads/2012/12/SAA-PDF.pdf (Accessed: 23 April 2017)

Social Audit Network (SAN) (2017) Available at: www.socialauditnetwork.org.uk (Accessed: 16 April 2017)

Social Impact Scotland (2017) Social IMPact measurement for Local Economies (SIMPLE). Available at: www.sel.org.uk/impact-assessment (Accessed: 17 April 2017)

Wydick, B. (2015) The impact of TOMS Shoes. Available at: www.acrosstwoworlds.net/?p=292 (Accessed: 23 April 2017)

Benchmarking CSR: Frameworks, Standards, Certifications and Indices 9

Learning outcomes

By the end of this chapter, students should be able to:

- articulate the importance of using CSR benchmarking of various types
- identify existing and emerging CSR frameworks, standards, certifications and indices

- explain the importance and limitations of using each of the benchmarking types
- apply these frameworks to improve a company's CSR
- align a company towards one or more benchmarking standards.

Case study   The UN Global Compact and The Boyner Group – Putting a human face to a global market

The UN Global Compact was initiated at the World Economic Forum (WEF) in Davos, 1999, in a yearly forum that aims to improve the state of the world by engaging business, political, academic and other leaders of society to shape global, regional and industry agendas. The UN Secretary-General at the time, Kofi Annan, said on this occasion: 'Unless globalisation works for all, it will work for nobody', and called on business to put a 'human face to a global market' (UN, 1999).

Together with the fast-growing trend of globalisation, business was publically perceived as profiting at the expense of communities and the environment. High-profile clashes and protests between companies and civil society erupted around the world. It was becoming evident that the single-minded goal of profit at any cost was detrimental to societies and destructive to the environment. Essentially, business was threatening the very elements that underpinned its own existence and the UN responded by engaging business in a large-scale and much-needed transformation.

In a consultation process, unprecedented in scale and range, the UN met with more than 1,500 stakeholders from business, civil society, local networks, UN partners and governments to discuss the question: how can the UN Global Compact deliver responsible business action worldwide? This question aligns with the UN Sustainable Development Goals (SDGs) as they were adopted by business through the Global Compact in August 2015 and by the heads of state a month later in a historic UN summit. These goals universally apply to all humankind and require countries and business to mobilise efforts to end all forms of poverty, fight inequalities and tackle climate change, while ensuring that no one is left behind.

The UN Global Compact, which resulted from the extensive consultation, is a principle-based framework to promote universal social and environmental principles, in line with the SDGs. The framework addresses problems such as poverty, child

(Continued)

labour, human rights violation and climate change on a global scale. These goals outline new markets and opportunities for companies all over the world, as well as ways of conducting existing business. The Global Compact's goal is to work with businesses worldwide to adopt sustainable and socially responsible policies based on ten principles in the areas of human rights, labour, the environment and anti-corruption and to report on their implementation. It is the largest corporate sustainability or CSR initiative in the world, with over 13,000 corporate and non-corporate participants from 170 countries in 2017.

For example, Boyner Grup in Turkey, a large fashion retail operator, has undertaken collaborative efforts to empower disadvantaged young women in a country with low female labour force participation. In Turkey, young women who were raised in foster care are particularly affected by social stigmatisation, conservative gender roles and lack of access to higher education and work. In response, Boyner Grup partnered with not-for-profit organisations, foundations, government entities and the UN Population Fund (UNFPA) and developed a two-phase project addressing the needs of such women. The project unified the partners' efforts to help these young women in their educational progress and prepare them for the job market through self-development training, access to networks and individual mentoring. In phase I (2008–2012), the project offered empowerment training, self-development and transformational mentoring, while in phase II (2013–2015), it focused on capacity building, monitoring and evaluation procedures within the government agencies responsible for foster care. The project reflected SDG #5 (achieve gender equality and empower all women and girls), the Universal Declaration of Human Rights, and the UN Global Compact Principles 1 and 6.

As a result of this project, by 2015, 57 per cent of the young women who participated in the training had entered the labour market, 25 per cent had decided to continue higher education and 18 per cent were commencing their job search. Most of the young women still keep in close contact with the project team and their mentors and consult them for their educational and professional decisions. In general, the young women have gained self-esteem and increased their knowledge about their rights and opportunities. In addition, the project resulted in handbooks for guiding other social projects in Turkey dealing with disadvantaged youth. Finally, the project has evaluated changes in the behaviour and attitude of more than 700 people, informed more than 16,000 people and raised the awareness of more than 1,380,000 people in Turkey.

According to the UN Global Compact mission statement, it is possible to create a sustainable and inclusive global economy that delivers lasting benefits to people, communities and markets. To make this happen, the UN Global Compact acts as a driver for change, which on the one hand supports companies in doing business responsibly by aligning their strategies and operations with the ten principles, and on the other hand, the UN Global Compact takes strategic actions to advance broader societal goals, such as the UN SDGs. All this is achieved with a strong emphasis on collaboration and innovation, modelling the approach to sustain business that benefits society holistically.

Questions

1. In the initiation of the UN Global Compact in 1999, the then Secretary-General, Kofi Annan called on business to put a 'human face to a global market'. What do you think was meant by this? Why was this important? Has this been achieved at any level?
2. While the UNGC was a strong player and promoter in the development and adaptation of the SDGs, its principles did not change. How do the ten principles of the UNGC align (or not) with the SDGs? What can be changed to achieve a better alignment?
3. Find another company that is a strong member of the UNGC. How does it implement the ten principles?
4. If you were a manager of a company that wanted to become a UNGC member, how would you convince the board to do so? What would you need to do to become a member?

Reference

United Nations (1999) 'Secretary-general proposes global compact on human rights, labour, environment, in address to world economic forum in Davos'. Available at: www.un.org/press/en/1999/19990201.sgsm6881.html (Accessed: 7 May 2017)

Further reading and links

Cetindamar, D. (2007) 'Corporate social responsibility practices and environmentally responsible behavior: The case of the United Nations Global Compact', *Journal of Business Ethics*, 76(2): 163–76.

Kell, G. (2003) 'The global compact', *Journal of Corporate* Citizenship, 11: 35–49.

Seebacher, D. (2017) Pomegranate Arils: The Boyner Group's approach to empowering young women in Turkey. Available at: www.unglobalcompact.org/docs/issues_doc/human_rights/boyner-group-case-example.pdf (Accessed: 6 May 2017)

Sethi, S. P. and Schepers, D. H. (2014) 'United Nations global compact: The promise–performance gap', *Journal of Business Ethics*, 122(2): 193–208.

UN Global Compact (2017a) UN history – A giant opens up. Available at: http://globalcompact15.org/report/part-i/un-history-a-giant-opens-up (Accessed: 17 May 2017)

UN Global Compact (2017b) The ten principles of the UN Global Compact. Available at: www.unglobalcompact.org/what-is-gc/mission/principles (Accessed: 24 May 2017)

UN Global Compact (2017c) Global Compact+15: Business as a force for good. Available at: www.youtube.com/watch?v=gCfMFppotJg (Accessed: 6 May 2017)

UN Global Compact (2017d) The unmet need. Available at: www.youtube.com/watch?v=hBRLRehpVY0 (Accessed: 19 May 2017)

(Continued)

UN Sustainable Development (2017) Sustainable development goals. Available at: https://sustainable development.un.org/topics/sustainabledevelopmentgoals (Accessed: 17 May 2017)
Voegtlin, C. and Pless, N. M. (2014) 'Global governance: CSR and the role of the UN Global Compact', *Journal of Business Ethics*, 122(2): 179–91.

Introduction: Evaluation of CSR performance

As we are starting the ninth chapter of this book, a strong case for strategic CSR emerges, but it can also be overwhelming. Where do we start? How do we know that we are taking the right direction? How do we prioritise our CSR aspects and efforts? How do we ensure that our CSR is well structured, embedded and holistic?

For this reason, benchmarking the company's CSR is an important aspect of strategic CSR. It can serve in measuring the company's social impact, as was discussed in the previous chapter, as well as assist in CSR reporting, which will be covered in the next chapter.

There are various approaches towards CSR benchmarking. Some companies simply examine their own social impact (including their input, outputs, outcomes and impact) or measure their own social return on social investment and report on it. They can then compare their results to other companies or examine how they have improved over the years. Others, however, prefer having external frameworks, guidelines and standards that allow them to check their CSR performance against lists of principles, values and corporate actions that are provided by indices and certifying bodies.

When companies use external CSR benchmarking, it is easier for them to compare themselves to others and identify any gaps in CSR performance. It also allows external bodies to rank companies according to their CSR and can therefore guide socially responsible consumers and investors in their decision making on where to put their money. Furthermore, since many corporate leaders are still driven by a sense of competition and ranking, external benchmarking could incentivise them to improve their CSR, in addition to other motivations.

While existing benchmarking tools can help and guide companies, it is sometimes difficult to know which path to take. According to Koerber (2009), the last three decades have seen the growth of various CSR codes, frameworks, standards, guidelines, norms and initiatives (e.g. the UN Global Compact, ILO Standards, OECD Guidelines for Multinational Enterprises, ISO 14001, Global Reporting Initiative, Global Sullivan Principles, SA 8000, AA1000 Series) as a response to the call for greater responsibility of business. Gilbert and Rasche (2008) proposed considering such 'standardised ethics initiatives' as promising approaches that complement efforts by legislation to better address social and environmental issues. According to these authors, standardised ethics initiatives represent predefined norms and procedures for corporate conduct with regard to social and/or environmental issues. Furthermore, adherence to these standards is ensured either by the organisation itself, its stakeholders or independent institutions (e.g. auditing bodies).

With a staggering number of CSR and sustainability certifications, standards and indices (over 500 in 2017), many companies find it difficult to know which ones will serve them best. To address this confusion, Leipziger (2003) has identified six different ways to classify standards: focus (e.g. process or performance focused); method of development (e.g. unilateral or multilateral); scope (e.g. social and environmental); stakeholder focus (e.g. employees or shareholders); sector (e.g. finance); and geographical region. In addition, Ligteringen and Zadek (2005) classified frameworks into three groups: 1. normative frameworks that provide guidance to firms on what they should do; 2. process guidelines that provide guidance to firms on what to measure and how to communicate what they do; and 3. management systems that provide detailed guidance to firms on how to integrate the management of social and environmental impacts into the organisation's operations.

When deciding on which benchmarking tools or standardised ethics initiatives to adopt, companies need firstly to define their stakeholders and their stakeholder approach (Gilbert and Rasche, 2008; see also Chapter 3). Corporate and CSR leaders then need to ask: what is the purpose of our benchmarking? To which stakeholder groups are we striving to demonstrate our commitment? What do these stakeholders care about? And what is the best way to reach them? Answering these questions will assist in choosing the most relevant frameworks and standards for the company and its stakeholders.

For example, stock market indices, such as the Dow Jones Sustainability Index, are a good way for listed companies to demonstrate to existing and potential investors their commitment to sustainability. On the other hand, having a clear certification such as the Rainforest Alliance or Fairtrade on products can help inform socially responsible consumers that the certified product is good for society and/or the environment. Some standards, such as the International Organization for Standardization (known as ISO) family of standards, can help inform and involve employees in the work that the company does in this area. Obviously, strategic CSR requires working with a broad set of stakeholders and therefore combining several such tools could be the most effective way of doing so.

In this chapter we will cover a small sample of each of the following: general CSR frameworks (such as the UN Global Compact); standards (such as ISO 26000 or SA8000); certifications (such as Fairtrade and Rainforest Alliance); and stock market indices (such as the Dow Jones Sustainability Index). Given the hundreds of benchmarking tools that currently exist on the market, this chapter will only briefly provide a taste of what is out there, and companies can search for additional tools that are more suitable for their needs and the requirements of their stakeholders. It should also be noted that there are additional ranking bodies such as Fortune 100 Best Companies To Work For or Forbes' Companies with Best CSR

Reputation, which are not covered in this chapter but also offer some benchmarking opportunities for companies.

Frameworks and guidelines

CSR frameworks provide some ideas of what values and principles should guide companies that strive to be responsible and sustainable. Some of these frameworks were covered as CSR theories in Chapter 2 but can be used as guidelines for CSR. For example, the CSR stages presented can guide companies in improving their CSR and achieving the Civil Stage, which is enhancing long-term economic value by overcoming any first mover disadvantages and realising gains through collective action (Zadek, 2004). Another example is the CSR congruence model (Haski-Leventhal et al., 2017), which suggests responsible companies demonstrate both socially responsible identity (in their values and what they stand for) and socially responsible behaviour (in their actions, philanthropy, employee involvement, etc.). These frameworks and others can help guide companies, providing some general principles and aspirations. Although they are not as detailed as the standards and certifications, which will be presented next, they can serve as a general compass.

The UN Global Compact (UNGC)

The opening case of this chapter presented a well-known framework: the UN Global Compact (UNGC). As was explained above, the UNGC emerged in time of extreme capitalism and globalisation in the face of ethical meltdowns and corporate scandals. Although the UN is an inter-governmental organisation that was established after World War II in order to prevent further global wars, over the years its mission became much broader and the stakeholders the organisation engages with diversified greatly. As such, in the year 2000 it was understood that governments alone could not (and perhaps should not) address all the issues that humanity faces and that businesses, which were often a part of the problem, can also become part of the solution. To achieve this, the UN developed a framework of ten principles that should guide business (through an impressive consultation process), which became a Compact with many signatory companies (over 13,000 in 2017). These ten principles are based on internationally agreed conventions and treaties, such as the Universal Declaration of Human Rights, the International Labour Organisation's Declaration on Fundamental Principles and Rights at Work, the Rio Declaration on Environment and Development and the UN Convention Against Corruption. The principles will be detailed and explained next, with some guidelines on what companies can do to achieve each, based on the UNGC Handbook (UN Global Compact, 2010).

The ten principles of the UNGC

Human rights

Human rights (such as freedom, unlawful imprisonment, torture and execution) are liberties that are legally protected in municipal, national and international law. They are fundamental rights inherited by all human beings regardless of their gender, ethnos, religion or location, 'to which a person is inherently entitled simply because she or he is a human being' (Sepúldeva et al., 2004: 3). Human rights are universal in the sense that they are applicable everywhere and are always egalitarian in the sense that they should be the same for everyone.

The first two principles of the UNGC hold companies responsible and accountable to these principles, directly and indirectly:

Principle 1: Businesses should support and respect the protection of internationally proclaimed human rights.

Principle 2: Make sure that they are not complicit in human rights abuses.

Companies should make sure they are not complicit in human rights abuses in any of the three following ways:

- *Direct complicity*: occurs when a company provides goods or services that it knows will be used to carry out the abuse.
- *Beneficial complicity*: occurs when a company benefits from human rights abuses even if it did not positively assist or cause them – for example, by buying cheap products from suppliers who abuse human rights.
- *Silent complicity*: occurs when the company is silent or inactive in the face of systematic or continuous human rights abuse (this is the most controversial type of complicity, it is the most difficult to enforce and is least likely to result in legal liability).

To align with the first two principles, the UN Global Compact (2010) suggests an effective human rights policy and human rights due diligence to help companies address (though will not eliminate) the risk of being implicated in human rights violations, by knowing and showing that they undertook every reasonable step to avoid involvement.

Labour

Labour rights are extremely relevant to business and include the highest number of principles (four out of the ten). Based on the International Labour Organisation's (ILO) Declaration on Fundamental Principles and Rights at Work, these four principles are aimed at ensuring that employees in the entire value chain gain access to their basic rights, such as freedom of association and no slavery. The four labour principles are:

Principle 3: businesses should uphold the freedom of association and the effective recognition of the right to collective bargaining.

All employers and workers can freely and voluntarily establish and join groups (such as trade unions) for the promotion and defence of their occupational interests. When employees join forces, they have stronger bargaining power and can therefore better achieve some fundamental rights. However, in many places around the world, if employees try to join a group, they get beaten and/ or thrown into jail and responsible corporations need to ensure that such practices are not taking place in their operations.

Principle 4: the elimination of all forms of forced and compulsory labour.

By right, labour should be freely given and employees should be free to leave in accordance with established rules. Forced or compulsory labour is any work or service that is done under the threat of some form of punishment and penalty (such as physical abuse) and for which that person has not offered himself/herself voluntarily. It should be noted that paying employees or offering other forms of compensation does not necessarily indicate that the labour is not forced or compulsory.

One major problem we currently face is the massive use of human trafficking for cheap labour, which is modern day slavery. Annually, approximately 600,000 to 800,000 people are trafficked across international borders and additionally millions more are enslaved in their own countries. Trafficking is usually done through the use of force (direct and violent, or psychological), fraud or coercion to exploit a person for forced labour and sex work. With this problem being so massive, it is a major responsibility of business to ensure that no trafficked humans are part of their supply chains.

Principle 5: the effective abolition of child labour.

Child labour is defined as work that deprives children of their childhood, their potential and their dignity (the International Labour Organisation or ILO). It is estimated that 168 million children are currently in child labour globally, and a more severe issue is that half of these young children work in hazardous work environments. Encouragingly however, child labour has declined by one-third in the last 15 years.

Child labour is a form of exploitation that is a violation of a human right and it is the declared policy of the international community and of almost all governments to abolish child labour. While the term 'child' covers all girls and boys under 18 years of age, not all under-18s must be removed from work: the basic rules under international standards distinguish what constitutes acceptable or unacceptable work for children at different ages and stages of their development.

ILO conventions provide the framework for national law to prescribe a minimum age for admission to employment or work that must not be less than the age for completing compulsory schooling and in any case not less than 15 years. Lower ages are permitted for transitional periods – in countries where economic and educational facilities are less well-developed, the minimum age for regular work generally is 14 years and 12 years for 'light work'. The minimum age for hazardous work is 18 years for all countries.

And yet in many developing countries children as young as 8 or 10 are forced to work in difficult conditions, earning very little to support their families. Child labour damages children's physical, social, mental, psychological and spiritual development; deprives children of their childhood and their dignity; and prevents them from attaining education and sometimes from seeing their families again. Being associated with child labour is not only immoral and illegal but can also be damaging to the company's reputation and result in boycotts and other actions against it.

What can companies do? It is essential to develop awareness and understanding of the causes and consequences of child labour; to identify the issues and determine whether or not child labour is a problem within the business (particularly for companies in specific industry sectors with geographically distant supply chains), and do everything in their power to avoid child labour. Some companies even build schools to ensure that children will gain education at a young age and not be part of the workforce.

Principle 6: the elimination of discrimination in respect of employment and occupation.

Discrimination means treating employees differently or less favourably because of characteristics that are not related to their merit or the inherent requirements of the job, such as race, colour, gender, religion, political opinion, national extraction, social origin, age, disability, HIV/AIDS status, trade union membership and sexual orientation. Discrimination can arise in a variety of work-related activities, including (but not limited to): access to employment, to particular occupations, promotions and to training and vocational guidance.

Discrimination is not only unethical, but it also does not make business sense. It leads to disruptive tensions and results in reduced access to talents, skills and competencies. Consequently, the resentment generated by discrimination will affect the performance of individuals and teams in the company. To address this, companies need to be aware of the diversities that may exist in the workforce, respect anti-discrimination laws, embrace diversity and introduce measures to promote equality.

Mini case study   LEGO

The LEGO Group, founded in 1932, is a well-known Danish toy manufacturer, with over 7,000 employees, and products sold in over 130 countries. The LEGO Group declares that it is committed to the development of children's creativity and imagination and it became a UN Global Compact signatory company in 2003. Even prior to this (since 1997), the LEGO Group has had a code of conduct that requires suppliers to observe the ILO conventions on labour rights, the OECD guidelines, the Universal Declaration of Human Rights and local legislation. The LEGO Group code of conduct addresses issues such as child labour, compensation and working hours, discrimination, coercion and harassment, health and safety, freedom of association, environment and sub-suppliers. The organisation has worked with Save the Children particularly to address the child labour issue. These actions are aimed to ensure that LEGO is being produced under decent working conditions. To achieve this, the LEGO Group employs local, experienced and independent auditors to carry out inspections at suppliers (UN Global Compact, 2010). ·

Reference

UN Global Compact (2010) Implementing the UN Global Compact. Available at: www.unglobalcom
    pact.org/docs/news_events/8.1/dk_book_e.pdf (Accessed: 12 May 2017)

Environment

The prominence of the natural environment was covered in Chapter 5, under sustainability. We discussed there the importance of providing for the needs of current generations while ensuring the needs of future ones. The next three principles are aligned with this approach.

Principle 7: businesses should support a precautionary approach to environmental challenges.

The key to a precautionary approach, from a business perspective, is the idea that prevention is better than remediation. It is more cost-effective to take early action to ensure that environmental damage does not occur rather than try to fix the problem later. Precaution involves the systematic application of risk assessment, risk management and risk communication. When there is risk of harm, decision makers need to apply precaution to avoid environmental damages. To assess such risks, companies need to involve scientific-technological evaluation, economic cost–benefit analysis and political considerations.

Principle 8: undertake initiatives to promote greater environmental responsibility.

In the 1992 Rio Earth Summit, the role of business and industry in the sustainable development agenda was established in these words: 'Business and industry should increase self-regulation, guided by appropriate codes, charters and initiatives integrated into all elements of business planning and decision-making and fostering openness and dialogue with employees and the public.' The Rio Declaration further states that business has the responsibility to ensure that activities within its own operations do not cause harm to the environment. As explained in Chapter 5, there is a strong business case for being environmentally sustainable, including efficiency, reduced costs and tax benefits (in some countries).

To achieve Principle 8, companies need to define a vision, policies and strategies to include the three aspects of sustainable development: economic prosperity, environmental quality and social equity. They also need to develop sustainability targets and indicators; establish a sustainable production and consumption programme to take the organisation beyond compliance in the long term; and work with product designers and suppliers to improve environmental performance and extend responsibility throughout the value chain.

Principle 9: encourage the development and diffusion of environmentally friendly technologies.

Environmentally sound technologies protect the environment, are less polluting, use all resources in a sustainable manner, recycle waste and products and manage residual waste. They include a variety of clean production processes and pollution prevention technologies as well as end-of-pipe and monitoring technologies. Environmentally sound technologies can be applied to reduce the day-to-day operating inefficiencies, emissions of environmental contaminants, worker exposure to hazardous materials and risks of environmental disasters. By using environmentally friendly technologies, companies can be more efficient and innovative, boost their performance and protect the only planet that we have.

Principle 9 may be achieved by changing the process or manufacturing technique; changing input materials; making changes to the product design or components; and reusing materials on site. Furthermore, this principle can be achieved at a strategic level by establishing a policy on the use of environmentally sound technologies; making information available to stakeholders that illustrates the environmental performance; and refocusing research and development on 'design for sustainability'. Companies can also use life cycle assessment (LCA) in the development of new technologies and products, and employ environmental technology assessments (EnTA).

Anti-corruption

The last of the ten UNGC principles focuses on corruption, which often stands in the way of addressing all the other nine principles. It is a lot more difficult to address human and labour rights and protect the environment when the institutes in charge of assuring these rights at a local level are corrupt.

Principle 10: businesses should work against corruption in all its forms, including extortion and bribery.

Corruption can take many forms that vary in degree from the minor use of influence to institutionalised bribery. The UNGC adopted the definition of corruption as the abuse of entrusted power for private gain. The OECD (2011) defines extortion thus: 'the solicitation of bribes is the act of asking or enticing another to commit bribery. It becomes extortion when this demand is accompanied by threats that endanger the personal integrity or the life of the private actors involved.'

Principle 10 therefore commits signatories not only to avoid bribery, extortion and other forms of corruption, but also to proactively develop policies and concrete programmes to address corruption internally and within their supply chains. Companies need to work collectively and join civil society, the UN and governments to realise a more transparent global economy.

In addition to moral and instrumental motivations to address corruption, the rapid global development of rules of corporate governance is also prompting companies to focus on anti-corruption measures as part of their mechanisms of expressing corporate sustainability. Businesses face high ethical and business risks and potential costs when they fail to effectively combat corruption in all its forms. All companies, large and small, are vulnerable to corruption and the potential for damage is considerable. Business can face legal and reputational risks and financial costs due to corruption. To address this, companies need to introduce anti-corruption policies and programmes within their organisations, report on their work done to combat corruption and share experiences and best practice. They need to join forces with industry peers and with other stakeholders to scale up anti-corruption efforts and create fair competition for all.

Questions for reflection and discussion

1. Examine the ten principles of the UNGC. Why do you think they were chosen? What is the overarching goal?
2. What do you think is missing from the ten principles? What else should business achieve?

OECD Guidelines for Multinational Enterprises

The *OECD Guidelines for Multinational Enterprises* are recommendations addressed by governments to multinational enterprises operating in or from adhering countries. Together with applicable laws and standards, the guidelines provide non-binding principles and standards for responsible business conduct in a global context. The Declaration and the Guidelines were adopted by the OECD in 1976 and revised in 1979, 1982, 1984, 1991, 2000 and 2011. Each of the OECD countries sets up a National Contact Point, an entity responsible for the promotion of the Guidelines on a national level.

The OECD Guidelines aim to ensure that the operations of multinational enterprises are in line with government policies, to strengthen the basis of mutual confidence between enterprises and the societies in which they operate, to help improve the foreign investment climate and to enhance the contribution to sustainable development made by multinational enterprises. The Guidelines cover business ethics on the following topics: human rights; employment and industrial relations; environment; combating bribery, bribe solicitation and extortion; consumer interests; science and technology; competition and taxation.

For example, regarding the environment, the Guidelines say that enterprises should take due account of the need to protect the environment, public health and safety and generally to conduct their activities in a manner contributing to the wider goal of sustainable development. This is followed by eight specific guidelines on the environment and commentary.

Also offered are some general policies, such as the ones below, that all multinational companies should adopt:

1. Contribute to economic, environmental and social progress with a view to achieving sustainable development.
2. Respect the internationally recognised human rights of those affected by their activities.
3. Refrain from seeking or accepting exemptions not contemplated in the statutory or regulatory framework related to human rights, environmental, health, safety, labour, taxation, financial incentives or other issues.

Questions for reflection and discussion

1. What are the main similarities and differences between the UNGC and the OECD Guidelines?
2. Find a company that works according to the OECD Guidelines and explain what it did to align its operations to the Guidelines.

Standards

CSR standards are voluntary, are usually third-party assessed and relate to environmental, social, ethical and safety issues. Companies adopt such standards to demonstrate the performance of their organisations or products in specific areas. There are over 500 standards, and the pace of introduction has increased dramatically in the last two decades. The trend started in the late 1980s and 1990s with the introduction of Ecolabels and standards for organic food and other products, and now there are many formal standards to cover almost every aspect of CSR discussed in this book.

The basic premise of sustainability standards is twofold. Firstly, they emerge in areas where national and global legislation was weak but where consumers and non-profit organisations demanded action. Secondly, an increasing number of companies that sell directly to consumers or to other businesses desired to demonstrate their level of sustainability in order to sell more products. For example, campaigns by Global Exchange and other non-profits against the purchase of goods from sweatshop factories by the likes of Nike and other leading brands, led to the emergence of social welfare standards such as the SA8000 and others. In addition, since standards are very detailed and comprehensive, they serve as detailed guidelines on how to achieve social and environmental responsibility.

ISO 26000 (Guidance on social responsibility)

ISO, the International Organization for Standardization that was founded in 1947, promotes worldwide proprietary, industrial and commercial standards. It is headquartered in Geneva, Switzerland and in 2017 was working in over 160 countries. Being the world's largest developer of voluntary international standards, ISO facilitates international trade by providing common standards across nations. The organisation has thus far created approximately 20,000 standards that cover almost every aspect of organisational quality, from manufactured products and technology to food safety, agriculture and healthcare.

Among its many standards, ISO developed a family of standards related to environmental management that exists to help organisations minimise the negative effects of business operations on the environment (i.e. cause adverse changes to air, water or land); comply with applicable laws, regulations and other environmentally oriented requirements; and continually improve in the above.

ISO 26000 (Social Responsibility) was developed by over 500 experts and published in 2010. It provides guidance on how businesses and organisations can operate in a socially responsible way. According to ISO's website (2017), 'this means acting in an ethical and transparent way that contributes to the health and welfare of society'. In addition to providing definitions and information to help organisations understand and address social responsibility, the standard emphasises the importance of actions, results and improvements in performance on social responsibility. However, it does not contain requirements and, therefore, in contrast to ISO management system standards, is not certifiable and only acts as a guide.

The ISO 26000 standard provides guidance on seven key principles of social responsibility: accountability, transparency, ethical behaviour, respect for stakeholder interests, respect for the rule of law, respect for international norms of behaviour and respect for human rights. It assists organisations from all sectors of the economy to recognise their social responsibility and engage stakeholders in their CSR. According to ISO, although the Standard was developed before the SDGs were, organisations that take action according to the practical recommendations offered in ISO 26000 will necessarily contribute to the SDGs. The organisation's website offers a guide on the link between the two.

ISO 14000 family of environmental management standards

ISO declares that it has developed standards that help organisations (including businesses, governments and non-profits) to take a proactive approach in managing environmental issues. The ISO 14000 family of environmental management standards aims to help meet the challenge of climate change by defining standards for greenhouse gas accounting, verification and emissions trading, and to measure the carbon footprint of products. To achieve this goal, ISO has developed nearly 600 International Standards for monitoring various climate change aspects, such as the quality of air, water and soil.

ISO 14001 is the world's most recognised framework for environmental management systems. It is implemented all around the world and helps organisations manage the environmental impact of their activities in a better way as well as to demonstrate sound environmental management. Although certification of conformity to the standard is not a requirement of ISO 14001, by the end of 2007 over 154,000 certificates had been issued in 148 countries.

Other standards from this family include the ISO 14004, which complements ISO 14001 by providing additional guidance and useful explanations. The environmental auditing standard, ISO 19011, provides guidance on principles of auditing, managing audit programmes and the conduct of audits. ISO 14031 provides guidance on evaluating environmental performance and addresses the selection of suitable performance indicators so that performance can be assessed against criteria set by management.

SA8000 (Social accountability)

Other standardisation bodies, such as Social Accountability Accreditation Services, also offer CSR and sustainability standards, such as the SA8000. SA8000 is an auditable certification standard that encourages organisations to develop, maintain and apply socially acceptable practices in the workplace. Developed in 1997 in consultation with trade unions, not-for-profits, civil society organisations and companies, SA8000 is aimed at increasing social responsibility, particularly towards employees (what was referred to earlier in this book as 'internal CSR'). As it can be applied worldwide to any company in any industry, it is a useful tool in measuring, comparing and verifying social accountability in the workplace.

SA8000 is aimed at certifying certain aspects of management related to CSR: respect for human rights, respect for the rights of workers, protection against exploitation of children, guarantees of safety and health at work. The Standard covers eight performance criteria: child labour; forced and compulsory labour; health and safety; freedom of association and right to collective bargaining; discrimination; disciplinary practices; working hours; and remuneration. For example, SA8000 states that a working week should be no more than 48 hours and that overtime should be voluntary, not regular, paid for and not exceed 12 hours per day. In a way, SA8000 can help address issues that arise with modern slavery.

Certifications and labels

When consumers want to buy a product, they often do not have full access to the information and knowledge required to establish if the product is sustainable and was manufactured in a socially responsible manner. They cannot tell if children were a part of the workforce that made the product, if farmers were paid fairly and if the produce is really organic. Consumers cannot go to the local farms in Africa and check the conditions in which the cocoa they are drinking was made. However, given the fast-growing trend of consumer social responsibility and the increasing number of people who care about these issues, many companies wanted to overcome the information asymmetry that did not allow consumers to know how good their brand is or how sustainable their products are. In addition, public trust in big corporations is declining rapidly. Governments alone cannot address global issues, particularly in the face of globalised trade. A trustworthy third party was required to help consumers gain the information they needed, help them buy sustainable products and rebuild this lost trust. As such, it is no wonder that since the 1980s a vast amount of certification bodies have emerged, particularly in the developed world, to inform consumers about what is happening in the supply chains of the products they buy, particularly from the developing world.

These third parties, such as the Fairtrade and Rainforest Alliance, offer auditing services, which are paid for by the companies. When the companies meet their standards, they gain permission to use the third-party organisation's logos/labels on their products. It should also be noted that some companies use their own certifications and labels, such as 'Whole Trade' by Whole Foods Market. Like the benchmarking tools covered in this chapter, there are hundreds of such logos and certifications, but we will cover here some of the most commonly used ones.

Fairtrade

> With over 1.65 million farmers and workers, thousands of campaigners, traders and companies around the world, Fairtrade stands to make important contributions to the Sustainable Development Goals. Our new five-year strategy outlines the world we want to see and how we aim to contribute to achieving it. (Fairtrade International, 2017)

'Fairtrade' is a product certification system designed to enable consumers to identify products that meet agreed environmental, labour and developmental standards. Overseen by a standard-setting body (Fairtrade International or FLO), receiving the Fairtrade label involves the independent auditing of producers to ensure that the product meets agreed standards. The most distinguishing feature of the Fairtrade label is the guarantee of a minimum price for suppliers and a social premium that goes to the co-operative and not to the producers directly. According to the organisation's website, Fairtrade is about 'stable prices, decent working conditions and the empowerment of farmers and workers around the world'. It performs development work and promotes a political vision of an alternative economy, with the main objective of empowering small producers and providing them with access to, and improving their position on, global markets.

Fairtrade mainly certifies products such as chocolate, coffee, tea, vanilla, cotton and gold, as these products (and others) are usually extracted from the developing world and are more likely to benefit from the use of child and forced labour. According to Fairtrade, when consumers purchase products with the Fairtrade mark, they are 'supporting farmers and workers as they work to improve their livelihoods and provide better support to their communities'. The Fairtrade mark shows consumers that the ingredients in the product have been produced by small-scale farmer organisations or plantations that meet internationally agreed Fairtrade social, economic and environmental standards. For most Fairtrade goods there is a minimum price set to cover the cost of sustainable production for that product in that particular region. If the market price for that product is higher than the minimum price defined by Fairtrade, then producers should receive the market price.

Rainforest Alliance

The Rainforest Alliance started in the 1980s as a social movement to save the rainforests that industry was destroying and it was later turned into an organisation committed to conserving rainforests and their biodiversity by certifying products and informing consumers. According to the organisation's website, the Rainforest Alliance is a 'growing network of people who are inspired and committed to working together to achieve our mission of conserving biodiversity and ensuring sustainable livelihoods. Through creative, pragmatic collaboration, we aim to rebalance the planet by building strong forests and healthy communities around the world' (Rainforest Alliance, 2017).

The Rainforest Alliance certified label is awarded to businesses, farms and forests that meet the organisation's environmental and social standards. One key element of this label is the elaboration and implementation of a detailed plan for the development of a sustainable farm management system in order to assist wildlife conservation. Another objective is to improve workers' welfare by establishing and securing sustainable livelihoods for the workers and their families.

The Rainforest Alliance's work is guided by an approach that the health of the planet is linked to the wellbeing of those whose livelihoods depend on the land and forests. As everyone has a vital role to play in strengthening this relationship, the Rainforest Alliance provides training to farmers and foresters, works with businesses committed to sustainability, and motivates consumers and citizens to adopt sustainable lifestyles.

There are some differences between Fairtrade and the Rainforest Alliance. Firstly, the Rainforest Alliance label requires only 30 per cent of the coffee to be from certified farms, whereas with Fairtrade, 100 per cent needs to be certified. However, with Rainforest Alliance, if less than 100 per cent of the product is certified, the percentage must be indicated beneath the Rainforest Alliance logo and companies that do this have to sign an agreement to scale up to 100 per cent. This allows an entry point for small and medium enterprises (SMEs), providing them with the chance of becoming more ethical.

Ethical fashion standards

Ethical fashion is becoming a fast-growing trend, with a growing number of clothing shoppers wanting to buy clothes that are not only fashionable and low priced but also ethical. In 2017, the famous young actress, Emma Watson, declared she would only wear designers' clothes that are ethically made and are eco-friendly, which further increased the interest in ethical fashion. While touring around to promote the *Beauty and the Beast* film, Watson created an Instagram account called 'The Press Tour' to document the outfits she wore and explain how they were sourced and made.

The general definition of ethical fashion focuses on minimising harm to people and the environment or the creation of 'positive impacts [by] a designer, a consumer choice, or method of production' (Thomas, 2008: 533). In contrast, fast fashion is about clothes that are cheap, do not last long, are not sustainably sourced, and can be seen as disposable. Fast fashion comes with a much higher price tag than the ones attached to the clothes in the shop: it has a massive negative impact on the environment (due to unsustainable supply chains and the amount of waste produced by throwing away millions of tons of garments and textiles every year) and on the people who produce fast fashion. In order to still make a profit on a T-shirt sold for a few dollars, companies hire cheap, forced and/or child labour in developing countries, where employees receive very low wages and minimal humane conditions to work in. While employees have been working in extremely poor conditions for decades, it was the 2013 collapse of the Rana Plaza building in Bangladesh and the death of 1,129 people that raised many people's awareness of the real cost of unethical fashion and consumer demand for ethical fashion.

MADE-BY aims to address sustainability in the fashion industry by offering 'transparency solutions' to directly address the struggles that brands and retailers have faced in gaining supply chain traceability. Transparency Solutions (http://transparencysolutions.co.uk) is a consultancy that gives companies the tools and guidance to create a successful transparency programme and supports them to use this information to improve the sustainability of their supply chains. MADE BY also offers a MODE Tracker – a holistic, transparent and verified progress tracking tool to support fashion brands and retailers in improving their sustainability performance through measuring and communicating year-on-year progress.

In addition, Child Labor Free (CLF) is a foundation aimed to provide an accreditation and certification system along the whole value chain of a product, which guarantees that the product is free from child labour. It does so by asking fashion brands to upload a report on various aspects of the business, while also conducting a limited external assessment. The tool mainly relies on companies' self-reports and does not audit on site.

The Higg Index was developed by the Sustainable Apparel Coalition (SAC), which is a coalition of companies from the fashion industry interested in producing and selling apparel in a sustainable and ethical way. The members of the coalition include dozens of companies, from large corporations such as H&M and Nike to smaller companies, not-for-profit organisations (including Fairtrade) and governmental organisations. Each Higg Index module comprises questions developed by the SAC's members, stakeholders and experts, from foundation-level measures (such as basic compliance) to medium-level to aspirational-level (such as advanced and far-reaching sustainability policies). Higg users accrue points for every policy or practice that they follow and receive the highest number of points for positively answering the highest-level questions. SAC members generate standardised performance scores that can be shared with current and future supply chain partners around the world at the click of a button. Scores are anonymised and aggregated, allowing businesses to benchmark their results against the industry and serve as a powerful incentive to strive for greater improvements and raise the sustainability bar.

Slave Free Trade

Over 45 million people are trapped in slavery today. Some are trafficked, while some have no choice but to work in horrific conditions. Over 70 per cent of businesses admit there is probably slavery in their supply chain (Slave Free Trade, 2017).

Slave Free Trade audits company supply chains against the eight pillars of its framework. Products and services achieving Slave Free Trade's audit standard will be certified and licensed to use the slave-free product label. Once certified, the organisation will continually monitor each supply chain to ensure that it continues to be free of slavery and exploitative labour practices.

Slave Free Trade has a vision of the world where slavery is something that happened in the past; a world where everybody is emancipated and companies respect humanity and human rights. Slave Free Trade's mission aligns with the UN SDG 8.7: to eradicate modern slavery by enabling and motivating business to clean slavery from their supply chains. This organisation, which is based in Geneva, does so by informing and mobilising consumers, investors, suppliers, insurers and governments to demand slave-free products. The organisation's mission is to enable business to clean up its supply chain so it can achieve a level of integrity whereby its products and services can be certified as slave free with an easy to recognise label.

EXERCISE

1. Find products that are labelled and certified. Have you noticed these labels before? What kind of information do they provide on the product? Would it make you more likely to buy these products? Why?
2. Find two certification labels in addition to the ones presented in this chapter. What additional information do they provide?
3. Choose one label (either from this chapter or from the ones you have identified) and discover what companies need to do to be able to use this label. What did you learn from this?

Indices

Since the 1990s, there has been a significant growth in the number of CSR indices by financial institutions such as stock markets, with the overriding goal being to describe the financial performance of companies meeting certain CSR requirements. The first CSR indices were developed in the US, when Dow Jones started to publish the Sustainability Index in 1999. In the following year, Calvert Funds started to publish the CSR index, followed by the FTSE4Good Index in the UK in 2001. These indices are conducted by CSR rating agencies, which are committed to an evaluation of corporate social performance based at least in part on non-financial criteria (Scalet and Kelly, 2010).

These and other indices usually offer criteria that companies need to meet in order to be included in the list. More importantly, because they measure similar companies (often according to industry as well), indices offer ranking between companies and can identify which company is doing better than others in terms of sustainability and responsibility.

The launch of indices by financial institutions is usually driven by two motives: firstly, to establish a benchmark for the companies involved in CSR activities; and secondly, to represent a real reference point for investors making their investment decisions based on the environment, social and governance aspects of the investee. It is part of socially responsible investment (or SRI; see Chapter 7) and such investors are usually motivated to know how well the firms they invest in do, both in sustainable terms and in financial terms. Indeed, Adam and Shavit (2008) showed that when all firms are publicly ranked according to SRI index parameters, sustainability and CSR indices could create a market incentive for increased investment.

The investment of various funds into CSR portfolios has resulted in a growing interest in the companies that are part of such indices, in what they do well and in the gaps they need to address. On the other hand, this phenomenon leads to a situation where individual companies are more and more interested in belonging to such indices. Therefore, it can be stated that not only does growing interest in CSR lead to an origin of indices and dedicated investment funds, but also that CSR indices motivate companies to apply individual CSR criteria to business activities run by them. For the purpose of illustration, we will examine two American indices, although many countries have their own.

Dow Jones Sustainability Index

Launched in 1999, the Dow Jones Sustainability Index (DJSI) was the first global index tracking the financial and environmental performance of the leading sustainability-driven companies worldwide. As such, the DJSI provides asset managers and other interested parties with reliable and objective benchmarks to manage sustainability portfolios. The Index represents the top 10 per cent of the largest 2,500 companies in the Dow Jones Global Total Stock Market Index based on long-term economic, environmental and social criteria.

The DJSI is managed by an external body (Sustainable Asset Management or SAM, which is now called RobecoSAM). SAM identifies global sustainability using a corporate sustainability assessment. According to the SAM website (2017), the DJSI offers benchmarking information for investors who have recognised that 'sustainable business practices are critical to generating long-term shareholder value' and for those who wish to 'reflect their sustainability convictions in their investment portfolios'. They further argue that the DJSI combines the experience of an established index provider with the expertise of a specialist in sustainability investing to select the most sustainable companies from across 60 industries.

The DJSI World Index applies a rules-based component selection process based on the companies' total sustainability scores resulting from the annual

RobecoSAM corporate sustainability assessment. Only the top-ranked companies within each industry are selected for inclusion in the DJSI. It should be noted that no industries (such as tobacco companies) are excluded from this process. However, for investors who wish to limit their exposure to controversial activities, RobecoSAM and S&P Dow Jones Indices also offer the DJSI Indices with exclusion criteria such as armaments and firearms, alcohol, tobacco, gambling and adult entertainment.

The DJSI family of indices comprises global, regional and country benchmarks such as DJSI World, DJSI North America, DJSI Europe, DJSI Asia Pacific, DJSI Emerging Markets, DJSI Korea, DJSI Australia and DJSI Chile. All DJSI indices are calculated in both price and total return versions and are disseminated in real time.

Examining the DJSI press release from 2016 (see RobecoSAM, 2017), it is reported that the highest improvement (compared to previous years) was found in the area of corporate citizenship and philanthropy. An increase of 22.09 per cent shows that companies increasingly approach their corporate citizenship activities in a strategic manner, with defined priorities that are aligned with their business drivers, allowing companies to leverage their strengths, brand and employees to have the maximum impact on the beneficiaries. This demonstrates that strategic CSR is now strongly recognised as a best CSR practice. However, the least improved criteria is Labor Practice Indicators and Human Rights. With a decline of 34.82 per cent (mostly due to newly introduced questions focusing on human rights), it is clear that this is a developing area of interest for companies and only a few have the tools to comprehensively assess, mitigate and remediate human rights risks.

The index is always presented in alphabetical order of the industries and the top-performing companies (sustainability wise) in each industry. For example, in 2016, LG Electronics Inc. was the top performer in the Consumer Durables & Apparel industry category, Nestlé in Food, Beverage & Tobacco, and Unilever in Household & Personal Products. The full list can be found on the RobecoSAM website (www.robecosam.com).

EXERCISE

1. Find the most recent DJSI ranking. Take three of the top-ranking companies and look into their CSR.
2. Do you agree that these are the best-performing companies in their industry? Substantiate your answer with examples.
3. What did you learn from this exercise?

NASDAQ OMX: Green Economy Index

NASDAQ (National Association of Securities Dealers Automated Quotations), founded in 1971, is an American stock exchange and the second-largest exchange in the world. NASDAQ publishes many indices on financial performance of its listed companies, such as the NASDAQ Composite and NASDAQ-100 index (which was introduced in 1985 alongside the NASDAQ 100 Financial Index to track the largest 100 companies in terms of market capitalisation).

As the world's first electronic exchange, NASDAQ developed several sustainability indices, including the OMX Green Economy Index. Many of the NASDAQ-listed companies excel in innovation, sustainability and dedication to environmental causes and it was therefore important to rank them accordingly. In 2012, NASDAQ OMX became a founding member of the UN Sustainable Stock Exchanges initiative on the eve of the UN Conference on Sustainable Development (Rio+20).

The OMX Green Economy Index provides information on the financial performance of companies that are part of the green economy, working to enhance economic development based on the reduction of carbon usage (see Chapter 5). Companies must be involved in the reduction of fossil-sourced fuels, products, services and lifestyles to be considered for selection in this Index.

Lessons and implications

With the increased emphasis on corporate responsibility and sustainability and the ever-growing expectations of many stakeholders that the firms they work with, buy from and invest in will demonstrate these traits, a strong need has emerged for CSR guidance. The vast amount of benchmarking tools, including hundreds of standards, certifications and indices, were created for this purpose.

Examining the various benchmarking tools presented in this chapter, there is clear emphasis on internal CSR compared to external CSR. Many of these standards examine the way that companies treat their own employees and their suppliers' employees. Human and labour rights are the main issues in the UN Global Compact, OECD Guidelines for Multinational Enterprises, ISO 26000, SA8000, Fairtrade and the Rainforest Alliance.

The second most common theme found in the benchmarking tools covered here is the natural environment. With climate change, environmental issues are becoming extremely important and therefore find their way to most guidelines and standards. The least discussed CSR aspect in these tools is corporate philanthropy, and yet, based on the DJSI recent media release (of the 2016 Index), this area is where companies excel. It is not surprising, given that it is easier to write a big cheque to a not-for-profit organisation than to work towards fixing human rights issues along the entire supply chain.

These benchmarking tools or standardised ethics initiatives offer not only appropriate instruments for companies who want to increase their level of sustainability and responsibility, but also inform many stakeholders, from consumers and employees to governments and investors, about the social performance of the companies they care about. They bring a new level of transparency to business conduct and although most of them are voluntary, non-binding and not enforceable, some companies are ranked and held accountable even when not choosing to participate. As standardised CSR is quickly becoming the new 'business as usual', companies that lag behind may not be seen favourably in the future by their existing and potential stakeholders.

Summary

The last three decades have seen the growth of various CSR codes, frameworks, standards, guidelines, norms and initiatives as a response to the call for greater responsibility of business. In this chapter, we have covered four groups of benchmarking tools: frameworks and guidelines, standards, certifications and indices. Other benchmarking tools exist and there are many more examples in each group.

The chapter started with a case study on the UN Global Compact and elaborated on its ten principles around human rights, labour, the environment and anti-corruption. We discussed each principle and what companies need to do to address them. Even companies that are not signatories to the Compact should follow these principles as they meet international and national conventions, declarations and laws. We further examined the OECD Guidelines for Multinational Enterprises, which are recommendations addressed by governments to multinational enterprises operating in or from countries that adhere to these guidelines. Together with applicable laws and standards, the guidelines provide non-binding principles and standards for responsible business conduct in a global context.

Next, standards provide more detailed lists of principles and actions that should be undertaken by businesses that desire such accreditation. CSR standards are voluntary, usually third-party assessed and relate to environmental, social and ethical issues. Companies adopt such standards to demonstrate the performance of their organisations or products in specific areas. To illustrate, the chapter detailed several such standards, including the ISO 26000, the ISO 14000 family of environmental standards and SA8000, all of which focus on human and labour rights and the environment in addition to other CSR aspects.

To inform consumers about the sustainability of products and the responsibility of the companies which sell them, certifications were developed. Certified companies are usually allowed to use a label or a logo of the certifying third party on their products so that consumers can be easily informed about the sustainable nature of the product. There are currently hundreds of such certifications and in this chapter we examined Fairtrade, the Rainforest Alliance, MADE-BY and Slave Free Trade.

Finally, there is significant growth in the number of CSR indices by financial institutions such as stock markets, with an overriding goal to describe the economic situation of the companies meeting certain CSR requirements. Such indices often rank companies according to both their CSR and financial performance, providing vital information to investors, shareholders and other stakeholders. Financial institutions such as Dow Jones, NASDAQ and others now contribute to the CSR movement due to such indices.

Together, the vast amount of benchmarking tools help to shape and promote CSR. They help guide companies in developing their own CSR as well as protecting human rights, labour rights and the environment. Together, they can help achieve the SDGs and a better future for CSR, business and society.

General questions

1. There are currently hundreds of CSR standards and certifications. Why do you think we need so many? Would it be better if we only had one label combining all metrics? Why?

2. Choose three benchmarking tools portrayed in this chapter. What do you see as the main benefits and limitations of each?

3. Some companies are accused of doing 'blue washing'. If greenwashing is about using sustainability as a marketing stunt with no real action (see Chapter 11), blue washing is about aligning with the UN blue logo and becoming a UN Global Compact signatory without real action. What is the danger with blue washing? What can be done to avoid it?

4. Some research suggests that there is a correlation between being on the top list of sustainability indices and financial performance. What could be the various explanations for such correlation?

5. If you were a manager of a large firm, which benchmarking tool would you choose to use and why? What obstacles would you need to overcome in order to adopt or implement the benchmarking tool?

Key definitions

- Standardised ethics initiatives are promising approaches that complement efforts by legislation to better address social and environmental issues (Gilbert and Rasche, 2008).
- Standardised ethics initiatives represent predefined norms and procedures for organisational behaviour with regard to social and/or environmental issues (Gilbert and Rasche, 2008).
- CSR standards are voluntary, usually third-party assessed, and relate to environmental, social, ethical and safety issues. Companies adopt such standards to demonstrate the performance of their organisations or products in specific areas (Koerber, 2009).
- The UN Global Compact is a UN initiative aimed at encouraging businesses worldwide to adopt sustainable and socially responsible policies and to report on their implementation. It is a principle-based framework for businesses, stating ten principles in the areas of human rights, labour, the environment and anti-corruption.
- Human rights (such as freedom, unlawful imprisonment, torture and execution) are freedoms that are legally protected in municipal, national and international law. They are fundamental rights inherited by all human beings regardless of their gender, ethnos, religion or location (Sepúldeva et al., 2004).
- The *OECD Guidelines for Multinational Enterprises* are recommendations addressed by governments to multinational enterprises operating in or from adhering countries.
- 'Fairtrade' is a product certification system designed to allow people to identify products that meet agreed environmental, labour and developmental standards.

References

Adam, A. M. and Shavit, T. (2008) 'How can a ratings-based method for assessing corporate social responsibility (CSR) provide an incentive to firms excluded from socially responsible investment indices to invest in CSR?', *Journal of Business Ethics*, 82(4): 899–905.

Fairtrade International (2017) Available at: www.fairtrade.net (Accessed: 8 May 2017)

Gilbert, D. U. and Rasche, A. (2008) 'Opportunities and problems of standardized ethics initiatives: A stakeholder theory perspective', *Journal of Business Ethics*, 82(3): 755–73.

Haski-Leventhal, D., Roza, L. and Meijs, L. C. (2017) 'Congruence in corporate social responsibility: Connecting the identity and behaviour of employers and employees', *Journal of Business Ethics*, 143(1): 35–51.

International Labour Organisation (2017) Available at: www.ilo.org/global/lang--en/index.htm (Accessed: 7 May 2017)

ISO (2017) Available at: www.iso.org/about-us.html (Accessed: 7 May 2017)

Koerber, C. P. (2009) 'Corporate responsibility standards: Current implications and future possibilities for peace through commerce', *Journal of Business Ethics*, 89: 461–80.

Leipziger, D. (2003) *The corporate responsibility code book*. Sheffield: Greenleaf Publishing.

Ligteringen, E. and Zadek, S. (2005) The future of corporate responsibility codes, standards and frameworks. Available at: www.upj-online.de/fileadmin/user_upload/MAIN-dateien/Themen/Debatte/gri_aa_futureofcrcodes_2005.pdf (Accessed: 27 April 2017)

OECD (2011) *OECD guidelines for multinational enterprises*. Paris: OECD Publishing.

Rainforest Alliance (2017) Available at: www.rainforest-alliance.org (Accessed: 7 May 2017)

RobecoSAM (2017) Available at: www.robecosam.com (Accessed: 6 May 2017)

Scalet, S. and Kelly, T. F. (2010) 'CSR rating agencies: What is their global impact?', *Journal of Business Ethics*, 94(1): 69–88.

Sepúldeva, M., Van Banning, T. and Van Genugten, W. J. M. (2004) *Human rights reference handbook*. Ciudad Colón: University for Peace.

Slave Free Trade (2017) Available at: https://slavefreetrade.org (Accessed: 6 May 2017)

Thomas, S. (2008) 'From "green blur" to ecofashion: Fashioning an eco-lexicon', *Fashion Theory: The Journal of Dress, Body & Culture*, 12(4): 525–40.

UN Global Compact (2010) Implementing the UN Global Compact. Available at: www.unglobalcompact.org/docs/news_events/8.1/dk_book_e.pdf (Accessed: 12 May 2017)

United Nations (1992) UN Conference on Environment and Development. Available at: www.un.org/geninfo/bp/enviro.html (Accessed: 3 October 2017)

United Nations (1999) 'Secretary-general proposes global compact on human rights, labour, environment, in address to world economic forum in Davos'. Available at: www.un.org/press/en/1999/19990201.sgsm6881.html (Accessed: 7 May 2017)

Zadek, S. (2004) 'The path to corporate responsibility', *Harvard Business Review*, 82(12): 125–33.

Further reading and links

ISO (2017) Environmental management: The ISO 14000 family of international standards. Available at: www.iso.org/files/live/sites/isoorg/files/archive/pdf/en/theiso14000family_2009.pdf (Accessed: 19 May 2017)

ISO (2017) ISO 26000: Social responsibility. Available at: www.iso.org/iso-26000-social-responsibility.html (Accessed: 12 May 2017)

ISO (2017) ISO 26000 and SDGs. Available at: www.iso.org/files/live/sites/isoorg/files/archive/pdf/en/iso_26000_and_sdgs.pdf (Accessed: 15 May 2017)

ISO (2017) ISO and social responsibility. Available at: www.youtube.com/watch?v=jRajp8s9beI (Accessed: 19 May 2017)

RobecoSAM (2016) DJSI 2016: Review results September 2016. Available at: www.robecosam.com/images/review-presentation-2016.pdf (Accessed: 19 May 2017)

RobecoSAM (2017) Investment objective. Available at: www.sustainability-indices.com/index-family-overview/djsi-family-overview/#tab-1 (Accessed: 19 May 2017)

UN Global Compact (2017) The ten principles of the UN Global Compact. Available at: www.unglobalcompact.org/what-is-gc/mission/principles (Accessed: 14 May 2017)

CSR Reporting

10

Learning outcomes

By the end of this chapter, students should be able to:

- explain the importance of effective CSR reporting
- detail the variety of CSR reporting audiences and how having such diverse audiences affects the reporting process
- apply various reporting approaches and methods to disclose information about what the company does and what it should do
- employ existing reporting frameworks, such as the GRI, to a specific company
- acknowledge and address related challenges.

Case study   KPMG – Leading CSR reporting

KPMG is a global network of independent member firms, offering audit, tax and advisory services. The firms work closely with clients, helping them to mitigate risks and grasp opportunities. Member firms' clients include business corporations, governments and public sector agencies, and not-for-profit organisations that look to KPMG for a consistent standard of service based on high order professional capabilities, industry insight and local knowledge. KPMG member firms can be found in 152 countries and collectively they employ more than 189,000 people across a range of disciplines. Sustaining and enhancing the quality of this professional workforce is KPMG's primary objective.

KPMG's values include leading by example and being committed to the community as well as acting as responsible corporate citizens. KPMG's 51-page code of conduct details the firm's values and ethics. It states: 'Your voice counts. So speak up if something doesn't seem right.'

(Continued)

CSR and Citizenship at KPMG

KPMG's CSR and citizenship activities are aimed at helping build the capability of governments, aid agencies, civil society and businesses to address some of the world's most pressing challenges and realise positive change. KPMG's member firms work alongside clients to find solutions to pressing global issues of poverty, environmental sustainability, education and equality. KPMG is highly involved in internal and external CSR in too many areas to cover here, but a few examples can be found below.

KPMG has been a signatory of the UN Global Compact (UNGC) since 2002. KPMG reports on how it implements human rights, labour standards, environmental protection and anti-corruption against the UNGC Ten Principles. Furthermore, KPMG is committed to the Sustainable Development Goals (SDGs): it published six volumes of the SDG Industry Matrix, a report designed to help clients understand the opportunities the SDGs present. In particular, KPMG is committed to Zero Hunger Declaration (SDG 2), promoting corporate strategies that will result in zero stunted children under two years old, 100 per cent access to adequate food all year round, and sustainable food systems.

KPMG has an ingrained culture of diversity and inclusion, focusing on shared values, experiences and aspirations. KPMG Australia's Diversity and Inclusion programme covers seven key areas: gender, flexibility, ethnicity, generational, sexual orientation and gender identity, disability and family. Furthermore, the firm is committed to advancing environmental sustainability, and between 2010 and 2014 reduced its net emissions by 10 per cent. In addition, 27 per cent of its total purchased electricity comes from renewable sources. KPMG was awarded the 'sustainable firm of the year' by the International Accounting Bulletin for at least four consecutive years.

KPMG is devoted to education ('Lifelong Learning') based on SDG 4. For example, it globally supports Enactus, which is a community of student, academic and business leaders committed to using the power of entrepreneurial action to transform lives and shape a better, more sustainable world. KPMG leads the Enactus World Cup to support students from 36 countries in designing and implementing effective change projects aligned with the SDGs. As John Veihmeyer, the past chairman of KPMG International noted:

> At KPMG, we honor the core values that shape the culture across member firms, including a strong commitment to our communities. These deeply-held values are aligned with the UN Global Compact's 10 principles and they are part of the foundation of how we conduct business. We believe strongly that responsible business practices contribute to broad-based development and sustainable markets.

CSR Reporting at KPMG

KPMG is a leader in CSR reporting. As part of the firm's commitment to the UNGC, it publishes its 'Communication on Progress' reports and makes them available to the public. These reports help other companies capture their own implementation of the UNGC Principles.

Despite no statute under the *Corporations Act*, KPMG Australia was the first of the Big four accounting firms to voluntarily publish, in 2011, an audit Transparency Report (Transparency Reports are now mandatory) defining audit quality and reporting on our audit methodology and standards. KPMG has published several studies on CSR reporting, including the 'Count Me In' report on CSR reports' readers (2008) and in 2015, KPMG analysed carbon emissions reporting in CSR reports worldwide.

KPMG is deeply involved in the development and promotion of the Global Reporting Initiative (GRI), which are globally applicable reporting guidelines and standards, aimed to enable organisations to voluntarily report on their activities in the social, environmental and economic dimensions. In 2014, KPMG presented the True Value tool which can help to assess the relationship between the value a company creates and reduces for society and the value it creates for shareholders (social value and financial value).

In addition, KPMG leads the Task Force on Climate-Related Financial Disclosures (TCFD). The TCFD seeks to develop recommendations for voluntary climate-related financial disclosures that are consistent, comparable, reliable, clear, and efficient, while also providing decision-useful information to lenders, insurers and investors. KPMG was invited to join the TCFD Financial Stability Board (FSB), which was commissioned by the G20 to explore how organisations should disclose consistent information on climate-related financial risks they face.

In early 2017, KPMG Australia and the Climate Council published a report identifying companies' actions addressing climate change. Based on the Paris Agreement, the report identified gaps and challenges and their implications, as well as offered recommendations for driving strong responses and more meaningful disclosure.

KPMG is a leader and a 'game changer' in CSR reporting. Based on strategic CSR, the company ties its core operations and expertise to assisting other businesses in being more responsible and accountable. It offers the required knowledge and tools to support their clients and the business community and to offer better CSR reporting, as this is now rapidly becoming the mainstream. As was stated in their 2013 research report:

> *Companies should no longer ask whether or not they should publish a [CSR] report. We believe that debate is over. [...] The important questions now are "what?" and "how?"* (KPMG, 2013: 11).

(Continued)

Questions

1. Would you say that the work KPMG is doing in the area of CSR reporting is a reflection of strategic CSR? Why so? Refer to the definition of strategic CSR.
2. Reading KPMG's own report and surveys, why do you think CSR reporting is important? List at least three reasons.
3. KPMG's values are:

    a. we lead by example and act how we expect of each other and of our clients
    b. we respect individuals, their knowledge, skills and experience
    c. we challenge assumptions and strengthen our reputation as trusted and objective business advisers
    d. we are open and honest in our communication, sharing information, insight and advice
    e. we manage tough situations with courage and candour
    f. we are committed to our communities, acting as responsible corporate citizens
    g. we act with integrity, striving to uphold the highest professional standards, providing sound advice and rigorously maintaining our independence.

Do you find these values engaging? Do they align with your own values? Would it make you want to work for the firm? What needs to change?

Bibliography

KPMG (2008) Count me in: *The readers' take on sustainability reporting*. Amstelveen, The Netherlands: KPMG.

KPMG (2013) *The KPMG survey of corporate responsibility reporting 2013*. Amstelveen, The Netherlands: KPMG.

KPMG (2015) *The KPMG survey of corporate responsibility reporting 2015*. Amstelveen, The Netherlands: KPMG.

O'Leary, D.E. (2016) 'KPMG Knowledge Management and the Next Phase: Using Enterprise Social Media', *Journal of Emerging Technologies in Accounting*, 13(2): 215–230.

Links

KPMG Code of Conduct (2017) Available at: https://home.kpmg.com/content/dam/kpmg/pdf/2016/03/kpmg-code-of-conduct-latest.pdf (Accessed: 24 January 2018)

KPMG Corporate Responsibility page (2017) Available at: https://home.kpmg.com/cn/en/home/about/corporate-social-responsibility.html (Accessed: 11 May 2017)

KPMG Reconciliation Action Plan 2017–2020 (2017) Available at: https://home.kpmg.com/au/en/home/about/citizenship/reconciliation-with-indigenous-australia/reconciliation-action-plan.html (Accessed: 11 May 2017)

KPMG True Value (2014) Available at: https://home.kpmg.com/content/dam/kpmg/ae/pdf/introduction-kpmg-truevalue.pdf (Accessed: 24 January 2018)

KPMG Values and Culture (2017) Available at: https://home.kpmg.com/au/en/home/about/values-culture.html (Accessed: 17 May 2017)

Diversity and Inclusion (2017) Available at: https://home.kpmg.com/au/en/home/about/values-culture/diversity-inclusion.html (Accessed: 11 May 2017)

KPMG 2015 Survey on CSR reporting (2017) Available at: https://home.kpmg.com/ru/en/home/insights/2015/11/kpmg-international-survey-of-corporate-responsibility-reporting-2015.html (Accessed: 17 May 2017)

Video on the 2015 report (2017) Available at: https://www.youtube.com/watch?v=TdmLOyOTn18 (Accessed: 11 May 2017)

KPMG and the Task Force on Climate Related Financial Disclosurehttp://www.climateinstitute.org.au/verve/_resources/TCI0001_1.5_Policy_Brief_FINAL.pdf (Accessed: 18 July 2017)

https://home.kpmg.com/lu/en/home/events/2017/02/kpmg-webinar-on-the-fsb-task-force-on-climate-related-financial-.html (Accessed: 18 July 2017)

Introduction: From measurement to reporting

The last two chapters focused on two important aspects of measuring CSR. In Chapter 8, we discussed social impact, what it is and how to measure it. Chapter 9 examined various CSR benchmarking tools such as standards and certifications. The next stage is communicating the company's CSR, social impact and benchmarking by using CSR reporting.

Most countries demand financial reporting and disclosure of corporations and financial reporting is what corporations know and do. It uses accounting terms and language, numbers and dollar value of the company. It has one defined audience: shareholders and investors. The goal of the corporation is to maximise profit and as such these financial reports show how well (or not) it does exactly that. It shows the financial gains and losses but omits 'externalities' that do not affect its balance sheet. Business reporting is therefore defined as the public reporting of operating and financial data by a business enterprise (Lymer, 1999).

On the other hand, CSR reporting only emerged as a popular business trend in the 1970s (and then again in the 1990s). CSR reporting provides information about the economic, environmental and social impacts of the reporting company as well as information on governance and performance. Besides in a few European and other countries, such as Denmark, CSR reporting is not a compulsory practice. There is a greater variety regarding the audiences of these reports and what interests them (Ellerup Nielsen and Thomsen, 2007). According to KPMG (2013, 2015), nearly 75 per cent of the top 100 companies (by revenue, N100) produce a CSR report, which is similar to the results of the past year. Two-thirds of these companies use the global reporting initiative (GRI) guidelines and standards that are detailed below. There has been a dramatic increase in CSR reporting rates in the Asia Pacific, with 71 per cent of companies based in the Asia Pacific publishing CSR reports in 2013 compared to only 49 per cent in 2011. The 2015 rate of CSR reporting among the G250 was over 90 per cent.

CSR reporting might seem to be a straightforward task: companies communicate their CSR efforts using a report, which is then uploaded to their website. People download the report and read about how responsible and sustainable the company is. However, CSR reporting is anything but simple. There are several imperative questions companies need to ask themselves before starting to design and write their CSR reports. For companies that are interested in strategic CSR, it is important that the CSR report aligns with the company's mission and what it stands for.

The first question to be asked is: *why do we want to report on our CSR?* Is it about promoting the company's brand and reputation or is it about gaining a good reputation, legitimacy and trust? Is it about communicating our achievement in this area or part of stakeholder engagement? Is it about inspiring others to also increase their levels of responsibility and sustainability? Or do we only report because we must? Most companies report on their CSR for various reasons, but these must be clarified in advance.

Secondly, *who are the primary audiences* of this report and what interests these audiences? What are the best methods and communication channels to reach out to them? What do we need to communicate in our CSR reports that these audiences would find beneficial?

Thirdly, *what kind of reports* do we want to use? A basic report with a few pages on the website or a full CSR report? Should we report on our CSR in a separate report or add it to our annual report? What are the advantages and disadvantages of doing so for our company?

Fourthly, *who is going to write* the report and sign it off? Is it the job of Marketing and PR or is it something Finance and Accounting should do? Perhaps the CSR department? Should it be signed off by the CEO and should an external auditing body be involved? All these options signal different messages to the market and create a different type of report (and even CSR for that matter).

The aim of Chapter 10 is to offer information on the various CSR reporting options and provide tools that are available in order to make the right decision for the company. We will begin by detailing the roles and goals of

CSR reporting (the 'why') and examine how CSR reports can be an effective communication tool if done well. We will detail 'what' CSR reports usually focus on and what they should detail. We will then examine the 'how' of CSR reporting; discuss various options and how to choose between them. We will then present CSR reporting initiatives and research that could help guide corporate decision makers to report effectively and strategically on their CSR and discuss related challenges and tools.

Why CSR reports: The roles and goals of CSR reporting

CSR reporting is a key tool for communication with stakeholders about CSR activities. It forms a central charter for public relations, communicating and creating mutual understanding, managing potential conflicts and achieving legitimacy. CSR reporting is a way for organisations to provide information to different stakeholders regarding social and environmental issues (Golob and Bartlett, 2007).

CSR reporting takes a lot of time, effort and money to put together. Some companies ask themselves: should we not direct these resources to helping the community instead? Why should we spend large parts of our CSR budgets on reporting when this money can be used to support non-profit organisations? However, there are some very good reasons to invest resources in CSR reporting, particularly in terms of creating legitimacy and trust, leading internal and external stakeholder engagement, improving impact and creating a culture of transparency and accountability. CSR reporting has many benefits, and companies therefore have various motivations to report on their CSR. While the motivations and benefits of CSR reporting are not identical to those of CSR in general, there are some similarities and connections between the two.

Firstly, CSR reporting can increase the company's *legitimacy*, and several authors who have written about CSR reporting use the legitimacy theory (e.g. Patten, 1991; Golob and Bartlett, 2007). Legitimacy theory explains that when corporate management responds to the expectations of the community, governments and other stakeholders, the corporate gains more legitimacy, trust and a social licence to operate (Patten, 1991; Deegan et al., 2002). Legitimacy is a 'generalised perception or assumption that the actions of an entity are desirable, proper, or appropriate within some socially constructed system of norms, values, beliefs and definitions' (Suchman, 1995: 574). It is the basis of PR and sometimes of CSR. Effective CSR reports promote corporate brand and reputation and build trust and transparency. Such reports signal the corporate goodwill and its interest in the environment, employees and communities.

CSR reporting, just like auditing, standardisation and measuring social impact (see Chapters 8 and 9), allows a company to *measure and improve its CSR level*.

What gets measured gets managed, and CSR reporting forces companies to constantly measure their CSR, their input and impact. CSR reporting promotes an internal audit of what the company does and why it does it. It also encourages companies to examine the alignment between their CSR, their mission statement and overall strategy, to ensure that they are on the pathway to strategic CSR.

Thirdly, based on stakeholder theory, CSR reporting is an effective method of *stakeholder engagement*. Good CSR reports inform internal and external stakeholders about the company's CSR. Excellent reports enable a dialogue and an open conversation with the stakeholders. Reporting solicits feedback on performance from a growing number of stakeholders. However, it is vital to understand which stakeholders we are communicating with and what is the best way of doing so, as will be discussed later in this chapter. Companies engage in CSR for moral, relational and economic motivations (Aguilera et al., 2007) and CSR reporting could be identified as a tool for companies motivated by *relational* goals. Such companies value the relationship they have with a broad set of stakeholders and to maintain it, they demonstrate a good level of CSR and communicate it.

By disclosing social, environmental and governance information, enterprises often find that they can better *identify and manage issues* that influence their business success, including their financial success. CSR reporting can help companies measure the true costs of their operations, realise the cost of their externalities, understand the financial impact of their CSR and improve their overall sustainability, both financial and non-financial. This should also be of interest to *investors* (not just socially responsible ones). Good disclosure of non-financial information enables investors to contribute to a more efficient allocation of capital and better achieve longer-term investment goals.

Furthermore, reporting can help the company improve its *strategy*. CSR reports are increasingly seen as strategic documents that should offer a balanced, objective and reasonable assessment of almost every aspect of a firm's non-financial performance (and sometimes financial performance as well, as will be discussed below). It can help the company clarify its mission and strategy and sometimes feeds into its marketing strategy as well.

Other benefits of CSR reporting include *improved internal decisions making and reduced costs*. Organisations that produce social and environmental reports develop better internal control systems, improve their decision making and reduce costs, resulting in continuous improvements. This improved operational and process efficiency results in reduced risks and improved safety at work. This is particularly true for organisations that choose to report on their CSR issues and problems, not just on their successes and contribution (Khan et al., 2009). Pike (2000) stated that social reporting is valuable because it provides an informed basis for explaining the company's actions.

While it is possible to have good CSR without reporting, disclosure of CSR and other information is essential to help the company excel in its CSR for all of the aforementioned reasons. As Chapple and Moon (2005: 426) have asserted: 'we acknowledge the possibility that companies may behave responsibly without reporting this, but given the key theme in contemporary CSR is its reporting and accountability, we would not expect this to be widespread.'

The vast number of CSR reporting benefits detailed here can build a strong case for reporting and answer the 'why', although each company needs to identify its own benefits and motivations for CSR reporting. The next question is who we report to, which will be discussed in the following section.

> ## Questions for reflection and discussion
>
> 1. Examine all the benefits detailed here for CSR reporting. What other benefits can you think of?
> 2. What level of CSR reporting is required to achieve all these benefits?
> 3. What might be the disadvantages and challenges of CSR reporting?

Who are the CSR reports for?

In Chapter 3 we presented the stakeholder theory, which asserted that in addition to shareholders, each company has numerous stakeholders, who are any group or individual who can affect or is affected (positively or negatively) by the achievement of the organisation's objectives (Freeman, 1984). When shareholders are perceived as the only stakeholders of the company, it follows that only financial reports are required. But if the company also has a responsibility towards its employees, consumers, governments, the community and the environment (to name a few specific stakeholder groups), then it follows that reporting and disclosure of non-financial information, such as the company's positive and negative impact on these stakeholders, are an essential part of the company's stakeholder engagement.

As such, stakeholder theory and CSR reporting are connected for two reasons and require two processes. The first one involves the identification of stakeholders the company affects, both positively and negatively. Companies need to know who they affect and how, list those stakeholders and measure the impact on them. While many CSR reports only focus on the positive impact on the community, more comprehensive CSR reports identify all major stakeholders and discuss both the negative and positive impacts on these stakeholders. This could include, for example, the negative impact on the environment (and what we are doing to fix it); the positive impact on the community (going beyond just input in terms of how much money was donated or how many hours were volunteered; see Chapter 8); and the positive and negative impact on employees (including physical and psychological wellbeing, gender equity, etc.).

The second aspect of stakeholder engagement and CSR reporting requires companies to ask themselves: who is the report for? Which stakeholders are going to read it? Why do they read it and what do they want to find in this report? This demands another stakeholder analysis and a gathering of essential information about the CSR report's readers. In a way, this requires some marketing tools for identifying the market segments you are communicating with, gathering information about them (demographic, motivations, benefits) and conducting market research to gain feedback on this specific product being CSR reported. This is not to say that CSR reporting is merely a marketing and PR activity but that marketing knowledge and tools can help in serving the organisation in communicating effectively to the stakeholders and achieving a 'buy-in' from them.

Identifying the stakeholder groups the company is communicating with through its CSR report will not only determine the messages, the language, the content and the design of the report, but it will also determine how the report is delivered. If it is on the company's website, where do we put it? Some companies put their CSR reports in the 'investor relations' page, as it combines financial and non-financial information in these reports and the companies want shareholders to know about their sustainability and CSR. Others place it in a CSR, sustainability or community page, whereas some companies feature it on their homepage, signalling that this defines the company. Sometimes there is a shift over the years. For example, PUMA (see mini case study below) used to publish its reports under 'investor relations' and now does so under 'sustainability'.

One of the stakeholder groups that could be the target of CSR reporting are current and potential *employees* (internal stakeholders). As employees increase their interest in CSR, gain pride and develop their commitment based on values and social responsibility (see Chapter 7), it is becoming more important than ever before for companies to communicate their CSR efforts and impact to their employees. And yet not enough companies communicate to their employees that the CSR report is now available for them to read. In addition, potential employees often read CSR reports to gain a better understanding of the company they are considering working for and to examine the value congruence with this company. This is evident from the findings of a survey conducted in the UK and the US, which found that 88 per cent of British businesses believe that social responsibility will be more important in the future in recruiting and retaining employees (Simms, 2002). However, many companies use their CSR reports to present employee satisfaction level, gender equality in the workplace, health and safety of their employees or employee participation in CSR (Ellerup Nielsen and Thomsen, 2007), but do not communicate directly with employees in their report.

In addition, companies communicate with *consumers*, who sometimes look for information about a company they buy from, particularly if this company attracts public attention for social/environmental responsibility or irresponsibility.

Disclosing information on social and environmental issues may minimise the risk of consumer boycotts (Adams and Ambika, 2005). Furthermore, when consumers understand corporate activities, criticism is reduced, leading to improved reputation and communication and a competitive advantage (Khan et al., 2009).

EXERCISE

1. Pick a CSR report of any company that you know.
2. Try to understand which stakeholders it communicates with through the report.
3. What messages are sent to each group of stakeholders?
4. Does the style of the report and the communication channel (e.g. where the report can be found) affect who is going to read the report?
5. Which other stakeholders should the company address?

As was explained in the opening case of this chapter, KPMG conducts ongoing surveys on CSR reporting. In 2008, the organisation conducted a survey with report readers and published the *Count Me In* survey results (KPMG, 2008), based on a study of nearly 2,300 readers and non-readers from around the world. KPMG found that publishing a sustainability report had a strong positive impact on readers' perceptions of the company, and that readers wanted to see a stronger role for stakeholders in reporting. Readers believed reporters are most likely to omit failures from their sustainability reports but said it is important for them to understand the negative impact of the company whose report they are reading and to see what the company is doing about these issues. The main reasons why people were reading CSR reports were: 'I want to understand the specific sustainability issues of the company'; 'I use it for my general understanding of the company'; and 'I want to learn from it by means of benchmarking'. The last item could indicate that other companies read the report in order to learn from it and benchmark their own CSR. Importantly, 90 per cent of readers said their views of a reporter had been influenced by reading its sustainability report. Of these, 85 per cent developed a more positive opinion of the organisation. These results build a strong case for CSR reporting.

What companies report about

Based on who the report is for, the content and the topics of the CSR report should follow. When the main stakeholders of these reports are the communities in which the company operates, the report mainly focuses on contribution to the community, particularly in terms of the amount of money that was donated or the number of hours given on a voluntary basis by the company's employees. When the main audience is employees, companies then report on their internal CSR, particularly on employee welfare and wellbeing, gender equality in the workplace and employee involvement in their CSR. When companies define the government as the main stakeholder of the report, there will be more information on contribution to the public good, working with the UN and complying with laws and regulations.

Some research shows that companies tend to focus on the 'three Ps' of sustainability – planet, people and profit – in their CSR reports (Ellerup Nielsen and Thomsen, 2007). Studying companies in Denmark, these authors show that CSR reports focus on employees, local communities and society, the environment, corporate governance and business strategy, with only a few demonstrating some objective measurements. Other sources discuss CSR report content under ESG (environmental, social and governance; see Brown et al., 2009).

According to KPMG (2013), CSR reports should include the following seven topics (see also Figure 10.1):

1. *Strategy, risk and opportunity*: CSR reporting should include a clear assessment of related risks and opportunities and should explain the actions it is taking in response.
2. *Materiality*: CSR reports should demonstrate that a company has identified the CSR issues with the greatest potential impacts (i.e. that are the most material) both on the business itself and its stakeholders.
3. *Targets and indicators*: Companies should use measurable targets and key performance indicators and clearly report on progress and performance based on set targets and objectives.
4. *Suppliers and the value chain*: CSR reports should explain the social and environmental impacts of the company's supply chain (see Chapter 5), as well as the downstream impact of products and services and show how the company is managing those impacts.
5. *Stakeholder engagement*: Companies should identify stakeholders in their CSR reports, explain the process used to engage with stakeholders and the actions taken in response to their feedback (see Chapter 3).
6. *Governance of CSR*: Reports should make clear how CSR is governed within a company, who has responsibility for the company's CSR performance and how the company links CSR performance to remuneration.
7. *Transparency and balance*: CSR reports should be balanced and include information on challenges and setbacks as well as achievements.

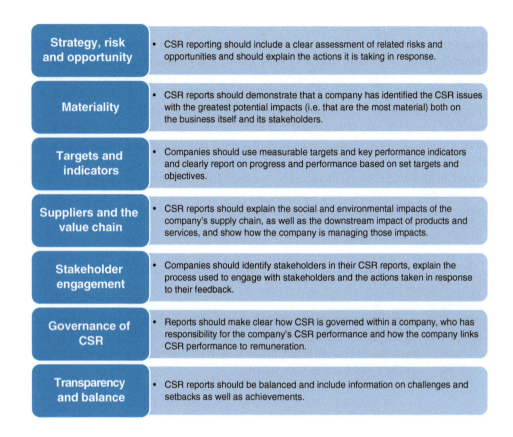

Strategy, risk and opportunity
- CSR reporting should include a clear assessment of related risks and opportunities and should explain the actions it is taking in response.

Materiality
- CSR reports should demonstrate that a company has identified the CSR issues with the greatest potential impacts (i.e. that are the most material) both on the business itself and its stakeholders.

Targets and indicators
- Companies should use measurable targets and key performance indicators and clearly report on progress and performance based on set targets and objectives.

Suppliers and the value chain
- CSR reports should explain the social and environmental impacts of the company's supply chain, as well as the downstream impact of products and services, and show how the company is managing those impacts.

Stakeholder engagement
- Companies should identify stakeholders in their CSR reports, explain the process used to engage with stakeholders and the actions taken in response to their feedback.

Governance of CSR
- Reports should make clear how CSR is governed within a company, who has responsibility for the company's CSR performance and how the company links CSR performance to remuneration.

Transparency and balance
- CSR reports should be balanced and include information on challenges and setbacks as well as achievements.

Figure 10.1 What companies should report on (based on KPMG, 2013)

Using CSR reporting as an effective communication tool

CSR reporting can also be analysed from a communication point of view. Effective CSR reporting can be seen as part of effective communication in which the sender of the message manages to encode it effectively so that the receiver of the message may decode it and understand the intended meaning. This basic communication process model (Shannon and Weaver, 1949) can be used to ensure that companies manage to come across as they intend to and capture the essence of their values and CSR in a way that will engage and inspire their stakeholders.

Another important theory of communication that can be used in this context is the signalling theory (Spence, 1974), according to which, in a situation of information asymmetry, companies signal their qualities by sharing information with the market, in this case through CSR reports. Indeed, there is a great information asymmetry in the current market, where companies often know more about their consumers than vice versa, and it is very hard for consumers and other stakeholders to gain access to information about the company. CSR reports can help alleviate this asymmetry to a certain extent and create a better information disclosure culture.

Finally, communication is not a one-way street. Although the communication cycle has a sender and a receiver, effective communication is about creating an ongoing dialogue, open communication channels and shared meaning. When companies invite stakeholders to engage in their CSR, provide knowledge and even help write their CSR story, it is more meaningful for everyone. When stakeholders have open communication channels to provide feedback on CSR reports, both positive and negative, companies can learn and improve.

How to report: Reporting options

According to Exter (2012), there are various ways in which companies can report on their CSR, from basic reporting, full CSR reporting and advanced reporting, to integrated and game-changing reporting. In this section, we will cover the different options for companies to choose from, given why they report, to whom and on what, as well as where they are in their CSR journey.

Basic reporting

Basic reporting usually comprises a few brief pages on the company's website. These brief reports are usually compiled and developed by the company's marketing and/or PR departments. Usually, these are not strategic documents, they are not aligned with the company's core operations and are disconnected from the company's annual report (financial disclosure). The motivation for such reporting is mainly compliance. Companies at this stage will only provide a CSR report because they must, either due to regulations (in some countries this is compulsory) or due to market demand and competition. In addition, such brief reports tend to focus more on the input of the company (how much money was donated to charity) than on the impact the company creates, as this takes more time and effort to analyse. Brief reports were more popular in the 1990s, but most companies nowadays have a full CSR report (KPMG, 2015).

Full CSR reports

A full CSR report is a stand-alone document on the company's CSR efforts. This is more comprehensive than the previous version, being longer and focusing on a larger number of issues, such as those covered in the previous section of this chapter (e.g. ESG or 'planet, people and profit'). These reports are at least ten pages long, usually somewhere between 50–100 pages. In the last few years, companies have moved away from intensive textual reports, which not many people read, to a visualised report, with many graphs, charts, images and an easy-to-follow analysis. These reports are usually compiled together by the CSR and marketing teams.

Full CSR reports usually include the mission statement of the company and an introduction by the CEO to signal the importance of CSR and how embedded it is in the company and aligned with its strategy. It is usually a one-way communication but opens the door to some level of stakeholder engagement.

Advanced reporting

In advanced reports, CSR is integrated into the business operations, in which the leadership of the business is integral to the development of the report. The CSR team usually writes advanced reporting and the organisational executive leadership, including the CEO, leads it. It is part of strategic CSR as the reporting aims to be holistic, covering both positive and negative impacts, and explains how the company aims to increase what is good and address the challenges. Advanced reporting often uses some reporting framework such as the global reporting initiative; it is longer, includes much more information and demonstrates higher levels of transparency compared to previous reports. It is aimed at ongoing stakeholder engagement and an open conversation that would benefit everyone involved.

Integrated reporting

Some leading companies have begun to integrate all their information statements into one single document in the form of integrated reporting. Integrated reporting provides information on the company's strategy, corporate governance, performance and prospects in such a way as to reflect the commercial, social and environmental context in which it operates (Frias-Aceituno et al., 2013). Integrated reports offer a clear and concise statement of how the organisation operates and how it creates and maintains value. It focuses on medium- to long-term goals and offers a holistic view of the company's responsibility. It is therefore aligned with and serves strategic CSR.

Integrated reporting is the integrated representation of a company's performance in terms of both financial and other relevant value-related information. It shifts away from the view that the triple bottom line (financial, environment and social) requires three different reports (and strategies for that matter), and rather signals that it is the combination and alignment of all three that create a company that is strategically responsible.

Over half of reporting companies worldwide (51 per cent) now include CSR information in their annual financial reports. This is a striking rise since 2011 (when only 20 per cent did so) and 2008 (only 9 per cent). The direction is clear and with more than half of companies researched now including CSR data in their financial reports, this can arguably be considered as standard global practice (KPMG, 2013).

Game-changing reporting

Some companies go above and beyond CSR reporting, taking a step beyond what is required. Some companies – not many – are game-changers in reporting, leading the way and impacting the way that others report. This could be due to innovative reporting methods, channels and/or the topics they report on.

Such reports are holistic as they cover everything that the company does, align all CSR aspects and lift the benchmark. Such reports are usually not only created by the CSR or marketing departments but are based on the entire organisation's effort: with the finance department involved, design thinking being utilised and the creativity and passion of many internal and external stakeholders being included. Such reports are developed with a long and genuine engagement of various stakeholders in a constant open dialogue.

Game-changing reports offer more than data. They offer a mindshift, whole-systems thinking and a recapture of the role of business in society. As they are holistic, such companies usually only have one integrated report in which the financial and the social value of the company are combined. The social value of the financial performance and the financial value of the social performance are both discussed.

One such innovative method is 'true cost accounting'. True cost examines the real costs of producing a product or the costs of the supply chain of the company (currently mainly focusing on food). Due to the dangerous idea of externalities, which has been covered in the book several times, companies (and therefore shareholders and consumers) do not pay the full price of manufacturing. Often, governments with tax revenue from people who do not invest in or even buy from a company, pay to fix the pollution and waste created by the company. Governments must address the social and environmental problems caused directly and indirectly by business. A few companies, such as PUMA (see mini case study below), dare to ask: what if we were to pay for all of this? In their reports, externalities are integrated into the organisation's balance sheet and the entire business model changes to take into account the true cost of everything that the company does.

Mini case study   PUMA

PUMA is a German multinational company that designs and manufactures athletic and casual footwear, apparel and accessories. PUMA employs more than 10,000 people worldwide and distributes its products in more than 120 countries. The company was founded in 1948 by Rudolf Dassler and became a public company in 1986. In 2007, PUMA became part of the French group Kering and in 2011 the company completed its conversion from a German public limited company to a Societas Europaea, the EU-wide equivalent, changing its name from PUMA AG Rudolf Dassler Sport to PUMA SE. At the same time, Franz Koch replaced the long-serving Jochen Zeitz as the firm's CEO and started to lead a vision of sustainability, CSR and business for peace in the company. PUMA became involved in a number of inspirational activities, such as signing a 'peace agreement' with Adidas (which was founded by Rudolf Dassler's brother, and the two did not talk to one another for decades). PUMA initiated sporting games between kids from conflicting countries and supported the Peace One Day organisation: 'PUMA Peace makes sports equipment donations as we think that sports has the power to overcome hostile boundaries, bringing people together in peace' (PUMA, 2012).

The company's 2012 annual report received a lot of attention and was referred to by Exter (in her lecture) as a 'game-changing' report. It was an integrated report, aimed at shareholders and other stakeholders together. It discussed PUMA's financial and social performance. The report says:

> As a leading Sportlifestyle company we have the opportunity, and the responsibility, to contribute to a better world, now and for the generations to come. Our sustainability concept, PUMAVision, along with our 4Keys – Fair, Honest, Positive and Creative – guides us on our way to put this vision of a better world into practice. (PUMA, 2012: 13)

What made this a remarkable report, which is covered in CSR textbooks (e.g. Blowfield and Murray, 2014), is that PUMA decided to incorporate its 'externalities' and set out a mission to place value on its GHG emissions, water use, land use, air pollution and waste caused by its operations worldwide by 2016. It committed to doing so in three stages: 1. gathering data on emissions and resource use; 2. calculating the financial values of the above; and 3. focusing on the beneficiaries of the economic impacts of PUMA's operations.

This would have been a remarkable report, but to date PUMA has only published data relating to stage 1. In 2013, CEO Koch was replaced by former football

(Continued)

professional Björn Gulden, and the agenda of the company changed dramatically. If the word 'sustainability' was mentioned over 400 times in the 2012 report, this was reduced to under 200 times in 2016. The word 'peace' disappeared altogether. The company does, however, still publish an integrated report and all of these reports can be found online.

Reference

Puma (2012) Business and sustainability report. Available at: http://about.puma.com/damfiles/default/sustainability/reports/puma-s-sustainability-reports/annual-reports/PUMAGeschaeftsbericht2012_en-98e88322bf37fe90049aaa6014d22af2.pdf (Accessed: 14 May 2017)

Questions

1. What were the benefits and advantages of PUMA's outstanding plan on its sustainability reporting?
2. What were the risks?
3. Why do you think PUMA diverted from its original plan?
4. Examine PUMA's 2012 and 2016 reports. What differences can you find between the two?
5. What else could PUMA do to excel in its CSR reporting?

CSR stages and reporting options

In Chapter 2, we presented Zadek's (2004) CSR stages model with five levels or stages of CSR: defensive, compliance, managerial, strategic and civil (see Figure 10.2). Although Zadek did not discuss reporting, we can connect these five stages of CSR to five levels of CSR reporting:

1. *The defensive stage* usually takes place when a company is accused of behaving unethically and does not take responsibility for its actions. Companies at this stage usually do not engage in CSR nor do they report it. If they do, it might be perceived by the public as 'greenwashing'.
2. At the *compliance stage*, the company complies with law, regulation and policy (be it external or internal). This would usually result in a brief report compiled by the marketing department and uploaded to the website.
3. At the *managerial stage*, companies embed societal issues in their core management processes and, as such, having a full CSR report fits their goals and actions.
4. At the *strategic stage*, companies integrate societal issues into their core business strategies. Similar to strategic CSR, companies align their responsibility,

sustainability and philanthropy with what they do and what their mission is. Since the approach here is more holistic, integrated reports are suitable.

5. At the *civil stage*, companies promote broad industry participation in corporate responsibility. They are CSR leaders and promote a wide-open conversation on the role of business in society. It is civil CSR that usually leads to game-changing reporting which the rest of the industry then tries to follow.

Stage	What organisations do	CSR report	Who leads it
Defensive	Deny practices, outcomes or responsibilities.	No report	No one
Compliance	Adopt a policy-based compliance approach as a cost of doing business.	Brief report	Marketing and PR
Managerial	Embed the societal issue in their core management processes.	CSR report	CSR team
Strategic	Integrate the societal issue into their core business strategies.	Integrated report	CSR + Finance + Marketing
Civil	Promote broad industry participation in corporate responsibility.	Game-changing report	The whole organisation and its stakeholders

Figure 10.2   CSR stages and CSR reporting (based on Zadek, 2004)

Global Reporting Initiative (GRI)

In Chapter 9, we discussed several benchmarking tools and frameworks that can assist companies in measuring their CSR. While many of these tools and frameworks require reporting (e.g. UNGC requires a 'communication on progress report') and others offer some guidelines on reporting (such as ISO), it is the Global Reporting Initiative (GRI) that has become the most commonly used reporting tool in the last 20 years (KPMG, 2013).

GRI is an independent non-profit organisation based in Amsterdam that promotes economic, environmental and social sustainability. Its mission is to develop and disseminate globally applicable sustainability reporting guidelines to enable organisations to voluntarily report on their activities in the social, environmental and economic dimensions. GRI achieves this mission by providing organisations with a comprehensive sustainability reporting framework that is widely used around the world. GRI's sustainability reporting framework enables organisations to measure and report their sustainability performance. According to GRI, by reporting transparently and with accountability, organisations can increase the trust that stakeholders have in them and in the global economy.

In the 1990s, CSR and CSR reporting became popular but lacked standardisation and consistency. As such, it was often difficult to read these reports, let alone compare them to other reports. In 1997, GRI was initiated and it is now the most used reporting framework in the world. GRI was developed in co-operation with the

UN Environment Program (UNEP) and it is particularly well established. The GRI offers a set of reporting principles and structured report content with indicators for economic, environmental and social sustainability (Brown et al., 2009).

As of 2016, the GRI standards are modular, interrelated and designed primarily to be used as a set, to prepare a sustainability report focused on material topics. The three universal standards (Foundation, General Disclosures and Management Approach) are used by every organisation that prepares a sustainability report according to GRI. The organisation can then choose from the topic-specific standards to report on its material topics – economic, environmental and/or social. There are six economic standards (the '200 series' such as financial performance, market presence and anti-corruption); eight environmental standards (the '300 series' including energy, water, biodiversity and emission standards); and 19 social standards (the '400 series', including several standards on employment and labour rights, several on consumer rights and one on local communities). A company can use all the GRI standards or select relevant ones to report on specific information. The flexibility, together with some specific and detailed guidelines, is what makes the GRI so popular.

EXERCISE

1. Go to the GRI website and download one of the standards.
2. Examine the standard and discuss it with one of your peers.
3. How detailed and specific is it? Is it too detailed?
4. What did you learn from it about CSR that you did not know prior to reading it?
5. How difficult do you think it would be to implement it?
6. Try finding a company that uses this standard and see how it reports on this aspect.

CSR reporting analysis model

Based on a study they conducted on CSR reporting in Denmark, Ellerup Nielsen and Thomsen (2007) offered a framework that can be useful for companies that desire to report on their CSR. It can assist organisations in using the questions raised in this chapter (why and how to report and to whom) and defining the goals and nature of their CSR reporting. The authors argued that the form and content of CSR reporting depend on contextual elements such as the size of the company, the specific stakeholder groups, the complexity of the issue, the ambition level and the nature of the engagement specified by the company.

This reporting framework resembles an open box (see Figure 10.3) with four sides. On the top side are the perspectives of the CSR report: people, profit or planet. Companies can be high or low on any of these dimensions or on all three. The right side of this box is about the CSR ambition of the company (or its motivation) which can range from low to high based on this scale: compliance-driven, profit-driven, caring, synergistic and holistic. CSR and CSR reporting are often derived from the company's values and motivations. Next, at the bottom, are the stakeholders' aspects, which examine which stakeholders' expectations are taken into account when reporting on CSR. Here, the authors chose to focus on employees, shareholders, customers, suppliers, media and NGOs, although other stakeholders can be added to this list (e.g. governments). Finally, the left side of the box examines the context of the report: is it local or global? Does the report discuss the history of the organisation? Does the CEO sign it off? (The last aspect is the least explained and not very clear.)

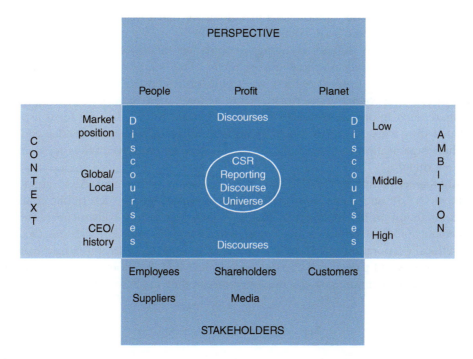

Figure 10.3   CSR reporting analysis model (Ellerup Nielsen and Thomsen, 2007)

While the framework was developed based on a very small sample of companies (only six organisations from Denmark), it still shows how many aspects are taken into consideration when writing and examining CSR reports.

Related challenges

As was stated in the introduction to this chapter, CSR reporting is anything but a simple and straightforward task, particularly if the company desires to do it well. It requires resources, including human resources, money, time, expertise, social networks and human capital. It is therefore not surprising that many companies in the past avoided this altogether or complied with a brief report. However, as was explained by KPMG (2013), CSR reporting is no longer an option. When 90 per cent of the top global companies publish such reports, the last 10 per cent are going to be highly criticised by various stakeholders.

The aim of this chapter is to provide some answers as to why CSR reporting is important and beneficial and what the various ways are in which companies can report. However, it requires ongoing stakeholder engagement to answer many of the questions raised in the chapter in order to develop not only an excellent report but also one that maximally serves the company and its stakeholders. There are very good frameworks, standards and guidelines that can assist the company in achieving this valuable goal, particularly the GRI.

One of the most difficult challenges companies face in CSR reporting is how much to report on their negative impact. While KPMG's report *Count Me In* (KPMG, 2008) suggested that report readers are highly interested in the negative aspects of CSR or even the company's performance in general, many companies are reluctant to share such information due to brand protection, the media and legal aspects. What if they were to report that they are still far from achieving gender equality in their organisation (but working on it) and then an employee takes legal action against them?

Another challenge is creating an open discussion with stakeholders about the company's CSR and about its report. Some companies create such public channels of communication but in doing so expose themselves to non-constructive criticism. Comments on the Internet can be negative and bloggers and CSR websites (such as the Ethical Corporation) often review CSR reports, and not always in a positive way. However, it is still part of stakeholder engagement and the more companies involve their stakeholders in the process, the less criticism they might face later on.

Reporting tips and tools

There are many CSR reporting tips and tools detailed throughout this chapter. Here is a brief summary:

1. Understand that CSR reporting is not just a task; it is a reflective practice. It requires reflections, raising questions and engaging in an open and sometimes brave conversation before the first letter is to be written. It requires a deep dive into corporate values, ambitions, CSR motivation and performance.

2. Bring as many stakeholders as possible to the table to help you answer the most important questions raised here: why do we report? To whom? How should we report? What do we report about? Employees, consumers and other stakeholders may not only have different answers to these questions, but could also take the company far beyond what it can do on its own.

3. Reports should be holistic and signal the importance of CSR to the company. Leaders focused on CSR reporting go beyond reporting on their input and their donations. They measure the positive and negative long-term impacts of everything that they do (including their corporate philanthropy and their supply chain) and engage in an open conversation on how to get better. Consider whether integrated reports are right for your organisation and how to become a game-changing player in this field.

4. Standards and sector framework mechanisms can help improve the content and quality of reports. Examine what other leading companies are doing in this space; and learn the frameworks, standards and guidelines that can help you improve your CSR and your reporting.

Summary

CSR reporting has become a popular trend since the 1990s with nearly 90 per cent of the top 250 global companies currently publishing such a report. However, it is not a simple task: it requires time, effort and resources and it demands reflection on why, what, how and to whom we report. Answering these questions is not an easy task but would assist in achieving effective CSR communication and reporting.

Companies report on their CSR for various reasons and when they do, they can achieve several prominent benefits. CSR reporting increases transparency, trust and legitimacy; assists the company in measuring its CSR and improving its performance; is an effective stakeholder engagement method; can promote the company's brand and good reputation; helps identify and address critical issues; and assists in developing the company's strategy, decision making and financial performance.

However, to achieve these benefits, companies need to apply their stakeholder engagement philosophy and activities. CSR reporting needs to address the interest and needs of various stakeholders, such as existing and potential employees, consumers, investors and the general public. To ensure it does just that, companies need to have an open conversation with their stakeholders, allow them to bring their concerns and ensure that the report addresses them.

Examining many CSR reports, companies often report on the 'three Ps' of sustainability (or the triple bottom line – people, planet and profits) or on their ESG (environmental and social responsibility and corporate governance). Many of them combine a report on their internal CSR (about their employees) with one detailing their external CSR. Regarding the latter, companies often only report on their input and not on the outcomes and long-term impact of their external CSR.

Based on the corporate values and where companies stand in their CSR levels, companies choose how to report on their CSR: from a brief report that is mainly done for marketing purposes, through full CSR reports and advanced reports to integrated reports and game-changing reports. Zadek's CSR stages framework can be used to align CSR stages with reporting methods.

Guidelines, such as the GRI standards and frameworks that were presented in this chapter and in the previous chapter, can assist companies to learn more about CSR reporting, understand what is required of them in this process, and improve their actual reporting and communications.

General questions

1. While there are many benchmarking tools (some of which were covered in Chapter 9), there is only one global initiative on CSR reporting that is commonly adopted. Why is this so? What are the advantages and disadvantages of this phenomenon?
2. In this chapter we have used stakeholder theory and Zadek's (2004) CSR stages to explain the differentiations in CSR reporting. What other theories and frameworks would be useful here?
3. Find two CSR/sustainability reports online and compare them. Which type of report do they publish (brief, full, advanced, integrated or game-changing)? What did you learn about the reporting companies? What is good about their reports? What can they do to improve them?
4. KPMG declares that the debate on whether or not to report is over. Do you agree? What does it mean for CSR? What about the 25 per cent of N100 and 10 per cent of G250 companies that do not report?
5. If you were the head of sustainability in a large corporation, how would you convince the board to report better on your CSR activities? What kind of report would you like your company to run and why?

Key definitions

- Business reporting is the public reporting of operating and financial data by a business enterprise (Lymer, 1999).
- CSR reporting provides information about the economic, environmental and social impacts of the reporting company as well as information on governance and performance.

- CSR reporting is a way for organisations to provide information for different stakeholders regarding social and environmental issues (Golob and Bartlett, 2007).
- Legitimacy is a generalised perception or assumption that the actions of an entity are desirable, proper or appropriate within some socially constructed system of norms, values, beliefs and definitions (Suchman, 1995).
- Integrated reporting provides information on the company's strategy, corporate governance, performance and prospects in such a way as to reflect the commercial, social and environmental context in which it operates (Frias-Aceituno et al., 2013).
- Integrated reports offer a clear and concise statement of how the organisation operates and how it creates and maintains value in the medium to long term, as well as a holistic view of the company responsibility.

References

Adams, C. and Ambika, Z. (2005) 'Corporate social responsibility: Why business should act responsibly and be accountable', *The Cost and Management*, 34(4): 10–17.

Aguilera, R. V., Rupp, D. E., Williams, C. A. and Ganapathi, J. (2007) 'Putting the S back in corporate social responsibility: A multilevel theory of social change in organizations', *Academy of Management Review*, 32(3): 836–63.

Blowfield, M. and Murray, A. (2014) *Corporate responsibility*. Oxford: Oxford University Press.

Brown, H. S., De Jong, M. and Lessidrenska, T. (2009) 'The rise of the global reporting initiative: A case of institutional entrepreneurship', *Environmental Politics*, 18(2): 182–200.

Chapple, W. and Moon, J. (2005) 'Corporate social responsibility (CSR) in Asia: A seven-country study of CSR website reporting', *Business & Society*, 44(4): 415–41.

Deegan, C., Rankin, M. and Tobin, J. (2002) 'An examination of the corporate social and environmental disclosures of BHP from 1983–1997: A test of legitimacy theory', *Accounting, Auditing & Accountability Journal*, 15(3): 312–43.

Ellerup Nielsen, A. and Thomsen, C. (2007) 'Reporting CSR: What and how to say it?' *Corporate Communications: An International Journal*, 12(1): 25–40.

Exter, N. (2012) *Cranfield on corporate sustainability*. London: Greenleaf Publishing.

Freeman, R. E. (1984) *Stakeholder management: Framework and philosophy*. Mansfield, MA: Pitman.

Frias-Aceituno, J. V., Rodriguez-Ariza, L. and Garcia-Sanchez, I. M. (2013) 'The role of the board in the dissemination of integrated corporate social reporting', *Corporate Social Responsibility and Environmental Management*, 20(4): 219–33.

Golob, U. and Bartlett, J. L. (2007) 'Communicating about corporate social responsibility: A comparative study of CSR reporting in Australia and Slovenia', *Public Relations Review*, 33(1): 1–9.

Khan, H. U. Z., Halabi, A. K. and Samy, M. (2009) 'Corporate social responsibility (CSR) reporting: A study of selected banking companies in Bangladesh', *Social Responsibility Journal*, 5(3): 344–57.

KPMG (2008) *Count me in: The readers' take on sustainability reporting*. Amstelveen: KPMG.

KPMG (2013) *The KPMG survey of corporate responsibility reporting 2013*. Amstelveen: KPMG.

KPMG (2015) *The KPMG survey of corporate responsibility reporting 2015*. Amstelveen: KPMG.

Lymer, A. (1999) *Business reporting on the Internet*. London: International Accounting Standards Committee.

Patten, D. M. (1991) 'Exposure, legitimacy, and social disclosure', *Journal of Accounting and Public Policy*, 10(4): 297–308.

Pike, A. (2000) 'When life is more than just a lottery: Management social reporting', *Financial Times*, 11(9): 31–2.

Shannon, C. E. and Weaver, W. (1949) *The mathematical theory of communication*. Urbana, IL: University of Illinois Press.

Simms, J. (2002) 'Business: Corporate social responsibility – you know it makes sense', *Accountancy*, 130(11): 48–50.

Spence, A. M. (1974) *Market signaling: Informational transfer in hiring and related screening processes*. Boston, MA: Harvard University Press.

Suchman, M. C. (1995) 'Managing legitimacy: Strategic and institutional approaches', *Academy of Management Journal*, 20(3): 571–610.

Zadek, S. (2004) 'The path to corporate responsibility', *Harvard Business Review*, 82(12): 125–32.

Further reading and links

Bebbington, J., Unerman, J. and O'Dwyer, B. (2014) *Sustainability accounting and accountability*. London: Routledge.

Exter, N. (2017) Types of CSR reporting options (video). Available at: www.think-sustainability.co.uk/sustain-affinity/view/types-of-csr-reporting-options (Accessed: 19 April 2017)

GRI Secretariat (2016) The GRI Sustainability Reporting Standards: The Future of Reporting. Available at: www.youtube.com/watch?v=AGqE4OO0_7g (Accessed: 14 May 2017)

Lexicon of Sustainability (2014) True cost accounting. Available at: www.youtube.com/watch?v=sej0w33BW2E (Accessed: 14 May 2017)

Luo, X. R., Wang, D. and Zhang, J. (2017) 'Whose call to answer: Institutional complexity and firms' CSR reporting', *Academy of Management Journal*, 60(1): 321–44.

Patten, D. M. and Zhao, N. (2014) 'Standalone CSR reporting by US retail companies', *Accounting Forum,* 38(2): 132–44.

Pérez, A. (2015) 'Corporate reputation and CSR reporting to stakeholders: Gaps in the literature and future lines of research', *Corporate Communications: An International Journal*, 20(1): 11–29.

PUMA (2016) Puma's sustainability reports. Available at: http://about.puma.com/en/sustainability/reports/puma-s-sustainability-reports (Accessed: 14 May 2017)

CSR and Marketing: Three Frontiers 11

Learning outcomes

By the end of this chapter, students should be able to:

- apply marketing knowledge and tools to promote responsibility and sustainability for societal benefits
- articulate the importance and advantages of CSR marketing together with related risk and understand how to do it well

(Continued)

- explain the complexity of CSR and its impact on consumer behaviour
- detail what is encompassed in ethical and sustainable marketing and why it is an essential part of strategic CSR
- describe what social marketing is and how companies are now using it as part of their CSR.

Case study   CSR marketing at H&M – Great achievements, enormous issues

Being the second largest polluting industry in the world, only second to the oil industry, the fashion sector offers an ample opportunity to increase its CSR. Fashion giant Hennes & Mauritz (H&M), a member of the UN Global Compact, has been focusing on sustainability in the last few years and using its CSR efforts in its marketing campaigns.

H&M, a Swedish company operating since 1947, is one of the world's leading fashion companies. Employing more than 160,000 people worldwide, the company operates over 4,400 stores in 66 markets. In 2016, the company's revenue reached US$25 billion. At the same time, H&M promotes sustainability and the circular economy as one of its core values, using its size and scale to advance a more 'circular, fair and equal fashion industry'. The company aims to use 100 per cent recycled or sustainable materials by 2030, as part of its overarching aim to become 100 per cent circular, as it aligns with UN SDG 12.

Its Conscious Exclusive collection, a fashion line for women, children and men, is made of sustainable materials (including a polyester made of plastics recycled from shoreline waste) and adheres to fair trade principles. The company has also published tips on more sustainable garment care practices. In terms of procurement, H&M has committed to source all cotton for its items from sustainable sources by 2020. In 2013, the company launched a global campaign on garment collection and recycling, with the aim of reducing the extent of clothing going into landfill. H&M accepts any unwanted clothing, of any brand and condition, in all of its stores worldwide. The clothes are either donated and sold as second-hand clothing, reused for other purposes (such as cleaning cloths) or recycled and turned into items such as insulation.

In addition to the efforts related to clothing itself, H&M seeks to improve the working conditions of employees in production countries, in line with UN SDG 8: 'Promote sustained, inclusive and sustainable economic growth, full and productive employment and decent work for all.' Since the collapse of an H&M supplier, a garment factory in Rana Plaza, Bangladesh, which killed 1,135 people, fashion consumers have demanded greater social responsibility. In the same year, H&M responded by taking a major step towards demonstrating its social responsibility, and made its supplier list public. Despite exposing H&M to a major business strategy risk, the company lists each factory's name and address, number of workers, worker interviews, information about the materials, information about the design team and how to take care of the garment. In addition, H&M published a sustainability commitment towards fair living wages, environmental performance in countries of operation and animal welfare. The company is now ranked as one of the top three most transparent fashion companies in the world and was even given a tick of approval by Oxfam for Christmas shopping in 2016.

But despite all these positive efforts, there are still some questions and issues raised about its CSR and sustainability and whether a fast-fashion company that manufactures an estimate of 550 million items a year can realistically promote sustainable solutions. YouTube videos demonstrate criticism of H&M sustainability and the conditions in the factories listed as H&M's suppliers (e.g. 'H&M conscious label not so conscious'). According to these videos, despite H&M transparency reports, employees still work in inhumane conditions, many for over the allowed limited time (by H&M and the international standards it commits to).

H&M nonetheless makes efforts to promote more sustainable fashion choices. Through its CSR marketing strategy, H&M campaigns for the recycling of clothes. Its advertisement from 2015, 'Close the loop', presented a range of fashion choices, and at the end of it, mentions the environmental value of recycling one single T-shirt: saving 2,100 litres of water. This is a distinct value proposition for clothes donors: rather than donating clothes to a charity shop, which may contribute to one more re-use of the garment, H&M aims to find an ultimate solution, completing the life cycle of garments.

The ad 'Bring it on' from 2017 shows a wide range of clothes that would no longer be worn, informs the viewer of H&M's initiative and makes a promise to recycle and re-use unwanted clothes, as well as to invest the profits of re-sales in research and innovation for 'closing the loop on textiles' and social improvement projects. Its Conscious Collection ad from 2017 discussed the increasing risk to our oceans of plastic and how fashion can be part of the solution, by turning plastic into clothes. These ads raise awareness of environmental issues and the solution offered by H&M, while promoting the company, its brand and products.

These marketing efforts result in an increase in revenue, but also in raised awareness of ethical fashion and sustainability. For example, the media and fashion magazines gave much attention to H&M's Conscious Collection, celebrating it and

(Continued)

commending it: 'H&M's new conscious exclusive collection turns discarded plastic into evening gowns", reported *Vogue* in 2017 (Farra, 2017).

Questions

1. What is your view on the drivers for marketing sustainable initiatives at H&M?
2. How does H&M's CSR marketing align with its core operations? What can be done to achieve a better alignment?
3. What ethical and unethical elements can you find in H&M's campaigns 'Bring it on' and 'Conscious exclusive'?
4. What are the risks and negative consequences of H&M'S marketing of its sustainability initiatives?
5. If you were a consultant working with H&M, how would you advise the company to change its CSR marketing? Why?

Bibliography

Blomqvist, K.H. and Posner, S. (2004) 'Three strategies for integrating CSR with brand marketing', *Market Leader*, 25 (Summer): 33–6.

Dach, L. and Allmendinger, K. (2014) 'Sustainability in corporate communications and its influence on consumer awareness and perceptions: A study of H&M and Primark', *Procedia-Social and Behavioral Sciences*, 103: 409–18.

Farra, E. (2017) 'H&M's new conscious exclusive collection turns discarded plastic into evening gowns', *Vogue*, 7 February. Available at: www.vogue.com/article/hm-conscious-exclusive-collection-exclusive-preview-bionic-yarn-natalia-vodianova (Accessed: 19 October 2017)

Giertz-Mårtenson, I. (2012) 'H&M: Documenting the story of one of the world's largest fashion retailers', *Business History*, 54(1): 108–15.

Shen, B. (2014) 'Sustainable fashion supply chain: Lessons from H&M', *Sustainability*, 6(9): 6236–49.

Links

DPM Production (2016) H&M conscious label not so conscious. Available at: www.youtube.com/watch?v=K7oRy1RyqdM&t=794s (Accessed: 1 June 2017)

H&M (2015) Conscious exclusive by H&M. Available at: www.youtube.com/watch?v=U2GEdMhGJR8 (Accessed: 1 June 2017)

H&M (2015) H&M close the loop: Sustainable fashion through recyclable clothes. Available at: www.youtube.com/watch?v=s4xnyr2mCuI (Accessed: 1 June 2017)

H&M (2017) Care for your clothes. Available at: https://about.hm.com/en/sustainability/get-involved/care-for-your-clothes.html (Accessed: 1 June 2017)

H&M (2017) H&M Group at a glance. Available at: https://about.hm.com/en/about-us/h-m-group-at-a-glance.html (Accessed: 1 June 2017)

H&M (2017) H&M's conscious exclusive 2017 collection shows the beauty of sustainability. Available at: https://about.hm.com/en/media/news/general-2017/h-m_s-conscious-exclusive-2017-collection-shows-the-beauty-of-su.html (Accessed: 1 June 2017)

H&M (2017) The way to sustainable fashion. Available at: https://about.hm.com/en/sustainability/get-involved/the-way-to-sustainable-fashion.html (Accessed: 1 June 2017)

Leo, K. (2017) Why I don't shop at H&M. Available at: www.youtube.com/watch?v=jAgq74QCWpA&t=137s (Accessed: 1 June 2017)

Introduction: Holistic CSR and marketing

A majority of adults in the US (63 per cent) said in 2016 that they are dissatisfied with major corporations, compared to 48 per cent in 2001 (Gallup, 2016). On the other hand, the 2016 Edelman Trust Barometer revealed that trust in corporations has reached its highest level since the global financial crisis. In addition, 80 per cent of people agreed that a company should take specific actions to improve the economic and social conditions in the community where it operates. As such, it seems that CSR can help build public trust in corporations and their brands, if they devote their power and resources to creating a positive impact on society.

To achieve higher levels of trust, companies need to be strategic about their CSR as well as with the way they market it. Marketing corporate philanthropy while receiving negative publicity for what the company does in its supply chain is not going to achieve good results. Therefore, companies need firstly to *be* socially responsible and only then consider communicating this social responsibility through their marketing campaigns.

For too long CSR has been used solely as a marketing instrument without enough substance behind it. In the 2003 documentary *The Corporation*, there is a scene where a company is shown to be using under-aged girls to make its clothes and add a tag on them that promises to donate a dollar to charity in the US for each piece of garment sold. This is the kind of behaviour that destroys consumers' trust in big corporations and creates cynicism around CSR. The term 'greenwashing' was created to describe companies that only publicise their CSR without putting substantial action behind it. When this is done, consumers and other stakeholders not only lose trust in the company but also in CSR altogether.

On the other hand, when companies become strategic and holistic in their CSR efforts and work to meet the interests of a broad set of stakeholders, it could yield great results for their brand, affect consumer behaviour, trust and loyalty, and in turn achieve financial results. The paradox of CSR marketing is that when CSR is done only for marketing purposes, it is not effective. Only when consumers believe that the company is genuinely interested in doing good, will they also assist the company in doing well.

As such, this chapter will examine three important aspects of *CSR marketing*. Firstly, we will discuss whether, why and how companies should promote their CSR efforts. We will see that such marketing could unleash a high level of criticism if the company is not fully trusted. We will show the advantages and risks of promotion, discuss various strategies and examine how CSR impacts consumer behaviour and competitive advantage.

Secondly, we will discuss *ethical and responsible marketing*. If companies are to adopt the strategic CSR approach and be responsible, sustainable and ethical in everything that they do, then ethical and sustainable marketing should follow. While some people think that ethical/sustainable marketing is an oxymoron (a phrase of self-contradiction), there are a growing number of companies that demonstrate it is possible. We will explain what ethical marketing is, why it is important and what ethical and unethical marketing consists of, so that companies can adopt responsible practices and avoid unethical ones when it comes to their marketing.

Finally, we will show that as part of strategic CSR, companies are now starting to be involved in *social marketing*. Social marketing is not aimed at selling products or services, but rather at changing attitudes and behaviour to increase individual and societal wellbeing. Such social marketing campaigns that aimed to encourage people to stop smoking, donate organs or volunteer (to give just a few examples) used to be the sole territory of governments and not-for-profits, but these are now part of CSR and CSR marketing. The chapter will end with some best practice in CSR marketing.

CSR and marketing: Should we PR our CSR?

While marketing is aimed at increasing consumption and may therefore work against sustainability and responsible consumption, the following definition of marketing by the American Marketing Association demonstrates that it can still be part of CSR:

> Marketing is an organisational function and a set of processes for creating, communicating, and delivering value to customers and for managing customer relationships in ways that benefit the organisation and its stakeholders. (American Marketing Association, as cited in Maignan et al., 2005: 957)

This definition emphasises the importance of delivering value and the responsibility of marketers to be able to create meaningful relationships that provide benefits to all relevant stakeholders (Maignan et al., 2005). It does not define marketing as selling as much as possible, but rather as delivering value that will benefit all stakeholders, and therefore falls well under the definition of strategic CSR. Companies can create value by selling less – by selling long-lasting products that would be good for the consumer, the community and the environment. It might mean that companies need to shift from profit maximisation at any cost to making a sound and sustainable profit, but the former cannot be sustained in the long run, not with the impact it has created on our planet and the global community in the last few decades.

The increasing enthusiasm for CSR bas been echoed in marketing research and practice. In particular, scholars have examined consumer responses to CSR initiatives, the perceived importance of ethics and CSR among marketing practitioners, along with the related marketing benefits (Maignan and Ferrell, 2004). More and more companies have started to implement CSR, use their CSR efforts in their marketing and tell the world their CSR story. Marketing their social responsibility and sustainability could be very beneficial for companies, but only if they adopt a holistic approach and fix their negative impacts first. Let us examine two examples of CSR marketing by big brands and their consequences.

Firstly, in response to the increasing criticism levelled against its contribution to obesity and health problems, in 2013 Coca-Cola released a 2-minute TV advertisement that highlighted the company's dedication to keeping consumers healthy and preventing obesity (see YouTube, 2013). In the *Coming Together* campaign, Coca-Cola aimed to show how it contributes to people's health by reducing calories in many of its beverages, creating smaller serving sizes for healthier soda consumption and putting the calories per serving in plain sight on the front of cans and bottles. It also showed how the company donates money and time to programmes that focus on children's health and encouraged consumers to exercise by saying 'But beating obesity will take action from all of us, based on one simple and common-sense fact: all calories count, no matter where they come from. [...] and if you eat and drink more calories than you burn off, you will gain weight', while showing images of people exercising.

This campaign backfired very quickly. Consumer organisations in the US, the UK, Australia and elsewhere accused Coca-Cola of misleading the public. For example, the British Advertising Standards Authority banned the Coca-Cola television ad, saying it could mislead viewers about how easy it is to burn off the calories in the beverage. People said it is misleading to state that 'all calories count' in the same way – if you gain 300 calories from a can of Coke or from one avocado, the effect on your body is not going to be the same. Negative comments on YouTube and on other social media channels started to create a negative counter campaign.

Public health lawyer Michele Simon wrote: 'They are downplaying the serious health effects of drinking too much soda and making it sound like balancing soda consumption with exercise is the only issue, when there are plenty of other reasons not to consume too much of these kinds of products' (Strom, 2013). Professor Marion Nestle (2013) asserted in her blog that if Coke really wanted to help prevent obesity, it should stop targeting its 'Drink more Coke' marketing at children; targeting marketing at low-income minorities; lobbying to defeat soda taxes and caps on soda sizes; and fighting attempts to remove vending machines from schools.

While the saying is that there is no negative publicity, Coca-Cola had to pull the campaign and for several years it was very hard to even find it on the Internet (it was only recently uploaded to YouTube again by a private individual). What you can still find today is a parody of this campaign, such as the 'Honest Coca-Cola obesity commercial' (see Pemberton, 2013) with a voice-over, telling people how unhealthy these products are and that if you want to be healthy 'you shouldn't buy any of our products'. This version has attracted over 8 million views to date. On the other hand, when Coca-Cola did a cause-related marketing campaign for its small world machines in 2013, the reaction was quite positive. Placing vending machines in conflict-affected areas such as India and Pakistan, the company encouraged people to interact with 'the enemy' and showed that people thrive in peace. This cause-related marketing attracted nearly 2 million views on YouTube.

The second example is taken from Whole Foods Market, a company that is mentioned in this book several times. The 'Values Matter' commercial was launched in 2014 and declared:

> We want people and animals and the places our food comes from to be treated fairly. The time is right to champion the way food is grown and raised and caught. So it's good for us, and for the greater good, too. This is where it all comes to fruition. This is where values matter. Whole Foods Market, America's healthiest grocery store.

The campaign attracted the attention of the media and social media with hundreds of thousands of views and many comments and reactions. While most were positive, there were also negative reactions, particularly around animal rights. Since the ad declares the company wants to treat animals fairly, there were counter campaigns for Whole Foods Market to stop selling animal products, specifically rabbit meat.

EXERCISE

1 Watch the two ads by Coca-Cola (Pemberton, 2013) and Whole Foods Market (2014) on the Internet.
2 What kind of emotions did each of these ads evoke in you?
3 Did you feel more or less likely to buy from these companies after watching the ads? Why?
4 What can companies do to better promote their CSR?

These two examples demonstrate the risks and advantages of CSR marketing, which will be discussed next. We define *CSR marketing* as campaigns that are not directly aimed at selling products or services, but those that demonstrate the company's values, responsibility, sustainability and goodwill.

Since the 1990s there has been a sharp increase in cause-related marketing (or CRM), mostly promoting corporate philanthropy. These campaigns were part of a company's responsive CSR instead of strategic CSR (see definitions in Chapter 1 and 2), and sometimes demonstrated 'random acts of charity'. Their impact was not great, as they were not always aligned with what the company stood for.

Lii and Lee (2012) divided these campaigns into three categories: sponsorship, cause-related marketing and philanthropy. The authors explained that while these initiatives are associated with marketing and financial gain, the public also expects them to operate in a 'moral way' that is relevant and helpful to society. *Sponsorship* is a strategic investment, in cash or in kind (such as providing time or equipment), in an activity to access the exploitable commercial potential associated with the sponsored entity or event. *Cause-related marketing* involves a company's promise to donate a certain amount of money to a not-for-profit or to a social cause when consumers purchase the company's products/services. *Philanthropy* involves a firm making a contribution of money or in kind (people or equipment) to a worthy cause simply because the firm wishes to be a good citizen without any expectation of a benefit tied to that effort (Lii and Lee, 2012: 71).

These options mostly focus on corporate philanthropy and do not include marketing strategies that promote the company's values, responsibility and sustainability or *CSR marketing*, as it was defined above. CSR marketing could be directly about the company's own CSR actions, or a call from the company to the public to be more sustainable (such as the recycling campaign by H&M in the opening case study). In strategic CSR, companies use their resources, knowledge, talent and skills to promote the wellbeing of their stakeholders, including the community and the environment, and some campaigns such as that of Patagonia (see Chapter 5) do exactly this.

According to Marin et al. (2009), investing in CSR initiatives is an important strategic task that provides enduring consumer loyalty, based on intangible company assets. Marketing CSR to consumers means going beyond the conventional marketing mix and focusing on corporate intangible assets, such as values, reputation and the goodwill associated with being a good corporate citizen, into marketing initiatives in an effort to garner a sustainable competitive advantage.

Three strategies for CSR marketing

Blomqvist and Posner (2004) detailed three strategies for integrating CSR with brand marketing (see Figure 11.1). They explained that the business strategy must be the foundation upon which both the CSR and the brand strategy are built. In other words, CSR and CSR marketing should both fall under the definition of strategic CSR and align with what the company does and stands for. It should be holistic and proactive.

The first strategy is named the *integrated approach*. In this approach, the brand and CSR operate in synchrony. This is particularly effective when responsible business practices become a key driver of brand preference. A core strength of this approach is that companies can tell a single compelling story across all touchpoints: their mission, values, core operations, responsibility and sustainability. It works best for those companies in which CSR is a core company value, which impacts all aspects of the business. This would mean consistent performance across environmental, community, employee welfare, financial performance and corporate governance commitments. This approach is the most aligned with the ideas presented in this book.

In the *selective approach*, CSR manifests itself in specific and targeted ways, for example in the form of sub-brands or strategic partnerships. The selective approach is suitable for companies that do not (yet) have proof points across all CSR components (i.e. environment, community, employee welfare, financial performance and corporate governance) or when only a specific identifiable sub-segment of the target market places significant value on responsible business practices. An example of a selective approach is creating a strategic partnership with a third party such as Fairtrade or the Rainforest Alliance (see Chapter 9), and by doing so attracting some market segments to some of the company's products.

Finally, in the *invisible approach*, CSR may play an important strategic or philosophical role in guiding the company, but play a very understated role in external communications and initiatives. Many companies say they do not want to 'blow their own horn' and they prefer to be modest about their giving. This approach is based on the (religious) idea that giving should be done in secret and that

The integrated approach
- Brand and CSR operate in synchrony.
- Most aligned with strategic CSR.
- Beneficial for certain companies and markets.

The selective approach
- CSR manifests itself in specific and targeted ways, for example in the form of sub-brands or strategic partnerships.
- Suitable for companies that do not have proof points across all five CSR components.

The invisible approach
- CSR may play an important strategic or philosophical role in guiding the company.
- CSR plays a very understated role in external communications and initiatives.

Figure 11.1   Three CSR marketing strategies (based on Blomqvist and Posner, 2004)

if the company boasts about it, it is not true philanthropy. While there is merit in this approach, there are also important societal advantages to CSR marketing that should be taken into consideration when making a decision on adopting this approach. These advantages, as well as the related risks, will be discussed next.

Advantages and risks of CSR marketing

CSR marketing can have quite a few advantages for companies, consumers and society.

For the marketing *companies*, CSR promotion can lead to a brand that people are proud to affiliate themselves with. When companies are branded as good for the world, the concept resonates with consumers' social identity and their desire to be part of something greater than themselves. Social icons and purpose-driven brands such as Patagonia and Thankyou create strong emotional reactions among consumers and many of them not only buy from these companies but are also willing to volunteer for them, promote their brands and share their positive review with others. Given five choices, consumers most frequently selected 'being socially responsible' as the factor most likely to make them loyal followers of a particular brand or company (Marin et al., 2009). Over 80 per cent of consumers reported that they prefer buying from sustainable companies, boycott unsustainable ones, and 80 per cent tell their friends and family about a company's CSR efforts (Sustainable Brands, 2015). Word of mouth is one of the most effective marketing tools today (Kozinets et al., 2010) and when people talk about a company's CSR on social media, share it and 'like' it, the impact could be greater than any of the paid campaigns. When companies adopt strategic CSR (and strategic philanthropy; see Porter and Kramer, 2002) and share a meaningful narrative about this as part of their marketing strategy, it could create a strong competitive advantage.

For *consumers*, CSR marketing can provide information about the product they buy, how and where it was made, and allow them to make an informed consumption decision and choice. It could also shed light on why this product is a little more expensive or of a better quality than competing products. CSR marketing provides a solid value proposition for consumers, showing them that what they are getting is more than just a cheap product; it is a product that is ethical and fair and that could contribute to a better and more sustainable world. It allows consumers to increase their positive emotions and 'warm glow' when buying such products.

There are also great benefits of CSR marketing for *society* at large. When large corporations and well-known brands use their power to show that CSR is important, they can change the public perception of what CSR is altogether. It can also inspire other companies to follow suit and so awareness about CSR increases. Often, CSR marketing also guides consumers and other stakeholders on what they can do to increase sustainability, and therefore could contribute to a sustainable future.

Consumers and other stakeholders can then feel parts of the company's CSR by sharing information about their activities for society either directly with friends and peers or on social media. Purpose-driven marketing (or cause-related marketing) has a better chance of going viral than product-centred marketing.

However, to gain these benefits, CSR marketing should be ethical and truthful as well as aligned with the core activities of the firm. As can be seen in the two examples above, CSR marketing without enough responsibility and without a holistic approach to sustainability could backfire on the company. By telling the world how good they are, companies risk a higher level of criticism than by only selling products. Consumers do not always trust companies that 'blow their own horn', and may scrutinise all their activities. Even with a trusted brand such as Whole Foods Market, stating that they want to treat all humans and animals fairly, led to consumers demanding that they do so more holistically. These risks lead some companies to believe in 'damned if you do and damned if you don't' and to give up on CSR marketing or even CSR altogether. However, this could lead to even higher levels of criticism, particularly as CSR becomes the new 'business as usual'.

To achieve CSR marketing advantages while also reducing the related risks, Maignan et al. (2005) suggested firms implement CSR in marketing in the following way and by going through all these stages in the following order:

1. Discovering organisational norms and values
2. Identifying stakeholders
3. Identifying stakeholder issues
4. Assessing the meaning of CSR for the firm
5. Auditing current practices
6. Implementing CSR initiatives
7. Promoting CSR
8. Gaining stakeholder feedback.

This is not a linear process, but a cycle, as can be seen in Figure 11.2.

As explained by Lii and Lee (2012), CSR initiatives are difficult to manage and must be implemented carefully to avoid possible consumer scepticism. Creating and maintaining a state of closeness between the consumer and the company (identification and brand attitude) through a CSR initiative has the potential to generate positive behavioural responses towards the company.

Quick question

Read the case study of H&M again. What do you see as the advantages and the risks for this company in advertising its sustainability?

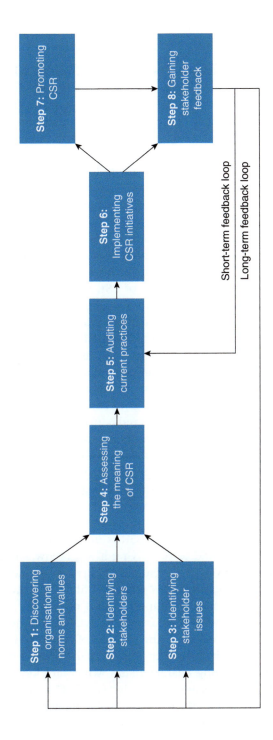

Figure 11.2   The stakeholder approach to CSR marketing (based on Maignan et al., 2005)

CSR and consumer behaviour

Consumer behaviour is 'the study of the processes involved when individuals or groups select, purchase, use or dispose of products, services, ideas or experiences to satisfy needs and desires' (Hawkins et al., 2004: 7). It is also concerned with the social and economic impacts that purchasing and consumption behaviour has on both the individual consumer and on broader society and the environment.

Research has suggested a positive relationship between a corporation's CSR activities and consumers' positive attitudes towards that corporation and its products (Rahim et al., 2011). While early research from the 2000s showed that CSR was still far from being the most dominant criterion in consumers' purchasing decisions and that traditional aspects such as price, quality and brand familiarity remained the most important choice criteria (see Marin et al., 2009), this is now changing rapidly (Sustainable Brands, 2015). CSR influences consumer behaviour at a time when consumers are demanding more out of organisations than simply a good-quality product at a low price. The impact of CSR on consumer behaviour occurs through consumer awareness, attitudes and overall evaluation of the company and its CSR. As such, strategic CSR and CSR marketing are both beneficial in order to create consumer loyalty and influence attitudes, intentions and consumption.

Firstly, for CSR to impact consumers' behaviour, there needs to be *awareness* of CSR in general and of the company's CSR in particular. With media and social media often reporting on social responsibility or irresponsibility, consumer awareness of CSR is increasing, with more and more consumers aware of sustainability and social responsibility issues (Sustainable Brands, 2015). Podnar and Golob (2007) showed that consumers, particularly young ones, expect companies to be legally responsible and to comply with ethical and philanthropic expectations. Secondly, consumers need to become aware of a specific firm's CSR level before this factor can impact their purchasing from this firm. Building awareness of the company's CSR is arguably the major purpose behind cause-related marketing (Mohr et al., 2001) and a key to connecting CSR to consumer behaviour.

However, awareness of the company's CSR is not enough. Consumers need to evaluate it positively (as opposed to perceiving it as greenwashing, for example). The influence of CSR initiatives on consumer loyalty and behaviour is mediated *positive evaluation of the company's CSR* (Marin et al., 2009). According to Marin et al. (2009), consumers evaluate a company based on whether the organisation acts in a manner consistent with supporting the welfare of the community and society. Company evaluation refers to the 'degree of "positiveness" or "negativeness" of the subject's global judgment of the company', based on the company's 'central, distinctive, and enduring characteristics, which are key components leading to the prestige of the organisation's identity' (2009: 67). Thus, individuals who are aware of the company's CSR efforts might display higher levels of identification than those who are not aware of such initiatives.

After awareness and positive evaluation, CSR can impact consumer behaviour on various levels, depending also on what is being marketed, or the *content of CSR marketing*. Lii and Lee (2012) showed that the three CSR marketing strategies detailed above yielded different consumer behaviour, with philanthropic campaigns creating significantly more favourable attitudes than cause-related marketing and sponsorship. Importantly, the relationship between CSR marketing and consumer positive attitudes was stronger when consumers perceived the brand as having a high CSR reputation. Similarly, Nan and Heo (2007) demonstrated that an ad with an embedded cause-related marketing (CRM) message, compared to a similar one without a CRM message, elicits more favourable consumer attitudes towards the company. Although we still need evidence to support this, we may assume that when a company adopts CSR holistically and becomes a CSR icon (Austin and Herman, 2008), it will result in more positive consumer behaviour compared to philanthropic campaigns or sponsorship, as there will be fewer negative corporate behaviours for consumers to criticise the company.

While these conditions are important, it is also essential to understand the 'attitude/behaviour gap' or 'values/action gap' when it comes to CSR and consumer behaviour (Young et al., 2010). For example, 30 per cent of UK consumers report that they are very concerned about environmental issues but most of them struggle to translate this concern into green purchases. The inability to afford a more expensive product or a lack of desire to spend additional funds, lack of time to search the required information and/or difficulty in accessing more sustainable products are some of the reasons for this gap. Sustainable and responsible companies need to ensure that the product is just as good as their competitors', that it is not much more expensive and that information and purchase are accessible for their CSR to actually lead to positive consumer behaviour. There is a growing demand for products that are of high quality, good price and that meet consumers' expectations around the

Figure 11.3 **The three aspects of consumer demand**

'goodness' of the product: good for them, good for society and good for the environment (Figure 11.3). Companies that are able to meet this demand while keeping their consumers informed may overcome this behavioural gap.

In summary, CSR may have a positive impact on consumer behaviour if there is suitable CSR marketing content, high levels of CSR awareness among consumers and a positive evaluation of the company's CSR. These could lead to intentions and positive attitudes, and when companies meet consumer expectation and demand, they can also overcome the behavioural gap, resulting in the desired consumer behaviour. This is illustrated in Figure 11.4.

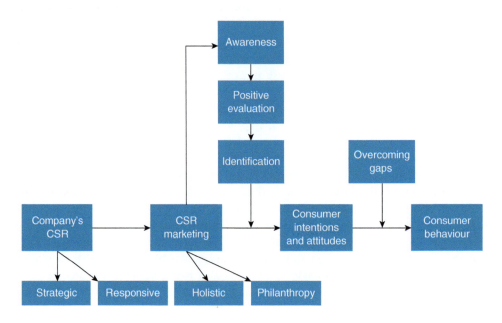

Figure 11.4   From CSR to consumer behaviour

CSR as a competitive advantage

When discussing CSR and marketing, it is also important to reflect on how CSR can enhance a company's competitive advantage in the market. Competitive advantage is the leverage that a business has over its competitors, which can be gained by offering clients a better and greater value proposition (Porter, 1985). It includes competencies, resources or skills that enable the firm to differentiate itself from its competitors and succeed over a sustained period of time.

In the past, value proposition focused mainly on the quality of the product and the price. Some companies achieved a competitive advantage by offering good value for money (high quality and low price), others did so by providing low-cost products which were of low quality (disposable goods, even disposable fashion as in the opening case of H&M), while yet others created a competitive advantage by offering a very high price for high quality, which some consumers prefer because they are perceived as luxury items. Michael Porter (1985) defined the two ways in which an organisation can achieve competitive advantage over others: cost advantage and differentiation advantage. While cost refers to the price, differentiation advantage refers to the quality of the product.

CSR offers a unique and novel value proposition to consumers: a social value proposition. Knowing that in buying certain products, employees and suppliers are paid fairly seems to matter to a growing number of people (Sustainable Brands, 2015). Corporations can use their charitable efforts to improve their competitive advantage by appealing to a different aspect of differentiation. By carefully analysing the elements of its competitive context, a company can identify the areas of overlap between social and economic value that will most enhance its competitiveness (Porter and Kramer, 2002).

Porter (1985) identified four elements of competitive context (see Figure 11.5), all of which can be applied to CSR:

1. *Factor conditions*: The quantity and quality of available business inputs, such as human and natural resources. Companies with better access to talent, technology and natural resources can outperform their competitors. In this context, internal CSR can help companies maximise the potential of their employees, and sustainability can help them increase their eco-efficiency, both of which could contribute to their competitive advantage.
2. *Context*: The context for strategy and rivalry includes markets, regulations and competition. The size of the market, the company's market share and the ability of others to easily penetrate the market can increase or decrease competitive advantage. In their article on creating shared value (see Chapter 2), Porter and Kramer (2011) asserted that markets are also determined by societal needs, not just financial needs. By addressing the needs of under-served societies, companies can also open up new markets and increase their competitive advantage. Furthermore, by being socially responsible and having a strong relationship with stakeholders, companies can proactively address issues that were otherwise addressed through regulations.
3. *Demand conditions*: The size and sophistication of local demand also affect competitive advantage. The higher the demand for the products and services a company sells, the better it would be positioned in the market. This is one of the major points of differentiation for companies with strong CSR, given the emerging evidence of consumer demand for ethical and sustainable products. When companies teach their stakeholders about sustainability, making it important for consumers, and then supply sustainable products, this would not only be good for the company but also for society and the environment.

4. *Related and supporting industries*: This aspect relates to the local availability
    of supporting industries and suppliers. Companies with better access to suppli-
    ers can gain a competitive advantage over others. Socially responsible
    companies work closely with their suppliers to ensure their wellbeing, thus
    creating a stronger relationship with them than their competitors. One of the
    key ways for creating shared value is through the development of local clusters
    with suppliers and other stakeholders, which in turn can help the company and
    its suppliers both be more successful. It is the change of mindset from a zero-
    sum game to a Win[6] approach (see Chapter 3) that can really help companies
    gain a better position in the market without 'crashing' suppliers, employees or
    even competitors.

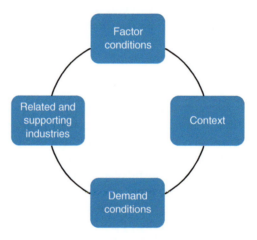

Figure 11.5   The four aspects of competitive advantage can be applied to CSR

In 2002, Porter and Kramer wrote about the competitive advantage of corporate
philanthropy. They explained that companies do not function in isolation from the
society around them and that their ability to compete depends heavily on the circumstances of the locations in which they operate. Social and economic goals are
not inherently conflicting but integrally connected, and companies that understand
'what is good for the community is good for business' could gain a competitive
advantage. To achieve this, companies need to focus on philanthropy that is connected to their business. Instead of focusing on 'random acts of charity', companies
should tie their giving to who they are, what they do and what they stand for.

   While this book is shifting away from corporate philanthropy to strategic CSR,
the concept of tying values, socially responsible identity and socially responsible
behaviour to what the company does is at the essence of strategic CSR. Based on
strategic CSR, it can be argued that companies that adopt a holistic view implement

CSR in their core operations and their entire value chain, and work with a broad set of stakeholders to achieve financial and social value over the medium to long term that will be able to maintain a competitive advantage in the coming years. It is possible that in the future all companies will be doing the same and as such strategic CSR will no longer be enough to maintain a competitive position in the market; but firstly, this might take a while, and secondly, there will always be companies that outperform others in this area.

Ethical and sustainable marketing

Up until the 1990s, the idea of 'ethical' (let alone 'sustainable') marketing seemed like an oxymoron (Murphy, 2010). The goal of marketing was to sell as much as possible, no matter what means to this end had to be taken. Lying to consumers, misleading them, targeting vulnerable groups, manufacturing demand – all was legitimate. After all, the only corporate responsibility is to maximise shareholder value, is it not?

In the 1990s, however, there began a change of discourse and as some companies and stakeholders started to realise that business needs to act responsibly, academic research and managerial practices started to examine what ethical marketing is all about. According to Murphy (2010), marketing ethics is the systematic study of how moral standards are applied to marketing decisions, behaviours and institutions.

Laczniak and Murphy (2006) explained that much of marketing activity can be viewed as systematic sales outreach by organisations to various members of the consumption community, and by extension to society. When exchange occurs, it has effects not only on the primary transacting parties (the consumer and the company) but also on society and the environment, which is the reason why marketing has ethical ramifications. Marketing is not only about maximising consumption but also about increasing societal wellbeing, which is why it is also the focus of business ethics (see Chapter 4).

Professional organisations such as the American Marketing Association (AMA), which was mentioned above, have documented the required ethical considerations and developed a professional code of conduct to achieve this purpose. The AMA mission statement includes the goal of advancing the thought, application and ethical practice of marketing. Similarly, the Academy of Marketing Science commits its members to the highest of ethical standards.

Seven basic practices of normative marketing ethics

In their article, Laczniak and Murphy (2006) offered up normative marketing ethics, which focuses on what companies need to do to ensure that their marketing is as ethical and responsible as the rest of their CSR efforts. They developed seven 'basic practices' (see Figure 11.6), which are based on some of the ethical principles discussed in Chapter 4. These are:

1. *Ethical marketing puts people first*: This is in line with the Kantian principle of never using people as the means to an end, only as the end itself (Formula for Humanity; Kant and Ellington, 1994). This is vital for ethical marketing and ethical business management. When marketers see consumers as people instead of only as revenue generators, when they perceive them as individuals with families or as little children who deserve to be healthy and happy, it might stop them from marketing unsafe or unhealthy products. People should never be treated merely as cogs in the marketing system, whether they are customers, employees, suppliers, distributors or some other stakeholders.

2. *Ethical marketers must achieve a behavioural standard in excess of the law*: This principle is similar to Carroll's (1979) definition of CSR, which is going beyond basic legal requirements. As of today, many unethical practices are still legal in many countries and it takes high standards of marketing ethics to not apply them in order to maximise profit. Ethics, including marketing ethics, embodies higher standards than law and implies assuming more responsibilities.

3. *Marketers are responsible for whatever they intend as a means or an end with a marketing action*: Marketing practice can be divided into three distinct components: the intent of the action; the means or method by which the practice is implemented; and the end or consequences of the strategy or tactic. As such, marketers need to be ethical about their intentions and motivation (e.g. to sell as much as possible); ensure that they have the means to achieve this (e.g. sell unhealthy food to children); and take responsibility for the outcome (e.g. child obesity and illness).

4. *Marketing organisations should cultivate better (i.e. higher) moral imagination in their managers*: In this context, moral imagination is the ability to morally reason to creative ethical solutions when encountering an ethical question. This implies that even if the CEO of the company that the marketer works in or the company that hires the marketing agency aim for unethical behaviour, marketers should adopt higher standards and act according to their values. This is one of the more difficult practices to adopt, particularly as people need to provide for their families and to not risk their jobs. It might create the ethical dilemmas we discussed in Chapter 4.

5. *Marketers should articulate and embrace a core set of ethical principles*: There are several marketing codes of ethics and marketers should know them well and adopt them. There are five ethical precepts which are detailed below. Two of them (non-malfeasance and non-deception) are regularly included in business codes of conduct and the other three principles (protection of vulnerable markets, distributive justice and stewardship) advocate an elevated level of

ethical responsibility that is likely to stimulate greater debate and challenge among marketing practitioners because they demand a much higher threshold of required moral obligation.

6. *Adoption of a stakeholder orientation is essential to ethical marketing decisions*: As explained in Chapter 3, stakeholder theory is based on the notion that every company has a broad set of stakeholders, including consumers, society and the environment. Strategic CSR is managing the company in the best interest of all these stakeholders. As such, marketing to increase consumption beyond what society and the environment can endure is not sustainable or responsible. Keeping the broad set of stakeholders in mind and avoiding 'externalities' for someone else to fix can help marketers behave ethically.

7. *Marketing organisations ought to delineate an ethical decision-making protocol*: The ability of managers to ethically reason is an essential part of ethical marketing. To achieve this, managers and marketers need to have ethical awareness and the ability to frame an ethical issue, articulate the stakeholders who would be affected by the decision, select a relevant ethical standard (e.g. legal, utilitarian, moral values or justice), conduct an ethical analysis and make an ethical decision – and on top of all that, keep a protocol of this process, which can sometimes be very difficult to do. However, as challenging as it seems, this is an incredibly important practice to strive for which can ensure ethical marketing.

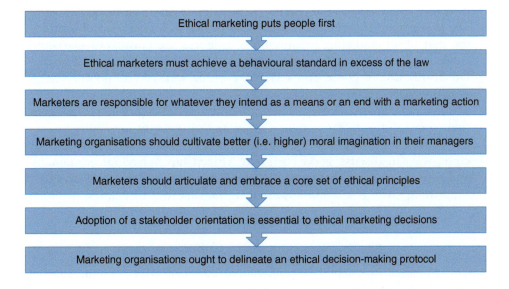

Figure 11. 6   The seven practices of ethical marketing (based on Laczniak and Murphy, 2006)

Five essential ethical precepts for enlightened marketing

Laczniak and Murphy (2006) also detail five essential principles for ethical marketing. These principles are aligned with the above seven practices and are often found, in one form or another, in marketing codes of ethics:

1. *The principle of non-malfeasance*: Marketers should knowingly do no major harm when discharging their marketing duties. This principle demonstrates its value by enshrining the assurance of product health and safety into the practice of ethical marketing.

2. *The principle of non-deception*: Marketers ought to never intentionally mislead or unfairly manipulate consumers. Grounded in virtue ethics (see Chapter 4), this involves considerations such as articulating the specific type of product claims that might mislead reasonable consumers. It takes honesty to become trustworthy.

3. *The principle of protecting vulnerable market segments*: Vulnerable market segments include children, the elderly, the mentally disabled and the economically disadvantaged. Such vulnerable market segments might be easily susceptible to exploitation by dishonest marketers who are in a position to manipulate information and transactions. Firms that exploit the marketplace illiteracy of children (e.g. selling junk food in primary schools), the low information-processing capability of the mentally feeble or the economic desperation of the poor (e.g. payday loan stores) are likely violators of this principle, regardless of the legality of these marketing practices.

4. *The principle of distributive justice*: This principle suggests an obligation on the part of all marketing organisations to assess the fairness of marketplace consequences resulting from their collective marketing practices. It implies a fair distribution of goods and services, even to 'weaker' and poorer segments of the market.

5. *The principle of stewardship*: This principle reminds marketing managers of their social duties to the common good and of their responsibility to act for the betterment of their host environments and community. Under this principle, we can discuss good corporate citizenship behaviour, sustainability and responsibility so that companies understand they need to always do the right thing, even if it is not specified in the first four principles.

Marketing codes of ethics

As was explained in Chapter 4, professional codes of ethics are the rules that govern the conduct of members in a given profession. Marketing also has several general and specific codes of ethics. For example, the AMA declares that it commits itself to promoting the highest standard of professional ethical norms and values for its members. Its code of conduct states that:

> as marketers, we recognise that we not only serve our organisations but also act as stewards of society in creating, facilitating and executing the transactions that are part of the greater economy. In this role, marketers are expected to embrace the highest professional ethical norms and the ethical values implied by our responsibility towards multiple stakeholders. (American Marketing Association, 2017)

The three 'ethical norms' of AMA are quite similar to the aforementioned principles and include:

1. *Do no harm.* This means consciously avoiding harmful actions or omissions by embodying high ethical standards and adhering to all applicable laws and regulations in the choices we make.
2. *Foster trust in the marketing system.* This means striving for good faith and fair dealing so as to contribute towards the efficacy of the exchange process as well as avoiding deception in product design, pricing, communication, and delivery of distribution.
3. *Embrace ethical values.* This means building relationships and enhancing consumer confidence in the integrity of marketing by affirming these core values: honesty, responsibility, fairness, respect, transparency and citizenship.

Questions for reflection and discussion

1. Examine the opening case study of H&M.
2. Which principles and practices of ethical marketing do you think H&M adopts? What others should it adopt?
3. Are there additional practices and principles you can think of to ensure ethical marketing?

Sustainable marketing

As explained in Chapter 7, there is now a movement towards mindful and sustainable consumption which implies consumers restraining themselves in acquisitive, repetitive and aspirational consumption (Sheth et al., 2011). Mindful and sustainable consumption calls for a new orientation and practices in marketing. As Sheth et al. (2011) argue, it is mistakenly assumed that the sole job of marketers is to sell as much as possible, and that their primary task gets defined as creating and maintaining demand, regardless of long-term consequences. In contrast, different market conditions require different roles from the marketing function, and in markets where overconsumption is prevalent, a first step for marketers is to refrain from over-marketing. This means avoiding aggressive pricing and promotions, over-hyped advertising and other hard-sell techniques.

Sheth et al. (2011) used the 'four Ps' of marketing (product, price, promotion and place) and showed how each of these can become a means for sustainable marketing. This is not only good for business as it creates trusted brands and consumer loyalty, it is also good for society and the environment. In the near future, it might become the only option.

> *Product*: A product is a tangible good or an intangible service that meets a specific customer need or demand. Products can be designed with attributes that help reduce repetitive consumption. For example, Patagonia offers products that are more durable and easier to repair and recycle. Many consumers are keen to know about the attributes of the product beyond where it was made and from what materials, and brands should provide this information. The product mix may be expanded to include multiple-use products, multi-user or shared-use products in product–service combinations. Finally, the product and its packaging should be made with minimal impact on the environment while it is being manufactured, transported, sold and used. This includes (but is not limited to) the materials used (e.g. recycled and recyclable) and the processes involved.

> *Price*: Price refers to the actual amount the end user is expected to pay for a product. Price is probably the best mechanism to regulate demand and consumption. Price increase in fuel, gasoline and fresh produce can make consumers aware of the impact of excessive consumption. Pricing based on full internalisation of environmental and social costs can help in a shift away from both acquisitive and repetitive consumption (see PUMA's case in Chapter 10). The emphasis in marketing should not be on 'cheap' but on quality and value, and items should be priced so they are easily disposable.

> *Promotion*: Promotion includes all marketing communication strategies and techniques. Advertising and communication strategies can play key roles in leading aspirational and sustainable consumption and lifestyles, and they can be used to educate consumers and other stakeholders on sustainability and involve them in efforts to reduce negative environmental impact. An increase in promotion that celebrates the sustainability of a product raises awareness of environmental issues and can increase consumers' involvement in the process. The H&M campaign on recycling clothes is part of this movement.

> *Place*: Place is the way that the product is provided to the customer (e.g. online and via mail or in the supermarket). H&M uses its stores (place) to allow consumers to

recycle clothes. Amazon uses place (online shop and Kindle) to reduce the number of printed books. While sustainability may or may not be the main motivation for these initiatives, these companies still have a positive impact on sustainability.

Quick question

What else can marketers and organisations do to increase sustainability via marketing? What might be the positive and negative consequences of sustainable marketing?

Unethical marketing and greenwashing

Some unethical marketing tactics which have been used by companies and marketers for years would not have existed if they were to act according to the above principles. For example (Laczniak and Murphy, 2006):

- High-pressure selling tactics in certain sectors of the financial services or real estate industries (e.g. junk bonds).
- Coercion in the channel distribution, such as demands for price concessions by the channel partner which has a significant economic leverage.
- Unethical psychological manipulation, such as the utilisation of fear and stereotyping.
- The sexual exploitation of women (and other groups) in advertising for attention-getting purposes.
- Price gouging in times of product shortage, such as in the aftermath of hurricanes or other natural disasters.
- Stereotyping of specific groups in society through marketing campaigns.

One of the worst examples of unethical marketing is when companies lie about how responsible and sustainable they are. Known as *greenwashing*, companies use the desire of consumers and people to buy from honest, ethical and trustworthy companies and put CSR or sustainability in their marketing campaigns without any real substance behind it. Greenwashing is 'the act of misleading consumers regarding the environmental practices of a company (firm-level greenwashing) or the environmental benefits of a product or service (product-level greenwashing)' (Delmas and Burbano, 2011: 66). It is the intersection of two corporate behaviours: poor environmental performance and positive communication about environmental performance (Delmas and Burbano, 2011). It is particularly unethical to lie about how responsible you are, and this is precisely why people lose trust in companies and in CSR marketing. 'The skyrocketing incident of greenwashing can have profound negative effects on consumer confidence in green products, eroding the consumer market for green products and services', wrote Delmas and Burbano (2011: 64).

Why do companies greenwash? Because there is a market for it. Because they can. Because it sometimes pays off. At least in the short term. The consumer market for green products and services was estimated at US$230 billion in 2009, and many companies thought they could just yield the benefits without putting the effort into actually becoming sustainable. At the same time that BP was involved in one of the worst manmade disasters of all time with its Gulf oil spill in 2010, BP positioned itself as a 'green' company, with matching slogans, a green marketing campaign (Beyond Petroleum) and green logos. Its website celebrates its sustainability efforts, while it will take decades to reverse the damage done to the environment, if it is even possible. Unfortunately, it worked and the small impact the damage had on its sales and prices (4.2 per cent decline in the company's prices relative to competitors and a 3.6 per cent decline in sales) was reversed only four months after the disaster (Frick, 2014). According to Delmas and Burbano (2011), the drivers of greenwashing include market external drivers (consumer demand, investor demand and competitive pressure), organisational drivers (firm characteristics, incentive structure and culture, the effectiveness of intra-firm communication and organisational inertia) and individual psychological drivers (optimistic bias, narrow decision framing and hyperbolic intertemporal discounting).

Social marketing by business

The last frontier that will be discussed in this chapter is social marketing. At the beginning of this book we discussed the concept of business as a force for good and how if business would use its resources, talent and knowledge to address social issues, there is no limit to what could be achieved. As part of this movement, business can use its marketing strategy to address social problems and environmental issues through social marketing.

Social marketing is the use of marketing principles and tools to influence human behaviour and attitudes in order to benefit society. It is a strategic or planning process, or systematic application of techniques, used for the benefit of individuals or society rather than for commercial gain (Carins and Rundle-Thiele, 2014). Kotler and Zaltman (1971: 5) defined social marketing as the 'design, implementation and control of programs calculated to influence the acceptability of social ideas'. It occurs when organisations use marketing to improve both customers' and society's wellbeing (Kotler and Armstrong, 2010). For example, marketing campaigns to help people to quit smoking, explain the importance of volunteering or organ donations, raise awareness about climate change and global social problems or stop people from drinking and driving all have something in common. They are not aimed (most of the time) at selling us something, but rather at changing our behaviour (e.g. smoking) or our attitudes (e.g. racism) in order to increase individual and societal wellbeing.

For years, social marketing was the sole responsibility of governments and not-for-profits. Business used marketing to sell products while governments and not-for-profits used marketing to change behaviours and attitudes in order to improve societal wellbeing. Governments were involved in social marketing as it helped them achieve their overall goals for society, increase their political power and save tax money. Not-for-profit organisations were involved in social marketing to increase awareness of the social/environmental issue they were trying to address as part of their mission and to raise money and recruit volunteers.

However, in recent years companies have started to get involved in social marketing as well, often as part of their CSR efforts. Social marketing can benefit society and it is an effective way for companies to utilise their resources to do good for the world. This is shifting away from corporate philanthropy to strategic CSR. Bhattacharya et al. (2008) illustrated this by explaining that a company that supports dental health can engage in corporate philanthropy (e.g. donating money to organisations that maintain children's dental health), in cause-related marketing (a percentage of toothpaste purchases goes to this organisation) or by using corporate social marketing programmes that promote actual behaviour change, such as running a campaign to increase individual dental care and health.

Ben & Jerry's (2017) has been involved in social marketing for many years, affecting people's attitudes (with its 'If it's melted it's ruined' campaign to raise awareness of climate change) and stands by its values ('Love who you want to love' campaign for marriage equality). The Body Shop runs social marketing campaigns to raise awareness of human trafficking. Other companies use social marketing to address the 'side-effects' of their business, such as AT&T's (2016) social marketing campaign 'Close to home' to stop people from texting and driving. Pfizer runs campaigns to encourage people to quit smoking.

In 2017, Airbnb Australia ran a social marketing campaign on marriage equality, 'Until we all belong' (Airbnb, 2017a), with the support of other companies including Qantas, the national airline. The initiative called on Australians to show their acceptance of marriage equality and commit to wearing a bespoke ring until same-sex marriage was recognised in Australia. Thousands of these rings were sold within 24 hours on eBay at cost. The video attracted nearly half a million views on YouTube. It is aligned with the general campaign of Airbnb: 'Belong anywhere'. Another social marketing campaign by the same company is a better example of strategic CSR. In February 2017, Airbnb launched a global campaign 'We accept' (Airbnb, 2017b), with the goal to raise awareness of and change attitudes towards diversity. The related ad, which was aired during the Super Bowl (and just as President Trump tried to pass his 'travel ban'), shows the merging faces of people from different backgrounds together with these words: 'We believe – no matter who you are, where are you from, who you love or who you worship, we all belong. The world is more beautiful the more you accept. #WeAccept'. The video was watched on YouTube five million times. This campaign goes hand in hand with Airbnb's strategic CSR. Being a company that hosts people anywhere, Airbnb says its goal is to provide short-term housing for 100,000 people in need over the next five years through its hosts and through partner organisations. The company will contribute US$4 million over the next four years to the International Rescue Committee to help meet the most critical needs of displaced populations globally.

These examples and many others show how creative businesses can be when they get involved in social marketing and when instead of marketing a product, they market a cause. This in turn makes consumers see the company in a different light and creates a strong emotional attachment to the brand. If consumers feel that companies are engaged in broad social issues and that they care about the wellbeing of their stakeholders, they trust them more, as the Edelman 2016 survey (in the introduction to this chapter) showed.

Similarly to sustainable marketing above, the 'four Ps' of social marketing are different to traditional marketing. The *product* is the desired change that social marketing is trying to achieve, together with the associated benefits (e.g. quitting cigarettes). The *price* is the related costs or barriers the target audience faces in making the desired change (e.g. difficult to give up smoking or gaining weight as a result). The *placement* in this context is where the audience can access products or services (e.g. helpline or medicine); and the *promotion* relates to the communications, messages, materials, channels and activities that will effectively reach the target audience (e.g. social media campaign).

CSR marketing: Best practices

CSR can be related to marketing in three ways: promoting the company's values, sustainability and social responsibility; ethical and sustainable marketing; and business being involved in social marketing to increase societal wellbeing. Based on some of the most effective examples that were discussed in this chapter, there are 'best practices' or 'inspirational practices' to align CSR and marketing:

Promote the cause, not the company. When companies want to promote their CSR, it is best to promote the causes and values the company stands for, not the company itself. If companies do discuss the work that they do, it is better to talk about the impact they create (only if there is evidence for it) instead of the input they put into it. Consumers and other stakeholders do not emotionally engage with how much money a company gave to charity last year, but with the difference it made in people's lives. Importantly, do not sell products at the same time. When McDonald's ran the McHappy Day campaign in 2009 it featured its products, which could be perceived negatively.

Discover what is important for the company and the reasons it is involved in CSR. As part of strategic CSR, it is important to tie CSR marketing to the company's strategic planning and core operations. Social marketing that is genuinely trying to make a difference while also relating to what the company stands for, such as in the example of Airbnb, might have the best effect.

Use storytelling tools to share the story of the organisation. Instead of using numbers and data, tell a compelling story with a beginning and an end (for now) on the difference the company made and of its purpose. KPMG is now engaged in purpose and leadership to engage its staff in 'changing the world' and uses storytelling to achieve its goals (Pfau, 2015). Storytelling in marketing is only just beginning to unfold and it has great potential for CSR marketing.

These tools can help the company to enhance its brand, but if it is responsible the goal can no longer be to sell as much as possible at any cost. Companies need to align with the movement towards more responsible consumption. In addition, CSR marketing campaigns must be based on truth and honesty. The damage of dishonest marketing is not limited to the company but could also have a large impact on other businesses and on society, as fewer people trust corporations and CSR.

Summary

There are three frontiers to CSR and marketing: CSR marketing, ethical marketing and social marketing. Together with strategic CSR, all three can impact the company, consumers and society at large, as well as all other stakeholders.

Firstly, it is important for companies to share what they do in the area of CSR through *CSR marketing*. Many companies do remarkable things through their CSR but the world does not necessarily know about them. CSR marketing allows companies to share with the world what they do for the world (their story of impact), engage stakeholders in this conversation, inform consumers about the benefits of the products they buy and inspire other companies to also take the CSR path. It is particularly effective when CSR is strategic and holistic.

The impact of CSR on consumer behaviour occurs through consumer awareness, attitudes and overall evaluation of the company and its CSR. As such, strategic CSR and CSR marketing could both create consumer loyalty and impact attitudes, intentions and consumption, if done well. Strategic CSR could create a competitive advantage for companies in markets where a growing number of consumers care about societal and environmental issues.

The second frontier discussed in this chapter was *ethical marketing*. Drawing on the various approaches to ethics and business ethics, which were presented in Chapter 4, ethical marketing is about doing the right thing when marketing products and services. While some people believe ethical and sustainable marketing is an oxymoron, the last two decades have presented us with related practices, principles and examples to show that it is possible. It requires a change of mindset, philosophical approach and the change of many current marketing practices; however, the end result is not only better but necessary.

The third and last frontier is *social marketing*. Strategic CSR is about embedding CSR in everything that we do, including utilising marketing strategies and resources to contribute to societal wellbeing. Social marketing is not aimed at selling products but at changing behaviour and attitudes to increase individual and societal wellbeing. There are some remarkable examples of what businesses do in this area, and they are fast growing.

All three frontiers can be used to enhance the company's brand and consumer emotional attachment to it. This could result in happier consumers, prouder employees, shareholders who are better off and societal and environmental wellbeing. However, these benefits are conditioned with being genuinely responsible and sustainable. Otherwise, there may be a negative impact not only on the company and its brand, but also on the way many people see CSR and, in turn, on our world.

General questions

1. Many companies avoid CSR marketing as they think 'blowing their own horn' might be negatively perceived by society. Do you agree? What are the reasons for overcoming this perception? Use a few examples to build your argument.
2. Find a company that promotes its CSR efforts (outside the ones presented in this chapter). How does it make you feel? What can the company do to improve it CSR and its CSR marketing?
3. Many people say that ethical or sustainable marketing is an oxymoron (self-contradicting). What examples show that this is so? What counter examples might show that ethical and sustainable marketing is possible?
4. When companies are blamed for selling products that are harmful to the individual or to the environment, their first line of defence is usually that they are only 'meeting demand'. Do you agree? Why? What needs to change?
5. Social marketing was for many years the sole responsibility of governments and not-for-profits. What are the advantages and risks of the business sector getting involved in changing people's behaviour and attitudes?

Key definitions

- CSR marketing involves campaigns that are not directly aimed at selling products or services but demonstrate the company's values, responsibility, sustainability and goodwill.
- Sponsorship is a strategic investment, in cash or in kind (such as providing time or equipment), in an activity to access the exploitable commercial potential associated with the sponsored entity or event (Lii and Lee, 2012).
- Cause-related marketing involves a company's promise to donate a certain amount of money to a not-for-profit or to a social cause when consumers purchase the company's products/services (Lii and Lee, 2012).
- Philanthropy involves a firm making a contribution of money or kind (people or equipment) to a worthy cause simply because the firm wishes to be a good citizen without any expectation of a benefit tied to that effort (Lii and Lee, 2012).
- Consumer behaviour is the study of the processes involved when individuals or groups select, purchase, use or dispose of products, services, ideas or experiences to satisfy needs and desires (Hawkins et al., 2004).
- 'Company evaluation' refers to the degree of 'positiveness' or 'negativeness' of the subject's global judgement of the company, based on the company's central, distinctive and enduring characteristics, which are key components leading to the prestige of the organisation's identity (Marin et al., 2009).
- Consumer–company identification is the degree to which a consumer's self-definition overlaps with that same consumer's perceived traits of a firm (Lii and Lee, 2012: 70).
- Marketing ethics is the systematic study of how moral standards are applied to marketing decisions, behaviours and institutions (Murphy, 2010).
- 'Greenwashing' is the act of misleading consumers regarding the environmental practices of a company (firm-level greenwashing) or the environmental benefits of a product or service (product-level greenwashing) (Delmas and Burbano, 2011).
- Social marketing is the use of marketing principles and tools to influence human behaviour and attitudes in order to benefit society. It is a strategic or planning process, or systematic application of techniques, used for the benefit of individuals or society rather than commercial gain (Carins and Rundle-Thiele, 2014).

References

Airbnb (2017a) Until we all belong. Available at: www.youtube.com/watch?v=0Y4EqF0PR4E (Accessed: 5 October 2017)

Airbnb (2017b) We accept. Available at: www.youtube.com/watch?v=yetFk7QoSck (Accessed: 5 October 2017)

American Marketing Association (2017) Statement of ethics. Available at: www.ama.org/ AboutAMA/Pages/Statement-of-Ethics.aspx#StatementofEthics (Accessed: 1 June 2017)

AT&T (2016) Close to home – it can wait. Available at: www.youtube.com/watch?v=jtQ9H1MrrPo (Accessed: 5 October 2017)

Austin, J. E. and Herman, B. (2008) 'Can the virtuous mouse and the wealthy elephant live happily ever after?', *California Management Review*, 51(1): 77–102.

Ben & Jerry's (2017) Love who you want to love. Available at: http://livead.com.br/en/ works/cases/ben-jerrys/love-who-you-want-to-love (Accessed: 5 October 2017).

Bhattacharya, C. B., Sen, S. and Korschun, D. (2008) 'Using corporate social responsibility to win the war for talent', *MIT Sloan Management Review*, 49(2): 37–44.

Blomqvist, K. H. and Posner, S. (2004) 'Three strategies for integrating CSR with brand marketing', *Market Leader*, 25 (Summer): 33–6.

Carins, J. E. and Rundle-Thiele, S. R. (2014) 'Eating for the better: A social marketing review (2000–2012)', *Public Health Nutrition*, 17(7): 1628–39.

Carroll, A. B. (1979) 'A three-dimensional conceptual model of corporate performance', *Academy of Management Review*, 4(4): 497–505.

Coca-Cola (2013) Coca-Cola small world machines: Bringing India & Pakistan together. Available at: www.youtube.com/watch?v=ts_4vOUDImE (Accessed: 4 October 2017)

Delmas, M. A. and Burbano, V. C. (2011) 'The drivers of greenwashing', *California Management Review*, 54(1): 64–87.

Edelman (2016) Trust barometer. Available at: file:///Users/mq20112236/Downloads/2016tr ustbarometerglobalresults-160117210706.pdf (Accessed: 1 June 2017)

Frick, W. (2014) 'Study: Green advertising helped BP recover from the Deepwater Horizon spill', *Harvard Business Review*, 5 February. Available at: https://hbr.org/2014/02/study-green-advertising-helped-bp-recover-from-the-deepwater-horizon-spill (Accessed: 1 June 2017)

Gallup (2016) Majority of Americans dissatisfied with corporate influence. Available at: www.gallup.com/poll/188747/majority-americans-dissatisfied-corporate-influence.aspx (Accessed: 1 June 2017)

Hawkins, D. I., Best, R. J. and Coney, K. A. (2004) *Consumer behavior: Building marketing strategy* (9th edn). Boston, MA: McGraw-Hill Irwin.

Kant, I. and Ellington, J. W. (1994) *Ethical philosophy: The complete texts of grounding for the metaphysics of morals, and metaphysical principles of virtue, part II of The metaphysics of morals, with On a supposed right to lie because of philanthropic concerns*. Indianapolis, IN: Hackett.

Kotler, P. and Armstrong, G. (2010) *Principles of marketing*. Englewood Cliffs, NJ: Pearson Education.

Kotler, P. and Zaltman, G. (1971) 'Social marketing: An approach to planned social change', *The Journal of Marketing*, 35(3): 3–12.

Kozinets, R. V., De Valck, K., Wojnicki, A. C. and Wilner, S. J. (2010) 'Networked narratives: Understanding word-of-mouth marketing in online communities', *Journal of Marketing*, 74(2): 71–89.

Laczniak, G. R. and Murphy, P. E. (2006) 'Normative perspectives for ethical and socially responsible marketing', *Journal of Macromarketing*, 26(2): 154–77.

Lii, Y. S. and Lee, M. (2012) 'Doing right leads to doing well: When the type of CSR and reputation interact to affect consumer evaluations of the firm', *Journal of Business Ethics*, 105(1): 69–81.

Maignan, I. and Ferrell, O. C. (2004) 'Corporate social responsibility and marketing: An integrative framework', *Journal of the Academy of Marketing Science*, 32(1): 3–19.

Maignan, I., Ferrell, O. C. and Ferrell, L. (2005) 'A stakeholder model for implementing social responsibility in marketing', *European Journal of Marketing*, 39(9/10): 956–77.

Marin, L., Ruiz, S. and Rubio, A. (2009) 'The role of identity salience in the effects of corporate social responsibility on consumer behavior', *Journal of Business Ethics*, 84(1): 65–78.

McDonald's (2009) McHappy Day. Available at: www.youtube.com/watch?v=XGYMcjnuGcM (Accessed: 17 April 2017)

Mohr, L. A., Webb, D. J. and Harris, K. E. (2001) 'Do consumers expect companies to be socially responsible? The impact of corporate social responsibility on buying behavior', *Journal of Consumer Affairs*, 35(1): 45–72.

Murphy, P. E. (2010) 'Marketing, ethics of', *Wiley Encyclopaedia of Management*. Chichester: Wiley.

Nan, X. and Heo, K. (2007) 'Consumer responses to corporate social responsibility (CSR) initiatives: Examining the role of brand–cause fit in cause-related marketing', *Journal of Advertising*, 36(2): 63–74.

Nestle, M. (2013) 'Coca-Cola fights obesity? Oh, please', *Food Politics*, 16 January. Available at: www.foodpolitics.com/2013/01/coca-cola-fights-obesity-oh-please (Accessed: 19 October 2017)

Pemberton, J. (uploaded by) (2013) The honest Coca-Cola obesity commercial. Available at: www.youtube.com/watch?v=bHhCP5ad-zM (Accessed: 1 June 2017)

Pfau, N. B. (2015) 'How an accounting firm convinced its employees they could change the world', *Harvard Business Review*, 6 October. Available at: https://hbr.org/2015/10/how-an-accounting-firm-convinced-its-employees-they-could-change-the-world (Accessed: 1 June 2017)

Podnar, K. and Golob, U. (2007) 'CSR expectations: The focus of corporate marketing', *Corporate Communications: An International Journal*, 12(4): 326–40.

Porter, M. E. (1985) *Competitive advantage: Creating and sustaining superior performance*. New York: Free Press.

Porter, M. E. and Kramer, M. R. (2002) 'The competitive advantage of corporate philanthropy', *Harvard Business Review*, 80(12): 56–68.

Porter, M. E. and Kramer, M. R. (2011) 'Creating shared value', *Harvard Business Review*, 89(1/2): 62–77.

Rahim, R. A., Jalaludin, F. W. and Tajuddin, K. (2011) 'The importance of corporate social responsibility on consumer behaviour in Malaysia', *Asian Academy of Management Journal*, 16(1): 119–39.

Sheth, J. N., Sethia, N. K. and Srinivas, S. (2011) 'Mindful consumption: A customer-centric approach to sustainability', *Journal of the Academy of Marketing Science*, 39(1): 21–39.

Strom, S. (2013) 'In ads, Coke confronts soda's link to obesity', *New York Times*, 14 January. Available at: www.nytimes.com/2013/01/15/business/media/coke-tv-ads-confront-obesity-and-sodas-role.html (Accessed: 19 October 2017)

Sustainable Brands (2015) Study: 81% of consumers say they will make personal sacrifices to address social, environmental issues. Available at: www.sustainablebrands.com/news_and_views/stakeholder_trends_insights/sustainable_brands/study_81_consumers_say_they_will_make_ (Accessed: 1 June 2017)

Whole Foods Market (2014) Values Matter Anthem | Values Matter | Whole Foods Market. Available at: www.youtube.com/watch?v=5DCow4J-pDE (Accessed: 1 June 2017)

Young, W., Hwang, K., McDonald, S. and Oates, C. J. (2010) 'Sustainable consumption: Green consumer behaviour when purchasing products', *Sustainable Development*, 18(1): 20–31.

YouTube (2013) Coca-Cola coming together. Available at: www.youtube.com/watch?v=SKi2 A76YJlc (Accessed: 1 June 2017)

Further reading and links

Airbnb (2017) Until we all belong: The acceptance ring. Available at: www.youtube.com/watch?v=0Y4EqF0PR4E (Accessed: 1 June 2017)

Airbnb (2017) We Accept | Airbnb. Available at: www.youtube.com/watch?v=yetFk7QoSck (Accessed: 1 June 2017)

American Marketing Association (2017) Statement of ethics. Available at: www.ama.org/AboutAMA/Pages/Statement-of-Ethics.aspx#StatementofEthics (Accessed: 1 June 2017)

Australian Food News (2013) 'Coke launches anti-obesity campaign in Australia but "be healthy" Coke banned in UK', *Australian Food News*, 24 July. Available at: www.ausfoodnews.com.au/2013/07/24/coke-launches-anti-obesity-campaign-in-australia-but-%E2%80%98be-healthy%E2%80%99-coke-ad-banned-in-uk.html (Accessed: 1 June 2017)

Breene, S. (2013) 'Coca-Cola launches health-focused ad campaign in 2013', *Greatist*, 14 January. Available at: https://greatist.com/health/coca-cola-health-campaign-011413 (Accessed: 1 June 2017)

Ferrell, O. C. and Gresham, L. G. (1985) 'A contingency framework for understanding ethical decision making in marketing', *The Journal of Marketing*, 49(3): 87–96.

Hollensen, S. (2015) *Marketing management: A relationship approach*. Englewood Cliffs, NJ: Pearson Education.

Kotler, P., Roberto, E. and Hugo, H. (1991) *Social marketing*. Berlin: Econ-Verlag.

Kotler, P., Roberto, N., Lee, N. and Lee, N. (2002) *Social marketing: Improving the quality of life*. Thousand Oaks, CA: Sage.

Pemberton, J. (uploaded by) (2013) The honest Coca-Cola obesity commercial. Available at: www.youtube.com/watch?v=bHhCP5ad-zM (Accessed: 1 June 2017)

Sirgy, M. J. (2001) *Handbook of quality-of-life research: An ethical marketing perspective* (Vol. 8). Berlin: Springer Science & Business Media.

Whole Foods Market (2014) Values Matter Anthem | Values Matter | Whole Foods Market. Available at: www.youtube.com/watch?v=5DCow4J-pDE (Accessed: 1 June 2017)

The Way Forward: Making the Shift   12

Learning outcomes

By the end of this chapter, students should be able to:

- explain the importance of moving an organisation towards CSR and of doing it well
- apply organisational change concepts and frameworks to CSR
- detail more specific processes around sustainability and responsibility
- discuss related challenges and how to overcome them
- describe the future of CSR and the significance of being prepared for it today.

Case study   Google's journey towards CSR

Since Larry Page and Sergey Brin started Google in 1995 out of their dormitory at Stanford University, the company has dominated the way we retrieve information as well as many other aspects of our lives. Google employs over 50,000 employees ('Googlers') in 50 countries and it earned a revenue of approximately US$89.5 billion in 2016. The company's vision statement is 'to provide access to the world's information in one click' and the mission is 'to organise the world's information and make it universally accessible and useful'. The company's philosophy is centred around integrity, innovation, unconventional organisational practices and making data-driven decisions. Google embodies the motto 'Don't be evil' and places importance on creating long-term value for all its stakeholders.

During the two decades that have passed since Google was established, the company has made changes to demonstrate CSR by displaying high levels of dedication to making the world a better place. Ten years after Google started as a company, it launched Google.org, the philanthropic arm and foundation of Google, with Dr Larry Brilliant as its executive director. The goals of the foundation were focused on global development, global public health and climate change. Google.org is hybrid in nature, as it has a charitable purpose at its core while simultaneously keeping in mind profit and the strategic delivery of its initiatives (Rana, 2008).

Google is committed to the 1 per cent pledge that was set up by the corporation Salesforce through which companies pledge to give 1 per cent of their products, time and money to charity. When Google.org was initially established, the foundation donated approximately US$20 million to various causes and organisations such as the Acumen Fund and the Seva Foundation. Today, the foundation annually donates US$100 million in grants to its various partner organisations. The culture of Google has influenced the way Google.org operates and makes decisions, causing the company to develop partnerships with organisations that are innovative and pioneers in their area of work.

Since 2005, Google has been aligning its CSR with what the company stands for. The company works to help not-for-profit organisations by providing them with access to Google products, services, funding, expertise and volunteers to help run specific programmes. Google helps not-for-profit organisations to use technology in order to alleviate global challenges and reduce inequalities, either in their local communities or on a global scale. GoogleServe encourages all employees to volunteer their time and expertise to organisations of their choice, and over 5,000 Googlers have contributed 250,000 hours to 400 projects globally in 2016 alone, using their engineering, marketing and operational expertise to help partners create social impact. Through its employee Matching Gift programme, Google matches the contributions that every Googler makes to a non-profit of the Googler's choice, and through the past year the organisation has donated US$50 million to more than 12,000 non-profit organisations.

Google has made some organisational changes over the years to increase its environmental sustainability. In the past, Google avoided disclosing information regarding its energy usage, which caused environmental organisations to criticise the company for its lack of transparency. However, since 2011, Google has revealed data on its carbon emissions, showing that its footprint is greater than that of the entire country of Laos or of the UN's operational footprint. This tremendously high footprint drove the company to drastically reduce its energy consumption by measuring its power usage and distributing energy more optimally across its locations. It was one of the first companies to invest in renewable energy, and it was promised that by the end of 2017, all of its offices and data centres would be running on 100 per cent renewable energy. The company also partnered with the Environmental Defense Fund (EDF) in the US to capture information on air quality in an area using Street View cars, enabling utility companies to make informed decisions about repairs and project improvements. Google operates more than 200 cafés and 1,000 self-service kitchens across its offices, requiring them to invest heavily in fresh produce. In an effort to address the issue of food wastage, the company started to purchase and use produce that would typically be deemed 'ugly' or wasted because of cosmetic standards. Google now takes its energy and food consumption very seriously, working to modify its supply chain to make it more sustainable.

In addition, Google demonstrates inclusion and gender diversity in its people recruitment and management. Having realised the under-representation of women and members of ethnic communities in the technology space, the company now makes an effort to hire people from diverse backgrounds. An estimated 40 per cent of Google's workforce comprises people of diverse ethnic groups, with approximately 31 per cent of its workforce comprising women. Additionally, 24 per cent of the company's employees in leadership positions are women, which is far above the current standard. The company uses its CSR activities as an incentive and a strategy for employee engagement to attract and retain talented people, with a focus on millennials and younger employees who demonstrate concern for environmental and social issues (Belfo and Sousa, 2011). Through its work and efforts, the company strives to provide not only its employees but also the global community with benefits that facilitate empowerment and growth (Belfo and Sousa, 2011).

(Continued)

Questions for reflection

1　Based on Google's philosophy and values, what values do you think a company should consider when trying to change its organisational culture to become more sustainable?
2　What factors contributed to Google being recognised as one of the most sustainable companies in the world?
3　From what you know about Google, what else can the company do to increase its CSR and sustainability?
4　How can a company engage its employees in developing environment-related initiatives?
5　Referring to this case study, what role does a company's leadership play in influencing change towards sustainability?

Bibliography

Bansal, P. and La Ber, M. (2008) *Google's way – don't be evil*. Boston, MA: Harvard Business School.
Belfo, F. and Sousa, R. D. (2011) 'Workforce incentives at IT companies: The Google case', *IADIS International Journal*, 9(2): 69–84.
Edelman, B. and Eisenmann, T. R. (2011) *Google Inc*. Boston, MA: Harvard Business School.
Edelman, B. and Eisenmann, T. R. (2014) *Google Inc. in 2014*. Boston, MA: Harvard Business School.
Rana, S. (2008) 'From making money without doing evil to doing good without handouts: The Google.org experiment in philanthropy', *Journal of Business and Technology Law*, 3: 87–96.
William Davidson Institute (2012) *Google Energy's Shift into Renewables*. Michigan: ERB Institute.

Links

Google (2017) Diversity. Available at: www.google.com/diversity (Accessed: 1 June 2017)
Google (2017) Giving back. Available at: www.google.com/intl/en/giving/people.html#gift-matching (Accessed: 1 June 2017)
Google (2017) Google.org + learning equality: Closing global education gaps. Available at: www.youtube.com/user/Googleorg (Accessed: 1 June 2017)
Google.org (2017) Available at: www.google.org (Accessed: 1 June 2017)
WCS (2015) Kate Brandt, Google. Available at: www.youtube.com/watch?v=ocTk16eUqw0 (Accessed: 1 June 2017)

Introduction: Changing for a sustainable future

As we start the last chapter of this book, it is important to reflect on everything that was discussed in the previous chapters and how to implement it. Throughout this book, we have discussed strategic CSR and why it is an effective way to achieve genuine responsibility and sustainability in every organisation and in the business world today. We have discussed the stakeholders of the organisation and how imperative it is to move beyond stakeholder prioritisation to stakeholder integration and involvement. We examined business ethics and the various (philosophical and practical) approaches to doing the right thing and what it means for everyday business management. We talked about environmental sustainability and why it is an urgent business and global issue in the face of the rapid climate change we are facing. We saw the shift towards responsible management and leadership, what it means to lead an organisation responsibly and why it is the leadership style that really counts. We inspected ways to involve stakeholders in the CSR efforts of the company, from employees and consumers to shareholders and investors.

We next moved to discuss the ways that companies communicate their CSR to the world and to their own stakeholders – how they measure their social impact, how they benchmark the organisation against frameworks and standards, how they report on CSR and how they use marketing strategies to not only promote their own CSR but to promote the wellbeing of the communities in which they operate. This final chapter will focus on implementing CSR in a company and the future of it for all companies.

Firstly, we will concentrate on implementing all of the CSR aspects presented in this book as an organisational change. To do so, we will discuss several frameworks for organisational change in general and inspect how they can be implemented in a company so it can become responsible and sustainable. We will also detail several specific frameworks on integrating CSR into the organisation.

Secondly, we will discuss the implications of the CSR movement for the business world in general. A shift in mindset and in managerial practice is already taking place but there is a lot more that business needs to do to achieve the wellbeing and prosperity of everyone. Some of the issues humanity faces require an immediate, holistic and collaborative response from the entire business sector. Business as usual is no longer a valid option and we will discuss what the future of CSR holds and ten CSR trends that could become the foci of CSR in the next decade.

Organisational change

Organisational change occurs when an organisation makes a transition from its current state to some desired future state. Managing organisational change is the process of planning and implementing change in organisations in such a way as to minimise employee resistance and cost to the organisation while simultaneously maximising the effectiveness of the change effort (Ganta et al., 2014). For this purpose, organisations undergo a change management process, which is a structured approach to shifting/transitioning individuals, teams and organisations from a current state to a desired future state (McShane et al., 2012).

These commonly used definitions can be easily applied to organisational change towards CSR and sustainability, by simply defining the future state or desired outcomes in relevant terms. However, a more fundamental and radical transformation is required in the approach towards organisational change. These definitions and many others focus on overcoming the resistance to change and on 'shifting' and 'transitioning' employees as if they were goods in a warehouse. However, to become fully socially responsible, internally and externally, we could argue that employees need to be perceived as people who might play a role in this process. Most change management processes fail (Kotter, 2002) because they are conducted top-down and outside-in. To successfully implement change, employees need to be respected and involved in the process. This rings true particularly in the context of conducting organisational change towards being responsible, which also implies internal responsibility towards employees.

In Chapter 7, we discussed how employees can be involved in organisational CSR efforts, via employee-led CSR, employee engagement and participation. If organisations are to successfully implement changes towards responsibility and sustainability, employees can be a remarkable source of innovation and positive energy to drive the change, implement it and sustain it for the long term. Furthermore, outstanding companies in this area, such as Whole Foods Market and Unilever, also involve their consumers, investors and other stakeholders in this process.

As such, change management towards CSR can be defined as an approach to involving various stakeholders in shifting the organisation from the current state to a sustainable and responsible future state. In order to do so, let us examine several organisational change frameworks and see how they can be implemented to achieve strategic CSR holistically and enduringly. But first, five imperative questions are to be asked and answered.

Five imperative questions

There are five imperative questions that any company needs to ask itself prior to undertaking the journey towards strategic CSR. These questions can be raised and answered by all stakeholders of the company, not just its formal leadership. They focus on the essence of the change, its direction and the manner to achieve it as they present the where, why, what, who and how of organisational change towards CSR.

1. *Where* do we want to be?

   The question of 'where' is about the vision of the company, not just for itself but also for the society and the environment in which it operates. What if we could really make a difference to the world? What will the company look like in ten years if we change accordingly? What will the world look like? What is our vision for a better world and how can we help achieve it?

2. *Why* do we need to change?

As discussed in Chapter 6, it is essential to start with a 'why'. This is true for any organisational change and particularly for one towards CSR. If the company does not have a strong enough 'why' that resonates with employees, the employees might resist the change. According to Sinek (2011), people make decisions with the part of the brain that is in charge of their emotions, and as such they need to emotionally engage with the 'why'. The good news is that CSR and sustainability, if done well, could offer a strong enough 'why' for this change. Being the best in the world may not be a strong enough motivator, but being best *for* the world might be.

3. *What* needs to change?

The question of the 'what' is particularly important in the context of strategic CSR given how holistic it is and how it needs to be aligned with the strategic planning of the company. As such, companies that undergo substantial changes towards CSR need to examine their entire business strategy, including mission and vision, culture and values, leadership and workforce, practices and policies, supply chain and value chain. All of these aspects and others have been discussed in this book. In addition, companies sometimes change their organisational structure towards CSR by making it flatter and more inclusive.

4. *Who* will be part of the change?

We tried to answer this question in Chapter 3 on stakeholder management, and in Chapter 7 on involving stakeholders in the company's CSR efforts. In other words, everyone potentially can be (and perhaps should be) part of this change. Employees can lead CSR and participate in the effort; suppliers can help sustain the supply chains; consumers can be involved and informed on the changes and be guided to make better choices, and so on. The question of who should lead the change towards CSR is answered differently by different companies: some just ask someone from the organisation to also lead CSR (e.g. the HR director), while others employ CSR officers and create CSR departments. Some companies believe it is the CEO of the company who should be leading the change while others involve all stakeholders throughout the entire organisation. While there is no right or wrong way of doing so, the last option is more aligned with the concept of strategic CSR.

In this context, it is also important to mention the role of change agents in conducting change. According to Kurt Lewin (1946), a change agent is anyone who possesses enough knowledge and power to guide and facilitate the change efforts. Many companies (e.g. PwC) map their CSR champions and involve them in every step towards CSR as internal change agents. While CSR champions are usually paid employees, they can also be from any other stakeholder group.

5. *How* will we achieve the vision?

Achieving a vision to be a responsible company requires a blueprint or a plan towards the change. Similar to the transformational leadership framework (see Chapter 6), companies need to develop a vision, communicate it, model it and create a commitment of all stakeholders towards it. In order to answer the 'how' question on organisational change towards sustainability, we will present a few general and specific frameworks which can assist companies in taking the first step towards this change and ensure they do it well.

Force field analysis model and CSR

You may recall that in the second chapter of this book we cited Kurt Lewin (1946), who said 'there is nothing so practical as a good theory'. Lewin was a German psychologist and a pioneer in the area of social, organisational and applied psychology. As he had to exile from Germany in World War II, Lewin moved to the US and became well-known for his scholarly work, particularly in the areas of organisational leadership and change. His force field analysis model is still one of the most utilised theories in organisational change, even though it was created over 60 years ago (Coghlan and Brannick, 2003), which proves his statement on theory to be true.

The force field analysis model is a framework on change that can be used in the context of CSR (see Figure 12.1). On the left side, the axis moves up from current conditions (in our case, low CSR) to desired conditions (strategic CSR). In order to get to the desired conditions and future, we need to examine and change the driving and restraining forces. In the first out of three stages of this process, before the change, the driving and restraining forces are equal in their power and therefore a certain status quo (or equilibrium) is created and may persist for years. In many organisations, the driving forces towards CSR and sustainability are not strong enough to overcome the resisting forces and the company remains at the low CSR level. This was the case in most companies until the 1990s.

In the second stage, referred to by Lewin as 'unfreezing', the driving forces are increased, pushing the organisation towards the desired conditions. In the case of CSR, these driving forces could be internal or external. *Internal drivers* for change could be a change in *leadership*, such as a new CEO (as in the case of Paul Polman and Unilever; see case study in Chapter 6) or a change in the mindset of the leader (e.g. when John Mackey learned more about animal rights, decided to become

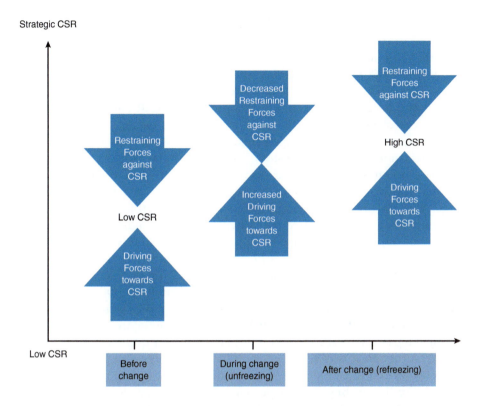

Figure 12.1   Force field analysis model applied to CSR (based on Lewin, 1946)

vegan and to change many of the practices at Whole Foods Market). Driving forces could also originate within the *employees*, who become more engaged in sustainability issues and vocalise their desire to work for an employer that is responsible. As discussed in Chapter 7, employee-led CSR is becoming more common in many workplaces around the world and many such initiatives increase the driving forces towards a more sustainable future. Another internal change that could become a driving force towards CSR is when a company changes its *mission and values* and as a result people start to expect the entire company to change. While these changes are mostly positive, internal drivers for change may also include a *crisis*. A financial crisis or a crisis in the relationship with employees and unions (including strikes and industrial actions), could lead the organisation to re-examine the way it treats employees and other stakeholders and move into change. In 2015, criticism of Amazon and the way it treats employees on social media could be seen as such a driver for change.

In addition, there are *external drivers* for change. One of the biggest drivers towards CSR is when companies see what their *competitors* are doing in this area.

When the drivers towards CSR in general were discussed in Chapter 1, we mentioned how 'social icons' such as Ben & Jerry's and The Body Shop showed other companies that it is not only possible to be a purpose-driven company but that it could also pay off. Many companies tried to imitate what such social icons did, but too often it was only superficial. In recent years, we have seen more companies inspiring others to adopt a holistic approach to CSR and sustainability, and the many cases presented in this book may serve to exemplify this and inspire action. External drivers for change can also originate with *external stakeholders*, such as consumers and/or investors. In recent years, consumer pressure and action (including social media campaigns, creating films on companies they buy from and boycotting certain brands) have become a powerful driver for change. While many companies try to avoid doing anything at first by denying any wrong-doing, others realise that when consumers signal to a company that they are not happy with its sustainability and responsibility levels, it is a great opportunity to address the issues and grow. Sometimes this solution is not holistic at first (e.g. see the cases of H&M and Nestlé in this book), but over time it may change the company, its actions and what it stands for. Other external drivers for change could come from *governments and governmental organisations* and a change in regulations and legislation. For example, in 2011 the Australian government passed a carbon pricing scheme (carbon tax) as the Clean Energy Act 2011. Although it was repealed in 2014 by the following government, many companies started to implement some changes, such as becoming carbon neutral, knowing that if they are not prepared, similar future legislation may result in a loss of profits and power. In addition, the UN SDGs (see Chapter 5) drove many companies to change their practices to align with the global goals towards 2030. Finally, an *external crisis*, such as natural disasters and the impact of climate change, might drive some companies towards environmental sustainability and CSR. Figure 12.2 summarises some of the driving forces towards change, although others also exist.

Internal drivers for change	External drivers for change
• Leadership • Employees • Mission and values • Internal crisis	• Competitors • Consumers and investors • Governmental organisations • External crisis

Figure 12.2   Internal and external driving forces towards CSR

However, as explained by Lewin, it is not enough to increase the driving forces to implement change. Unless the restraining forces are managed and decreased, they will become a counter power to the driving forces and prevent the change. CSR and sustainability are still opposed by many stakeholders, from current business leaders who only focus on economic growth to consumers who only want to pay the least amount possible; from investors and shareholders who believe the only role of the company is to maximise its profit to employees who do not want to see their company change; from governments who give in to lobbying by strong and irresponsible businesses to suppliers who are not ready to change their own methods of business conduct to align with the change of the company they supply to, and the public who may be cynical about CSR, having seen too much greenwashing to support the change. This list was not written to deter companies from trying to become more sustainable, but it is a good reminder of what can happen when the change towards CSR is only superficial instead of strategic. It is important to involve each of the aforementioned stakeholder groups in the change to ensure that it is accepted and undertaken, while managing the expectations and needs of all stakeholders.

Appreciative inquiry

As we saw at the beginning of this chapter, the very approach to change is what often results in change failure. Focusing on the problem (what is wrong with our organisation); failing to provide a strong enough 'why' for the change; seeing employees and other stakeholders as passive pawns in this process; and assuming change is about overcoming resistance are some of the reasons that many organisational changes do not last long. The idea that people are creatures of habit and will always resist change often becomes a self-fulfilling prophecy. We are all happy to change – get married, have children, buy a house, move countries and be promoted – as long as we see a reason for the change and as long as we know that the change will serve us or the people we care about. This different approach is at the core of *appreciative inquiry*, a framework for organisational change that focuses on the positive aspect of change, and that is what makes it desirable in many corporations and in large-scale changes.

Appreciative inquiry (Cooperrider and Srivastva, 1987) is based on positive psychology and positive organisational change. Emerging research in positive psychology shows that by focusing on the positive rather than the negative aspects of life we can improve organisational success and individual wellbeing. As such, instead of focusing on problems and on what is wrong, appreciative inquiry concentrates on the positive strengths of the organisation (and people) and on its possible future. The process searches for strengths and capabilities and uses them for further success and wellbeing.

The 'four-D' model of appreciative inquiry is a blueprint for the pathway to change and it is most suitable for change towards strategic CSR (see Figure 12.3). In fact, David Cooperrider, the father of appreciative inquiry, used it to increase corporate citizenship and to coin the phrase 'business as an agent of world benefit'.

It should be noted that the process aims to be a whole-organisation process, not a top-down one. As such, all the employees and leadership of the organisation, and sometimes additional stakeholders as well, participate in an appreciative inquiry summit where they go through the four stages, or four Ds, of appreciative inquiry. Firstly, they *discover* what is wonderful about the organisation they work in – what its strengths are, where its biggest assets lie. In the context of CSR, it might be about identifying what the company is already doing or what great assets it has (e.g. strong leadership, devoted employees) that can be used to drive sustainability. The next stage, *dream*, is usually very engaging as people start dreaming together of what could be. Instead of thinking 'what if we fail', participants start thinking 'what if we fly'. Imagining what a sustainable future will look like for their organisation and for the world can be highly engaging. The third stage, *design*, involves design thinking and deciding on the actual future to work towards all the dreams and visions that have emerged in the previous stage. Design involves the process of dialogue, in which participants listen with selfless receptivity to each other's models and assumptions and eventually form a collective model for thinking within the team and create a common image of what should be. Finally, the organisation commits to its new destiny and *delivers* on the future dream.

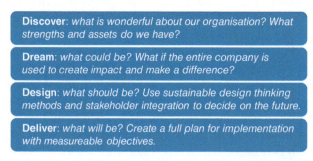

Figure 12.3   Appreciative inquiry (based on Whitney and Cooperrider, 1998)

Appreciative inquiry was used to drive some phenomenal changes. Professor David Cooperrider was invited to lead the Global Compact Leaders Summit in 2004, and appreciative inquiry was used to engage leaders from all sectors of the economy in reimagining the future of business and the world. In 1999, working with David Cooperrider, and using appreciative inquiry techniques, the Dalai Lama hosted the Interreligious Friendship Group in Jerusalem, Israel to promote peace between religions. Based on appreciative inquiry, the Dalai Lama Center for Peace & Education has developed the Heart-Mind Inquiry (1999), which is designed to engage parents, children and key stakeholders in a change process focusing on the social and emotional learning and development of young people in their families, schools and community.

Appreciative inquiry was used by Cooperrider to develop the concept of 'business as an agent of world benefit'. Similar to the ideas presented in this book, this approach focuses on the positive potential of companies to use all their resources to benefit the world. The Fowler Center for Business as an Agent of World Benefit is aimed at advancing the scholarship and practice of flourishing enterprises. On its website (2017) the Center says:

> The Fowler Center's primary focus is on for-profit organizations that use their core activities to create value for society and the environment in ways that create even more value for their customers and shareholders; its primary vehicle for effecting change is Positive Organizational Science and Appreciative Inquiry. We are drawing on expertise and tools such as design, sustainable value, Appreciative Inquiry, and systems thinking to build and maintain prosperity and flourishing.

Kotter's eight steps for organisational change

In his book *The Heart of Change* (2002), Kotter explained that most change management processes fail. Kotter emphasised that in order for organisational change to be effective, particularly in large organisations, it is not enough to offer people the rationale behind the change, but instead employees need to be emotionally involved. We can therefore assume that when the change is about becoming a purpose-driven organisation, focusing on creating a better future for society and sustaining our planet, people might be more likely to engage emotionally and work together to achieve the new goals. This was the case, for example, with the Sustainable Living Plan at Unilever (2017), which required a whole-organisation change. The buy-in from employees and their emotional involvement in the process was very high. Let us examine Kotter's eight steps and apply each one to the context of strategic CSR:

1. *Establish a sense of urgency*: Originally, Kotter suggested using economic crisis and competitive realities to achieve this. In the case of CSR, demonstrating to employees the urgency around climate change and the burning issues society

faces could create a different sense of urgency. Knowing that we need to achieve the SDGs by 2030 could also create such a sense of urgency.

2. *Form a powerful coalition*: In this step, companies are to create a group with enough power to lead the change effort and develop strategies to achieve that vision. Since strategic CSR is about working with a broad set of stakeholders, creating coalition through stakeholder integration and working with all internal and external stakeholders to create and achieve a purpose-driven vision may increase the likelihood of success.

3. *Create a vision*: Here, the company needs to create a vision to help direct the change effort and develop strategies for achieving that vision. In the context of this book, it is about a vision of being best for the world and how the company can serve the community. In 2017, Mark Zuckerberg, the CEO of Facebook, wrote an open letter to all its stakeholders on how the vision and mission statement of the social media giant will need to change to address societal needs. Zuckerberg wrote:

> On our journey to connect the world, we often discuss products we're building and updates on our business. Today I want to focus on the most important question of all: are we building the world we all want? […] This is a time when many of us around the world are reflecting on how we can have the most positive impact. I am reminded of my favourite saying about technology: 'We always overestimate what we can do in two years, and we underestimate what we can do in ten years.' We may not have the power to create the world we want immediately, but we can all start working on the long term today. In times like these, the most important thing we at Facebook can do is develop the social infrastructure to give people the power to build a global community that works for all of us.

The new vision that Zuckerberg goes on to offer is about five aspects of community development: supportive community, safe community, informed community, a civically engaged community and an inclusive community. This is a vision that resonates with Facebook employees and users.

4. *Communicate the vision*: Similar to the discussion in Chapter 6 on transformational leadership, communicating the vision needs to be emotionally engaging, using storytelling and metaphors to allow others to see what the visionary person sees. Companies need to use every channel and vehicle of communication possible to share the new vision and strategies with all their stakeholders. An important aspect of this step is leading by example, which makes the responsible leadership discussed in Chapter 6 an essential part of success.

5. *Empower others to act on the vision*: In Chapter 6, we discussed the importance of shared leadership as part of responsible leadership. Strategic CSR requires the embedding of it in every part of the organisation and among all employees, suppliers and other stakeholders. People need to be involved and empowered

to lead the change. Using a whole-organisation method such as appreciative inquiry could assist in facilitating this.

6. *Plan for and create short-term wins*: According to Kotter, at this stage, organisations need to incentivise and reward employees who are involved in the change. However, based on the approach of this book and in many other scholarly works (e.g. self-determination theory), people are motivated by purpose more than by rewards. People are not horses and incentivising them with carrots could sometimes have the opposite effect than intended, as external motivators tend to decrease internal ones (Ryan and Deci, 2000).

7. *Consolidate improvements and produce still more change*: Kotter explains that at this stage, organisations need to change 'systems, structures and policies' to align with the new vision and hire and develop employees who can implement it. This is also true for CSR. Strategic CSR implies changing the value chain of the organisation, the entire system and core operations to adopt a holistic approach. Companies need to make sure that they do not celebrate their CSR while causing harm to people, animals and the planet. It is also important to develop employees' awareness and passion for CSR and to hire people with a strong value congruence.

8. *Institutionalise new approaches*: This is a crucial stage for leading an organisational change towards strategic CSR. While the initial energy and excitement around being 'best for the world' may start to decline, companies need to constantly and consistently work to ensure that it is on the right path to CSR.

CSR-specific change management frameworks

In addition to the above general frameworks, such as the force field analysis or appreciative inquiry, which were originally designed to fit organisational change for any purpose, goal or vision, there are some organisational change frameworks that are tailored to the specific goals of CSR or sustainability.

Maignan et al. (2005) offered a stakeholder approach to CSR marketing, which was presented in Chapter 11. It comprises eight steps, which could also be used to implement an organisational change towards CSR, particularly as it begins with identifying the main stakeholders, their respective salience and their main issues of concern. It continues with the understanding of what CSR means to the company and the auditing of current practices. This may help companies understand and develop their personal vision to apply it more holistically. The sixth step, prioritising and implementing CSR changes, is at the heart of this chapter. Although the Maignan et al. article does not expand greatly on how this should be done, the authors explain that in the planning of this change it is important for organisations to distinguish between CSR challenges according to how much investment they require and how urgent they are. The last two stages are CSR marketing and gaining stakeholders' feedback, which were covered previously.

Cramer (2005) offered a similar framework for organisational change towards CSR with six implementation activities. Like Maignan et al. (2005), Cramer also begins with the stakeholders but emphasises the importance of the new vision as the second stage (see Figure 12.4). She further suggests differentiating between short-term and long-term strategy to implement CSR. The next two steps are similar to what Kotter (2002) suggests: implement a change to the organisational systems and processes. Finally, Cramer discusses the importance of communicating the change internally and externally.

Cramer's (2005) six CSR implementation activities	Listing the expectations and demands of the stakeholders.	Maignan et al.'s (2005) stakeholder approach to CSR implementation	Discovering organisational norms and values.
	Formulating a vision and a mission with regard to CSR and creating a code of conduct.		Identifying stakeholders.
	Developing short- and longer-term strategies with regard to CSR and creating a plan of action.		Identifying stakeholder issues.
	Setting up a monitoring and reporting system.		Assessing the meaning of CSR for the firm.
	Embedding the process by rooting it in quality and management systems.		Auditing current practices.
			Promoting CSR.
	Communicating internally and externally about the approach and the results obtained.		Gaining stakeholder feedback.

Figure 12.4   Cramer vs. Maignan et al.'s approaches to CSR implementation

Questions for reflection and discussion

Examine Figure 12.4 which details two sets of steps towards CSR implementation.

1.   How are they different in their basic approach to CSR?
2.   Which one is better aligned with strategic CSR and why?
3.   Which one is easier to follow and implement?

The integrative framework

Maon et al. (2009) offered an integrative framework for implementing change towards CSR while using the force field analysis model and other frameworks.

The model refers to Lewin's three phases (before change, unfreeze and refreeze) but uses instead four stages: sensitise, unfreeze, move and refreeze. Prior to the shift, there is the *sensitising* stage, in which top management becomes aware of the importance of sustainability and CSR issues. Next, managers *unfreeze* past practices associated with the status quo. Unlearning old habits is critical to the development of CSR as old assumptions (such as profit should be maximised at any cost) can stand in the way of the unfreezing stage and the overall change. In the *moving* stage, the organisation is guided towards a new set of assumptions and culture. Identifying the need to adopt a holistic CSR approach is just the start of the change process. In the third stage, to effect a new state, managers must *refreeze* the new cultural assumptions. At this stage, employees learn to adopt the new assumptions and the CSR culture. Figure 12.5 summarises the four stages and what needs to be done in each.

It is important to note how this framework is aligned with strategic CSR. It is based on ongoing conversations with stakeholders, and suggests an 'integrated CSR strategic plan for the entire organisation', which embeds CSR in the organisational strategy. It also includes communicating CSR efforts and continually evaluating and improving them until CSR is 'institutionalised' in the organisation.

While this framework is important as it uses both the force field model and the literature on the learning organisation to draw a detailed picture of the process

Stage	Action	Activities
Sensitise		1. Raising CSR awareness inside the organisation.
Unfreeze	Plan	2. Assessing corporate purpose in a societal context:
		a. Uncovering organisational systems, as well as corporate norms and values.
		b. Identifying key stakeholders and critical stakeholder issues.
		3. Establishing a vision and a working definition for CSR.
		4. Assessing current CSR status:
		a. Auditing current CSR norms, standards and practices.
		b. Benchmarking competitors' CSR practices, norms, standards and practices.
		5. Developing a CSR-integrated strategic plan:
		a. Embedding CSR in organisational strategy.
Move	Do	6. Implementing a CSR-integrated strategic plan:
		a. Implementing organisational initiatives and strategies linked to CSR.
		7. Communicating about CSR commitments and performance.
	Check/	8. Evaluating CSR-integrated strategies and communication:
	Improve	a. Evaluating, verifying and reporting on CSR progress.
Refreeze	Mainstream	9. Institutionalising CSR.

Figure 12.5 **Integrative framework for implementing CSR (based on Maon et al., 2009)**

towards strategic CSR, it is very focused on a top-down approach. Organisational change towards CSR, however, could originate and even be led by employees or other stakeholders.

The six insights towards sustainability

The 'Six Insights' is a paper offering an innovative approach to organisational change towards sustainability. Based on action research undertaken with several big corporations in Australia, reflective practice and cases, Hunting and Tilbury (2006) offered a process aimed at helping people and organisations think through the implications of their choices and behaviours and the risks and opportunities of current behaviours in relation to the goal of sustainability. Figure 12.6 displays the six insights, which are detailed below.

Figure 12.6   Six insights towards sustainability (based on Hunting and Tilbury, 2006)

Insight 1: Adopt a clear, shared vision for the future. Visioning is a highly creative process, which opens up possibilities. Based on appreciative inquiry, the authors suggest to define a vision and look at 'what can be' rather than taking a negative 'problem-solving' approach to sustainability. Acknowledgement of different perspectives helps to build the shared vision and gets the necessary 'buy-in' from all stakeholders.

Insight 2: Build teams, not just champions. While it was suggested above that change agents and champions can help lead organisational change, the 'Six Insights' paper states that a team-based approach is vital to get an organisation-wide buy-in to sustainability, and it is therefore essential to include as many people in the change as possible. As well as collaborative decision making, participation encourages the sharing of information and prevents knowledge being withheld and used as a source of power. It is important to discover why some people want to get involved and others don't, and what can build their involvement.

Insight 3: Use critical thinking and reflection. Critical thinking is about identifying the various elements of a change situation (including power structures and personal bias), reflecting on why things work or not and then using this deeper knowledge to build a path to your vision. Critical thinking and reflection can help organisations understand the effect levers (such as leadership, power, politics, hierarchy, structure, information flows and personal bias) have on change and develop practical steps to change using the levers.

Insight 4: Go beyond stakeholder engagement. While strategic CSR is very much about engaging with a broad set of stakeholders, Hunting and Tilbury (2006) suggest companies ask themselves why they engage with stakeholders – is it to minimise risk or is it a genuine interest in the input of others so the company can collectively make change for sustainability? To change for sustainability, organisations need to work more proactively with a variety of other organisations and share information, issues and practices until a 'tipping point' for sustainability is reached. This requires rethinking the traditional stakeholder engagement approach and building cross-sectorial partnerships.

Insight 5: Adopt a systemic approach. Systems thinking looks at the whole (the 'bigger picture'), accepts uncertainty and ambiguity; expands our worldview; recognises that there are many ways of learning; and encourages more participatory and holistic approaches to identifying better sustainability strategies. Sustainability has to not only have a 'whole institution' approach but also an 'outside institution' approach, which implies continually working with external stakeholders in partnerships for sustainability.

Insight 6: Move beyond expecting a linear path to change. It is important for companies to realise that the process of change for sustainability needs to be more iterative and reflective, addressing issues as they occur and often taking a branch path for a while. It is not a linear shift from point A to point B but rather the change process needs to be more flexible and potentially more opportunistic too, and this may lead to more innovative, productive and unexpected outcomes.

Implementing strategic CSR

Chandler (2017) suggested implementing strategic CSR in two waves. In the short to medium term, companies can take the following actions:

1. *Executive investment*: the organisational leadership needs to change policy and strategy to embed CSR in every part of the organisation.
2. *CSR officer*: creating positions or departments to implement CSR.

3. *CSR vision*: creating a vision for the future of the company within society and communicating this vision to internal and external stakeholders.
4. *Performance metrics*: changing performance and rewards systems in the organisation so that sustainability and responsibility are recognised.
5. *Integrated reporting*: a firm-wide audit with published results are integrated into the annual report (see Chapter 10).
6. *Ethics code and training*: developing a comprehensive ethics code may assist the company in encouraging CSR throughout the firm and its supply chain, and in training employees and suppliers so that the code is used and implemented.
7. *Ethics helpline*: companies need to develop a platform to allow whistleblowers to come forward without risking their jobs (see Chapter 4).
8. *Organisational design*: this is about redesigning the structure of the organisation and its procedures so that strategic CSR is implemented and respected.

In addition to these steps, Chandler (2017) also details some long-term actions:

1. *Stakeholder involvement*: while Chandler (2017) suggests building a two-way open communication channel with stakeholders as a long-term activity, it could also be argued that this might be the first activity to take in the journey towards strategic CSR.
2. *Managing the message*: communicating strategic CSR is important to gain a buy-in from as many stakeholders as possible, including through social media.
3. *Corporate governance*: a committed board of directors with structural reforms is essential to reinforce CSR throughout the organisation.
4. *Activism and advocacy*: corporate activism can help to define the firm's identity by creating a link between the brand and the social causes it promotes. This can be done, for example, via social marketing (see Chapter 11).

The way forward: Challenges and opportunities

Changing an entire organisation towards CSR and sustainability is not an easy task. To embed CSR as a holistic approach while fully involving all the internal and external stakeholders (which may amount to tens of thousands or even millions of people) might seem like an overwhelming task. It is not enough to change the CEO or for the CEO to have a compelling vision for the company.

The journey towards strategic CSR can be long and difficult, but it is easier than other organisational changes as it offers a stronger 'why'. There are many companies who have undertaken this journey in the past and it is important to hear their stories and look at the pathways they created while moving their organisations forward. There are companies who are pioneers and leaders in this area, some that understood the importance of CSR before others (early adopters), while others are taking longer to change. In 2018, companies who still lag behind may find themselves ridiculed and criticised, with negative actions taken against them by various stakeholders.

Some of the common challenges in the journey towards CSR is that a narrow view is established in the culture of the company. At such companies, for example, people who bring in more money, no matter how unethical their actions may be, are celebrated and recognised. Profit is the only focus of the organisational leadership and its annual reports. Externalities are something to be abused to make more profit. It is not an easy task to change such a culture and it may take a while, but with the right leadership and vision it can be done, as we saw in many of the case studies in this book.

Another challenge is apparent when many internal and external stakeholders push towards sustainability and CSR but the leaders of the company (including the CEO and the board) are not interested. Or they are interested but see it only as a marketing stunt. While a strong business case for CSR, detailing the financial and brand gains of CSR, may help convince them, it might only encourage them to greenwash. Storytelling and showcasing other companies may inspire them to change. No person or a company is an island, and with enough internal and external influence even self-interested CEOs may change their mindset, and there are many such examples from the last few decades.

Some companies are full of good intentions but they are not sure how to become more sustainable and responsible. Based on the phrase 'the way to hell is paved with good intentions' we learn that good intentions alone are not going to be enough. The good news is that knowledge and tools are widely available today in books (such as this one), journal articles, media articles, blogs, social media, and so on. CSR is undergoing a professionalisation process and there are related university degrees, networks and centres to help companies not only start this journey, but to also become fully socially responsible.

Finally, some companies, particularly small and medium enterprises (SMEs), are reluctant to be more socially responsible due to the related costs, both financial and non-financial (including time and effort). It is true that becoming more sustainable may require some investment of time and money, particularly at first, but it can also save companies future costs, make them more efficient and help them achieve marketing results beyond what a paid ad in the local newspaper could ever buy.

Remember, 'it always seems impossible until it is done' (Nelson Mandela).

The future of CSR

'The best way to predict the future is to create it.' (Abraham Lincoln)

Over the last four decades, the world has witnessed a shift in the business world – from a narrow view of business responsibility (the only social responsibility is to maximise profit) to a broad set of responsibilities, towards society and the environment. In the very recent past, companies thought they had nothing to do with saving the environment and now we have companies with sustainable living plans and commitments to the SDGs. Some CEOs of large corporations have started to sound like the head of Greenpeace. We have witnessed a shift from no responsibility to corporate philanthropy and greenwashing to strategic CSR, where it is embedded in every aspect of the company. We can see a slow transformation from a linear economy to a circular economy. It is comparable to witnessing the Titanic making a shift just before it hits the iceberg. The ship is big and the shift seems too slow and sometimes not sharp enough, but unless the shift is there, we will hit the iceberg.

We still do not have perfect companies, impeccable CEOs or flawless people. But it is encouraging to see how many firms are now striving to be better for the world instead of being best in the world, focusing on how they can serve society instead of on how society can serve them. Some of them are more genuine in their efforts than others, but it is important to also remember that some companies started off with using CSR for marketing only, but later adopted a more holistic approach.

Examining the last four decades and the changes that have occurred in just over a generation, it is possible that the next generation's business world will be quite different to ours. Carroll (2015) recently predicted three possible scenarios. In the *gloomy scenario*, CSR will be a passing trend. When companies discover another way to engage their consumers or if there is another global recession, CSR might fade from the scene and eventually disappear from the agenda. Carroll does not think this is very likely. Given the high pressure to act on environmental issues and the raised awareness of businesses, governments, consumers and employees, it is not likely that businesses will be able to wash their hands of their responsibility. As Paul Polman said, 'the world we want is an enormous responsibility, and this is not going to change any time soon.'

At the other extreme is the *hopeful scenario*. On this optimistic view, companies the world over would significantly grow their CSR commitments and programming and the ideas embedded within them would move from the transactional to the transformational. CSR would become so strong that it may no longer be a competitive advantage but instead an enormous global power for change. Companies will be proactive and holistic, using their resources and power to make this world better. Carroll does not see this as a likely scenario, but given how the world has changed since he first offered a definition of CSR in 1979, there is hope.

The *probable scenario* will likely rule the day over the foreseeable future, according to Carroll. There is significant evidence that CSR has been consistent and stable in its popularity and at least three driving forces (business acceptance, global growth and academic proliferation) have kept it alive and well. 'Business as an institution in society has increasingly accepted the idea that it is a multi-purpose social institution, an adaptive learning institution, and that its legitimacy in society and the world over is tied to public acceptance and approval, particularly in free economies' (Carroll, 2015: 94).

Given the emerging challenges and business innovations and solutions in the last few years, we can foresee ten future trends of CSR that companies need to be aware of today and start preparing for in the near future:

1. *A holistic approach*: The shift from corporate philanthropy and random acts of charity to strategic CSR, which is more holistic and genuine, is going to continue. Call it strategic CSR, conscious capitalism or circular economy, the business approach needs to change. CSR will no longer sit with the company's marketing people but with CSR departments and finance, working with many other people within and outside the organisation to achieve change. Organisational leadership will be tested not just by quarterly profits but by five-year plans to overcome societal and environmental challenges. Companies will start to realise that they cannot create societal and environmental harm in their core operations only to give some money to charity. And if they do not realise it themselves, stakeholder pressure could show them it is so. We are still not there yet but perhaps ten years from today many companies will have adopted a holistic view of CSR, and the ones lagging behind will be condemned by society.

2. *Responsibility in the entire value chain*: A supply chain in which companies strive to be responsible and sustainable in each of its parts could be the future of CSR. Auditing and standardisation will require companies such as H&M to go back to all their suppliers' suppliers and move beyond compliance. It will not be enough to just get the Fairtrade label if it is very easy for reporters and consumers to scratch the surface of companies' supply chain to find forced and child labour. Companies will have to be more efficient with natural resources, even if they are not socially and environmentally responsible, simply because they will become more and more scarce. Manufacturing will need to change

dramatically to reduce carbon emissions, toxic materials and waste and an impact on the environment that could last for centuries. Laws and regulations are likely to change, and it would be a good business move to be proactive and prepare for this future change today.

3. *End of modern slavery*: People who are earning less than US$2 and are working in slavery conditions, human trafficking and child labour should all become something of the past. Although it is hard today to imagine supply chains without modern slavery, it was also hard for owners of sugar and corn plantations in the US to imagine it 200 years ago. Many people lost their lives in the US, fighting to stop slavery, but we still have slavery today in many parts of the developing world. As more countries follow China, Bangladesh and Korea to overcome poverty, companies who want to use poverty to create modern slavery will soon run out of countries. Companies can still make a sound profit while paying people a liveable wage and ensuring that they are not working in slavery conditions. Children belong in school, not in dirty factories or hot fields where they work for up to 20 hours per day for cents. Once more, it may become the law in many developed countries (as is the law today in the UK and soon in Australia) not to enslave people in supply chains, and companies have an opportunity today not just to comply with future laws but to stop slavery before it needs to become illegal. Organisations such as Slave Free Trade can help companies achieve this.

4. *CSR in the age of robots and AI*: Harari (2017) claims that with so many of today's jobs to be replaced by robots, machines and artificial intelligence (AI), we might witness the most unequal society in history. We already live in a society with a smaller than ever 'upper class' and a larger than ever 'lower class'. In 2015, the 61 richest people in the world had the same amount of wealth as the 2.5 billion poorest people. If you think this is inconceivable, a year later it was only the eight richest people in the world. This is unjust and unsustainable. However, Harari claims we will soon be moving to a world where a growing number of people will be 'useless' as they will not be able to find any job due to robots and AI replacing them. It might be the end of slavery as companies will not need people in manufacturing anymore but the risks are even greater. Harari says that governments will no longer be incentivised to ensure people's health and well-being if they are not employable. There will also be a drastic decline in tax revenue, which will no longer allow governments to take care of people.

The automation of work will create a great opportunity for a few companies to become very rich. For example, instead of having thousands of taxi companies with drivers, one corporation will control the algorithm that regulates the entire transport market of self-driven vehicles. 'All the economic and political power which was previously shared by thousands is now in the hands of a single corporation, owned by a handful of billionaires', wrote Harari (2017).

However, with so many people losing their jobs and incomes, the market could also shrink dramatically as only a few would be able to afford goods and services. We could witness unprecedented levels of refugees and displacement, conflict and war due to the largest unemployment level in history. CSR will have new meanings, possibly the decision to employ people despite the ability to automate the entire supply chain, or finding new ways to ensure people's wellbeing. There are even discussions on the rights of robots and AI.

5. *End of disposable and soft plastic*: In the last century, since plastic was invented, we have been using it in rapidly growing amounts to hundreds of millions of tons every year. Because it is cheap and can be easily moulded, plastic now replaces many materials used in the past. However, its true cost is yet to be revealed. Since the 1950s, one billion tons of plastic have been discarded, of which approximately 10 per cent reaches the oceans and destroys marine life. Most of it gets to landfill, where it does not degrade for hundreds of years. Soft plastic, such as the supermarket bags which are used by the millions each day, can break into smaller parts and pollute water, soil and air for generations. Plastic bags are now banned in many countries (such as the Netherlands and Spain) while consumers and other stakeholders strive to pressure governments and companies to stop the use of them in many other places. But the future trend is not just based on the magnitude of the problem but also on the accessibility of solutions, such as sustainable plastic (Vilela et al., 2014). Some solutions include recyclable and recycled plastic, reusable bags and environmentally friendly packaging.

   If plastic is changed, replaced or banned in the future, the impact on companies will be enormous. Plastic is used in vast amounts to package and deliver goods (often unnecessarily, such as packaging one small toy in layers of thick plastic). Companies that want to prepare for this future trend might innovate today with ideas on how to remove as much plastic as possible from their supply chain, and offer alternatives to consumers.

6. *True cost of externalities*: As was mentioned several times in this book, one of the causes of corporate social irresponsibility is the notion of externalities. When a child or a person learns that no matter what they do and what the consequences of their actions are, someone else will fix the problems for them, all sense of responsibility is lost. Similarly, when corporations learned over the years that no matter how much harm they caused to society and the planet, governments and not-for-profits would 'clean up the mess', the result was corporate social irresponsibility. It is only when companies start realising the true costs of their actions and take responsibility for them that they can truly claim to have CSR. Puma and other companies started calculating the true cost of their externalities and adding it to their annual reports. True cost accounting is a recent CSR trend that could become more prominent in the future. It will

impact companies' profit and the price of goods and products in the future, and therefore it would be prudent to prepare for it by reducing the risk and the negative externalities of the company as of today.

7. *Purpose-driven organisations, leaders and marketing*: Purpose is the new black. Books and media on purpose, such as *Start with the Why* (Sinek, 2011) and *Conscious Capitalism* (Mackey and Sisodia, 2014), are more popular than ever before. People are looking to live a meaningful life and have meaningful jobs, and purpose-driven organisations with a strong sense of responsibility can offer this. After decades of telling us to find happiness through consumption, people have begun to discover that consumption provides only short-term pleasure, but not happiness, and it can also have many negative impacts. Many people try to find meaning through other channels, such as religion or volunteering. We are just starting to discover the impact that CSR has on people's sense of meaningfulness, and it is a wave that is yet to come. Leadership is no longer about directing employees what to do through punishment and reward, and is not even about having a vision for the company. The outstanding business leaders of today hold a strong sense of purpose and ensure everyone around them has a strong sense of purpose too, as was echoed in Mark Zuckerberg's commencement speech at Harvard in 2017 (see Chapter 6). Similarly, we are just starting to see the shift towards purpose-driven marketing, where instead of marketing products, companies enhance their brand by sharing their purpose with consumers.

8. *New levels of transparency*: In the future, companies will need to get used to being more transparent and disclosing more information. Companies such as Nike and H&M list their supplier factories for everyone to read. It is possible that in the future, consumers will be able to see what is going on in these factories through live streaming so they can judge for themselves whether the conditions these workers are exposed to are good enough. Companies such as Thankyou use their products to share information with consumers on the problems and issues they are trying to address, the solutions and the impact made (through Track Your Impact). Consumers now use smartphone apps to find out more information on where their clothes came from and an increasing number of watchdog organisations demand higher levels of transparency by exposing what companies actually do. Greenwashing will be a lot harder to do in the future as the use of it will backfire and consumers will demand to know what companies really do in the area of their declared responsibility. New levels of transparency could unleash new waves of innovation by the companies. They will need to walk the talk and talk the walk like never before. It is therefore only pragmatic to fix core operational issues today, before getting exposed in the near future.

9. *Innovative ways to communicate to and engage stakeholders*: Stakeholder engagement and involvement are becoming an important part of CSR for many companies. Whole Foods Market, for example, involves all its stakeholders and

integrates them in the management process of the organisation. Singtel enables employees, consumers and investors to take an active part in its CSR. Companies will soon need to move beyond stakeholder prioritisation to full involvement and integration and discover innovative ways to do so. Inviting a few consumers to a board meeting was innovative in 2005, but we can now involve an unlimited number of stakeholders using social media, apps and the channels that are yet to be created. Companies that do it well, while also being fully transparent to their stakeholders, will gain an emotional attachment and strong leadership from their stakeholders.

10. *The professionalisation of CSR*: CSR has only emerged as a strong business approach in the last four decades and for many years it lacked the aspects of a distinct profession. There is a growing body of CSR managerial knowledge (including hundreds of books, thousands of articles and related journals); networks and guilds of CSR managers, conferences and global summits; and a recognition that people who manage CSR need to have certain levels of access to the knowledge and network to perform their jobs. Although there is no entry requirement (such as a license in other jobs, e.g. law, medicine or social work), more and more universities are offering a degree that can be used to perform a CSR job (e.g. MBA in Sustainability). The days in which a CSR position was given to someone from HR or to an employee who simply liked the idea of doing something in this area will soon be over. The professionalisation of CSR work implies that companies can gain the required knowledge and talent to do CSR and do it well.

Questions for reflection and discussion

1. Based on the knowledge gained in this book, which three trends do you think will dominate the next few years?
2. Are there other trends that you think might emerge?

Epilogue

As we reach the end of this book, it would be good to reflect on our goals and what we achieved. The aim of this book was to emphasise the importance of the holistic approach to CSR. CSR is not just corporate philanthropy, corporate volunteering or waste management. It is beyond auditing, benchmarking and marketing. It is more than stakeholder management. Strategic CSR is about tying CSR to the company's strategy and its core operations in a manner that enables the company to be good and ethical, respectful and sustainable in everything that it does. It is not about being perfect but it is about utilising all the power, resources, knowledge and talent the company holds, to improve our world.

The challenges we face as a global society are so enormous that they might seem overwhelming. There is no one person or one company, as great as they might be, that can address it alone. However, if all the big corporations worked together to address some of the issues that we face, poverty, hunger, slavery and inequality could be demolished way before the year 2030. Climate change is not going to be easily reversible but business can take substantial action to mitigate its consequences and move beyond doing no harm to making a real contribution to saving this planet. However, we cannot afford another decade of corporate social irresponsibility – by then it could be too late. The time to act is today.

Our generation is fortunate to have a remarkable window of opportunity to fix problems caused by previous generations with the aim of saving future generations. Knowledge is available and easy to reach more than ever before. People are purpose-driven and connected like no other period in history. The world is hungry and eager for solutions and the business world can become an agent for the benefit of the world. Companies, big and small, will need to decide whether to act and become CSR pioneers on history's page or to continue to use our planet like an open sewer and exploit people and nature and be condemned by current and future generations.

The aim of this book was to provide business students and current and future business leaders with inspirational examples of how some companies take on these challenges. It was about introducing readers to the existing body of knowledge, theories, models and concepts, but more importantly, about enabling students and managers to apply these frameworks and offering managerial tools. In each chapter, we discussed positive examples of CSR and suggested many managerial tools, some of which could easily be implemented to achieve a strong social impact.

As manifested by the UN Supported Principles for Responsible Management Education (PRME), business schools have an important role to play in preparing students for their jobs, which is far from just maximising profit. This book and many other textbooks on the topic of CSR are here to help serve the same goal. By teaching MBA and business students all that we can about CSR, business management education can also become an agent of world benefit.

The book does not cover all possible frameworks or solutions but it has offered a good toolkit to start the journey with. The most important message is that what is required is a change in mindset and motivation for business, those people who lead it and those people who work in it. The rest will follow.

Summary

The aim of this chapter was to discuss ways and approaches to implement strategic CSR and all its aspects presented in previous chapters. As such, we started with an understanding of how organisational change is defined and how it should be modified to become a CSR tool. We examined five imperative questions for companies to consider before starting the journey towards CSR. We then presented three general organisational change frameworks (force field analysis, appreciative inquiry and Kotter's eight steps) and applied them to the context of CSR.

Several specific frameworks for implementing CSR were discussed in this chapter. Many of them list several steps that need to be taken in order to increase levels of CSR and sustainability. Some are more innovative than others, but all discuss the importance of working with a broad set of stakeholders at every stage of the change.

There are many challenges for organisations that desire to implement a holistic change towards strategic CSR, such as the establishment of a narrow view in the organisational culture; a lack of leadership support and resistance from stakeholders; a lack of knowledge on how to implement CSR; and concern regarding costs. However, all of these challenges also present great opportunities for business to change, unlearn and learn.

In addition to organisational change in specific companies, we also need to examine the overall change in the business sector. For this purpose, we elaborated on ten future CSR trends that are based on urgent issues and emerging solutions. While it is hard to know what the future holds, if the same trends that we are witnessing today grow and become mainstream, it would be prudent to prepare for the future by changing our business approach and practices today. There are various scenarios of CSR in the future and given the positive approach of this book, we can assume the hopeful one is the one that will prevail.

General questions

1. Why do you think organisations need to change towards CSR and plan this change carefully?
2. While most approaches to and frameworks of organisational change focus on problems and overcoming resistance, others are focused more on creating a desired future. Which ones do you think are more relevant to CSR and why? Use one framework to build your argument.
3. Most of the specific CSR implementation frameworks begin with the stakeholders or involve them at some stage. Using stakeholder theory, provide three reasons why stakeholder involvement and integration are an essential component of such an organisational change. Can this also be applied to organisational change that is not CSR related?
4. What do you think the future of CSR would look like? What current trends and antecedents would enable this future? What can be done by all of us to ensure the desired CSR future?
5. If you were the CEO of a company about to address all your employees about the future of the company, what would you say to get them engaged and involved? How would you convince them and other stakeholders to change and move towards strategic CSR?

Key definitions

- Organisational change occurs when an organisation makes a transition from its current state to some desired future state.
- Managing organisational change is the process of planning and implementing change in organisations in such a way as to minimise employee resistance and cost to the organisation while simultaneously maximising the effectiveness of the change effort (Ganta et al., 2014).
- The change management process is a structured approach to shifting/transitioning individuals, teams and organisations from a current state to a desired future state (McShane et al., 2012).
- Change management towards sustainability is defined as an approach to involve various stakeholders in shifting the organisation from the current state to a sustainable and responsible future state.
- Force field analysis is an organisational change framework that focuses on the three stages from current conditions to desired conditions (before change, unfreeze and refreeze) while focusing on the driving and restraining forces (Lewin, 1946).
- Appreciative inquiry is an organisational change strategy focusing on what is positive and what could be, instead of the problems. It includes four stages to change: discover, dream, design and delivery (Cooperrider & Srivastva, 1987).

References

Carroll, A. B. (1979) 'A three-dimensional conceptual model of corporate performance', *Academy of Management Review*, 4(4): 497–505.

Carroll, A. B. (2015) 'Corporate social responsibility', *Organizational Dynamics*, 44(2): 87–96.

Chandler, D. P. (2017) *Strategic corporate social responsibility: Sustainable value creation* (4th edn). Thousand Oaks, CA: Sage.

Coghlan, D. and Brannick, T. (2003) 'Kurt Lewin: The "practical theorist" for the 21st century', *Irish Journal of Management*, 24(2): 31–7.

Cooperrider, D. L. and Srivastva, S. (1987) 'Appreciative inquiry in organizational life', *Research in Organizational Change and Development*, 1(1): 129–69.

Cramer, J. (2005) 'Company learning about corporate social responsibility', *Business Strategy and the Environment*, 14(4): 255–66.

Dalai Lama Center for Peace & Education (1999) Heart-mind inquiry. Available at: http://dalailamacenter.org/programs/programs-development/appreciative-inquiry (Accessed: 5 October 2017)

Fowler Center for Business as an Agent of World Benefit (2017) Main website at Weatherhead School of Management, Case Western Reserve University. Available at: https://weatherhead.case.edu/centers/fowler (Accessed: 5 October 2017)

Ganta, C. V., Chittabbai, V. and Babu K. N. (2014) 'Managing organizational change', *International Journal of Combined Research & Development*, 2(2): 2321–41.

Harari, N. Y. (2017) 'Are we about to witness the most unequal societies in history?', *Guardian*, 24 May. Available at: www.theguardian.com/inequality/2017/may/24/are-we-about-to-witness-the-most-unequal-societies-in-history-yuval-noah-harari?CMP=Share_iOSApp_Other (Accessed: 1 June 2017)

Hunting, S. A. and Tilbury, D. (2006) *Shifting towards sustainability: Six insights into successful organisational change for sustainability*. Sydney: Aries.

Kotter, J. P. (2002) *The heart of change: Real-life stories of how people change their organizations*. Boston, MA: Harvard Business Press.

Lewin, K. (1946) 'Force field analysis', in J. E. Jones and J. W. Pfeiffer (eds), *The 1973 Annual Handbook for Group Facilitators*, pp. 111–13. San Diego, CA: University Associates.

Mackey, J. and Sisodia, R. (2014) *Conscious capitalism: Liberating the heroic spirit of business*. Boston, MA: Harvard Business Review Press.

Maignan, I., Ferrell, O. C. and Ferrell, L. (2005) 'A stakeholder model for implementing social responsibility in marketing', *European Journal of Marketing*, 39(9/10): 956–77.

Maon, F., Lindgreen, A. and Swaen, V. (2009) 'Designing and implementing corporate social responsibility: An integrative framework grounded in theory and practice', *Journal of Business Ethics*, 8: 71–89.

McShane, S., Olekalns, M. and Travaglione, T. (2012) *Organisational behaviour: Emerging knowledge, global insights*. Sydney: McGraw Hill Australia.

Ryan, R. M. and Deci, E. L. (2000) 'Self-determination theory and the facilitation of intrinsic motivation, social development, and well-being', *American Psychologist*, 55(1): 68–78.

Sinek, S. (2011) *Start with why: How great leaders inspire everyone to take action*. London: Penguin.

Unilever (2017) Sustainable living. Available at: www.unilever.co.uk/sustainable-living (Accessed: 5 October 2017)

Vilela, C., Sousa, A. F., Fonseca, A. C., Serra, A. C., Coelho, J. F., Freire, C. S. and Silvestre, A. J. (2014) 'The quest for sustainable polyesters: Insights into the future', *Polymer Chemistry*, 5(9): 3119–41.

Whitney, D. and Cooperrider, D. L. (1998) 'The appreciative inquiry summit: Overview and applications', *Employment Relations Today*, 25(2): 17–28.

Zuckerberg, M. (2017) 'Building global community', *Facebook*, 16 February. Available at: https://www.facebook.com/notes/mark-zuckerberg/building-global-community/10154544292806634/ (Accessed: 1 June 2017)

Further reading and links

Boston College Center for Corporate Citizenship (2016) CSR & the future. Available at: www.youtube.com/watch?v=nLgO9P8CZMg (Accessed: 1 June 2017)

CBK CUHK (2013) CSR in China: Past, present and future. Available at: www.youtube.com/watch?v=8kgaNmK62xs (Accessed: 1 June 2017)

Izzo, J. (2011) *Stepping up: How taking responsibility changes everything*. Oakland, CA: Berrett-Koehler.

Kanani, R. (2012) 'The future of CSR', *Forbes*, 9 February. Available at: www.forbes.com/sites/rahimkanani/2012/02/09/the-future-of-corporate-social-responsibility-csr/#40b703c54a71 (Accessed: 1 June 2017)

McPherson, S. (2017) '6 CSR trends to watch in 2017', *Forbes*, 19 January. Available at: www.forbes.com/sites/susanmcpherson/2017/01/19/6-csr-trends-to-watch-in-2017/#5d6c8465b1cc (Accessed: 1 June 2017)

SpaceWolfTube (2011) What's so hard about organisational change? Available at: www.youtube.com/watch?v=Ulx7-uUmK_Q (Accessed: 1 June 2017)

TEDx Talks (2016) Organizational change through sustainability | Tim Cole | TEDxHerndon. Available at: www.youtube.com/watch?v=ULnwLeM_YkM (Accessed: 1 June 2017)

TEDx Talks (2016) The era of corporate social responsibility is ending | Rachel Hutchisson | TEDxWilmington. Available at: www.youtube.com/watch?v=N8dXNzCIVxg (Accessed: 3 June 2017)

Visser, W. (2011) *The age of responsibility: CSR 2.0 and the new DNA of business.* Hoboken, NJ: Wiley.

Visser, W. (2012) 'Future trends in CSR', 3 April . Available at: www.waynevisser.com/articles/future-trends-in-csr (Accessed: 1 June 2017)

Williams, O. F. (2014) 'CSR: Will it change the world? Hope for the future: An emerging logic in business practice', *The Journal of Corporate Citizenship*, 53(18): 9–26.

Index